90 0473032 2

LANDSCAPE

the richest historical record

edited by Della Hooke

Society for Land dies
supplementary series 1

Published by
The Society for Landscape Studies

© The Society for Landscape Studies and the individual authors, 2000
Registered Charity No 278393

British Library Cataloguing in Publication Data
A catalogue record for this book is available from the British Library
ISBN 0 9539711 Paperback

Front cover: View from Cader Idris, Wales
© D. Hooke

This book is available from Graham Brown (membership secretary)
6 Canbury Close, Amesbury, Wiltshire SP4 7QF

Printed in Great Britain by Silk & Terry Ltd, Birmingham

Contents

Preface

Robert A. Dodgshon

The scale of time over which the landscapes of Britain have evolved makes it particularly appropriate that we should celebrate the passing of the millennium with a volume that takes stock of what we now know about them. Yet whilst these landscapes span a great depth of time, their purposeful study is a product of relatively recent times. Few would quibble with the claim that the study of landscape history was launched, symbolically if not actually, by W. G. Hoskins' classic volume on the making of the English landscape, a book first published in 1955. Whilst there had been many local studies of landscape before this date, Hoskins' text was the first to offer a large-scale or broad-brush synthesis of landscape history, to bring together a vast array of work and knowledge into a coherent story of succession, one that attempted to establish trends, patterns, discontinuities and phases in a style that not only made it eminently usable as an academic text, but also, accessible to the wider public. Since it was published, though, much new research has been carried out. Out of this research have come new ideas and themes that are starting to build a fuller and much revised interpretation of landscape history compared to that outlined in Hoskins' text.

The confident way in which writers like Hoskins separated the landscapes of prehistory from those of history and portrayed events like the Anglo-Saxon conquest as a new beginning in the history of the countryside, one that implanted the village, open fields and other institutions into it, has been undermined. Far more survived on after the end of prehistory in terms of patterns of settlement, boundaries and estates than ever was appreciated by earlier generations of landscape historians. The much quoted analogy of the landscape as a palimpsest - a parchment that is re-used successively but which never quite manages to erase the text created by each successive use - has never been more applicable than it is now, perfectly capturing the lived-in face of the British landscape.

As this volume admirably illustrates, the gradual reworking of the debate over our landscapes has been sustained by different disciplines. Indeed, it is over two decades since Michael Beresford urged document-focussed landscape historians to put on their boots. All involved in the debate would agree that his call has been heeded, with landscape archaeology establishing itself as one of the most productive and vital parts of the contemporary debate. Given that, potentially, more evidence lies in the landscape itself than is buried in archives, this vigorous growth of landscape archaeology has been both inevitable and welcome. Yet just as we have learnt to bring the document and spade together, so also, have we learnt to see landscape in more rounded terms. Thanks to the early pioneer work of geographers like H. Clifford Darby on habitats like the Fens, and the work of botanists like Max Hooper and Oliver Rackham on hedgerows and woodland respectively, we have learnt to more fully appreciate the contribution that the history of all the different habitats and biotopes that make up the landscape can make to its wider history. In short, just as the landscape itself was the work of many hands and interests, so also, has its history been the product of many hands and interests. By conveying this new richness of debate and methodology, *Landscape, the Richest Historical Record* summarises the study of landscape history in 2000 as successfully as Hoskins' overview of 1955.

Mental and material landscapes in prehistoric Britain

Richard Bradley

ABSTRACT

It has been difficult to understand the evolution of the prehistoric landscape because the evidence from the Neolithic and early Bronze Age is dominated by specialised forms of monuments and that of the later Bronze Age and Iron Age by settlements, enclosures and field systems. But that problem arises more from different traditions of research than from differences in the material being studied. One way of providing a more integrated study is through considering the symbolism of different kinds of monuments in relation to the landscapes in which they were set. This suggests that we might think in terms of three successive phases in which ritual and everyday activities were closely connected with one another. The first consists of traditions of monuments that recalled an ancestral past, real or imagined, in Continental Europe. The second involved monuments whose proptypes were to be found in the natural topography of Britain itself. In a final phase the main focus of symbolic elaboration was the house.

KEYWORDS:

Prehistoric, ritual monuments, domestic landscapes

INTRODUCTION

This paper celebrates the twenty-first anniversary of the journal *Landscape History*. It also marks the anniversary of the Society for Landscape Studies. Two decades hardly register on a prehistoric time scale, and yet they saw a major transformation in the very field which the Society exists to study.

It would not be too much to claim that the history of the journal spans an important transition in the ways in which prehistoric landscapes are investigated in this country. It was founded in the heyday of one kind of landscape archaeology, and to some extent its pages still bear the imprint of that kind of thinking. At the same time, it reaches this anniversary at a time when a quite different kind of landscape archaeology is coming into vogue.

How can we characterise these competing approaches? The principles that were widely accepted in the late 1970s had three sources in prehistoric archaeology. There was detailed topographic analysis based on careful field survey, which was a tradition with a continuous history from pioneers like Crawford to the work carried out by the Royal Commissions (Bowden 1999). There was the evidence of large-scale rescue excavation which unearthed the plans of entire settlements, and linking both approaches there was the fashion for economic archaeology. This grew out of the approaches advocated by Grahame Clark and received a new stimulus from a group of researchers in Cambridge led by Eric Higgs. It emphasised the importance of human adaptations to the natural environment and pioneered new methods of retrieving and analysing ancient food remains (Higgs 1972). Taken together, these constituted a 'settlement' or 'landscape archaeology' that broke free of the increasingly sterile studies of artefacts and chronologies that had dominated the post-war years. It was the same feeling of dissatisfaction that led to the rise of the New Archaeology.

By 1990 the situation had changed. After twenty years the innovations of the 1970s seemed commonplace and research had lost some of its momentum. The rather inflexible approaches to archaeological science advocated two decades before had come under fire (Thomas 1990) and landscape archaeology itself became increasingly conventional. Now the term was applied to virtually any large field project.

That attack on archaeological science formed only part of a wider critique of the assumptions associated with the New Archaeology. Material culture studies assumed a fresh significance, but this time the main concerns were with the ideas expressed by artefacts in the past (Hodder 1982). Social archaeology came into its own through a rapprochement with anthropology, and this led to a renewed interest in ritual and the use of monuments. Inspired by contemporary developments in history and geography, prehistorians rediscovered landscape studies. Like the portable objects which were being analysed in new ways, entire landscapes might have carried specific meanings and values. Again it was necessary to move beyond the documentation of their outward form to consider how they would have been experienced in prehistory (Tilley 1994).

To some extent that is the situation in which archaeologists find themselves today, but it is a stance that has already created problems, for there is a fine line between studying how people reacted to landscapes in the past and presenting one's own responses to those places as if they had a wider significance. That is particularly troubling when the research lacks an explicit methodology. The best projects have been those that bring newer and older methods together, and the weakest are the ones that can only be assessed by repeating the exercise on the ground.

Whilst some researchers claim to be undertaking a new form of landscape archaeology, the older methods still dominate the work carried out in the field. There has been no diminution in the amount of survey or excavation, but the two approaches to the landscape take little account of one another, with the result that the subject is fractured down the middle. Most archaeologists are studying what I would term 'material' landscapes – that is to say, the minutely physical evidence of where people lived and how they gained their livelihood (Fowler 1983; Barker 1985). Others are investigating purely 'mental' landscapes – the superstructure of meanings and values through which particular landscapes were experienced in prehistory (Bender 1993; Hirsch & O'Hanlon 1995; Ucko & Layton 1999; Ashmore & Knapp 1999). The division is a damaging one, and it has its consequences for the organisation of research. At the risk of over-simplification, the study of material landscapes is based on the examination of settlements, land use and food remains, whilst mental landscapes are interrogated through studies of monuments, artefact deposits and the natural topography into which they were set.

This distinction is unproductive, but it is hard to break it down. It is based on quite different versions of the past. The conflict is ultimately between two propositions: either we can understand the lives of ancient people without making any attempt to see the world through their eyes; or the rituals and beliefs of prehistoric communities played such a dominant role that is no longer necessary to discuss how they obtained their food. The debate has certainly cleared the air, but what is needed is a more generous approach that brings both schools of thought together.

This paper explores the connections between these competing landscape archaeologies and does so by considering the prehistoric sequence in the British Isles from the Neolithic period to the middle of the Iron Age. Before that time, there is too little information to sustain this kind of approach and by the later years of the Iron Age the landscape is better investigated in relation to that of the Roman period. To cover 4,000 years in little over 4,000 words must involve some simplifications and so I shall describe the prehistoric sequence in very general terms; I shall not be able to take into account many of the regional variations from the general pattern. At the same time, I do not want this account to be so abstract that it can only be understood by prehistorians. For that reason I shall comment on five successive landscapes and their wider significance, each of them drawn from a well-researched area of England or Wales. Each section will be built around a *vignette* of a specific landscape whose basic character is well understood. I shall also illustrate the kinds of monuments that can be found there. In every instance my concerns are much the same: to sketch the basic character of these successive landscapes; to consider the relationship between the different levels of analysis summarised in the title of my paper; and to ask how far those particular situations characterise Britain as a whole. The literature on prehistoric Britain is vast. In order to keep the bibliography within bounds I shall refer, wherever possible, to monographs and edited volumes rather than single papers.

THE EARLIER NEOLITHIC: A LANDSCAPE OF MEMORY

The first illustration (Fig. 1.1) shows a number of crop-mark monuments on the gravels of the Great Ouse Valley (Clark & Dawson 1995). Comparison with excavated sites identifies at least three distinct forms. There are small oval enclosures which are most probably the remains of long barrows or related earthworks. There are more rectilinear features that we can identify as cursus monuments, and set back from the river there is the site of a causewayed enclosure (Megaw & Simpson 1979, ch. 3). More detailed plans of excavated monuments on the Fen edge also appear in this drawing: the long barrow at Haddenham in Cambridgeshire (Hodder & Shand 1988) and a nearby causewayed enclosure (Hodder 1992, ch. 15).

The obvious temptation is to take this evidence literally and to treat the entire area as a specialised 'monument complex' or 'ritual landscape' (see Topping 1997). That same could be said about many other groups of earlier Neolithic monuments, but this interpretation is based on some misleading assumptions. Ritual is a form of human behaviour which takes place in many different settings, yet by using the term 'ritual landscape' we suggest that in prehistory it was confined to specialised monuments. The excavation of earlier Neolithic settlements shows that this was not the case. It may be better to suggest that certain practices took a more public form in some locations than in others. The term 'ritual landscape' also suggests that communal events of this kind took place well away from the occupation sites of the same period. There may be instances in which this suggestion is correct, but there is no reason to treat them as the norm. Fieldwork and environmental analysis often show that monuments were closely integrated into the domestic landscape.

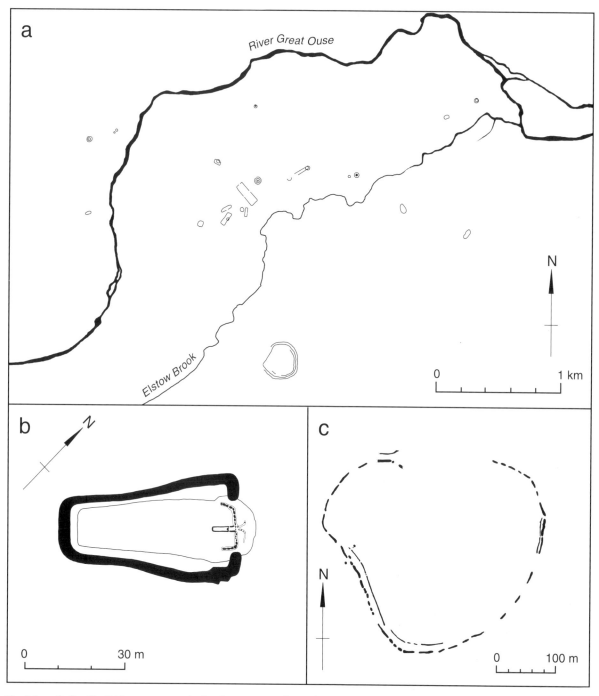

Fig. 1.1. a: Earlier Neolithic monuments in the Great Ouse Valley (after Clark & Dawson 1995); b: outline plan of the Haddenham long barrow (after Hodder & Shand 1988); c: outline plan of the Haddenham causewayed enclosure (after Hodder 1992). Drawing: Steve Allen.

One reason for the confusion has been the idea that Neolithic communities were more mobile than was once supposed. There is only limited evidence for crop cultivation and in many areas it has been difficult to identify houses or lasting settlements, despite the most careful search. Domesticated livestock may have been more important than cereals, particularly in lowland Britain (Thomas 1999, ch. 2). Unfortunately, these observations have created unnecessary problems. It is all too easy to assume that groups of mobile cattle herders came into contact only at specialised monuments. This may be true of some of the causewayed enclosures on the chalk, but there is no reason to extend the argument to other areas. The distribution of monuments was not necessarily related to mobility and the 'paths' that play such a large part in recent literature are entirely hypothetical.

A second assumption is that the evidence from southern England can be extended to other parts of Britain and Ireland. This is unjustified. Apart from causewayed enclosures, related monuments have a wide distribution, but in some areas the settlement pattern was very different. Houses are found regularly in highland Britain, from southern and western Scotland to Orkney and Shetland, and Irish archaeologists have experienced no difficulty in locating them in the field (Darvill & Thomas 1996). Moreover, many of these structures are in areas well suited to year-round settlement. They can be associated with finds of grain and even with land divisions and often they are located close to more specialised monuments. The prevailing model may explain the situation in the south, but it is not consistent with the evidence from other areas. There was much more variation than is commonly supposed.

How are we to interpret the monuments that have dominated the study of the landscape in recent years? They do not seem to be related directly to the process of food production, although causewayed enclosures could have been used, among other things, for the exchange of agricultural products. The mental landscape of the earlier Neolithic is dominated by an origin myth. With the exception of the cursus, which is an elaborate form of mortuary enclosure or long barrow, the main types of monumental architecture originated on the Continent, together with domesticated crops and animals. There they had a quite specific source. The long barrows are best interpreted as representations of a type of house which had actually gone out of use before the Neolithic period began in Britain. It seems possible that the original inspiration for these structures was provided by one specific practice in the Linear Pottery Culture and its successors (Hodder 1990, pp. 142-56; Bradley 1998, ch. 3). Long houses seem to have been abandoned and left to decay whilst they were structurally sound. This appears to have happened every generation, raising the possibility that it took place on the death of one of the occupants. The house of the living was transformed into the house of the dead, and by the end of the period in which these buildings were constructed their characteristic form was already being copied by burial mounds.

In the same way, the earliest causewayed enclosures were directly integrated into the pattern of everyday life. Some of them actually enclosed groups of houses, whilst others were built to mark the positions of settlements that had recently been abandoned. After that time, the pattern of settlement in northern and western Europe changed and it seems as if human activity was dispersed across larger areas of the landscape. But earthwork enclosures of exactly the same form continued to be built, although now they were mainly used in rituals and the treatment of the dead. Just as the form of the long barrow commemorated the houses of a remote past, the form of these earthworks contains a memory of a kind of settlement which no longer existed (Bradley 1998, ch. 5). Both contributed to 'the symbolic construction of community' (Cohen 1989). It was not until this development had happened that Neolithic material culture was adopted in Britain.

If this sequence has been interpreted correctly, it would mean that the major monuments that dominate the landscape of earlier Neolithic Britain recalled the mythical origin of the inhabitants, in a remote past and a distant area. There is no particular reason to suppose that this reconstruction of the past was accurate, but it was one of the features that gave their landscape its identity.

THE LATER NEOLITHIC: MICROCOSM AND MACROCOSM

The second illustration (Fig. 1.2) shows a series of buildings and a circular enclosure. The drawing has been designed to illustrate the continuum that exists between the simple round houses of this period, some of them with a square central hearth or other feature, the massive timber circles associated with major enclosures and even the form of the henge monuments themselves. In fact this is only a sample, for there are henges with stone settings at their centre and the series could continue by illustrating the situation of these earthworks in the natural topography. Thus Durrington Walls is located inside the limits of a dry valley, whilst other monuments of the same type occupy the middle of a large natural basin, whose horizon echoes the form of the perimeter earthwork (Bradley 1998, ch. 8). The important point is that there is such a continuum. It seems as though there was no clear-cut distinction between the ritual and domestic worlds.

To a large extent the evidence of field archaeology supports this idea. Although many of the major monuments are located near to earlier examples, there is little to show that they were set apart from the main concentrations of human activity during the later Neolithic period. It may be that many of the major groups of earthworks would have been accessible from a larger region, but nonetheless their distribution is limited to the more productive soils which could have supported a resident population. The problem is that it is all too tempting to regard these sites as central places or even to consider some of the enclosures as settlements themselves. The results of field survey certainly show that much activity was going on near to these sites, but it was not limited to their surroundings and the distribution of artefacts continues over an altogether larger area (Richards 1990).

In fact it is in the very period when the great henge monuments were built that we find evidence for a widening of the settlement pattern. There are new clearance episodes in the pollen record and the distribution of datable artefacts extends to many places which are thought of as marginal land today. Some of these may have been used on an occasional basis (Bradley 1978, pp. 106-14). There is a paradox here, for, with certain exceptions, the monuments of the later Neolithic

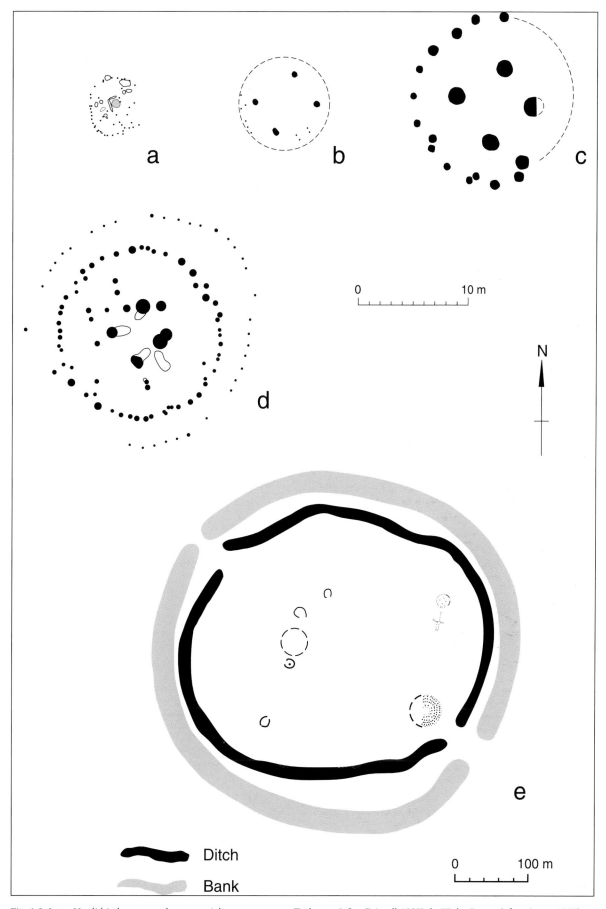

Fig. 1.2. Later Neolithic houses and ceremonial monuments. a: Trelystan (after Britnell 1982); b: Wyke Down (after Green 1997); c: Durrington Walls (after Wainwright & Longworth 1971); d: Machrie Moor (after Haggarty 1991); e: the Durrington Walls henge (after Wainwright & Longworth 1971 with additions). Drawing: Steve Allen.

are larger than their predecessors, whilst the comparatively rare domestic structures can be small and insubstantial (Darvill & Thomas 1996). The flint industry of the period suggests that in southern England certain places may have been used on a more lasting basis, yet there is little evidence to suggest that cereal farming was of comparable importance to stock raising (Thomas 1999, pp. 23-9). As so often, the evidence from the Northern Isles has a very different character.

The artefact assemblages recovered by excavation extend along a continuum from relatively simple deposits to others with a much more specialised character, as shown by their composition and the ways in which they had been committed to the ground. Some of the more distinctive groups of artefacts come from settlement sites, again suggesting that any rigid distinction between the ritual and domestic worlds would be inappropriate here. Rather, it seems as if there was a continuous range of variation. Structured deposits are most obvious when they are found within specialised monuments, but they also occur across the surrounding landscape. On the other hand, it seems to be true that the most varied assemblages are located near to major monuments (Barrett, Bradley & Green 1991, pp. 79-84).

Such a continuum is reflected by the buildings of the later Neolithic. As we have seen, they take much the same form across a wide range of structures, from a stake-built house with a central hearth to the massive timber circles found inside henge monuments. In the same way, their circular form is often echoed by the perimeter of these enclosures and even by the ways in which those monuments are placed within the wider landscape. It is possible to interpret this relationship in two different ways. Perhaps the ceremonial centres of this period were conceived as 'big houses': public buildings which symbolised the integrity of the communities who used them (De Boer 1997). They were massively enlarged versions of the ordinary dwellings of this period, yet their purely symbolic character is obvious from the ways in which some of them were rebuilt in stone (Gibson 1998). On the other hand, that does not explain the circular ground plan of so many different kinds of monument. Perhaps that developed because those enclosures were seen as microcosms of the landscapes in which they were built (Bradley 1998, ch. 8); that same image may have extended down to the individual house. If so, then it suggests that the architectural distinctions between dwellings and public buildings were only a matter of degree. Each part of the later Neolithic landscape expressed the same organisation of space. Where the earlier Neolithic world had been constructed around an origin myth, during this period the mental and material landscapes were the mirror images of one another.

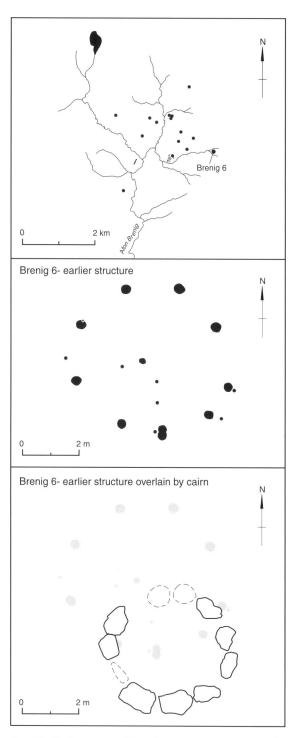

Fig. 1.3. Outline plan of the Bronze Age cemetery at the Brenig (after Lynch 1993) with details of the timber building on Site 6 and the cairn overlying it. Drawing: Steve Allen.

THE EARLIER BRONZE AGE: SETTLING THE DEAD

Figure 1.3 illustrates a single landscape: the Bronze Age cemetery at the Brenig in North Wales (Lynch 1993). Again we can consider this at a number of different scales. On one level it is a cemetery of mounds and cairns: one of the few to be excavated and published in modern times. On another, it illustrates a round cairn and the plan of the circular building which was buried beneath it. The entire group of monuments is located in a valley with a series of springs, but it is clear from environmental evidence that the main settled area was on the lower ground some distance beyond the cemetery. That was where cereals were grown, whilst the area around the monuments was used mainly as pasture. That is not to deny that the valley had been occupied before the monuments were constructed and there is evidence of another building and a group of domestic artefacts from the excavated area.

In some ways the Brenig encapsulates the principal features of the earlier Bronze Age landscape, but in others it is perhaps a little unusual. There are many regions where burial mounds appear in groups and sometimes in more formal patterns, but quite often these were located in relation to other monuments that had been built during the Neolithic period. In this case that does not seem to have happened. Instead the cemetery was an entirely Bronze Age creation. It contains a whole array of small circular monuments, from elaborated natural mounds to complex burial cairns and from open timber circles to stone-walled enclosures. It encapsulates many of the characteristic forms taken by monuments during this period.

Unfortunately, such monuments have dominated the archaeology of the earlier Bronze Age. The Brenig is unusual in containing reasonably well-preserved evidence of domestic occupation, but in other ways it is typical. It is located beyond the apparent limits of the earlier Neolithic landscape and, like many other sites of this character, it is found in an area that was first colonised during the later Neolithic. In fact there are two main characteristics of domestic settlement at this time. The first is a continual extension of the settlement pattern into areas which today we would regard as marginal land. For the most part these regions had not been settled since the Mesolithic period (Bradley 1978, pp. 106-14). There is environmental evidence for the removal of trees, for cultivation or stock raising and for far-reaching changes in the character and productivity of the soils. Such areas sometimes went of out use again during the earlier Bronze Age and, whilst a number sustained a longer period of occupation, very few were still occupied by the Iron Age. Although these developments are sometimes attributed to a worsening climate, the local soils were so brittle that this sequence was almost inevitable. It led to the formation of many areas of heathland and moorland which take the same form today.

The expansion of settlement in these areas occurred in parallel with changes in the agricultural regime on the more stable soils, although so few settlements survive that the most useful information is provided by environmental evidence. This would suggest that cereal growing gradually increased in importance in the most productive areas, where it seems to have resulted in local episodes of erosion (Evans 1990). There remains very little evidence of field or land boundaries, perhaps because cultivation did not take place in fixed plots. Rather, it shifted its position from one generation to another, with the result that it obliterated most of the traces of domestic buildings. Nor did it lead to the formation of permanent field divisions. This pattern may be preserved at some of the sites in the uplands which have escaped the effects of later farming (Spratt & Burgess 1985), but it has to be admitted that the dating evidence is not altogether satisfactory. In just a few areas, such as Dartmoor and the North Sea coast, there are indications that land-holding was reorganised during this period, but that development is best considered in the following section of the paper.

The evidence from the Brenig and other barrow excavations suggests that some of the settlements may not have been located far from the burials of this period. The smaller, simpler mounds may have been placed quite close to the houses and it is only the larger monuments – those associated with the most elaborate graves – that were far away. These were often located on high ground where they would have been visible on the horizon. It is no longer correct to think in terms of *individual* burials at this time, for some of the mounds, and even some of the graves, contained more than one set of human remains. On the other hand, these were deposited singly and very often each was accompanied by its own selection of artefacts (Petersen 1972). The positions of the newer burials took account of those that were already present on the site, suggesting that they were organised in a prescribed sequence (Last 1998) In the same way, the positions of the different barrows often acknowledged those of the other monuments, with the result that the funerals of this period may have assumed an increasingly complex character (Mizoguchi 1992; Barrett 1994, ch. 5). The interrelationships between the separate burials and the monuments where they were placed was perhaps one of the ways in which social relationships were worked out.

What of the house found beneath the funerary cairn at the Brenig? Finds like this are fundamental to our understanding of the landscape during this period. It is roughly the same size as that cairn and it is not the only example in upland Britain to be found in direct association with a burial monument (Lane 1984). It might suggest an even closer association between the living and the dead, but this time in terms of ideas rather than physical geography. That may be why the turves used to build one of the round barrows at the Brenig came from the settlement area. Perhaps such a monument was seen as a representation of the house and a lasting memorial to its occupants. If that is true – and the evidence is necessarily tenuous – then the great barrow cemeteries must surely be viewed as the settlements of the dead, organised according

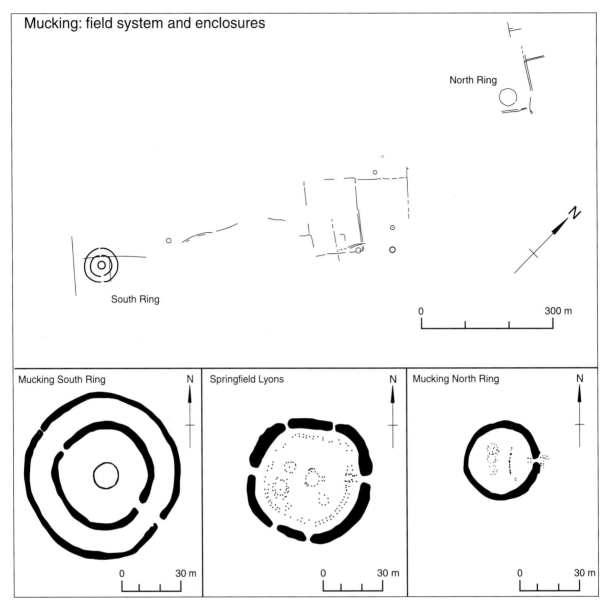

Fig. 1.4. Outline plan of the later Bronze Age enclosures at Mucking, Essex, and associated round barrows / round houses and fields (after Clark 1993). The insets show the excavated features inside both these enclosures as well as those on a comparable site at Springfield Lyons (after Buckley & Hedges). Drawing: Steve Allen.

to principles of alliance and descent and lending a permanence to the earlier Bronze Age landscape that it did not have in daily life. As land use intensified during that period, settlements may have changed their character, but the most obvious indications of a new sense of community come from the ideal image presented by the barrow cemetery.

THE LATER BRONZE AGE: DIVIDING THE LAND

The next illustration (Fig. 1.4) brings together a number of later Bronze Age sites in Essex: Mucking North and South Rings (Bond 1988; Clark 1993) and the defended enclosure at Springfield Lyons (Buckley & Hedges 1987). In this period field evidence is widely available and it is more difficult to select representative examples.

I have chosen to feature Mucking for several reasons. The excavations were conducted under difficult conditions and not all of them have been properly published, but even so this complex contains four elements of vital importance to any understanding of the later Bronze Age landscape: isolated round houses, small burial mounds, a field system and two defended enclosures, each of them associated with circular buildings. In the case of Mucking North Rings it is clear that an open settlement had existed immediately outside the earthwork.

This juxtaposition of elements is largely new, although it is anticipated by developments late in the preceding period, in particular those on Dartmoor (Fleming 1988). Small funerary monuments are integrated with field boundaries in the same manner as a number of the houses; indeed, it is sometimes difficult to distinguish between these circular buildings and the round barrows used during the same period. As we have seen, this may not be fortuitous, as earlier Bronze Age burial mounds could have referred to the domestic sphere. At the same time, the major enclosures illustrated in Fig. 1.4 also adopt a circular plan and, like the round houses of this period, their principal entrances are towards the east or south-east. The interiors of Mucking South Rings and Springfield Lyons are dominated by larger circular buildings, and, taken together, these are now the most impressive features of the local landscape. At Mucking, then, it seems as if the domestic and funerary arenas had been brought together and that both conformed to the same organisation of space.

That sketch inevitably over-simplifies the situation. Small round barrows like those found at Mucking were the successors of those of the earlier Bronze Age, but they did not continue to be created throughout this period. Rather, they went out of use by about 1200 B.C., after which time the remains of the dead are no longer found in specialised monuments (Brück 1995). In some cases they were associated with settlements, whilst in others they are found in rivers together with deposits of metalwork. A second qualification is equally important. The ring-works typified by those at Mucking and Springfield Lyons are not found throughout the country. They are mainly a feature of eastern England, although related earthworks may have existed in Wessex, north Wales and Ireland. Their chronology is quite distinctive too. They first appear around 1200 B.C. and most of the sites date from the early first millennium, the period when round barrows had largely gone out of use (Needham & Ambers 1994).

Even with these qualifications, the evidence summarised in Fig. 1.4 can stand for a more general transformation in the British landscape, but the evidence must be handled with care. It is all too tempting to suppose that for whatever reasons – a retreat from marginal soils, population pressure, the need to provide for an élite – the landscape of Britain was radically reorganised, but in fact the geographical extent of that reorganisation has yet to be established and recent research suggests that the process extended over a considerable period of time. Field systems were established in some regions long before this process extended to neighbouring areas and not all the land that was enclosed at this time remained in occupation (Yates 1999). Although this applies particularly to the river gravels of southern England, the same process can be recognised on the chalk, where longer earthwork land divisions have an equally volatile chronology (Bradley, Entwistle & Raymond 1994). Even less is known about the character of the later Bronze Age economy, and here opinion is divided. The field systems found on the river gravels do not seem to have been used in the same ways as their equivalents in upland areas. They seem to have been more important in stock raising than the growing of crops. Similarly, the ditched land divisions found in some parts of the downland can be interpreted in various ways. They may reflect a new emphasis on sheep farming, or they may be territorial divisions enclosing the land of individual communities who practised a mixed economy. Whatever the solution to these problems, it is true to say that the pollen record shows a significant number of new clearances during this period and suggests a greater emphasis on crop cultivation.

It would be easy to suppose that ritual activity played a less important role as the landscape was restructured around the needs of food production, but in fact ritual and practical concerns were closely intertwined. Some of the field systems adopted a solar alignment and the dead were buried close to the settlements. Their remains can sometimes be found associated with houses and land divisions (Brück 1995). Specialised deposits of artefacts, including metalwork, occur within the domestic landscape or on its edges and once round barrows went out of use there is little to suggest the creation of a special class of ceremonial monuments. The only exceptions are the curious timber structures associated with finds of fine metalwork discovered in watery locations, and they are very rare (Pryor 1992).

The focus of ritual life was now the settlement and its surroundings. The circular form of the barrows retained its original importance but now it was associated mainly with the houses. The ring-works that were built during this period conformed to the same symbolism, and the entrances to both kinds of structure provided an important focus for symbolic elaboration. By the end of this period the house had become the focus of ritual and domestic life. The mental and material landscapes of my title were the same.

THE EARLY AND MIDDLE IRON AGES: THE NEW SYNTHESIS

The latest edition of Barry Cunliffe's book *Iron Age Communities in Britain* runs to 685 pages (Cunliffe 1991). My contribution has a word limit. So much is known about Iron Age landscapes in the British Isles that my treatment must be very selective indeed. The last section of this paper shows how the merging of ritual and domestic life that happened in the later Bronze Age led to a new kind of synthesis during the following period. As so often before, this left a distinctive mark on the landscape.

My final example comes from Dorset (Fig. 1.5; *cf.* Bowen 1990). It illustrates the developed landscape of late prehistory on the chalk and contains a number of distinctive elements, some of them no doubt originating in the later Bronze Age. There are large areas of fields, long ditched

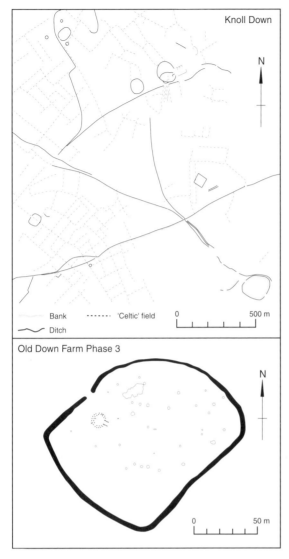

Fig. 1.5. A segment of the late prehistoric landscape close to the hill fort of Buzbury Rings in Dorset (after Bowen 1990), together with a plan of the excavated features of the early Iron Age settlement at Old Down Farm, Hampshire (after Davies 1981). Drawing: Steve Allen.

land divisions, a variety of earthwork enclosures which probably contained houses, and a major hill-fort. Accompanying these is the outline plan of an enclosed settlement on the Hampshire chalk which shows it at the beginning of the Iron Age when it was dominated by a round house and a number of storage pits (Davies 1981).

There is considerable regional variation in every part of Iron Age Britain but for our purposes certain widespread features do stand out, for they seem to have their origins in the distinctive landscape of the later Bronze Age. First, houses continued to play a major role in the domestic and ritual life of the community and were often the focus for specialised deposits of artefacts and both human and animal bones. Normally these buildings adhered to a solar alignment and the internal space appears to have been organised about an axis extending through the centre of the porch; on some sites the entrance of the enclosure

follows the same convention (Fitzpatrick 1997). Near to the houses there were a variety of granaries and pits. In recent years it has become clear that after their practical function was over many of the corn storage pits were used for offerings of artefacts, meat joints, animal burials and human remains (Hill 1995). These had an extremely stereotyped composition and the presence of agricultural tools among these collections suggests that people may have connected the farming cycle with the fertility of the human and animal population. Indeed, these same ideas could have extended to the regeneration of the dead themselves.

Marking the edges of the settled area there was often an enclosure ditch and this provided an ideal context for further offerings of this kind (Hill 1995). Others have been identified in the base of land boundary ditches. These finds are important in two ways. Firstly, they include human remains, from isolated bones to entire bodies, in a period when the evidence for formal burials is very limited indeed. At the same time, the places where they are found seem to be associated with the process of food production. The evidence for such rituals is widely distributed about the Iron Age landscape, but it is most obvious in the monumental enclosures that are usually described as hill-forts. Here recent excavations have identified the positions of temples or shrines, located amongst the specialised structures used for storing grain. At South Cadbury it even seems as if these shrines were modelled on the architecture of the granaries on the site (Downes 1997). Temples do not occur in isolation until the later part of the Iron Age, suggesting that it was important to integrate them into the domestic domain.

The effect of these arguments is to suggest that the production of food in the Iron Age landscape was attended by special rituals. These took place inside the settlements, at hill-forts and even along the boundaries that enclosed the areas of farmland. No longer were such ceremonies undertaken in special locations and even the number of river finds diminished during this period. The everyday concerns of food production were imbued with special meanings so that a landscape like that illustrated in Fig. 1.5 would have been much more than an orderly arrangement of agricultural resources. It was both a mental landscape and a material landscape. The integration of those two worlds that began so strikingly in the Bronze Age reached its apotheosis.

BIBLIOGRAPHY

Ashmore, W., & Knapp, A. B. (eds), 1999. *Archaeologies of Landscape* (Oxford).

Barker, G., 1985. *Prehistoric Farming in Europe* (Cambridge).

Barrett, J., 1994. *Fragments from Antiquity* (Oxford).

Barrett, J., Bradley, R., & Green, M., 1991. *Landscape, Monuments and Society* (Cambridge).

Bender, B. (ed.), 1993. *Landscape: Politics and Perspectives* (Oxford).

Bond, D., 1988. 'Excavations at the North Ring Mucking Essex', *East Anglian Archaeol*, 43.

Bowden, M. (ed.), 1999. *Unravelling the Landscape: an inquisitive approach to archaeology* (Stroud).

Bowen, H. C., 1990. *The Archaeology of Bokerley Dyke* (London).

Bradley, R., 1978. *The Prehistoric Settlement of Britain* (London).

Bradley, R., 1998. *The Significance of Monuments* (London).

Bradley, R., Entwistle, R., & Raymond, F., 1994. *Prehistoric Land Divisions on Salisbury Plain* (London).

Britnell, W., 1982. 'The excavation of two barrows at Trelystan, Powys', *Proc Prehist Soc*, 48, pp. 133-201.

Brück, J., 1995. 'A place for the dead: the role of human remains in Late Bronze Age Britain', *Proc Prehist Soc*, 61, pp. 245-77.

Buckley, D., & Hedges, J., 1987. *The Bronze Age and Saxon Settlement at Springfield Lyons: interim report* (Chelmsford).

Clark, A., 1993. *Excavations at Mucking, vol. 1: Site Atlas* (London).

Clark, R., & Dawson, M., 1995. 'The prehistoric and Romano-British landscape in Bedfordshire: recent work', in *Chiltern Archaeology: recent work*, ed. R. Holgate (Dunstable), pp. 56-67.

Cohen, A., 1989. *The Symbolic Construction of Community* (London).

Cunliffe, B., 1991. *Iron Age Communities in Britain* (3rd edn, London).

Darvill, T., & Thomas, J. (eds), 1996. *Neolithic Houses in North-west Europe and Beyond* (Oxford).

Davies, S., 1981. 'Excavations at Old Down Farm, Andover', *Proc Hampshire Field Club*, 37, pp. 81-163.

De Boer, W., 1997. 'Ceremonial centres from the Cayapas (Esmeraldas, Ecuador) to Chillicothe (Ohio, USA)', *Cambridge Archaeol J*, 7, pp. 225-53.

Downes, J., 1997. 'The shrine at South Cadbury Castle: belief enshrined?', in *Reconstructing Iron Age Societies*, ed. A. Gwilt & C. Haselgrove (Oxford), pp. 145-52.

Evans, J. G., 1990. 'Notes on some Late Neolithic and Early Bronze Age events in long barrow ditches in southern and eastern England', *Proc Prehist Soc*, 56, pp. 111-16.

Fitzpatrick, A., 1997. 'Everyday life in Iron Age Wessex', in *Reconstructing Iron Age Societies*, ed. Gwilt & Haselgrove, pp. 73-86.

Fleming, A., 1988. *The Dartmoor Reaves* (London).

Fowler, P., 1983. *The Farming of Prehistoric Britain* (Cambridge).

Gibson, A., 1998. *Stonehenge and Timber Circles* (Stroud).

Green, M., 1997. 'A second henge and Neolithic buildings uncovered on Wyke Down, Cranborne Chase, Dorset', *Past*, 27, pp. 1-3.

Haggarty, A., 1991. 'Machrie Moor, Arran. Recent excavations at two stone circles', *Proc Soc Antiq Scotland*, 121, pp. 51-94.

Higgs, E. (ed.), 1972. *Papers in Economic Prehistory* (Cambridge).

Hill, J. D., 1995. *Ritual and Rubbish in the Iron Age of Wessex* (Oxford).

Hirsch, E., & O'Hanlon, M. (eds), 1995. *The Anthropology of Landscape* (Oxford).

Hodder, I., 1982. *Symbols in Action* (Cambridge).

Hodder, I., 1990. *The Domestication of Europe* (Oxford).

Hodder, I., 1993. *Theory and Practice in Archaeology* (London).

Hodder, I., & Shand, P., 1988. 'The Haddenham long barrow: an interim Report', *Antiquity*, 62, pp. 349-53.

Lane, P., 1984. 'Past practices in the ritual present: examples from the Welsh Bronze Age', *Archaeol Rev from Cambridge*, 5.2, pp. 181-92.

Last, J., 1998. 'Books of Life: biography and memory in a Bronze Age barrow', *Oxford J Archaeol*, 17, pp. 43-53.

Lynch, F., 1993. *Excavations in the Brenig Valley* (Bangor).

Megaw, J. V. S., & Simpson, D., 1979. *Introduction to British Prehistory* (Leicester).

Mizoguchi, K., 1992. 'The historiography of a linear barrow cemetery', *Archaeol Rev from Cambridge*, 11.1, pp. 39-49.

Needham, D., & Ambers, J., 1994. 'Redating Rams Hill and reconsidering Bronze Age enclosures', *Proc Prehist Soc*, 60, pp. 225-43.

Petersen, F., 1972. 'Traditions of multiple burial in Later Neolithic and Early Bronze Age England', *Archaeol J*, 129, pp. 22-55.

Pryor, F. (ed.), 1992. 'Current research at Flag Fen', *Antiquity*, 66, pp. 439-531.

Richards, J., 1990. *The Stonehenge Environs Project* (London).

Spratt, D., & Burgess, C. (eds), 1985. *Upland Settlement in Britain. The Second Millennium BC and After* (Oxford).

Thomas, J., 1990. 'Silent running: the ills of environmental archaeology', *Scott Archaeol Rev*, pp. 2-7.

Thomas, J., 1999. *Understanding the Neolithic* (London).

Tilley, C., 1994. *A Phenomenology of Landscape* (Oxford).

Topping, P. (ed.), 1997. *Neolithic Landscapes* (Oxford).

Ucko, P., & Layton, R. (eds), *The Archaeology and Anthropology of Landscape* (London).

Wainwright, G., & Longworth, I., 1971. *Durrington Walls. Excavations 1966 - 1968* (London).

Yates, D., 1999. 'Bronze Age field systems in the Thames Valley', *Oxford J Archaeol*, 18, pp. 157-70.

Human-environment interactions in prehistoric landscapes: the example of the Outer Hebrides

Kevin J. Edwards, Ymke Mulder, Tim A. Lomax, Graeme Whittington and Ken R. Hirons

ABSTRACT

Quaternary scientists, archaeologists and historical geographers have a history of working together on landscape and environmental studies. This paper deals with the Outer Hebrides – an area which is perceived by many as featuring a rather homogeneous landscape, in spite of its geographical variability. The archipelago has predominantly peat-covered uplands and lowlands, with a narrow, mainly western, coastal fringe of sandy, calcareous grassland (machair). Water, either fresh or sea, is rarely far from view.

The persistence of this 'landscape' over the last ten millennia was thought to have been confirmed in 1979 with the publication of a paper on a site in Lewis which presented evidence for a sustained grass-sedge-heathland in which woody plants played a minor role. The two decades since then have seen much palynological research from the Outer Hebrides. Surprisingly, much of this work paints a very different picture: one where woodland is likely to have been a major entity; where the spread of peat, in places, has been a feature of only the last few thousand years; and where human activity from Mesolithic hunter-gatherers to Neolithic and post-Neolithic agriculturalists, is arguably evident.

In this paper, the changing vegetational landscapes of the Outer Hebrides are examined together with a consideration of archaeological distributions. It is shown that woodland persisted, in general, for the first half of Postglacial time; that woodland reduction, from either natural or human causes, and highly variable spatially, was taking place at the same time as a human presence can be demonstrated; that fire is likely to have played a major role in promoting the development or maintenance of heathland; and that agricultural activities have led, in some locations, to major phases of soil erosion.

The importance of data limitations is emphasised, but palynology has the ability to reveal whole landscape changes, both natural and anthropogenic, as part of unbroken time series, something which is inaccessible by purely archaeological means. Like much interdisciplinary research, archaeological and environmental studies can complement each other extremely well, and the results emanating from the Outer Hebrides seem to justify the energy involved in their production.

KEYWORDS

Outer Hebrides, palynology, woodland, heathland, archaeology

INTRODUCTION

'Landscape' is interpreted elastically with regard to scale and composition (*cf.* Muir 1999). It can encompass the totality of elements which, in forming an often recurrent pattern, constitutes a landscape; or each such element may be deemed to represent a landscape. Landscapes are inextricably linked with the environments which contribute to their appearance and in which they are located. Interacting with their environments and landscapes, humans are influenced by them and modify them accidentally or intentionally.

Quaternary scientists, archaeologists and historical geographers have a history of working together on landscape and environmental studies. These stem especially from joint research dating from the middle part of the last century to the present (*e.g.* Clark 1954; Lambert *et al.* 1960; Simmons & Tooley 1981; Birks *et al.* 1988; Bell & Walker 1992; Butlin & Roberts 1995; Mellars & Dark 1998; Edwards & Ralston 1997; Edwards & Sadler 1999a; Mithen in press). Although the mutual interests of different practitioners have often led to studies which pay lip-service to co-operation, and a clash of ideologies is certainly not unusual (*cf.* Thomas, 1990; O'Connor, 1991), the past two decades especially have seen a propensity for more integrated studies, in which environment, landscape and human endeavour are seen as interrelated facets of an environment-human system (Barton *et al.*, 1995; Edwards & Sadler 1999b; Mithen 1999).

To review such an extensive and diverse field, and to do it justice, seems to us an impossible task within the compass of a contribution to this volume. Instead, we have elected to examine human-environmental interactions in the prehistoric landscape development of an extensive, supposedly 'marginal' area – the Outer Hebrides. The 'Long Island' has seen a tremendous amount of archaeological and environmental research over the last quarter century. It is not our intention to summarise the findings, but rather to demonstrate how palynology especially is contributing new perspectives to our understanding of such landscapes.

BACKGROUND

The Outer Hebrides of western Scotland (Fig. 2.1) are perceived by many as featuring a rather homogeneous landscape, in spite of their geographical variability (Boyd & Boyd 1990). The archipelago has predominantly peat-covered uplands and lowlands, with a narrow, mainly western, coastal fringe of sandy, calcareous grassland (machair). Water, either fresh or sea, is rarely far from view.

Maps of potential woodland distribution prior to the onset of large-scale clearance (McVean & Ratcliffe 1962; Bennett 1989) almost six millennia ago show the area as having been essentially unwooded other than for some patches of birch in eastern areas. Early pollen diagrams from Lewis, South Uist and Barra (Erdtman 1924; Harrison & Blackburn 1946; Blackburn 1946), with their limited range of fossil types depicted graphically as percentages of a tree pollen sum, tend to be disregarded or overlooked – they are numerically dominated, as presented, by non-arboreal taxa.

The publication of the investigations at Little Loch Roag, Lewis (Birks & Madsen 1979; Birks 1991), reinforced the pattern of a largely open 'landscape' in which a grass-sedge-heathland, in which woody plants played a minor role, had persisted for the last ten millennia (Fig. 2.2). The high quality data from Little Loch Roag signify an important statement on the vegetational and environmental history of the site. A major question arises, however, as to their representativeness.

In landscape terms, a superficially anomalous picture is provided by the fragmented stands of natural trees and shrubs in ungrazed and sheltered localities (Spence 1960; Currie 1979; Bennett & Fossitt 1988; Pankhurst & Mullin 1991). These hint at a potential woodland cover as do, in their way, the nineteenth-century plantations at Northbay, Barra (Watson & Barlow 1936; Geary & Gilbertson 1997) and Lews Castle, Stornaway, Lewis (Currie 1979) and commercial forestry (Blake 1966). The ubiquitous blanket peats of the Outer Hebrides hide a much more extensive distribution of woodland. Remains of pine, birch, alder, hazel and willow have been widely reported (e.g. Lewis

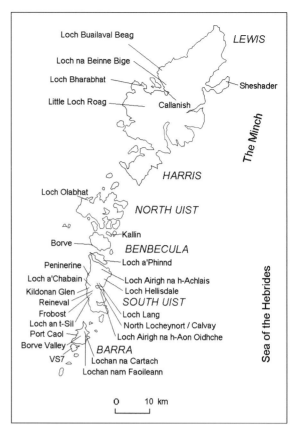

Fig. 2.1. The Outer Hebrides and the location of pollen sites mentioned in the text (for sources, see Table 1).

1906, 1907; Beveridge 1911; Elton 1938; Blackburn 1946; Wilkins 1984; Bohncke 1988; Fossitt 1996).

The early pollen data from Barra and South Uist are not, in fact, really arboreally mute. When they are re-cast with taxa expressed as percentages of total pollen, then some interesting facts emerge (cf. Fig. 2.3). Thus, maxima for tree plus shrub pollen percentages reach about 48 per cent (Lochan nan Faoileann), 63 per cent (Calvay) and 77 per cent (Stoneybridge). For Barra, Blackburn (1946, p. 48) observed that 'quite considerable numbers of forest trees grew on the better drained parts of the island'. Since the publication of the Little Loch Roag site in 1979, the Outer Hebrides have received a great amount of palynological attention (e.g. Bohncke 1988; Bennett et al. 1990, 1997; Edwards 1990, 1996; Edwards et al. 1995; Fossitt 1996; Lomax 1997; Mulder 1999). This would seem to suggest that many localities were wooded, that the spread of blanket peat occurred at different times, and that human agency was involved in prehistoric landscape change. Intriguingly the impact of people may be discernible in deposits of Mesolithic age – a period for which no material evidence of hunter-gatherers is known from the archipelago.

In this paper, discussion focuses particularly upon the evidence from previously unpublished pollen-analytical investigations. It will be shown that landscape change has been fundamental, and gradual or dramatic changes in the resource base available to human populations clearly occurred.

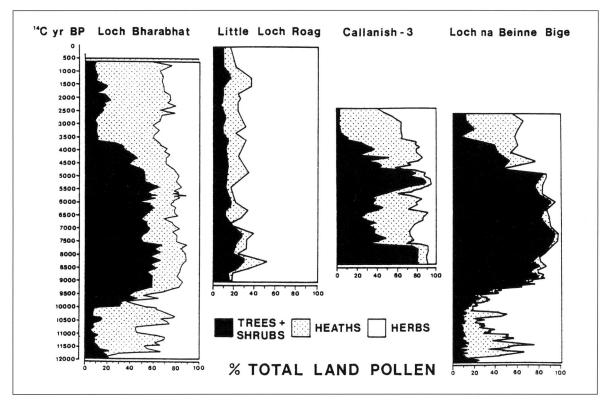

Fig. 2.2. Summary pollen diagrams from west Lewis (vertical axis in uncalibrated years B.P.; after Edwards 1996).

Unless indicated otherwise, all dates are quoted as calibrated radiocarbon (^{14}C) years before present (cal B.P.) based on the computer program CALIB 4.0 (*cf.* Stuiver & Reimer 1993). Archaeological distributions of selected monuments are shown in Figs 2.4-2.6. Plant and pollen nomenclature follow Stace (1997) and Bennett (1994) respectively. Selected data from pollen sites are presented in Figs 2.7-2.11. Where appropriate dating controls exist, the vertical axes of pollen diagrams are scaled in calendar years B.P. and dashed lines indicate 1,000 calendar year intervals from 6000 cal B.P. onwards, indicating the period covering Neolithic and later times.

THE PHYSICAL CONTEXT

The Outer Hebrides are separated from mainland Scotland and the islands of the Inner Hebrides by The Minch and the Sea of the Hebrides (Fig. 2.1). The archipelago is about 213 km in length with a coastline approximately 1800 km long (Boyd 1979; Angus 1997).

The islands are almost entirely composed of metamorphic gneisses and igneous rocks of Precambrian age, collectively known as Lewisian gneiss. On weathering, the gneiss tends to produce a subdued undulating landscape (Smith & Fettes 1979). The east coast plunges sharply to deep water, whereas the west coast is characterised by a submerged shelving platform and a shallow sea.

The islands were wholly glaciated during the last glacial maximum with the possible exception of the extreme north-west of Lewis (Peacock 1984; Sutherland & Walker 1984). Deglaciation led to severe erosion and formed a characteristic 'knock-and-lochan' landscape of rocky knolls and small peat- or water-filled hollows displayed to advantage in central North Uist (Gribble 1991; Hudson 1991).

It is likely that the area of the Outer Hebrides was much greater in the early Holocene (Postglacial) than it is today, perhaps forming one large island. A rise in sea-level, some 9.0 m since 9840 cal B.P. (Ritchie 1985), would have drowned the low-lying landscapes between the Uists and Benbecula, as well as the shallow areas of sand on Harris and Barra, creating a series of smaller islands (Boyd 1979).

The Outer Hebrides have been classified as 'hyperoceanic', with high precipitation, humidity and wind speeds, and a low annual temperature range (Angus 1991). Rain falls in measurable amounts three days out of every four when measured over a year (Manley 1979) with average levels of 1,100 mm at Stornoway and 2,610 mm at Loch Ashavat (Glentworth 1979). Precipitation exceeds evaporation during every month of the year except June (*ibid.*), and this long history of water surpluses has led to severe leaching of the soil and the formation of peaty podzols, gleys and peaty gleys, and blanket peat (Hudson 1991).

The winter is mild for the latitude and relatively free of frost and snow. The warmest months are July and August (12.9 °C mean daily temperature) and the coldest January and February (4.1 °C). The dominant factor in the climate appears to be

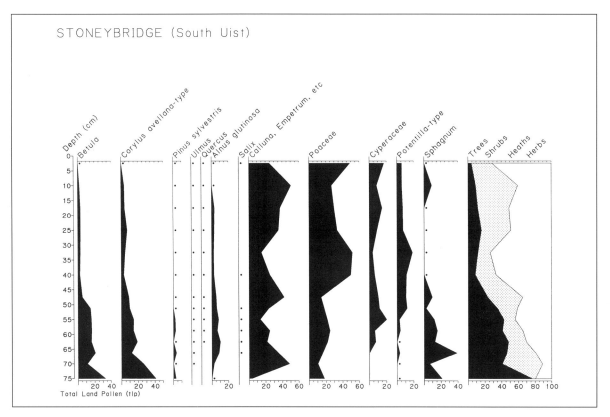

Fig. 2.3. Re-drawn pollen diagram from Stoneybridge, South Uist (Harrison & Blackburn 1946), with taxa expressed as percentages of total land pollen.

the strong and persistent wind; most of the island area is very exposed and gales are common (Birse & Robertson 1970).

Peat is the dominant soil on the islands today, but the peatland is considered generally unsuitable for agriculture apart for grazing (Glentworth 1979). The soils around the crofting townships generally consist of podzols and peaty brown soils. Further inland is the 'blackland' – undulating and hummocky land, with hollows filled with peat and lochs interspersed with bare rock. Along the east coast of the southern isles especially there is upland with steeper slopes, where peat and bare rock alternate, and heather moor and grassland can be found on better drained slopes. The rocky summits of these hills rise to 608 m in South Uist and 347 m in North Uist, while the highest mountains (up to 800 m O.D.) can be found in Harris.

An outstanding feature of the islands is the coastal plains of wind-blown and largely calcareous shell sand known as 'machair' (Ritchie 1979, 1991). In the Uists and Barra the machair covers about 10 *per cent* of the total land area, and stretches almost continuously along the west and north coasts, varying in width from a few metres to some 2 km (Figs 2.4-2.6). Because of its alkaline nature, the machair areas can support a rich and varied flora not found on any other part of the islands, as well as providing relatively productive pastoral and arable farmland (Ritchie 1967). The history of the machair has been extensively studied

(Ritchie 1967, 1979, 1985; Whittington & Ritchie 1988; Ritchie & Whittington 1994; Gilbertson *et al.* 1996, 1999; and Whittington & Edwards 1997). On present evidence it appears that the sands of the machair were originally derived from two sources: glacial sand deposited off the coast by the retreating Devensian ice-sheet, and postglacial shell sand. As the sea-level rose, these deposits were moved towards the land mass of the Hebrides, either as a continuous process or in a series of discrete events.

The oceanic climate and the soils have a significant impact on the vegetation. High precipitation and high wind speeds mean that montane plants tend to grow at much lower altitudes than in more continental areas, and that the growth of bryophytes such as the bog mosses (*Sphagnum* spp.) is favoured (Angus 1991). The wind speeds also stunt the upward growth of plants and, as in addition the winds are often salt-laden, particularly when they blow from the south or south-west, maritime species such as sea plantain (*Plantago maritima*) and the lichen *Ramalina siliquosa* may grow far inland (Currie 1979; Angus 1991).

THE HUMAN PRESENCE

The standing stones of Callanish (Calanais) and the broch of Dun Carloway, both located in west Lewis, may be the best known archaeological

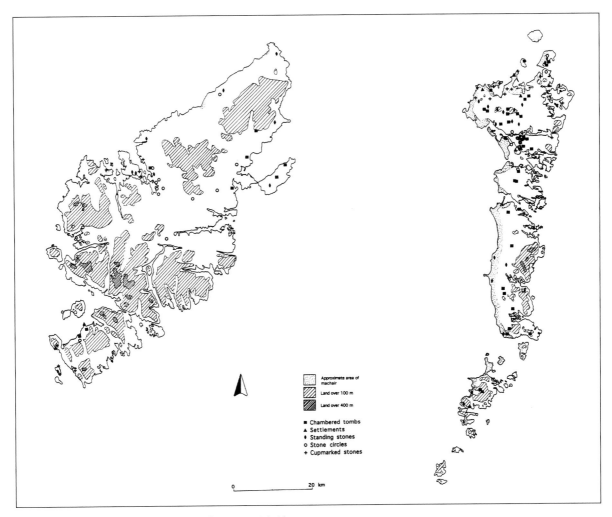

Fig. 2.4. Distribution of Neolithic sites in the Outer Hebrides.

monuments of the Outer Hebrides, but the distribution maps presented here (Figs 2.4-2.6; based on many sources including RCAHMS 1928, Henshall 1972, Armit 1996 and volumes of *Discovery and Excavation in Scotland*), despite the vagaries of discovery, indicate that a considerable population must have inhabited the islands at all stages of prehistory since the Neolithic. Much of the recent investigation has focused on the coastal areas, and in particular on the machair plains, where many sites have been revealed by erosion. The potential wealth of sites lying in the peat-covered inland areas has still to be explored.

THE MESOLITHIC

There is plenty of evidence for the presence of Mesolithic hunter-gatherers on the west coast of mainland Scotland and in the Inner Hebrides (Wickham-Jones 1994; Edwards & Mithen 1995), but no archaeological sites dating to the Mesolithic period have been found on the Outer Hebrides (Edwards 1996). Mesolithic people certainly had seaworthy boats (Finlayson & Edwards 1997) and so there is no reason to suppose that these vessels could not have reached the Outer Hebrides.

THE NEOLITHIC (FIG. 2.4)

The first archaeological evidence for settlement in the Outer Hebrides comes from the Neolithic period (*i.e. c.* 5800-4000 cal B.P.). The remains of ritual sites are plentiful and include standing stones, cup-marked stones, stone circles, stone settings, and chambered tombs. The last appear to be the earliest of these monuments, and are perhaps the most prominent archaeological feature of the islands, as their size makes them highly visible. Some forty-five chambered tombs have been recorded, with the greatest density on the island of North Uist, while Lewis, Harris and Barra have relatively few.

In contrast, only six settlement sites are recorded. Eilean an Tighe and Eilean Domhnuill on North Uist are both located on small islands in lochs (Scott 1951; Armit 1992a). Bharpa Carinish is an inland site discovered beneath the peat near the long cairn of Caravat Barp (Crone 1993). Northton and the Udal are sites located in the machair in Harris and North Uist respectively (Simpson 1976; Crawford n.d., 1996). Allt Chrisal is located on the rocky coastline of Barra (Foster 1995). The general picture of Neolithic settlement that is emerging is one of isolated small-scale

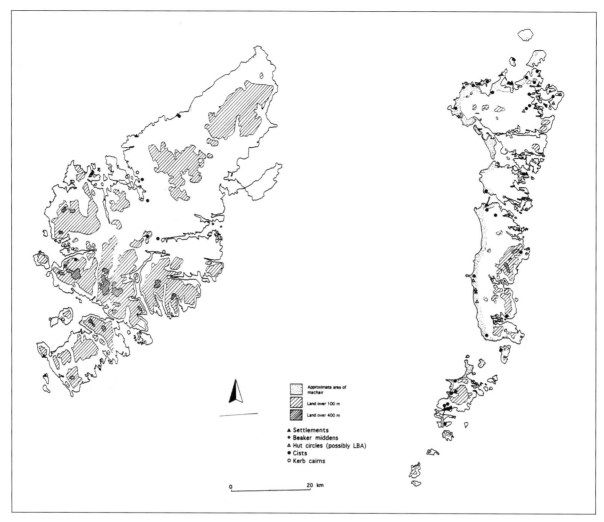

Fig. 2.5. Distribution of Bronze Age sites in the Outer Hebrides.

farming settlements, with one principal building, occupied perhaps by an extended family.

The range of plant remains found at the Neolithic sites suggests that a mixed economy using a variety of food sources, both cultivated and wild, was the norm for the islands (*cf.* Crone 1993; Boardman 1995; Armit in press) .

THE BRONZE AGE (FIG. 2.5)

Around 4000 cal B.P., large communal monuments appear to have become less significant, and individual burials, under small cairns or barrows or in stone cists became common. This period also saw the first appearance of Beaker pottery on settlement sites and in graves in the Outer Hebrides. A number of chambered tombs seem to have been sealed after a final Beaker burial – perhaps denoting the change from communal to single burial (Armit 1996). The appearance of Beaker pots has traditionally been seen as a sign of immigration, but arguments now revolve as much upon adoption (Parker Pearson 1999). At Allt Chrisal the Beaker period remains directly overlie the Neolithic levels, and Beaker ceramics appear to have been adopted at this site without

any break in the cultural tradition (Foster 1995). To date, there are no inland or island settlement sites from this period, and virtually all of the known sites have been found in the machair (Fig. 2.5), where they have generally been revealed by erosion (*e.g.* Ponting & Ponting 1984; Cowie 1987).

Towards the end of the Bronze Age there remains somewhat of a gap in the settlement evidence. There is also remarkably little evidence for funerary and ritual sites, although kerb cairns may have continued in use during this period and there is evidence for midden and cultivation at Baleshare (Barber forthcoming, quoted in Armit 1996), and presumably associated with a domestic site. At this time the characteristic settlement site in the southern Inner Hebrides was the hut circle. It is possible that such structures in the Outer Hebrides are also of late Bronze Age date, but also that settlement sites of the later Bronze Age may be obscured by later buildings. Underwater excavations at Dun Bharabhat, Lewis, suggest that this Iron Age site was occupied for some time in the first millennium B.C. before the dun was built (Harding & Armit 1990).

The Neolithic mixed economy based on

agriculture, hunting, gathering, fishing and fowling appears to have continued into the Bronze Age. Food remains in Beaker levels at Northton were similar to those found in the Neolithic deposits. Unlike these, however, the Beaker levels also contained abundant quantities of red deer. That arable agriculture was occurring is clear from ard marks, as at Rosinish. Botanical remains from that site in the form of carbonised grains, suggest that naked barley (*Hordeum vulgare* var. *nudum*) was the most important crop, with hulled barley and emmer wheat (*Triticum dicoccum*) forming an insignificant component (Shepherd & Tuckwell 1977). Protein analyses of residues from pots at Cladh Hallan, South Uist, revealed traces of cow's milk (Marshall *et al.* 1999).

THE IRON AGE (FIG. 2.6)

The Iron Age in Scotland is usually considered to start around the eighth century cal B.C. and to end with the first Roman invasion of Scotland in the late first century A.D., an event which appears to have had little influence on the material culture of the Outer Hebrides (Armit & Ralston 1997). The Iron Age witnessed a shift to monumental domestic architecture with roundhouses (brochs and duns) and wheelhouses, all built of stone and generally conspicuous in the landscape.

During the early Iron Age, when the Atlantic roundhouses were being built, there appears to have been a contraction of settlements into coastal areas (Armit 1992b). This may be due to the fact that the inland parts of the islands had started to suffer from peat bog spread by this time, thus becoming less productive and no longer useful for anything but rough grazing and peat-cutting (Barber & Brooks n.d.). There is little palaeo-economic evidence available from the Atlantic roundhouses because the bones from these sites, which were generally not located on the machair, tend to be poorly preserved (though sheep and pig bone were well represented in midden material at Dun Vulan (Parker Pearson & Sharples 1999) and red deer at the broch tower of Loch na Berie (Armit 1996). The mixed economy of the Neolithic and Bronze Age, though, appears to have persisted.

Some time at the end of the first millennium B.C., the people of the Outer Hebrides started building wheelhouses – single-storey, circular structures with a hearth in the centre and a

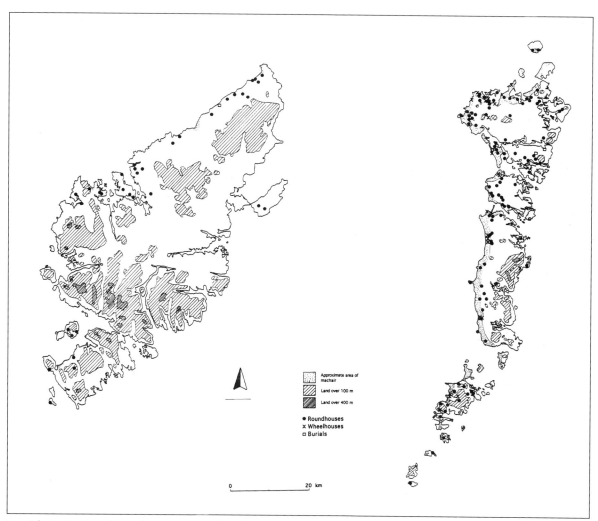

Fig. 2.6. Distribution of Iron Age sites in the Outer Hebrides.

periphery divided by radial piers, creating individual cells. The sites tended to extend outwards with secondary buildings and were often revetted into a sand-dune for extra stability, or built into earlier roundhouses. Unlike the roundhouses, however, most of the wheelhouses were built in the machair.

Few Iron Age burial sites have been identified in the Outer Hebrides. One possible reason is that the non-monumental nature of the graves makes them difficult to find, while lack of grave goods may make them difficult to identify. Ritual sites include pits, with apparent ritual and votive offerings, located within houses.

What is clear from the distribution maps is that the west lowland, and especially coastal areas, have produced most of the archaeological evidence for prehistoric occupation and use of the islands and there seems to have been a clear 'migration' towards the coast after the Neolithic, especially in the Uists and Barra.

THE DEVELOPMENT OF A WOODLAND STORY

If the paper by Birks & Madsen (1979) seemed in keeping with the open peat-covered landscapes of present-day Lewis, articles by Wilkins (1984) and Bohncke (1988) presented new (or re-discovered) perspectives. Wilkins's paper showed that macrofossils of birch (*Betula*), willow (*Salix*) and Scots pine (*Pinus sylvestris*) were widespread on Lewis (dating collectively to the period *c.* 10,240-4370 cal B.P.). Bohncke, from palynological studies at Callanish, 11 km north-east of Little Loch Roag, revealed that not only was birch locally very frequent (around 70 *per cent* of total land pollen), but that phases of woodland reduction and charcoal representation may signify woodland disturbance by Mesolithic hunter-gatherers (Fig. 2.2). Birks (1991, p. 35) reconciled the differences between the evidence from Little Loch Roag and that of the tree stumps by suggesting that the pollen reflected treeless vegetation at the *regional* scale, whereas the macrofossils reflected *local* areas of scrub in sheltered situations. Many of the macrofossil sites are not, however, very sheltered.

It might be suggested that the pollen data from Little Loch Roag reflect a local and not a regional picture. The high herbaceous content of the record would be expected from a valley mire in which peat was accumulating over the last 10,000 years and which provided local pollen and spore producers (especially grasses (Poaceae), sedges (Cyperaceae), heather (*Calluna vulgaris*), bog asphodel (*Narthecium ossifragum*) and bog moss (*Sphagnum*)) growing on and around the mire surface (for similar patterns, see Newell 1988, Mills *et al.* 1994 and Walker 1984). The lack of arboreal pollen could reflect the fact that woodland was not actually growing locally, or was not a major contributor to the pollen catchment area. Birks

(1991) acknowledged that (at the then time of writing) unpublished pollen data from South Uist (Bennett *et al.* 1990) revealed a substantial woodland component and that pollen spectra from organic sands in Benbecula and Grimsay (Whittington & Ritchie 1988) also indicated the possible local occurrence of woodland.

WOODLAND BECOMES THE NORM?

Since the publication of the Little Loch Roag site, the quantity of pollen data from the Outer Hebrides has expanded greatly. Figures 2.7-2.11 may be considered alongside other published (Walker 1984; Bohncke 1988; Whittington & Ritchie 1988; Bennett *et al.* 1990, 1997; Edwards 1990, 1996; Edwards *et al.* 1995; Brayshay & Edwards 1996; Fossitt 1996; Ashmore *et al.* 2000) and forthcoming (Brayshay *et al.*; Edwards & Craigie a, b; Lomax & Edwards; Mulder & Edwards) data.

It is becoming clear that the open vegetation of the Lateglacial (Edwards & Whittington 1994; Brayshay & Edwards 1996), dominated by such taxa as grasses, sedges and crowberry (*Empetrum nigrum*), gave way rapidly to a Holocene flora, from *c.* 11,500 cal B.P., in which arboreal (tree and shrub) elements became established. Expansions in juniper (*Juniperus communis*), willow (*Salix*) and especially birch (*Betula*) are immediate beneficiaries of climatic warming, to be followed from around 10,500 cal B.P. by hazel (*Corylus avellana*). Elm (*Ulmus*) and oak (*Quercus*) are present in lower percentages from *c.* 8800 cal B.P. and alder (*Alnus glutionosa*) from *c.* 8000 cal B.P. Consistent, but low quantities of ash (*Fraxinus excelsior*), rowan (*Sorbus aucuparia*) and aspen (*Populus tremula*) pollen are also found (not shown in the pollen diagrams).

The timing and abundance of these taxa, as for others, varies considerably. Thus, hazel was expanding at Loch Airigh na h-Aon Oidche from about 11,000 cal B.P., but from 8500 cal B.P. at Reineval. Percentages of *Corylus* reach 66 *per cent* at Lochan na Cartach, but only 17 *per cent* at Reineval. This kind of exercise could be played out for any taxon and reflects the mosaic nature of the vegetation, the taphonomic properties affecting the different pollen records and the variable quality of site chronologies. It is not possible to discuss the important methodological points arising from these here, but two issues will be addressed – the validity of the woodland record and the broad woodland patterns.

The more recently produced pollen records may be showing high quantities of woodland pollen, but the issue of the actual extent and density of woodland is not a simple one (Tipping 1994; Bennett *et al.* 1997; Edwards & Whittington 1997). The wood remains in peat prove the presence of at least pine, birch, hazel, alder and willow in some of these localities. The question of elm and oak establishment in the islands remains uncertain, although it has been argued (Bennett *et al.* 1990; Brayshay & Edwards 1996) that their consistent and high pollen percentages (*e.g.* 15 *per cent* for *Quercus* at Loch Lang, 10 *per cent* for *Ulmus* at Loch Hellisdale) are best explained by their local presence rather than a pollen source in mainland areas. A potential route towards unravelling some of the difficulties is to look not at pollen percentages, but at absolute pollen abundance – in other words, to use pollen influx (numbers of grains accumulating in a year) as a proxy measure of vegetational density. If woodland pollen influx in the islands is similar to that found in mainland areas assumed to have been wooded, then this may provide supporting evidence for the local presence of woodland in the islands. Many caveats should be invoked (Edwards in press), but in a preliminary comparison of pollen influx values for selected woodland taxa at sites in the Outer Hebrides and Fife, it might reasonably be inferred that the Outer Hebrides sites had a strong local presence of at least birch and hazel, and that the woodland cover was probably less dense than that of lowland Fife. Furthermore, fossil percentages for all Outer Hebridean taxa are greater than found in modern percentage samples from the same area (Fossitt 1994; Brayshay *et al.* in press), although this is less impressive for pine, oak and elm.

What is apparent is that birch-hazel woodlands dominate most pollen assemblages during the first half of the Postglacial and that major reductions in inferred woodland cover occur at different times, generally to be replaced by blanket peat and heath. The summary cumulative curves of trees, shrubs, heaths and herbs in the pollen diagrams (Figs 2.7-2.11) show these features very well and Table 2.1 summarises maximum arboreal pollen (AP) percentages for a fuller selection of Outer Hebridean sites. The variability is of considerable interest (*cf.* Fig. 2.2): the arboreal frequencies at the west Lewis sites of Loch na Beinne Bige and Callanish reach 90 *per cent* of TLP (total land pollen), whereas values for the more easterly sites of Loch Bharabhat and Loch Buailaval Beag attain 65 *per cent*. This may well be reflecting the deleterious effects of exposure and salt-spray on the more coastal sites. In South Uist, Loch a'Phuinnd is located only 3.5 km from Loch Airigh na h-Achlais yet its arboreal pollen content is considerably lower (58 *per cent* as opposed to 80 *per cent*), perhaps due to the relatively sheltered location of the latter site, 3 km inland. The series of westerly South Uist sites (Loch a'Chabain, Kildonan Glen, Frobost and Loch an t-Sìl) reach 74-79 *per cent* AP, yet the site of Reineval, less than 1 km from Frobost, produced an AP maximum of 42 *per cent*, presumably because Frobost is located in a relatively sheltered area, while Reineval lies at higher altitude in the centre of a large, exposed basin. The coastal sites, and especially inter-tidal peats, are more complex. The

deposits at Peninerine, South Uist and Kallin, Grimsay (admittedly for a time period which may post-date *c.* 6800 cal B.P.) have 38 *per cent* AP, whereas Port Caol, Barra, displays a massive 95.3 *per cent* of arboreal pollen (88 *per cent Betula*) in one spectrum (birch was on-site as evidenced by the macro-remains in the peat). Loch an t-Sìl, as noted, reached 74 *per cent* AP, but it lies immediately to the east of the machair and during the first half of the Holocene it would have been even further from the sea (currently 1.1 km) than those sites presently located in inter-tidal locations.

Sub-peat samples from Sheshader, east Lewis (Newell 1988) and spot samples from Bharpa Carinish, southern North Uist (Crone 1993) also have high quantities of woodland pollen (mainly hazel and birch), but the samples come from mineral soils and possibly suffer from differential preservation.

THE DECLINE OF WOODLAND, THE SPREAD OF PEAT AND SAND, AND A HUMAN DIMENSION?

Although both the eastern side and western sides of the islands had considerable woodland cover at some stage in the early Holocene, the timing for the decline of trees and shrubs is somewhat different (Table 2.1). There seems to be a pattern whereby most of the Lewis sites, and those from the eastern sides of South Uist and Barra, saw woodland decline after 5910 cal B.P. The dates at other sites for which a main AP fall (as opposed to a gradual decline) is detectable, spread between estimated dates of 8590 (Loch Bhuailaval Beag, Lewis) cal B.P. and up to 6150 cal B.P. for a series of western South Uist sites. This may well indicate that the earlier declines are reflecting continuous and natural influences deriving from their westerly locations (such as exposure to wind and salt), whereas the later falls in AP are a response to more sudden impacts of which human disturbance from Neolithic times seems most likely. In most cases, reductions in woodland pollen were matched by expansions in taxa indicative of peatlands, especially *Calluna,* Cyperaceae, *Potentilla*-type (cinquefoil/tormentil) and *Sphagnum*.

To what extent are anthropogenic influences evident in the palynologically-derived environmental record? This topic will be examined in the context of the conventional cultural periods.

THE MESOLITHIC

The decline in trees and shrubs during what elsewhere would be seen as Mesolithic times was an asynchronous event, and could be due to a number of different factors, including changes in climate, the progressive deterioration of soils, and human impact. At many sites the decline in trees and shrubs is rather gradual, which, as Brayshay

TABLE 2.1. MAXIMA IN ARBOREAL (TREE + SHRUB) POLLEN PERCENTAGES (TO NEAREST PERCENTAGE VALUE) AND DATES (TO NEAREST TEN YEARS) FOR PRINCIPAL DECLINE IN ARBOREAL POLLEN FOR SITES IN THE OUTER HEBRIDES

Site	Max.AP %	Start date of main AP fall (cal yr B.P.)	Source
Loch Bharabhat, Lewis	65	4730	Lomax 1997
Loch Bhuailaval Beag, Lewis*	65	8590	Fossitt 1996
Loch na Beinne Bige, Lewis	90	5640	Lomax 1997
Callanish, Lewis	90	4570	Bohncke 1988
Little Loch Roag, Lewis	30	5930	Birks & Madsen 1979
Loch Olabhat, North Uist	75	5910	Mulder 1999
Kallin, Grimsay	38	-	Whittington & Ritchie 1988
Borve, Benbecula	83	-	Whittington & Edwards 1997
Loch a☐Phuinnd, South Uist*	58	4470	Fossitt 1996
Loch Airigh na h-Achlais, South Uist	80	5600	Mulder 1999
Peninerine, South Uist	38	-	Whittington
Loch a☐Chabain, South Uist	78	6150	Mulder 1999
Kildonan Glen, South Uist	79	-	Brayshay & Edwards 1996
Reineval, South Uist	42	-	Edwards & Hirons
Frobost, South Uist	75	7980	Mulder 1999
Loch an t-S☐l, South Uist	74	8440	Edwards & Hirons
Loch Hellisdale, South Uist	81	-	Brayshay & Edwards 1996
Loch Lang, South Uist*	60	4850	Bennett et al., 1990
North Locheynort, South Uist	60	8080	Edwards & Hirons
Loch Airigh na h-Aon Oidhche, South Uist	64	4110	Edwards & Hirons
Port Caol, Barra	95	-	Brayshay & Edwards 1996
Borve Valley	34	-	Ashmore et al., 2000
Lochan na Cartach, Barra	87	4700	Brayshay & Edwards 1996

* AP values expressed as percentages of total land pollen except for the asterisked sites for which values are given as estimated percentages of total pollen and spores of terrestrial vascular plants.

& Edwards (1996) argue, could be indicative of climatic and pedogenic factors. At sites directly on the coast, such as Port Caol, Loch an t-Sìl and Kallin, as well as inter-tidal peat sites such as Peninerine and Borve, the appearance of sand in the stratigraphy suggest that the expansion of machair in that area may have had an effect on the vegetation, encouraging the growth of calcareous grasslands (Brayshay & Edwards 1996; Whittington & Edwards 1997). The primary taxa of blanket bog and heathland communities were already present on the island from the very start of the Holocene, and at many inland sites tree growth may simply have become unsustainable because of the progressive spread of peat in the area. How and when this happened will have depended at least partly on local vegetation, topography and hydrology. There may have been a general shift to wetter climatic conditions in western Europe around 7800 cal B.P. and this could have had a limiting effect on tree growth in the Outer Hebrides (Bell & Walker 1992).

In spite of the absence of known material remains for Mesolithic peoples in the Outer Hebrides, various pollen and related records point strongly towards phenomena which could be interpreted as reflecting the impacts of hunter-gatherers. At Callanish, Bohncke (1988) argued that sustained and dramatic decrease in *Betula* pollen (from ~72 down to 17 *per cent*), and increases in charcoal, *Calluna vulgaris*, Poaceae, *Potentilla*-type and *Pteridium aquilinum* (bracken), c. 9450-6060 cal B.P., could be evidence of burning by hunter-gatherer communities in order to assist in clearing woodland and create browse. At North Locheynort in South Uist there is also a sustained charcoal peak from 8110-5050 cal B.P. associated with reductions in trees and shrubs,

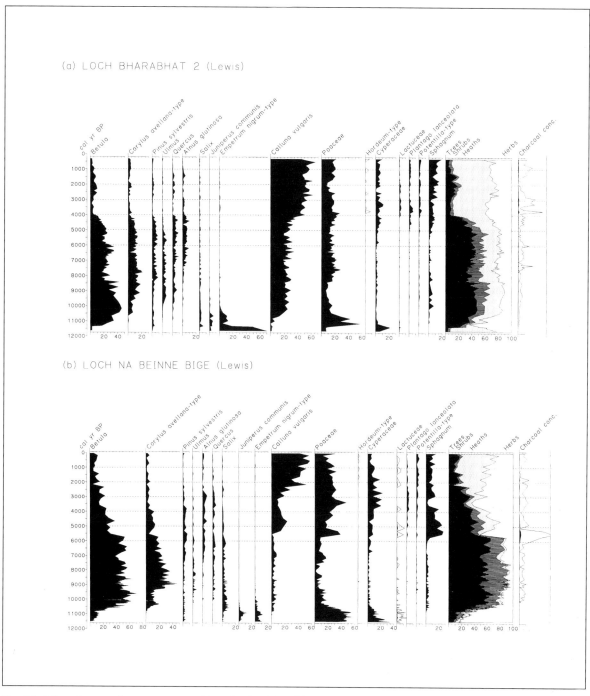

Fig. 2.7. Pollen diagrams from west Lewis: (a) Loch Bharabhat; (b) Loch na Beinne Bige.

which may also be attributable to human impact (Edwards 1990). The site at Loch an t-Sìl may be displaying evidence of two woodland clearance phases, lasting around a century each, at about 9000 and 8620 cal B.P. (Edwards 1996). Charcoal values are also high at Reineval, especially around 6810 cal B.P. Again this is accompanied by reductions in tree and shrub taxa, and could form evidence for a Mesolithic presence (Edwards *et al.* 1995). At Borve, an inter-tidal peat site on the west coast of Benbecula, there are rises in charcoal between 7680 and 7100 cal B.P., decreases in hazel and birch woodland and other changes, which the authors interpreted as possible evidence for

burning instigated by hunter-gatherers (Whittington & Edwards 1997) and similar changes are evident at Kallin. Virtually all these changes take place after 8890 cal B.P., a time when the Inner Hebrides are known to have been settled, but Bennett *et al.* (1990) have suggested that decreases in arboreal taxa and a rise in the charcoal curve at a somewhat earlier date (10,200 cal B.P.) at Loch Lang could also reflect human activity. If Mesolithic people and megafauna were present in the Outer Hebrides, then it must be supposed that evidence for them remains undiscovered beneath sea, sand and peat (Edwards 1996).

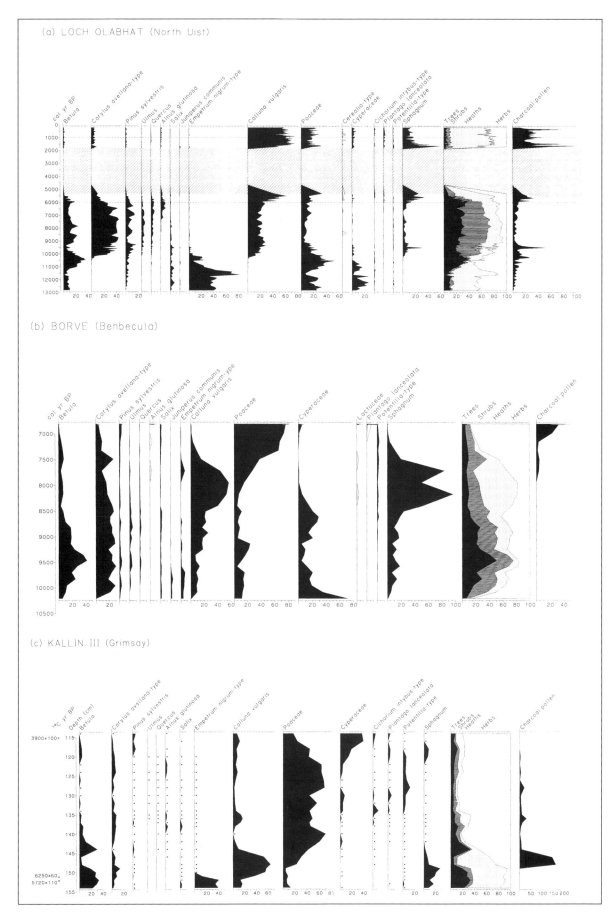

Fig. 2.8. Pollen diagrams from (a) Loch Olabhat, North Uist (shaded area is non-polleniferous); (b) Borve, Benbecula; (c) Kallin, Grimsay (vertical axis in uncalibrated years B.P.).

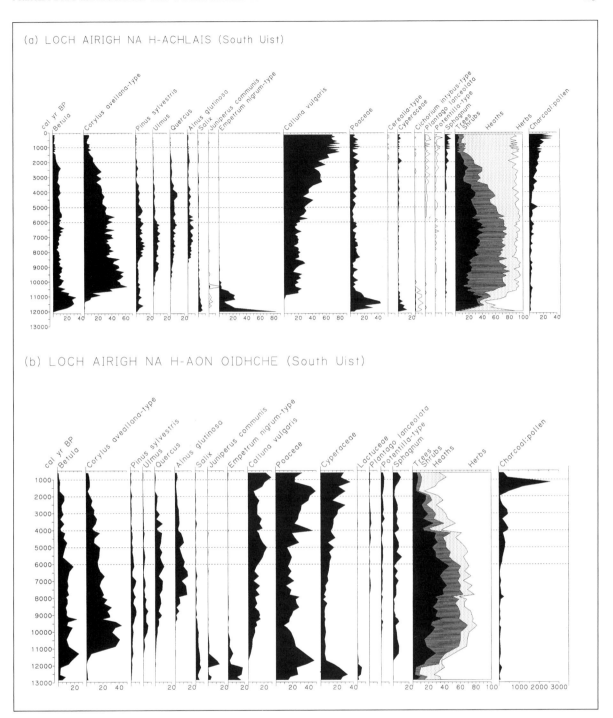

Fig. 2.9. Pollen diagrams from north-east and east South Uist: (a) Loch Airigh na h-Achlais; (b) Loch Airigh na h-Aon Oidhche.

THE NEOLITHIC

It has been observed above that most of the Lewis sites, and those from the eastern sides of South Uist and Barra, apparently saw woodland decline after *c.* 5910 cal B.P., *i.e.* from Neolithic times onward. This is very marked at Loch na Beinne Bige and Loch Olabhat and also to a lesser extent at Loch Airigh na h-Achlais and Loch Airigh na hAon Oidhche. In all cases *Betula* and *Corylus* are especially affected, but not solely. The classical 'elm decline' of *c.* 5800 cal B.P., the traditional marker of the start of the conventional Neolithic, can be seen in the profiles from a number of sites

including Loch Bharabhat, Loch na Beinne Bige, Loch a' Chabhain, Loch Airigh na h-Achlais and Loch Lang. *Ulmus* pollen representation has never been particularly high on the islands, however, and whether anthropogenic in origin or not, the elm decline is hard to detect.

Convincing evidence for Neolithic activity is particularly evident at Loch Olabhat in North Uist, a loch which actually contains the Neolithic settlement site of Eilean Domhnuill on its shore (Armit 1992a; Mulder & Edwards in press). Woodland at Loch Olabhat was greatly reduced from *c.* 5910 cal B.P. onwards, together with a strong increase in charcoal. The local community may have removed trees, not only to clear land for agriculture, but also as a source of building timber. The *Plantago lanceolata* (ribwort plantain) curve becomes continuous around the same time as woodland declines and, along with other indicators of pastoral agriculture, suggests that the area around the site may have been used for grazing. That arable agriculture was also taking place is suggested by the presence of Cerealia-type pollen (earlier instances are thought to derive from wild grasses) as well as arable weed indicators. Supporting macrofossil evidence for wheat and barley comes from Eilean Domhnuill (P. Grinter, pers. comm.). As trees and shrubs declined, *Calluna* heathland and peat bog taxa, such as *Sphagnum*, increased in prominence. It may well be that heath was deliberately managed by fire at this site or *Calluna* may have expanded into areas that had been opened up because of human interference. The process of clearing woodland in the area may have had a significant impact on the loch itself. From *c.* 5390 cal B.P. there is a very obvious erosional phase in the sedimentary sequence – organic mud is replaced by a silty clay in which very little pollen was preserved (indicated by the shaded area on Fig. 2.8). It is possible that the removal of trees led to changes in the natural hydrological systems in the area, which in turn led to increased erosion into the loch, and eventually a rise in water levels. Cultivation of what may have already been rather poor soils may also have contributed to the erosion. Eventually these changes appear to have affected Eilean Domhnuill itself – the settlement site was abandoned because of water inundation on at least one occasion during the Neolithic (Armit 1992a). The minerogenic sediment at Loch Olabhat forms a substantial deposit covering an estimated 3,500 calendar years, but whether it was deposited in one event followed by a long hiatus, or is the result of a series of erosional episodes (perhaps because of continued cultivation), cannot be determined.

The expansion of heathland as woodland is reduced during the Neolithic is seen well at Callanish, Loch na Beinne Bige and Loch Airigh na h-Achlais. The fact that palynological evidence of possible Neolithic impacts is not as apparent in some other cores does not signify a lack of early agriculturalists – the archaeological distributions for this period are widespread (Fig. 2.4) – but rather the difficulties in detecting changes in the pollen record when woodland was already reduced and where herbaceous 'cultural indicator' taxa are swamped by an increasing heath and peat bog component. Even in respect of the latter, however, the profile from Reineval is instructive. Its catchment area was virtually treeless prior to the Neolithic, but from 5170 cal B.P., *Calluna*-dominated heathland becomes far more prominent and high charcoal values between about 5170 and 1960 cal B.P. could suggest that the heathland was

being managed by fire. Two chambered tombs (Reineval and Barp Frobost) are located within 0.75 km of the site.

The greater part of the profile for Kallin in Grimsay (above 145 cm) probably covers the Neolithic. Here grass rather than heather dominates an area which had witnessed the loss of birch woodland. The spread of calcareous machair substrates, as seen earlier during the Mesolithic at Borve, Benbecula, was probably having a strong influence on the flora.

THE BRONZE AGE

The decline in woodland or the sustained presence of heathland and mire continued during the Bronze Age at most sites. At Loch Bharabhat, the fall in woodland pollen which had begun around 4740 cal B.P. became much more striking from *c.* 4150 cal B.P. and at Callanish the woodland decline also accelerated shortly after this. At both sites *Calluna* and charcoal expanded. Although these features are associated with the appearance of cereal-type pollen (*cf.* barley) at Loch Bharabhat and the continued presence of cereal-type at Callanish, the former site exhibits a clear decline in *Pinus*. This would seem to be the widespread and probably climatically-induced pine decline of *c.* 4500-4100 cal B.P. (Bennett 1984) and could indicate contemporaneous pressures emanating from both environmental and human sources. Similar patterns (apart from the cereal-type pollen) are evident at Lochan na Cartach, Barra. Investigations at the upland site of Borve Valley, Barra (Ashmore *et al.* 2000) revealed falls in woodland pollen and extensive mass movement of peat and soils within and beyond the Bronze Age and especially between *c.* 3200 and 1660 cal B.P. It was not possible to assign natural or anthropogenic causes to this, and although the authors noted marked human exploitation of the area during the Bronze Age, environmental aspects including slope inclination, heavy rainfall and soil impermeability may have been equally or more significant.

A useful indication of possible Bronze Age vegetational modification is provided (cautiously, given the nature of soil pollen spectra) from beneath a kerb cairn in Vatersay (Edwards & Craigie in press). It is inferred that the site upon which cairn VS7 was later to be built had originally had a vegetational cover dominated by heather, and grazing had encouraged the extension of grassland, forming a heath-grassland mosaic (Fig. 2.11). It is also posited that hazel was being conserved as part of a coppice system.

THE IRON AGE

The Iron Age and early historic periods are characterised by the continuation or expansion of heath and poor grassland. Very few areas seem to have retained much more than a token woodland

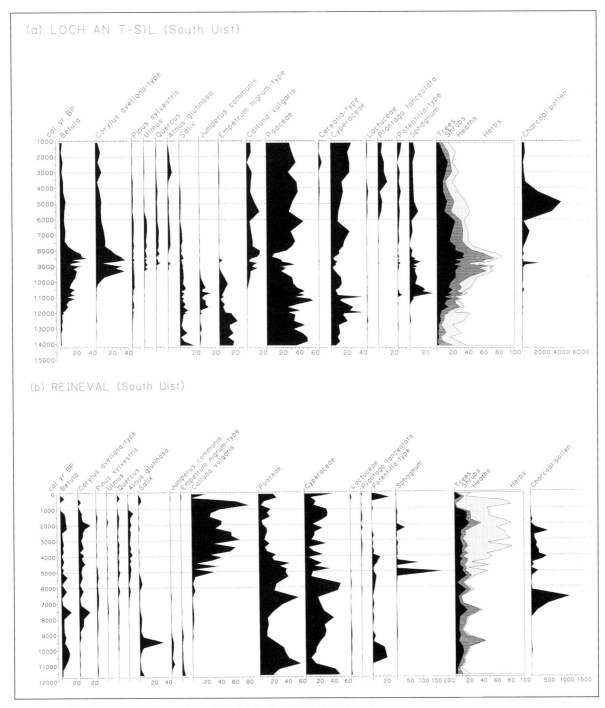

Fig. 2.10. Pollen diagrams from west South Uist: (a) Loch an t-Sìl; (b) Reineval.

presence and where, most usually, some birch remains (*e.g.* Loch na Beinne Bige, Loch Airigh na h-Achlais, Reineval) it does so temporarily. Heather pollen dominates many records with very high counts at Loch Bharabhat, Loch na Beinne Bige, Loch Olabhat, Loch Airigh na h-Achlais, Reineval and Lochan na Cartach. In some, but not all instances, these are associated with good charcoal representation. If fire was not directly involved with heathland management (*cf.* Edwards *et al.* 1995; Simmons 1996), then the charcoal may be reflecting domestic fires of a possibly increased human population (note the density of settlements, Fig. 2.6). Grassland rather than, or as

well as, heath is typical of several sites including the west Lewis cluster of Loch na Beinne Bige, Callanish and Loch Buailaval Beag, and the west coast, South Uist site of Loch an t-Sìl. This may denote an emphasis on grazing or equally, in the case of Loch an t-Sìl, the fact that calcareous additions to the peaty substrates favoured grasses.

The first appearance of cereal-type pollen is during the Iron Age at Loch na Beinne Bige and Loch Airigh na h-Achlais; it is even later at Loch a' Phuinnd, Frobost and Loch Lang; and it is absent from the Reineval, Loch Airigh na h-Aon Oidhche and Borve Valley profiles. If this is a true reflection of the status of cultivation in these areas, and not

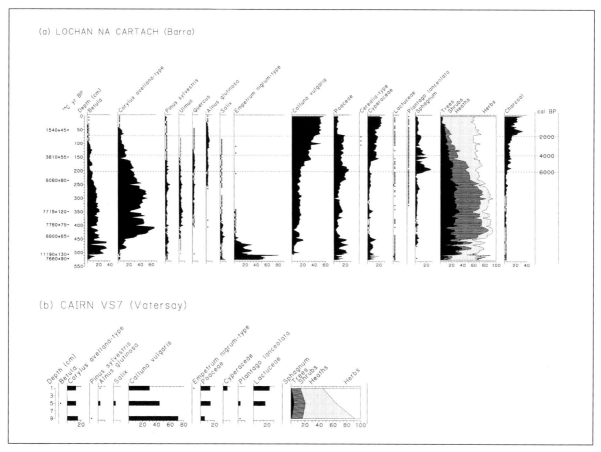

Fig. 2.11. Pollen diagrams from (a) Lochan na Cartach, Barra (vertical axis in uncalibrated years B.P.); (b) beneath kerb cairn VS7, Vatersay (soil pollen).

an artefact of sampling, then it seems to denote the lack or delayed adoption of arable in inland and eastern areas. Indeed, the two *Airigh* (Gaelic: 'shieling') sites of Loch Airigh na h-Achlais and Loch Airigh na h-Aon Oidhche did not witness final clearance until about 1360 cal B.P. (the latter site is relatively inaccessible, while the shieling designation, if not recent, could indicate their primary grazing role).

The Lewis site of Loch Bharabhat offers an interesting picture of human impact with sedimentological and palynological evidence for catchment disturbance from an inferred 2900 cal B.P. through to 800 cal B.P., but reaching a maximum *c.* 2340 cal B.P. Soil erosion was high throughout the Iron Age causing the deposition of inorganic materials, eroded peat and, paradoxically, old deteriorated pollen of woodland taxa. It is likely that the construction of the roundhouse, Dun Bharabhat, within the loch would have created considerable disturbance on the loch islet and in the catchment. This would have been in combination with agricultural activities at a time of deteriorating climate and soil impoverishment. Harding & Armit (1990) propose continuous occupation between the primary (monumental roundhouse) and secondary (post-collapse simple cellular building) phases, *c.* 2740 and 2000 cal B.P. – dates which can be accommodated by the palaeoenvironmental

evidence. Archaeological discoveries of peat ash and hearths show that peat was an important fuel resource, especially in the absence of widespread woodland. The cutting of peat for fuel or bedding is likely to have rendered peat deposits more susceptible to erosion.

CONCLUDING POINTS

The Outer Hebrides have obviously been settled since Neolithic times at least. The environmental evidence also points to a Mesolithic presence even if the material archaeological record of the earliest hunter-gatherers perhaps lies hidden beneath sea, sand and peat. Human modification of landscape, shown especially by the pollen-based vegetational record during Mesolithic and later periods, is difficult to disentangle from natural processes involving climate (particularly exposure from wind and salt-laden rain and not simply climate change), soil acidification, peat spread, the effects of sand movement and a retreating coastline as sea-levels rose. Prehistoric peoples probably accelerated processes such as heathland development and the spread of blanket peat which would have occurred naturally anyway.

What is evident is that many areas of the Outer Hebrides possessed a tree and shrub cover in which birch and hazel dominated, where pine, alder and willow were present and in which elm and oak may have figured. The density of such taxa remains to be demonstrated, but those pollen profiles featuring a good arboreal record not only reveal that the landscape had a concomitant woodland resource base, but also provide the means to assess anthropogenic impacts upon landscape. A pattern of woodland reduction with expansions in heather and 'cultural' pollen, together with microscopic charcoal, furnish circumstantial evidence for human engagement with the environment. The variable times at which this occurred is a further demonstration of the time-transgressive nature of human impact, or of the 'buffering' imposed by natural systems.

There are some clear limitations in the data sets, both environmental and archaeological, which hinder progress. The pollen evidence from areas where natural and human causes are difficult to disentangle, especially where many sites display little woodland or its loss at an early stage, are often complacent and lack good 'indicators' of specific types of impact. Although modern pollen studies can assist in interpretation (*cf.* Gaillard *et al.* 1992; Broström *et al.* 1998; Brayshay *et al.* in press), investigations which explore the association between modern and fossil records, almost certainly involving multivariate statistics, are required. It is regrettable that routine light microscopy is still unable to differentiate unequivocally between the large pollen grains of wild grasses and those of cereals. The former are frequent in Outer Hebridean pollen profiles, while the latter are also almost certainly present and reflected further by ard marks, macrofossils and quernstones from archaeological sites. Debates still surround the significance of microscopic charcoal (Edwards 1996, 1998; Tipping 1996), though the correspondence between inferred heathland spread and the charcoal-based fire record is compelling (Odgaard 1992; Edwards *et al.* 1995; Simmons 1996).

The archaeology of the Outer Hebrides is becoming better known (*cf.* Armit 1990a, 1996, in press; Branigan & Foster 1995, in press; Parker Pearson & Sharples 1999), but in spite of the seemingly good distributions of monuments (Figs 2.4-2.6), these can only represent current impressions. The forthcoming publication of intensive surveys (*e.g.* Branigan & Foster in press) will show the inadequacies of distributions which have accumulated from a knowledge of accessible, occupied areas, or as a result of archaeological visits or chance discoveries elsewhere. Numerous sites must be hidden beneath sand and peat. There always remains, of course, the problem of chronology where excavation or reliable radiometric dating has not taken place. This applies to the vast majority of sites. We may be happy to assign a Neolithic age to a chambered cairn, but hut circles could be Bronze or Iron Age. Furthermore, it remains the case that environmental evidence is not always gathered systematically (or at all) during archaeological excavation (though see, for example, Parker Pearson & Sharples 1999; Armit in press).

Pollen analyses from long peat and lake sediment sequences reveal whole landscape changes, both natural and anthropogenic, as part of unbroken time series. Typically, and the Outer Hebrides sites are no exception, long pollen profiles demonstrate that landscape impacts have been continuous, if variable in scale and intensity. The archaeological record (and palynology from archaeological materials) usually provides snapshots or time slices of restricted spatial extent, yet they also furnish colour and sometimes certainty. Palynology provides a constant reminder that landscapes were seldom forsaken totally, and a corrective to archaeological notions of abandonment based upon restricted data. In unison, like much interdisciplinary research, archaeological and environmental studies can complement each other extremely well, and the results emanating from the Outer Hebrides seem to justify the energy involved in their production.

ACKNOWLEDGEMENTS

Much of the fieldwork and evidence based on radiocarbon-dating has benefited from the financial support of the Leverhulme Trust, Historic Scotland, the Natural Environment Research Council, and the Universities of Birmingham, Sheffield and St Andrews. The assistance of Patrick Ashmore, Keith Branigan and staff at the NERC Radiocarbon Dating Laboratory, East Kilbride, are gratefully acknowledged. Ian Armit and Ian Whyte are thanked for their comments on a draft of the paper and Della Hooke is thanked for her patience.

BIBLIOGRAPHY

Angus, I. S., 1991. 'Climate and vegetation of the Outer Hebrides', in *Flora of the Outer Hebrides*, ed. Pankhurst & Mullin, pp. 28-31.

Angus, S., 1997. *The Outer Hebrides: the Shaping of the Islands* (Cambridge).

Armit, I. (ed.), 1990. *Beyond the Brochs: changing perspectives on the Atlantic Scottish Iron Age* (Edinburgh).

Armit, I. 1992a. *Eilean Domhnuill, Loch Olabhat, North Uist. Archive Rep Vol. 1.*

Armit, I., 1992b. *The Later Prehistory of the Western Isles of Scotland*, Br Archaeol Rep, Br ser 221 (Oxford).

Armit, I., 1996. *The Archaeol of Skye and the Western Isles* (Edinburgh).

Armit, I. (ed.), in press. *Eilean Domhnuill: Excavation of a Neolithic Settlement in Loch Olabhat, North Uist, Western Isles,* Dep Archaeol, Univ Edinburgh, Monogr Ser.

Armit, I., & Ralston, I. B. M., 1997. 'The Iron Age', in *Scotland: Environment and Archaeology, 8000 BC-AD 1000,* ed. Edwards & Ralston, pp. 169-93.

Ashmore, P., Brayshay, B. A., Edwards, K. J., Gilbertson, D. D., Grattan, J. P., Kent, M., Pratt, K. E., & Weaver, R. E., 2000. 'Allochthonous and autochthonous mire deposits, slope instability and palaeoenvironmental investigations in the Borve Valley, Barra, Outer Hebrides, Scotland', *The Holocene,* 10, pp. 97-108.

Barber, J., & Brooks, M., n.d. 'Excavation and survey in North Uist' (Unpubl ms).

Barton, R. N. E., Berridge, R. J., Walker, M. J. C., & Bevins, R. E., 1995. 'Persistent places in the Mesolithic landscape: an example from the Black Mountain uplands of South Wales', *Proc Prehist Soc,* 61, pp. 81-116.

Bell, M., & Walker, M. J. C., 1992. *Late Quaternary Environmental Change: physical and human perspectives* (London).

Bennett, K. D., 1984. 'The Post-Glacial history of *Pinus sylvestris* in the British Isles', *Quaternary Sci Rev,* 3, pp. 133-56.

Bennett, K. D., 1989. 'A provisional map of forest types for the British Isles 5000 years ago', *J Quaternary Sci,* 4, pp. 141-4.

Bennett, K. D., 1994. *Annotated Catalogue of Pollen and Pteridophyte Spore Types of the British Isles* (http://www.kv.geo.uu.se/pc-intro.html).

Bennett, K. D., Bunting, M. J., & Fossitt, J. A., 1997. 'Long-term vegetation change in the Western and Northern Isles, Scotland', *Bot J Scotland,* 49, pp. 127-40.

Bennett, K. D., & Fossitt, J., 1988. 'A stand of birch by Loch Eynort, South Uist, Outer Hebrides', *Trans Bot Soc Edinburgh,* 45, pp. 245-52.

Bennett, K. D., Fossitt, J. A., Sharp, M. J., & Switsur, V. R., 1990. 'Holocene vegetational and environmental history at Loch Lang, South Uist, Scotland', *New Phytol,* 114, pp. 281-98.

Beveridge, E., 1911. *North Uist: its Archaeology and Topography, with notes upon the early history of the Outer Hebrides* (Edinburgh).

Birks, H. H., Birks, H. J. B., Kaland, P. E. & Moe, D. (eds), 1988. *The Cultural Landscape – Past, Present and Future* (Cambridge).

Birks, H. J. B., 1991. 'Floristic and vegetational history of the Outer Hebrides', in *Flora of the Outer Hebrides*, ed. Pankhurst & Mullin, pp. 32-7.

Birks, H. J. B., & Madsen, B. J., 1979. 'Flandrian vegetational history of Little Loch Roag, Isle of Lewis, Scotland', *J Ecol,* 67, pp. 825-42.

Birse, E. L., & Robertson, L., 1970. *Assessment of Climatic Conditions in Scotland 2. Based on Exposure and Accumulated Frost* (Aberdeen).

Blackburn, K. B., 1946. 'On a peat from the island of Barra, Outer Hebrides. Data for the study of post-glacial history. X.', *New Phytol,* 45, pp. 44-9.

Blake, J. L., 1966. 'Trees in a treeless island', *Scott For,* 20, pp. 37-47.

Boardman, S., 1995. 'Charcoal and charred plant macrofossils', in *Barra. Archaeological Research on Ben Tangaval*, ed. Branigan & Foster, pp. 149-57.

Bohncke, S. J. P., 1988. 'Vegetation and habitation history of the Callanish area', in *The Cultural Landscape – Past, Present and Future*, ed. Birks, Birks, Kaland, & Moe, pp. 445-61.

Boyd, J. M. (ed.), 1979. *The Natural Environment of the Outer Hebrides, Proc R Soc Edinburgh,* 77B.

Boyd, J. M., & Boyd, I. C., 1990. *The Hebrides, a Natural History* (London).

Branigan, K., & Foster, P., 1995. *Barra. Archaeological Research on Ben Tangaval* (Sheffield).

Branigan, K., & Foster, P. (eds), in press. *From Barra to Berneray: archaeological survey and excavation in the Southern Isles, Outer Hebrides* (Sheffield).

Brayshay, B. A., & Edwards, K. J., 1996. 'Lateglacial and Holocene vegetational history of South Uist and Barra', in *The Outer Hebrides: the last 14,000 Years,* ed. Gilbertson, Kent & Grattan, pp. 13-26.

Brayshay, B. A., Gilbertson, D. D., Kent, M., Edwards, K. J., Wathern, P., & Weaver, R. E., in press. 'Surface pollen-vegetation relationships on the Atlantic seaboard: South Uist, Scotland', *J Biogeogr.*

Broström, A., Gaillard, M. J., Ihse, M., & Odgaard, B., 1998. 'Pollen-landscape relationships in modern analogues of ancient cultural landscapes in southern Sweden – a first step towards quantification of vegetation openness in the past', *Veg Hist & Archaeobot,* 7, pp. 189-201.

Butlin, R., & Roberts, N. (eds), 1995. *Human Impact and Adaptation: ecological relations in historical times* (Oxford).

Clark, J. G. D., 1954. *Excavations at Star Carr* (Cambridge).

Cowie, T., 1987. 'Barvas', *Discovery and Excavation in Scotland,* p. 62.

Crawford, I. A., 1996. 'The Udal', *Current Archaeol,* 147, pp. 84-94.

Crawford, I. A., n.d. *The West Highlands and Islands: a View of 50 Centuries. The Udal (N. Uist) evidence* (Cambridge).

Crone, A., 1993. 'Excavation and survey of sub-peat features of Neolithic, Bronze and Iron Age date at Bharpa Carinish, North Uist, Scotland', *Proc Prehist Soc,* 59, pp. 361-82.

Currie, A., 1979. 'The vegetation of the Outer Hebrides', *Proc R Soc Edinburgh,* 77B, pp. 219-65.

Edwards, K. J., 1990. 'Fire and the Scottish Mesolithic: evidence from microscopic charcoal', in *Contributions to the Mesolithic in Europe,* ed. P. M. Vermeersch & P. Van Peer (Leuven), pp. 71-9.

Edwards, K. J., 1996. 'A Mesolithic of the Western and Northern Isles of Scotland? Evidence from pollen and charcoal', in *The Early Prehistory of Scotland*, ed. T. Pollard & A. Morrison (Edinburgh), pp. 23-38.

Edwards, K. J., 1998. 'Detection of human impact on the natural environment: palynological views', in *Science in Archaeology: an agenda for the future*, ed. J. Bayley (London), pp. 69-88.

Edwards, K. J., in press. 'Palaeoenvironments of Late Upper Palaeolithic and Mesolithic Scotland and the North Sea area: new work, new thoughts', in *Mesolithic Scotland: the Early Holocene prehistory of Scotland and its European context,* ed. A. Saville, Soc Antiq Scotland, Monogr Ser (Edinburgh).

Edwards, K. J., & Craigie, R., in press. 'Soil pollen analyses associated with Bronze Age kerbed cairn VS7, Vatersay', in *From Barra to Berneray: archaeological survey and excavation in the Southern Isles, Outer Hebrides*, ed. Branigan & Foster.

Edwards, K. J., & Mithen, S., 1995. 'The colonization of the Hebridean islands of western Scotland: evidence from the palynological and archaeological records', *World Archaeol,* 26, pp. 348-65.

Edwards, K. J., & Ralston, I. B. M. (eds), 1997. *Scotland: Environment and Archaeology, 8000 BC-AD 1000* (Chichester).

Edwards, K. J., & Sadler, J. P. (eds), 1999a. *Holocene Environments of Prehistoric Britain, J Quaternary Sci*, 14 (*Quaternary Proc*, 7).

Edwards, K. J., & Sadler, J. P., 1999b. 'Striving for an environment-human consensus', *J Quaternary Sci*, 14 (*Quaternary Proc*, 7), pp. v-vii.

Edwards, K. J., & Whittington, G., 1994. 'Lateglacial pollen sites in the Western Isles of Scotland', *Scott Geogr Mag*, 110, pp. 33-9.

Edwards, K. J., & Whittington, G., 1997. 'Vegetation history', in *Scotland: Environment and Archaeology, 8000 BC-AD 1000*, ed. Edwards, & Ralston, pp. 63-82.

Edwards, K. J., Whittington, G., & Hirons, K. R., 1995. 'The relationship between fire and long-term wet heath development in South Uist, Outer Hebrides, Scotland', in *Heaths and Moorland: Cultural Landscapes*, ed. D. B. A. Thompson, A. J. Hestor & M. B. Usher (Edinburgh), pp. 240-8.

Elton, C., 1938. 'Notes on the ecological and natural history of Pabbay and the other islands in the Sound of Harris', *J Ecol*, 26, pp. 275-97.

Erdtman, G., 1924. 'Studies in the micropalaeontology of postglacial deposits in northern Scotland and the Scottish Isles, with especial reference to the history of woodlands', *J Linnean Soc*, 46, 449-504.

Finlayson, B., & Edwards, K. J., 1997. 'The Mesolithic', in *Scotland: Environment and Archaeology, 8000 BC-AD 1000*, ed. Edwards, & Ralston, pp. 109-25.

Fossitt, J., 1994. 'Modern pollen rain in the northwest of the British Isles', *The Holocene*, 4, pp. 365-76.

Fossitt, J. A., 1996. 'Late Quaternary vegetation history of the Western Isles of Scotland', *New Phytol*, 132, pp. 171-96.

Foster, P., 1995. 'Excavations at Allt Chrisal, 1989-1994. The excavations', in *Barra: Archaeological Research on Ben Tangaval*, ed. Branigan & Foster, pp. 49-99.

Gaillard, M. -J., Birks, H. J. B., Emanuelsson, U., & Berglund, B. E., 1992. 'Modern pollen land/use relationships as an aid in the reconstruction of past land-uses and cultural landscapes: an example from south Sweden', *Veg Hist & Archaeobot*, 1, pp. 3-17.

Gearey, B., & Gilbertson, D. D., 1997. 'Pollen taphonomy of trees in a windy climate: Northbay Plantation, Barra, Outer Hebrides', *Scott Geogr Mag*, 113, pp. 113-20.

Gilbertson, D., Kent, M., & Grattan, J. (eds), 1996. *The Outer Hebrides: the last 14,000 years* (Sheffield).

Gilbertson, D. D., Schwenninger, J. -L., Kemp, R. A., & Rhodes, E. J., 1999. 'Sand-drift and soil formation along an exposed North Atlantic coastline: 14,000 years of diverse geomorphological, climatic and human impacts', *J Archaeol Sci*, 26, 439-69.

Glentworth, R., 1979. 'Observations on the soils of the Outer Hebrides', *Proc R Soc Edinburgh*, 77B, pp. 123-37.

Gribble, C. D., 1991. 'The geology of the Outer Hebrides', in *Flora of the Outer Hebrides*, ed. Pankhurst & Mullin, pp. 14-18.

Harding, D. W., & Armit, I., 1990. 'Survey and excavation in West Lewis', in *Beyond the Brochs: changing perspectives on the later Iron Age in Atlantic Scotland*, ed. I. Armit (Edinburgh), pp. 71-107.

Harrison, J. W. H., & Blackburn, K. B., 1946. 'The occurrence of a nut of *Trapa natans* L. in the Outer Hebrides, with some account of the peat bogs adjoining the loch in which the discovery was made', *New Phytol*, 45, pp. 124-31.

Henshall, A. S., 1972. *The Chambered Tombs of Scotland*, Vol. 2 (Edinburgh).

Hudson, G., 1991. 'Geomorphology and soils of the Outer Hebrides', in *Flora of the Outer Hebrides*, ed. Pankhurst & Mullin, pp. 19-27.

Lambert, J. M., Jennings, J. N., Smith, C. T., Green, C., & Hutchinson, J. N., 1960. *The Making of the Broads*, R Geogr Soc Res Ser No. 3.

Lewis, F. J., 1906. 'The plant remains in the Scottish peat mosses. Part II. The Scottish Highlands', *Trans R Soc Edinburgh*, 45, pp. 335-60.

Lewis, F. J., 1907. 'The plant remains in the Scottish peat mosses. Part III. The Scottish Highlands and Shetland', *Trans R Soc Edinburgh*, 46, pp. 33-70.

Lomax, T., & Edwards, K. J., forthcoming. 'Pollen and related studies of human impact at Loch Bharabhat', in *Investigations at Dun Bharabhat, Bhaltos Peninsula, Lewis*, D. Harding, Dep Archaeol, Univ Edinburgh, Monogr Ser.

Lomax, T. M., 1997. 'Holocene vegetation history and human impact in western Lewis, Scotland', Unpubl Univ Birmingham PhD thesis.

Manley, G., 1979. 'The climatic environment of the Outer Hebrides', *Proc R Soc Edinburgh*, 77B, 47-59.

Marshall, P., Mulville, J., Parker Pearson, M., and Smith, H., 1999. 'Cladh Hallan Late Bronze Age and Early Iron Age settlement, South Uist', *The Western Isles Project. 12th interim report*, Dep Archaeol & Prehist, Univ Sheffield, pp. 1-7.

McVean, D. N., & Ratcliffe, D. A., 1962. *Plant Communities of the Scottish Highlands* (London).

Mellars, P., & Dark, P., 1998. *Star Carr in Context: new archaeological and palaeoecological investigations at the early Mesolithic Site of Star Carr, North Yorkshire* (Cambridge).

Mills, C. M., Crone, A., Edwards, K. J., & Whittington, G., 1994. 'The excavation and environmental investigation of a sub-peat stone bank near Loch Portain, North Uist, Outer Hebrides', *Proc Soc Antiq Scotland*, 124, pp. 155-71.

Mithen, S. J., 1999. 'Mesolithic archaeology, environmental archaeology and human palaeoecology', *J Quaternary Sci*, 14 (*Quaternary Proc*, 7), pp. 477-83.

Mithen, S. J. (ed.), in press. *Hunter-Gatherer Landscape Archaeology: the southern Hebrides Mesolithic project, 1988-1998* (Cambridge).

Muir, R., 1999. *Approaches to Landscape* (Macmillan).

Mulder, Y., 1999. 'Aspects of vegetation and settlement history in the Outer Hebrides, Scotland', Unpubl Univ Sheffield PhD thesis.

Mulder, Y., & Edwards, K. J., in press. 'Palynological studies of landscape change of Loch Olabhat and Eilean Domhnuill', in *Eilean Domhnuill: excavations of a Neolithic settlement in Loch Olabhat, North Uist, Western Isles*, ed. I. Armit, Dep Archaeol, Univ Edinburgh, Monogr Ser.

Newell, P. J., 1988. 'A buried wall in peatland by Sheshader, Isle of Lewis', *Proc Soc Antiq Scotland*, 118, pp. 79-93.

O'Connor, T. P., 1991. 'Science, evidential archaeology and the new scholasticism', *Scott Archaeol Rev*, 8, pp. 1-7.

Odgaard, B. V., 1992. 'The fire history of Danish heathland areas as reflected by pollen and charred particles in lake sediments', *The Holocene*, 2, pp. 218-26.

Pankhurst, R.J ., & Mullin, J. M., 1991. *The Flora of the Outer Hebrides* (London).

Parker Pearson, M., 1999. 'The Earlier Bronze Age', in *The Archaeology of Britain: an introduction from the Upper Palaeolithic to the Industrial Revolution*, ed. J. Hunter & I. Ralston (London), pp. 77-94.

Parker Pearson, M., & Sharples, N. (eds), 1999. *Between Land and Sea: excavations at Dun Vulan, South Uist* (Sheffield).

Peacock, J. D., 1984. *Quaternary Geology of the Outer Hebrides*, Rep Br Geol Surv, 16, No. 2.

Ponting, G., & Ponting, M., 1984. 'Dalmore', *Current Archaeol*, 91, pp. 230-5.

RCAHMS 1928. Royal Commission on the Ancient & Historical Monuments of Scotland. *Ninth Report with Inventory of Monuments and Constructions in the Outer Hebrides, Skye and the Small Isles* (Edinburgh).

Ritchie, W., 1967. 'The machair of South Uist', *Scott Geogr Mag*, 83, pp. 163-73.

Ritchie, W., 1979. 'Machair chronology and development in the Uists', *Proc R Soc Edinburgh*, 77B, pp. 107-22.

Ritchie, W., 1985. 'Inter-tidal and sub-tidal organic deposits and sea level changes in the Uists, Outer Hebrides', *Scott J Geol*, 21, pp. 161-76.

Ritchie, W., 1991. 'The geography of the Outer Hebrides', in *Flora of the Outer Hebrides,* ed. Pankhurst & Mullin, pp. 3-13.

Ritchie, W., & Whittington, G., 1994. 'Non-synchronous aeolian sand movements in the Uists: the evidence of the intertidal organic and sand deposits at Cladach Mór, North Uist', *Scott Geogr Mag,* 110, pp. 40-6.

Scott, W. L., 1951. 'Eilean an Tighe: a pottery workshop of the second millennium B.C.', *Proc Soc Antiq Scotland,* 85, 1-37.

Shepherd, I. A. G., & Tuckwell, A. N., 1977. 'Traces of Beaker period cultivation at Rosinish, Benbecula, Western Isles', *Proc Soc Antiq Scotland,* 108, 108-13.

Simmons, I. G., 1996. *The Environmental Impact of Later Mesolithic Cultures: the creation of moorland landscape in England and Wales* (Edinburgh).

Simmons, I. G., & Tooley, M. J. (eds), 1981. *The Environment in British Prehistory* (London).

Simpson, D. D. A., 1976. 'The later Neolithic and Beaker settlement site at Northton, Isle of Harris', in *Settlement and Economy in the Third and Second Millennia B.C.,* ed. C. Burgess & R. Miket, Br Archaeol Rep, Br ser 33 (Oxford), pp. 221-31.

Smith, D. I., & Fettes, D. J., 1979. 'The geological framework of the Outer Hebrides', *Proc R Soc Edinburgh,* 77B, pp. 75-83.

Spence, D. H. N., 1960. 'Studies on the vegetation of Shetland. III. Scrub in Shetland and in South Uist, Outer Hebrides', *J Ecol,* 48, pp. 73-95.

Stace, C., 1997. *New Flora of the British Isles* (2nd edn, Cambridge).

Stuiver, M., & Reimer, P. J., 1993. 'Extended ^{14}C data base and revised CALIB 3.0 ^{14}C age calibration program', *Radiocarbon,* 35, pp. 215-30.

Sutherland, D. G., & Walker, M. J. C., 1984. 'A late Devensian ice-free area and possible interglacial site in the Isle of Lewis, Scotland', *Nature,* 309, pp. 701-3.

Thomas, J., 1990. 'Silent Running: the ills of environmental archaeology', *Scott Archaeol Rev,* 7, pp. 2-7.

Tipping, R., 1994. 'The form and fate of Scotland's woodlands', *Proc Soc Antiq Scotland,* 124, pp. 1-54.

Tipping, R., 1996. 'Microscopic charcoal records, inferred human activity and climate change in the Mesolithic of northernmost Scotland', in *The Early Prehistory of Scotland,* ed. T. Pollard & A. Morrison (Edinburgh), pp. 39-61.

Walker, M. J. C., 1984. 'A pollen diagram from St. Kilda, Outer Hebrides, Scotland', *New Phytol,* 97, pp. 99-113.

Watson, E. V., & Barlow, H. W. B., 1936. 'The vegetation', in *The Natural History of Barra, Outer Hebrides,* ed. J. E. Forrest, A. R. Waterston & E. V. Watson, *Proc R Phys Soc Edinburgh,* 22, pp. 244-54.

Whittington, G., & Edwards, K. J., 1997. 'Evolution of a machair landscape: pollen and related studies from Benbecula, Outer Hebrides, Scotland', *Trans R Soc Edinburgh: Earth Sci,* 87, pp. 515-31.

Whittington, G., & Ritchie, W., 1988. *Flandrian Environmental Evolution on North-East Benbecula and Southern Grimsay, Outer Hebrides, Scotland,* O'Dell Mem Monogr No. 21, Dep Geogr, Univ Aberdeen.

Wickham-Jones, C. R., 1994. *Scotland's First Settlers* (London).

Wilkins, D. A., 1984. 'The Flandrian woods of Lewis (Scotland)', *J Ecol,* 72, pp. 251-8.

Characterising the landscape of Roman Britain: a review of the study of Roman Britain 1975 – 2000

Mark Corney

ABSTRACT

The evolution of the Romano-British landscape and the relationship between urban and rural economies is investigated. The contribution of the late Iron Age social and economic framework is discussed together with subsequent change in the structure and organisation of the rural landscape in association with the political and administrative reorganisation of the province.

KEYWORDS

Roman, rural landscape, urban landscape, industry, ritual, religion

INTRODUCTION AND REVIEW OF RECENT WORK

For far too long the study of Roman Britain has had an image problem. It would have been true some years ago to level the accusation that the archaeology of Roman Britain was dominated by site-oriented studies; specifically the triumvirate of villas, towns and forts. *The Archaeology of Roman Britain* (Collingwood & Richmond 1969), although an invaluable source in its time, epitomised the individual site and artefact specific approach to the topic. Neatly compartmentalised into separate headings, the total picture of the Provincial landscape was never attempted. Yet only one year after the publication of this volume, Phillips (1970), produced a regional landscape study of *The Fenland in Roman Times*. It is salutary to note that this was produced under the auspices of the Royal Geographical Society rather than an archaeological body. The lessons of the Fenland approach were slow to be adopted, much to the detriment of Romano-British studies. 1982 saw the publication of an important volume that presented a series of papers examining the Romano-British countryside (Miles 1982). Yet even as late as 1989 a major volume on *Research on Roman Britain 1960-89* (Todd 1989) contained only two papers out of a total of sixteen that attempted to examine broader landscape themes (Miles on The Romano-British Countryside and Potter on The Roman Fenland).

This state of affairs is regrettable, especially given the great increase in national air photographic cover and other non-intrusive mapping methods now available.

Studies of Romano-British sites have frequently presented site-specific data without reference to their broader landscape context; for example, until very recently our knowledge of villas *and* their potential estates has been lamentably poor. The same is largely true for non-villa rural settlement and, with a few notable exceptions, for the urban hinterlands of most Romano-British towns and larger nucleated settlements. The next few years should see major changes in this state of affairs.

Two major publications that have appeared during the period covered by this review should however be singled out for mention as examples of how it is possible to view the mass of data on Roman Britain from a new perspective. These are Millett's *The Romanization of Britain* (1990) and Hingley's *Rural Settlement in Roman Britain* (1989). The former work broke away from the neat compartmentalisation approach to the study of the Province, whilst Hingley's synthesis for the first time demonstrated the diversity of rural settlement and examined the topic within a socio-economic and theoretical framework familiar to prehistorians, but hitherto rarely attempted by students of Roman Britain.

RURAL SETTLEMENT AND LANDSCAPE

The last decade has however seen a great change in attitudes and approaches to the landscape of Roman Britain. Mention has already been made of Hingley's 1989 work on rural settlement. In addition, the evolution of more rigid methodologies and the application of an increasing number of refined field techniques are starting to pay dividends. The contribution of air photography cannot be overemphasised enough. The pioneering work of St Joseph during the immediate post-Second World War decades has matured into an increasingly structured programme of aerial reconnaissance involving flyers and photographers working at both regional and national levels. Many regional surveys are now available, with others in progress, and the development of a national standard of presentation for crop-marks and related features (Edis *et al.* 1989) has made comparisons much easier and meaningful. Coupled with increasingly rigorous field survey methodologies we are now beginning to see ways of quantifying and comparing regional trends in the Romano-British landscape.

A number of very important projects have appeared in print or are underway. Undoubtedly one of the most important regional studies to appear that has presented a detailed landscape analysis as well as developing new approaches to field methodology is the Maddle Farm Project on the Berkshire Downs (Gaffney & Tingle 1989). Here, carefully selective excavation has been complemented by an extensive programme of fieldwalking, landscape analysis and a consideration of artefact condition to build up a detailed picture of changing regimes of land use and management. It is a model of its kind and deserves a wider consideration and methodological application.

The publication of David Neal's work at Stanwick in Northamptonshire will similarly provide a detailed picture of the immediate environs of a major villa-based estate centre. Large-scale open area excavation has revealed a complex picture of buildings (including the 'villa' and a possible administrative block), compounds, tracks and other structures (Neal 1989). Similarly, the publication of Goodburn's work at Winterton on Humberside is also eagerly awaited. Study of rural and 'agricultural' buildings in Roman Britain (Morris 1979) strongly suggests a highly productive agrarian landscape. Many villas and non-villa settlements are associated with very large ancillary structures, many of which are best interpreted as barns. In terms of size and potential storage capacity some of these structures may be favourably compared with medieval tithe barns. At the Winterton villa, Humberside (Goodburn 1978), aisled building P is some 50 m x 10 m and at Spoonley Wood, Gloucestershire, another aisled structure measures approximately 25 m x 10 m and appears to have a 'loading platform' at its western end (RCHME 1976, p. 114). Such large structures have great implications for the productivity of the landscape in Roman Britain. From eastern England we have recently seen the publication of a Romano-British farm, one of the very few sites of this type to be thoroughly investigated, at Orton Hall, near Peterborough (Mackreth 1996). Here, a series of agricultural buildings of predominantly aisled form are grouped around a courtyard and represent a range of agrarian activities. The excavations have also demonstrated that occupation continues into the post-Roman period with post-built structures and sunken-floored buildings.

It is to be very much hoped that publication of large area investigations will stimulate further research into defining the broader landscapes around such sites. This will not be easy and no doubt there will be intense debate as to whether it can be convincingly achieved. Whatever the outcome, it has to be pursued. Few have dared to follow this path since Finberg's attempt to identify the estate around the Cotswold villa at Withington and to further suggest that much of this estate survived as a territorial unit into the Anglo-Saxon period (Finberg 1955).

More recently Hunn has undertaken work of great interest in the *Verulamium* area and has attempted to show the evolution of the urban hinterland landscape from the late Iron Age to medieval periods (Hunn 1992, 1994). Further examples of what can be achieved by integrating excavation results with air photography and environmental studies are also amply made by the reconstruction of an upper Thames Valley Romano-British landscape at Roughground near Lechlade (Allen *et al.* 1993). The results of this study should be compared with the earthwork survey of the environs of the Barnsley Park villa (RCHME 1976), only some 15 km from Roughground, to see how rapidly land division patterns can change; this underscores the regional variation present in the Romano-British landscape.

The landscapes of Romano-British settlements are still very poorly understood on the whole. It is becoming clear – as a general point – that many have correlations with the pattern of later prehistoric land divisions. Our understanding of this is still highly variable and strongly regionalised. In East Anglia, Williamson (1987) has shown that large areas of prehistoric land division are largely ignored by the Roman road network, yet the partial survival and recovery of the field plans in the modern landscape suggests that these systems continued to function despite this apparent disruption. More recent studies of the Roman landscape in eastern England have begun to demonstrate the diverse patterns of settlement and land use ranging from 'small towns' to villas and villages (Brown 1995). Clearer patterns of specialised, seasonal exploitation are also emerging in this region, most notably relating to salt production (Gurney 1986; de Brisay 1975).

Further to the north, the publication of major air photographic regional surveys has revealed an extensive series of landscapes of later prehistoric and Romano-British date across Lincolnshire (Bewley 1999), south Humberside (Jones 1988, 1999) and the Yorkshire Wolds (Stoertz 1997). Once again we can see a recurring theme of distinctive regional characteristics in both settlement form and land division. On the Yorkshire Wolds, Stoertz (*ibid.*, p. 67) has drawn attention to the conservatism of settlement and landscape form throughout the Roman period, with little variation in what are essentially Iron Age patterns of linear settlements with integral field systems into which a small number of villas have been inserted. South of the Humber, on the

Lincolnshire Wolds, Jones (1999, fig. 4) presents a picture of a different form including villas that appear to overlie earlier, possibly late prehistoric, settlements. Extensive areas of field systems are lacking although evidence for cereal production is present and Jones (*ibid.*, p. 78, citing Wilson 1993) suggests that field boundaries may have been formed in such a way as to leave no visible trace from the air.

In Wessex, most notably on Salisbury Plain, detailed survey by the late and much lamented RCHME, has demonstrated how prehistoric patterns of land division are modified and enhanced during the Roman period. This is a pattern also seen on the Marlborough Downs (Fowler 2000) and the Berkshire Downs (Gaffney & Tingle 1989; Bowden *et al.* 1993). On Salisbury Plain, the settlements and their contemporary landscapes, including possible dams across the heads of coombes, survive as substantial and extensive earthworks and provide a rare glimpse into a past landscape of international importance (Corney *et al.* 1994; Frere 1992, figs 20-22; English Heritage forthcoming; McOmish 1993). What immediately impresses one here is the variation in scale and morphology of settlements and their landscapes over a comparatively small area (just under 400 km^2) of chalk downland. Settlement types range from nucleated forms suggestive of a long term, 'organic' development such as Chisenbury Warren to probable planned examples like Knook East (Frere 1992, fig. 21) and those of linear configuration extending for up to 1.5 km along trackways, as at Chapperton Down, all with surrounding field systems (Bowen & Fowler 1966; Frere *ibid.*). Are these differences due to variation in economy, social status or date? It is difficult to give a definitive answer at present, but it is possible that the origins of the morphological variation may lie in the later Iron Age political and economic structure of the region where a number of socio-political units appear to meet (Corney forthcoming; Corney & Eagles forthcoming).

The Roman landscape on Salisbury Plain has also been used to promote the interpretation of the region as an Imperial Estate, largely based on the apparent lack of villas in the immediate area, an observation now known to be erroneous. Survey, primarily using geophysics supplemented by air photography, has located a number of villas on the periphery of Salisbury Plain (Corney *et al.* 1994). The pattern now emerging would appear to show a considerable number of villa-based 'estate centres' along the Avon Valley, Wylye Valley and the Vale of Pewsey, occupying the same general locations as the medieval and modern villages. The larger settlements on Salisbury Plain would appear to be deliberately sited within field systems to exploit the higher downland arable landscape. Comparison of the villas and their associated settlements when overlain onto a map of the post-Roman parishes and estates shows a close correlation. This is especially so in the Avon Valley, an area where Bonney (1976) first proposed a possible link between Romano-British boundaries, pagan Anglo-Saxon burials and early medieval estates, parishes and tithings. At the time of his study Bonney did not know that a number of his early medieval land units would prove to have Romano-British villas within them. The pattern now emerging would add further support to the thesis proposed by Bonney – elements of the pre-medieval landscape *can* survive into the present. This is an extremely important development and one that deserves to be looked at in closer detail and, if possible, identified in other central and western areas of Britain where, away from the primary zone of Anglo-Saxon settlement, greater survival of the Romano-British landscape may be reasonably expected.

Due to the presence of an office of the former RCHME in Wiltshire, coupled with ongoing research by the author, this is one county where we can now see the density of Romano-British settlement (Fig. 3.1) and associated landscapes. This pattern will no doubt be repeated when work at a similar level of intensity is undertaken (see also the RCHME 1980 atlas of archaeological sites in Northamptonshire).

Elsewhere in Wessex the detailed study and mapping of extensive areas at a common scale of 1:25 000 has allowed the prehistoric and Romano-British landscape to be looked at over an area extending from the outskirts of Blandford to the edge of Basingstoke (Palmer 1984; Bowen 1990). A study of the area plans in these volumes amply demonstrate both the density and morphological variety of settlement as well as the complexity of the chalkland landscape from later prehistory to the middle of the first millennium A.D. The region also shows a high degree of coincidence between certain types of late Iron Age enclosed settlements and the siting of later Romano-British villas. This is especially so in the case of 'banjo' enclosures, a distinctive late Iron Age form often associated with single and multiple ditch systems (Corney 1989, 1991; Perry 1970, 1972, 1982, 1986).

Such associations between later Iron Age settlements and Romano-British villas are, as has already been demonstrated, not confined to Wessex. The work by David Neal (Neal *et al.* 1990) at Gorhambury, near Roman *Verulamium*, has provided a detailed picture of the transition from a pre-conquest settlement to a Romanised villa complex whose layout is governed by the earlier landscape. This work has been further complemented by Hunn's landscape development study of the St Albans region (1994). In Gloucestershire, a first-century villa of pre-Flavian date was constructed of stone within a late Iron Age enclosure at The Ditches, North Cerney, near Cirencester (Trow 1988; Trow & James 1989). The enclosure has produced evidence of 'high status' and specialist activity

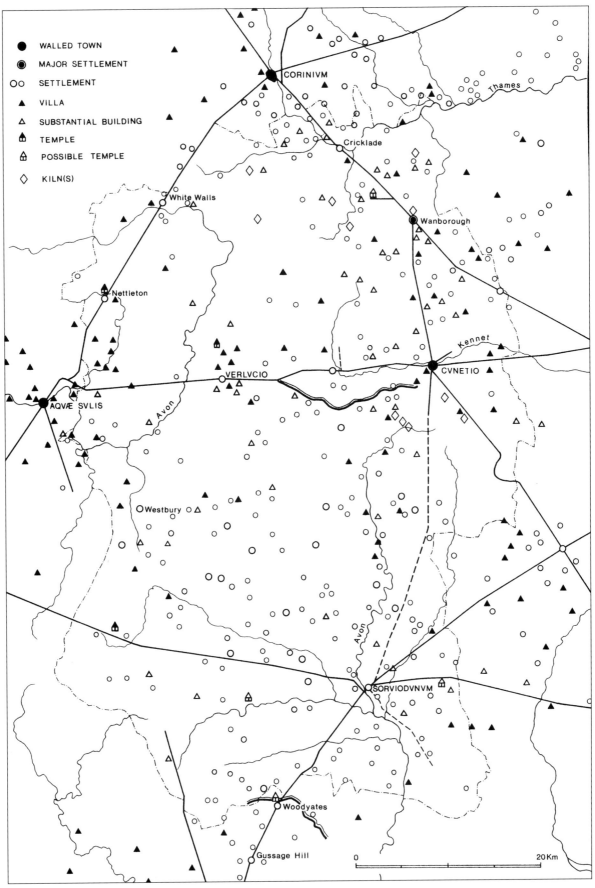

Fig. 3.1. Romano-British settlements in Wiltshire. Compiled from a variety of sources and ongoing research, the pattern clearly demonstrates the density of settlement and land use.

including imported ceramics, metalwork and Iron Age coin production.

Even when post-conquest activity does not ultimately result in the construction of a villa-type building, there is good evidence from many regions to demonstrate that occupation continued with little, if any, disruption. Much as with villas succeeding later prehistoric settlements, the evidence of continuity of settlement location is widespread across much of the country. The work of Pitt-Rivers (1887, 1888) in Cranborne Chase demonstrated this for the settlements at Rotherley and Woodcutts where late Iron Age settlements continued into the late Roman period. In the same region, Wainwright (1969, 1979) has demonstrated that the Iron Age settlements at Gussage All Saints and Tollard Royal continued to be occupied into the early second century A.D. On the north Hampshire chalk, a number of late Iron Age settlements in the Basingstoke area continued into the Roman period, for example Rucstalls Hill (Oliver & Applin 1978). In the south Midlands, a very close correlation between late Iron Age settlements and Romano-British villas and other settlement types has been noted in the vicinity of the north Oxfordshire Grim's Ditch, a possible Dobunnic *pagus* (Hingley 1988; Massey, pers. comm.).

If the settlements continued to be occupied then it is highly probable that their landscape settings of fields, managed woodland, pasture and tracks will also have survived and influenced later Roman land division and units. Naturally there will be exceptions, notably in areas of military control, areas where land is requisitioned for new urban and other foundations and, occasionally, confiscation of the holdings of criminals, supporters of rebellions and so forth.

Such studies strongly suggest that we may be able to see continuity of settlement and landscape at a number of levels, not just the presumed 'higher-status' villas. Furthermore it is quite possible that in many areas these patterns may also indicate a continuity of social and tenurial hierarchies during the first and second centuries A.D. Even if land and estates subsequently change hands (and given that Britain was under Roman rule for 350 years it would be surprising if this was not the case) the patterns established are essentially ones that originate before the invasion of A.D. 43. If this is so then we may be able to propose that the concept of private landownership (whether by individuals or small kin-based units) was established in some regions before the Roman conquest.

It is becoming increasingly clear over many parts of Britain that Romano-British settlement was far more extensive, and covered a greater topographical range, than in the medieval period. What factors are at play here? Is it a reflection of a larger population and climatic optimum? The patterns that we are seeing all raise new sets of questions to challenge those engaged in the study of the landscape over the coming decades.

The northern areas of Britain that came under Roman rule have not, until recently, seen serious work on the characterisation of their landscapes. For too long the Roman archaeology in this region has been dominated by the study of military remains and frontier works. In the last twenty years new attitudes and approaches have begun to prevail and at last we are starting to see closer examination of the impact of Rome on the landscape, the 'native' population and its infrastructure. In this region we have seen much greater use made of environmental methods, especially pollen analysis. Excavation has also played a role and the discovery of regular field systems sealed beneath Hadrian's Wall at Tarraby Lane near Carlisle points to the potential of the region (Smith 1978). The general picture appears to indicate an increase in open country and cereals (Clack & Haselgrove 1982) although east of the Pennines clearance and an increase in cereal cultivation may have commenced shortly before the Roman conquest (Huntley 1999). Detailed regional studies such as that of the Solway Plain (Bewley 1994) are, however, still rare.

In the other area of predominantly military control, Wales, serious study of the Roman landscape has not moved on a great deal since the 1984 study by Davies. The eastern region of the central Welsh Marches is however now under study as part of the Wroxeter Hinterland Project. This is an exciting project that will prove how an integrated survey methodology using the latest remote sensing techniques can be applied in a regional survey.

Studies of 'marginal' areas have faired somewhat better in the past decade. The numerous 'wetland' projects around the country are beginning to demonstrate the scale of Roman wetland reclamation, management and exploitation. This has been especially so in the Severn Estuary where Allen and Fulford (1986, 1987, 1992) have identified a large-scale programme of reclamation along the Gwent Levels inter-tidal zone. The level of investment identified by Allen and Fulford would strongly suggest that on the Gwent Levels we are seeing an act of Imperial policy towards the provision of 'new' land. This study complements the work by Rippon on the Somerset Levels (Rippon 1996) and may also be compared with the massive scale of early second-century A.D. Roman land management in the Fenland investigated by Jackson and Potter (1996) and the Fenland Project (Hall & Coles 1994).

Despite all of the evidence outlined above for a densely-settled and structured landscape across much of Roman Britain we still know depressingly little of landownership and tenure. We confidently talk of 'bailiff's' houses or 'principle' villas, 'estate villages' and the like without any clear and precise knowledge of *how* the landscape was viewed in terms of ownership, sale or transfer etc. In this context the recent discovery of a wooden stylus writing tablet from Roman London is of great importance. This describes the sale of a wood of five acres, probably in Kent, for the sum of 40 *denarii*. Tomlin has described it as '... a disconcerting survival ... because it implies what does *not* survive: records of the ownership of land, farm by farm, throughout the Roman province' (Tomlin 1996, p. 215). As already noted, the close association between villas and other Romano-British settlements with late prehistoric sites suggests a great deal of spatial and locational continuity, but the evolving mechanisms of tenure, ownership and legal status under Roman rule still elude us.

URBAN LANDSCAPES

The Roman conquest saw a dramatic change in the landscape with the great explosion of urban settlements. These cover a variety of types, from the planned *coloniae* and *civitas* capitals of the Graeco-Roman urban tradition to the so-called 'small towns', performing a variety of roles and frequently lacking signs of centralised core planning (Burnham & Wacher 1990). Urban sites of the 'small town' category are crucial to our understanding of regional ethnic identities (primarily as possible *pagus* centres that may originate in the pre-conquest period), market and economic functions. In addition a number of these sites have possible *mansiones* or *mutationes* that will have played a significant role in the local Roman administrative structure (Black 1995).

The study of Romano-British urbanism has been dominated by the tendency to concentrate on the area within a defensive circuit – even though the majority of defended towns do not receive these until the late second century at the earliest (an exception being the *coloniae*, see Webster 1988). This restrictive intramural viewpoint has, with a few notable exceptions, led to an incomplete understanding of Romano-British urban topography and their hinterlands. The survey of 'suburbia' by Esmonde Cleary (1987) was the first comprehensive study of the province to examine the urban landscape. Prior to this only a handful of site-specific studies had examined this question. Some were purely air photographic (*cf.* Barker 1985) whilst others combined a number of non-intrusive methods (*cf.* Corney 1984). The current work on the hinterland of the Cornovian *civitas* capital at Wroxeter is of tremendous importance, both for its results and the methodologies being employed. The final publication of the project promises to be a landmark in Romano-British studies.

The limited work to date has demonstrated how close the rural landscape came to some of the major towns in the province. At Wroxeter, Silchester and *Verulamium* the air photographic evidence shows fields, small plots and tracks close to the urban limits (Barker 1985; Corney 1984;

Hunn 1994). The nature of the relationship between town and country in Roman Britain has received some attention in regional studies, although the last major national synthesis was that by Rivet published as *Town and Country in Roman Britain* in 1964! Fulford (1982) provided a brief but incisive appreciation of the nature of this relationship but since then no major review has appeared. Whilst such an evaluation is well beyond the scope of this paper, there are a number of key areas that need to be reviewed.

A common feature of all Romano-British urban hinterland landscapes will have been the town cemeteries. These are located just beyond the settlements limits – a position specifically dictated by Roman law (Toynbee 1971), this being one of the few instances in Britain where we can actually recognise archaeologically a Roman legal requirement imposed on the landscape. The funerary treatment of the urban dead stands in contrast to rural patterns where we see far more regional variation and a stronger link between the dead and boundaries in the landscape (see Philpott 1991 for a detailed appraisal of Romano-British funerary traditions). Urban cemeteries are most frequently encountered along the major roads leading into the towns. Large-scale excavations over recent years have shown that many of these will have been very extensive and some contain a number of substantial funerary structures such as mausolea (*cf.* Poundbury outside of Dorchester, Farwell & Molleson 1993). Further extensive urban cemeteries have been published from Winchester (Clarke 1979) and Cirencester (McWhirr *et al.* 1982), to name but two. At Colchester, an extramural fourth-century cemetery at Butt Road (Crummy *et al.*1993) appears to have had a Christian church constructed within it, a location and pattern with strong parallels amongst the *Martyrium* churches of Gaul and the Rhineland.

At many urban sites, most notably the 'small towns', we can see suburbs or peripheral areas where a mix of industrial and agrarian activities are clearly being practised. At Water Newton, Roman *Durobrivae*, near Peterborough, detailed analysis of the air photographic evidence by Mackreth (1979) supplemented by limited excavation (summarised in Burnham & Wacher 1990) has revealed extensive areas of industry, mainly pottery kilns, interspersed with fields, paddocks and features best interpreted as agricultural in character. In East Anglia, at Brampton, Norfolk, fieldwork has revealed a concentration of over 140 pottery kilns located to the south-west of a defended 'small town' (Knowles 1977; Burnham & Wacher 1990). Elsewhere, potential villa-based estate centres have been identified within a few hundred metres of the urban limits, as at Godmanchester (Green 1978) and Great Casterton (Corder 1951, 1954, 1961).

Undoubtedly many of these settlements will have functioned as local marketing, manufacturing and redistribution centres across the province (*cf.* Hodder 1974). In some instances this may be a development of a situation that was already underway before the conquest of A.D. 43. A strong contender here is the 'small town' of *Cunetio*, modern Mildenhall in the Kennet Valley in Wiltshire. The Roman settlement succeeds a major late Iron Age regional centre (Corney 1997) that was closely linked to the Savernake pottery industry (Swan 1975). Recent re-evaluation of the origins of Savernake Ware has demonstrated the presence of a late Iron Age industry that was initially developed by the Roman military immediately after the conquest and which subsequently flourished until the mid third century (Hopkins forthcoming).

In the same vein, it is probable that the products of the Alice Holt/Farnham pottery industry were marketed from the nearby 'small town' at Neatham. In their study of this industry, Lyne and Jeffries (1979) mapped from air photographic and other sources an extensive area between Neatham and the main kiln sites to the east of the town. Here we can see an ordered landscape of tracks and fields integrated with villas, settlements and areas of intensive industrial use (*ibid.*, fig 4). This layout is quite regular in form and suggests the probability of a planned landscape. It has yet to be looked at in detail and whether it is of pre-Roman origin is still unknown. Areas of intensive industrial use such as these will also, by implication, have required extensive areas of managed woodland to provide fuel for the kilns and a reliable source of water – a point that obviously applies to all ceramic industries irrespective of whether or not they were close to an urban centre.

Within the framework of urban landscapes and industrial and manufacturing processes it should be remembered that a small number of nucleated sites of an urban character appear to be based entirely on highly specialised industrial activities. These are discussed further in the next section.

ROMANO-BRITISH INDUSTRIAL LANDSCAPES

Although the Roman Empire was an essentially rural- and agrarian-based entity it did also include areas of intensive industrial activity. Reference has already been made to some industries (mainly ceramics) where they are associated with urban and sub-urban landscapes (see above). Many more industrial activities are primarily rural based and can cover very large areas. Industrial activities in the Romano-British landscape range from relatively well-studied processes such as pottery manufacturing, iron production and salt making to less well documented activities such as stone quarrying. Clearly this is a difficult topic for study as in many locations post-Roman exploitation of the same resources and deposits will have removed or buried the evidence for Roman and earlier workings.

The major (and many lesser) pottery industries have been studied in detail over the past decades. Whilst extremely useful in terms of providing detailed typological sequences and broad economic patterns (*cf.* Fulford 1975; Young 1977; Tyers 1996), few have been successful in providing a detailed analysis of the landscapes within which these industries functioned or the woodland and water management regimes required for their maintenance.

The extraction of mineral deposits is well attested in Roman Britain although details are sorely lacking in most cases. The exploitation of gold deposits around Dolaucothi in Wales was initially studied by Lewis and Jones (1969) and more recently by Burnham (1997). Careful field-survey, air photography and selective excavation has revealed a complex picture of aqueducts and other features associated with the mining of the ore (*ibid*). The evidence to date also suggests that the Roman mining operations succeeded a prehistoric phase of exploitation.

The extraction of silver from argentiferous lead ore was the principle source of this precious metal in the Roman world. Extensive traces of Roman-period lead-mining have been recorded from Derbyshire, Wales, Shropshire and Somerset (see Jones & Mattingly 1990, pp. 179-95, for a useful summary of Roman mining in Britain). The high silver content of the Mendip lead deposits in Somerset led to exploitation of these ores from a very early date, probably by A.D. 49. On Mendip the principle lead-mining site is at Charterhouse-on-Mendip, Somerset (conveniently summarised in Burnham & Wacher 1990). This exceptionally well-preserved site is located high on Mendip adjacent to rich lead deposits that were exploited until the opening decade of the twentieth century. Although masked by subsequent workings it is highly likely that much remains to be recovered of the Roman lead workings and their surroundings. The settlement associated with the mining operations still survives as an extensive earthwork complex and displays an irregular street grid with the remains of a number of substantial buildings. The lack of even the most basic ground survey of this complex is a cause of some astonishment and concern.

Tin and copper are known to have been extracted during the Roman period, probably in many cases continuing a prehistoric tradition. In Cornwall, an increase in tin production during the later Roman period is linked to the decline in Iberian production, but details of the methods used, presumed to be primarily streaming, are scant (Quinnell 1986, pp. 129-30). Copper-working is known from Parys Mountain on Anglesey, Great Orme and Llanymynech in Shropshire. At the latter, extensive traces of galleries survive although little is yet known of the attendant settlement and processing landscape (Jones & Mattingly 1990, pp. 191-2).

Deposits of iron ore are relatively common in Britain and a number of major areas of Roman activity are known. Three of these, the Weald in Sussex, the Forest of Dean in Gloucestershire and the East Midlands cover very large areas and the impact on the landscape will have been considerable. Experiments in iron production based on furnaces excavated on Wealden sites show that 265 pounds of charcoal were required to produce 20 pounds of iron from 201 pounds of ore (Cleere 1971, p. 213). The woodland management required for charcoal production alone demonstrates the scale and environmental impact of Roman exploitation.

The Weald of Sussex was intensively exploited for its iron deposits (Cleere 1974; Cleere & Crossley 1986) and, in a break form the normal pattern of control for non-precious metals, appears to have been under state control. A number of the iron production sites have produced tiles stamped 'CLBR', indicating a connection with the '*Classis Britannica*', the Roman fleet based along the English Channel and North Sea coastline. At one site, Beauport Park, iron production is estimated to have produced as much as approximately 50,000 tonnes of slag.

In the Forest of Dean in Gloucestershire, recent investigations at the Woolaston villa by Fulford and Allen (1992) have shown the importance of river and sea transport to the local industry. Other iron-making sites in this region still await investigation and the full impact of Roman iron exploitation on the landscape, although likely to be considerable, still lacks a detailed regional survey.

The use of coal in Roman Britain is well attested from the numerous finds of coal on Romano-British settlements and from contemporary documentary sources (Dearne & Branigan 1995). No confirmed Roman period mines or workings have been identified to date although Dearne and Branigan (*ibid.*, p. 72) point to possible surface workings in northern Britain. A recent study of coal from Romano-British contexts has demonstrated that all of the major coalfields in England and Wales (with the exception of Staffordshire) were being exploited (Smith 1997).

Extraction of stone for building and sculptural purposes will have been another important aspect of the Romano-British industrial landscape. The study of this topic has been poorly served on a national basis. Williams (1971) has studied the sources in south-east England but similar regional studies are still wanting. Association with specific excavated structures can attest to the exploitation of certain types of building materials. For example, Purbeck marble is being quarried by *c.* A.D. 60-70, based on the presence of mouldings from the legionary bath-house at Exeter (Bidwell 1979, pp. 136-41), and Bathstone is being used for major architectural works in Bath by *c.* A.D. 60-75 (Blagg 1979). However, as with mineral extraction, later exploitation will in many cases have removed or buried the evidence of Roman activity. Lithological studies can demonstrate the approximate sources of many rock types and indicate the distances over which stone was transported. A study of the non-flint components of the third-century town wall at Silchester (Sellwood 1984) has shown that limestone was being transported to the site from the Bath region, a distance of 90 km.

RITUAL AND RELIGIOUS LANDSCAPES

Ritual and religious monuments are a relatively common feature of the Romano-British landscape and the past thirty years have seen a great deal of work on this topic. This has ranged from large-scale excavations (many prompted by the systematic looting of sites, such as Lamyatt Beacon (Leech 1986), and Wanborough, Surrey (O'Connell & Bird 1994)) to broader and theoretically-based studies examining contemporary attitudes, religious philosophies and re-use of earlier monuments (*cf.* Henig 1984; Dark 1993; Forcey 1998; Williams 1998).

There is an immense range and variation in site and monument form with a number of regional patterns discernible. Many rural sites cover extensive areas and have been demonstrated to have pre-Roman origins. At Hayling Island in Hampshire large-scale excavations recovered a sequence beginning in the late Iron Age with a circular timber building set within a fenced enclosure. By *c.* A.D. 60-70 this complex had been translated into stone and the comparatively early date for this change has led to the suggestion that the complex was linked with the contemporary luxurious dwelling at nearby Fishbourne (King & Soffe 1994). This continuity of a sacred space within the landscape can be observed over a large part of the Roman province. At Gosbecks, south of Colchester, a large stone temple of 'Romano-Celtic type' was built within a late Iron Age ditched shrine, was surrounded by a walled *temenos* and is probably associated with a further walled precinct, possibly a garden with a bath house, and a theatre (Hawkes & Crummy 1995, pp. 101-5). Such a complex has close parallels with the extensive sanctuaries that are such a dominant feature of the Gallo-Roman rural landscape (*ibid.*, p. 105). Further examples of these large rural complexes are known. At Frilford, in the Vale of the White Horse near Wantage, a succession of Iron Age and Roman shrines are associated with an amphitheatre and an extensive settlement (Hingley 1982). In 1997 a further example was discovered in woodland near Newbury in Berkshire. Covering at least 8 ha, this site still has substantial surface remains of the *temenos* boundary, circular and rectangular structures (probably shrines), and a possible theatre (Massey, pers com). At Wycomb, in Gloucestershire, a small town developed around another extensive religious complex that appears to include a theatre (Burnham & Wacher 1990).

Not all rural religious sites of the Romano-British period develop along such grand and formal lines. Some, possibly deliberately, remain isolated and lack the provision of extensive ancillary structures. At Cold Kitchen Hill, in Wiltshire, limited excavation coupled with ongoing air photographic and landscape analysis suggests that a major prehistoric ritual landscape, partially defined by cross-ridge dykes, was subject to minimal restructuring after the Roman conquest, yet the wealth of Romano-British material from the site, much of it votive in character, attests to ongoing and intensive activity.

In western England, notably western Wessex, the Cotswolds and Somerset, there is a marked concentration of Romano-British temples that display a close correlation with Iron Age hill-forts and other prehistoric monuments. In this area it is apparent that in some examples there appears to be a hiatus in recognisable activity from the late Iron Age until the third or fourth century A.D. This is certainly the case at Lydney in Gloucestershire (Wheeler & Wheeler 1932; Casey *et al.* 1999) where an extensive temple complex with guest-house, baths and other buildings is constructed in the late third century. Whilst at Brean Down, Somerset, a fourth-century temple is constructed immediately adjacent to a Bronze Age round barrow and within 400 metres of a small hill-fort (Ap Simon 1964; Burrow 1981). At Maiden Castle, Dorset (Wheeler 1943), and Uley, Gloucestershire (Woodward & Leach 1993), there is evidence for a ritual use throughout most of the Romano-British period, although it is only in the late third or fourth centuries that substantial buildings are constructed.

On the chalk uplands of the South Downs in Sussex and across much of the western region discussed above, the temples and shrines are placed on prominent local hill-tops. This pattern is so common that it has to be seen as a deliberate act. We need to visualise what these structures would have looked like when in use and the impact they would have had on the surrounding landscape. The general form of Romano-British (and Gallo-Roman, see Fauduet 1993) temples is based on a *tall*, central *cella*, either circular or multiangular, but more often square, surrounded by an ambulatory. Such structures would have dominated the landscape and will have been visible for a considerable distance.

The construction of many of the rural temples, shrines and major cult centres in stone during the later third and fourth centuries A.D. may reflect the general economic wealth and stability of *Britannia* during this period. This is also the principle period when the majority of the villas and substantial stone town-houses and other domestic structures are being constructed.

The association between prehistoric monuments and religious and ritual sites of Romano-British date has been a topic of much interest in recent years and a number of other factors, more closely related to a variety of ideological and theoretical issues, have begun to be explored (*cf.* Blagg 1986; Bradley 1987; Williams 1996, 1997). In some regions it is quite possible that rural temple and shrine location may be closely related with pre-Roman and Romano-British demographic and political patterns. Certainly in parts of northern and western Gaul there is very compelling evidence for many rural shrines to be associated with *pagus* and *civitas* boundaries.

The re-use of earlier monuments in the Romano-British landscape is not confined to the construction of substantial structures. Many prehistoric funerary and related monuments have produced Roman material. This can range from individual coins in round barrow ditches to evidence for the re-opening of neolithic long barrows and the deliberate placing of what are best regarded as votive deposits. This practice is visible across the landscape of Roman Britain and has been the subject of in-depth research by Williams (1998). It is of some additional interest to note that this phenomenon is not just confined to Britain, Dark (1993) has also observed a similar focus of Gallo-Roman ritual re-use of many megalithic monuments in Armorica – an area with links to Britain in the early post-Roman period.

The re-use of prehistoric barrows in the post-Roman period, primarily for pagan 'Anglo-Saxon' burials, has been well documented. The correlation between such burials and post-Roman boundaries has equally been noted and commented on at length (*cf.* Bonney 1976; Speake 1989). The recognition of this phenomenon also occurring during the Romano-British period raises many intriguing issues of liminality that have yet to be explored.

In northern Britain, an area with a large military presence, we can see not only the expected 'exotic' cults such as Mithraism that the Roman Army will have introduced. The importance and the recognition of local deities and locations is also well attested by a wide range of altars, with dedications ranging from regional deities such as *Brigantia* to more specific locations such as the 'well' dedicated to *Coventina* (Allason-Jones & McKay 1985).

The study of cemeteries and funerary monuments across the province have received attention at a number of levels. Of note is Philpott's (1991) study of Romano-British burial practices. This detailed study and analysis highlights a number of regional trends as well as broader patterns and practices and provides a useful base for further in depth regional study.

Apart from the general chronological changes through the Romano-British period, such as the move from cremation to inhumation as the dominant rite during the third century A.D., the location of burials and cemeteries is another area of considerable potential for revealing Romano-British attitudes to the landscape. In many areas there is a clear pattern of establishing rural cemeteries, many probably representing extended family groups, in close proximity to property and field boundaries. This is well illustrated by the cemeteries associated with the extensive suburban settlement outside of Roman Ilchester (Leach 1982), the rural settlements at Catsgore (Leech 1982), Bradley Hill, Somerset (Leech 1981), and Lynch Farm, Orton Longueville near Peterborough (Jones 1975). Such practices stand in contrast to the organisation of Roman urban cemeteries where strict laws and regulations governed the location of burials (excluding very young infants) well beyond the limits of the existing settlement.

Barrows of Roman date and of a distinctive monumental form are well known in eastern England with distinct clusters in Kent, Essex, Hertfordshire and Cambridgeshire (Jessup 1959). Less well known, and more importantly morphologically indistinguishable in their present condition from prehistoric barrows, are barrows of Roman date such as those excavated on Overton Hill in Wiltshire (Smith & Simpson 1960). Barrows of this type beg the question of whether they are conscious local tradition inspired by a deep-rooted folk memory of earlier periods – a theme examined by Williams (1998). In the upland areas of Roman Britain, ranging from Mendip to the Derbyshire Peaks, caves are used as burial places. This little-known aspect of Romano-British funeral archaeology has been the subject of a recent examination by Branigan and Dearne (1992).

The religious and ritual landscape of Roman Britain is one that still holds many areas of potential for understanding both indigenous 'native' and intrusive Roman attitudes and beliefs. How these relate to the contemporary social and political landscape has still to be explored in depth.

THE FUTURE

Despite the rather pessimistic opening statement at the beginning of this paper, it should be clear from the above that the study of the landscape of Roman Britain has advanced significantly in the past twenty-five years. Whether that advance can match that made in pre-Roman and post-Roman studies is another matter. There is still a very strong tendency towards site- and artefact-oriented studies in Roman Britain. These are undoubtedly important in providing refined economic, social and chronological data for further study and analysis. However, studies adopting the latest landscape survey techniques, such as employed by the Wroxeter Hinterland Project, are needed

across the entire province. We also desperately need a large number of comparable studies that will provide methodologically compatible data to highlight the regional similarities and differences across the Romano-British landscape. Similarly we need to see greater application of environmental sampling across the province to reconstruct the changing patterns of land use and exploitation from c. A.D. 43–450. With an enhanced environmental base we may be able to reinterpret or refine our views of some of the great mass of evidence derived from excavation, air photography and other sources as to how the landscape evolved and changed during the period of Roman administration.

An area of great potential and enormous interest is what becomes of the Romano-British landscape in the centuries following the cessation of Roman rule. The long-held view of a very rapid decline of the economic and social order is looking increasingly uncertain as our ability to recognise post-A.D. 410 archaeology increases. For many years the example of late and post-Roman Wroxeter was viewed as a one-off regional peculiarity. But the new campaign of excavations at Silchester have begun to elucidate a further lengthy fifth- and sixth-century sequence with recognisably Romanised features. The break up and decline of the province is clearly a complex issue with many regional factors and variations. The distribution of Germanic cemeteries (and more rarely, settlements) of fifth- and sixth-century date clearly shows that the transformation from a Roman to an early medieval landscape will differ considerably across the area of the former province. Relatively few workers in this sphere have a good working knowledge of both Romano-British and Anglo-Saxon archaeology. When this does occur, some extremely stimulating work can result. The study by Bruce Eagles (1994) of Wessex in the fifth to seventh centuries is a notable exception, as is the same author's (1997) study of the immediate post-Roman landscape of the Great Bedwyn villa in Wiltshire.

If we are to begin to really understand how the Romano-British landscape (and the later prehistoric landscape on which so much of Roman Britain is based) evolves into the extensively documented and studied medieval landscape there has to be much greater co-operation and understanding between Romanists and Medievalists. The breakdown of period barriers and the development of an ongoing dialogue between these two areas of study is the great challenge over the next twenty-five years of landscape studies.

BIBLIOGRAPHY

Allason-Jones, L., & McKay, B., 1985. *Coventina's Well: a shrine on Hadrian's Wall* (Newcastle-upon-Tyne).

Allen, J. R. L., & Fulford, M. G., 1986. 'The Wentlooge Level: a Romano-British saltmarsh reclamation in south-east Wales', *Britannia*, 17, pp. 91-117.

Allen, J. R. L., & Fulford, M. G., 1987. 'Romano-British settlement and industry on the wetlands of the Severn estuary', *Antiq J*, 67, pp. 237-89.

Allen, J. R. L., & Fulford, M. G., 1992. 'Romano-British and later geoarchaeology at Oldbury Flats: reclamation and settlement on the changeable coast of the Severn estuary', *Archaeol J*, 149, pp. 82-123.

Allen, T., Darvill, T., Green, L., & Jones, M. U., 1993. *Excavations at Roughground Farm, Lechlade, Gloucestershire: a prehistoric and Roman landscape* (Oxford).

Ap Simon, A., 1964. 'The Roman temple on Brean Down, Somerset', *Proc Univ Bristol Spelaeol Soc*, 10, pp. 195-258.

Barker, P., 1985. 'Aspects of the topography of Wroxeter (Viroconium Cornoviorum)', in *Roman Urban Topography in Britain*, ed. F. O. Grew & B. Hobley (London), pp. 109-17.

Bewley, R., 1994. *Prehistoric and Romano-British Settlement in the Solway Plain, Cumbria* (Oxford).

Bewley, R. (ed.), 1999. *Lincolnshire's Archaeology from the Air* (Gainsborough).

Bidwell, P., 1979. *The Legionary Bath-House and Basilica and Forum at Exeter* (Exeter).

Black, E. W., 1995. *Cursus Publicus, the Infrastructure of Government in Roman Britain*, Br Archaeol Rep, Br ser 241 (Oxford).

Blagg, T., 1979. 'The date of the temple at Bath', *Britannia*, 10, pp. 101-8.

Blagg, T., 1986. 'Roman religious sites in the British landscape', *Landscape History*, 8, pp. 15-27.

Bonney, D. J., 1976. 'Early boundaries and estates in Southern England', in *Medieval Settlement, Continuity and Change*, ed. P. H. Sawyer (London), pp. 72-82.

Bowen, C., 1990. *The Archaeology of Bokerley Dyke* (HMSO, London).

Bowen, C., & Fowler, P. J., 1966. 'Romano-British rural settlements in Dorset and Wiltshire', in *Rural Settlement in Roman Britain*, ed. C. Thomas, Counc Br Archaeol Res Rep No. 7 (London), pp. 43-67.

Bowden, M., Ford, S., & Mees, G., 1993. 'The date of the ancient fields on the Berkshire Downs', *Berkshire Archaeol J*, 74 (1991-3), pp. 109-33.

Bradley, R., 1987. 'Time regained: the creation of continuity', *J Br Archaeol Assoc*, 140, pp. 1-18.

Branigan, K., & Dearne, M. J. (eds), 1992. *Romano-British Cavemen*, Oxbow Monogr 19 (Oxford).

de Brisay, K. W., & Evans, K. A. (eds), 1975. *Salt: the study of an ancient industry* (Colchester).

Brown, A. E. (ed.), 1995. *Roman Small Towns in Eastern England and Beyond* (Oxford).

Burnham, B., 1997. 'Roman mining at Dolaucothi: the implications of the 1991-3 excavations near the Carreg Pumsaint', *Britannia*, 28, pp. 325-35.

Burnham, B. C., & Wacher, J., 1990. *The 'Small Towns' of Roman Britain* (London).

Burrow, I., 1981. *Hillfort and Hill-Top Settlement in Somerset in the First to Eighth Centuries A.D.*, Br Archaeol Rep, Br ser 91 (Oxford).

Casey, P. J., Hoffman, B., & Dore, J., 1999. 'Excavations at the Roman Temple in Lydney Park, Gloucestershire, in 1980 and 1981', *Antiq J*, 79, pp. 81-144.

Clack, P., & Haselgrove, S., 1982. *Rural Settlement in the Roman North* (Durham).

Clarke, G., 1979. *Pre-Roman and Roman Winchester, part 2, The Roman Cemetery at Lankhills*, Winchester Studies 3 (Oxford).

Cleere, H., 1971. 'Ironmaking in a Roman furnace', *Britannia* 2, pp. 203-17.

Cleere, H., 1974. 'The Roman iron industry of the Weald and its connexions with the *Classis Britannica*', *Archaeol J*, 131, pp. 171-99.

Cleere, H., & Crossley, D., 1986. *The Iron Industry of the Weald* (Leicester).

Collingwood, R. G., & Richmond, I. A., 1969. *The Archaeology of Roman Britain* (London).

Corder, P., 1951. *The Roman Town and Villa at Great Casterton: 1st interim report* (Nottingham).

Corder, P., 1954. *The Roman Town and Villa at Great Casterton: 2nd interim report* (Nottingham).

Corder, P., 1961. *The Roman Town and Villa at Great Casterton: 3rd interim report* (Nottingham).

Corney, M., 1984. 'A field-survey of the extra-mural region of Silchester', in Fulford, M. G., *Silchester Defences 1974-80*, Britannia Monogr 5 (London), pp. 239-97.

Corney, M., 1989. 'Multiple ditch systems and late Iron Age settlement in central Wessex', in *From Cornwall to Caithness, some aspects of British field archaeology*, ed. M. Bowden, D. MacKay & P. Topping, Br Archaeol Rep, Br ser 209 (Oxford), pp. 111-28.

Corney, M., 1991. 'The late Iron Age', in *Landscape Monuments and Society*, ed. J. Barrett, R. Bradley & M. Green (Cambridge), pp. 227-42.

Corney, M., 1997. 'The origins and development of the Romano-British small town at *Cunetio*, Mildenhall, Wiltshire', *Britannia*, 28, pp. 337-50.

Corney, M., Gater, J., & Gaffney, C., 1994. 'Geophysical investigations at the Charlton Villa, Wiltshire (England)', *Archaeol Prospect*, 1, pp. 121-8.

Corney, M., forthcoming. 'Romano-British settlement patterns in central Wessex'.

Corney, M., & Eagles, B., forthcoming. 'The boundary of *Civitas Durotrigium*: some pointers in south-west Wiltshire'.

Crummy, N., Crummy, P., & Crossan, C., 1993. *Excavations of Roman and Later Cemeteries, Churches and Monastic Sites in Colchester, 1971-88*, Colchester Archaeol Rep 9 (Colchester).

Davies, J. L., 1984. 'Soldiers, peasants and markets in Wales and the Marches', in *Military and Civilian in Roman Britain, cultural relationships in a frontier province*, ed. T. F. C. Blagg & A. C. King, Br Archaeol Rep, Br ser 136 (Oxford), pp. 93-127.

Dark, K. R., 1993. 'Roman-period activity at prehistoric ritual monuments in Britain and in the Armorican peninsula', in *Theoretical Roman Archaeology: first conference proceedings*, ed. E. Scott (Aldershot), pp. 133-46.

Dearne, M., & Branigan, K., 1995. 'The use of coal in Roman Britain', *Antiq J*, 75, pp. 71-105.

Eagles, B. N. E., 1994. 'The archaeological evidence for settlement in the fifth to seventh centuries AD', in *The Medieval Landscape of Wessex*, ed. M. Aston & C. Lewis (Oxford), pp. 13-32.

Eagles, B. N. E., 1997. 'The area around Bedwyn in the Anglo-Saxon period', in *The Romano-British Villa at Castle Copse, Great Bedwyn*, ed. E. Hostetter & T. N. Howe (Indiana), pp. 378-97.

Edis, J., Macleod, D., & Bewley, R., 1989. 'An archaeological guide to the classification of cropmarks and soilmarks', *Antiquity*, 63, pp. 112-26.

Esmonde Cleary, S., 1987. *Extra-Mural Areas of Romano-British Towns*, Br Archaeol Rep, Br ser 169 (Oxford).

Fauduet, I., 1993. *Atlas des Sanctuaires Romano-Celtique de Gaule: les fanums*, Éditions Errance (Paris).

Farwell, D. E., & Molleson, T. I., 1993. *Excavations at Poundbury 1966-80, Volume 2: The Cemeteries* (Dorchester).

Finberg, H. P. R., 1955. *Roman and Saxon Withington*, Univ Leicester, Dep Engl Local Hist Occas Pap No. 8.

Fowler, P. J., 2000. *Landscape Plotted and Pieced: landscape history and local archaeology in Fyfield and Overton, Wiltshire* (London).

Forcey, C., 1998. 'Whatever happened to the heroes? Ancestral cults and the enigma of Romano-British temples', in *TRAC 97, Proceedings of the Seventh Annual Theoretical Roman Archaeology Conference Nottingham 1997*, ed. C. Forcey, J. Hawthorne & R. Witcher (Oxford), pp. 87-98.

Frere, S. S., 1992. 'Roman Britain in 1991', *Britannia*, 23, pp. 255-308.

Fulford, M. G., 1975. *New Forest Roman Pottery: manufacture and distribution, with a corpus of pottery types*, Br Archaeol Rep, 17 (Oxford).

Fulford, M. G., 1982. 'Town and country in Roman Britain – a parasitical relationship?', in *The Romano British Countryside*, ed. Miles, pp. 403-19.

Fulford, M. G., & Allen, J. R. L., 1992. 'Iron-making at the Chesters Villa, Woolaston, Gloucestershire: survey and excavation 1987-91', *Britannia*, 23, pp. 159-215.

Gaffney, V., & Tingle, M., 1989. *The Maddle Farm Project: an integrated survey of prehistoric and Roman landscapes on the Berkshire Downs*, Br Archaeol Rep, Br ser 200 (Oxford).

Goodburn, R., 1978. 'Winterton: some villa problems', in *Studies in the Romano-British Villa*, ed. M Todd (Leicester), pp. 93-102.

Green, H. J. M., 1978. 'A villa estate at Godmanchester', in *Studies in the Romano-British Villa*, ed. Todd, pp. 103-17.

Gurney, D., 1986. *Settlement, Religion and Industry on the Roman Fen Edge, Norfolk*, East Anglian Archaeol, 31.

Hall, D., & Coles, J., 1994. *Fenland Survey: an essay in landscape and persistence* (London).

Hawkes, C. F. C., & Crummy, P., 1995. *Camulodunum II* (Colchester).

Henig, M., 1984. *Religion in Roman Britain* (London).

Hingley, R., 1982. 'Recent discoveries of the Roman period at Noah's Ark Inn, Frilford, south Oxfordshire', *Britannia*, 13, pp. 305-9.

Hingley, R., 1988. 'The influence of Rome on indigenous groups in the Upper Thames Valley', in *First Millennium Papers: Western Europe in the First Millennium BC*, ed. R. F. J. Jones, J. H. F. Bloemes, S. L. Dyson & M. Biddle, Br Archaeol Rep, Int ser 401 (Oxford), pp. 73-97.

Hingley, R., 1989. *Rural Settlement in Roman Britain* (London).

Hodder, I., 1974. 'The distribution of Savernake Ware', *Wiltshire Archaeol Mag*, 49, pp. 84-97.

Hopkins, R., forthcoming. 'Savernake Ware: a reassessment of the evidence'.

Hunn, J. R., 1992. 'The Verulamium *oppidum* and its landscape in the late Iron Age', *Archaeol J*, 149, pp. 39-68.

Hunn, J. R., 1994. *Reconstruction and Measurement of Landscape Change: a study of six parishes in the St Albans area*, Br Archaeol Rep, Br ser 236 (Oxford).

Huntley, J. P., 1999. 'A survey of the environmental evidence from Hadrian's Wall', in *Hadrian's Wall 1989-99: a summary of recent excavations and research*, ed. P. Bidwell & I. Carauna (Carlisle), pp. 32-49.

Jackson, R., & Potter, T., 1996. *Excavations at Stonea, Cambridgeshire 1980-85* (London).

Jessup, R. F., 1959. 'Roman barrows in Britain', *Latomus*, 58, pp. 853-67.

Jones, D., 1988. 'Aerial reconnaissance and prehistoric and Romano-British archaeology in northern Lincolnshire – a sample survey', *Lincolnshire Hist & Archaeol*, 23, pp. 5-30.

Jones, D., 1999. 'Romano-British settlements on the Lincolnshire Wolds', in *Lincolnshire's Archaeology from the Air*, ed. Bewley, pp. 69-80.

Jones, B., & Mattingly, D., 1990. *An Atlas of Roman Britain* (Oxford).

Jones, R. F. J., 1975. 'The Romano-British farmstead and its cemetery at Lynch Farm near Peterborough', *Northamptonshire Archaeol*, 10, pp. 94-137.

King, A., & Soffe, G., 1994. 'The Iron Age and Roman temple on Hayling Island', in *The Iron Age in Wessex: recent work*, ed. A. P. Fitzpatrick & E. Morris (Salisbury), pp. 114-16.

Knowles, A. K., 1977. 'Brampton, Norfolk: interim report', *Britannia*, 8, pp. 209-21.

Leach, P., 1982. *Ilchester: Volume I: Excavations 1974-5* (Bristol).

Leech, R. H., 1981. 'The excavation of a Romano-British farmstead and cemetery on Bradley Hill, Somerton, Somerset', *Britannia*, 12, pp. 177-252.

Leech, R. H., 1982. *Excavations at Catsgore 1970-3* (Bristol).

Leech, R. H., 1986. 'The excavation of a Romano-Celtic temple and a later cemetery on Lamyatt Beacon, Somerset', *Britannia*, 17, pp. 259-328.

Lewis, P. R., & Jones, G. D. B., 1969. 'The Dolaucothi gold mines, I: the surface evidence', *Antiq J*, 49, pp. 244-72.

Lyne, M., & Jeffries, R. S., 1979. *The Alice Holt/Farnham Roman Pottery Industry* (London).

Mackreth, D., 1979. 'Durobrivae', *Durobrivae*, 7, pp. 19-21.

Mackreth, D., 1996. *Orton Hall Farm: a Roman and early Anglo-Saxon farmstead*, East Anglian Archaeol, 76.

McOmish, D. 1993. 'Salisbury Plain', *Current Archaeol*, 135, pp. 110-13.

McWhirr, A., Viner, L., & Wells, C., 1982. *Romano-British Cemeteries at Cirencester*, Cirencester Excavation Reports II (Cirencester).

Miles, D. (ed.), 1982. *The Romano-British Countryside: studies in rural settlement and economy*, Br Archaeol Rep, Br ser 103 (Oxford).

Millett, M., 1990. *The Romanization of Britain* (Cambridge).

Morris, P., 1979. *Agricultural Buildings in Roman Britain*, Br Archaeol Rep, Br ser 70 (Oxford).

Neal, D., 1989. 'The Stanwick villa, Northants: an interim report on the excavations of 1984-88', *Britannia*, 20, pp. 149-68.

Neal, D., Wardle, A., & Hunn, J., 1990. *Excavation of the Iron Age, Roman and Medieval Settlement at Gorhambury, St Albans* (London).

O'Connell, M. G., & Bird, J., 1994. 'The Roman temple at Wanborough, excavation 1985-1986', *Surrey Archaeol Coll*, 82, pp. 1-168.

Oliver, B., & Applin, M., 1978. 'Excavations of an Iron Age and Romano-British settlement at Rucstalls Hill, Basingstoke, Hampshire, 1972-5', *Proc Hampshire Field Club*, 35, pp. 41-92.

Palmer, R., 1984. *Danebury: an Air Photographic Interpretation of its Environs* (London).

Perry, B., 1970. 'Iron Age enclosures and settlements on the Hampshire chalklands', *Archaeol J*, 126, pp. 29-43.

Perry, B., 1972. 'Excavations at Bramdean, Hampshire, 1965 and 1966, and a discussion of similar sites in southern England', *Proc Hampshire Field Club*, 29, pp. 41-77.

Perry, B., 1982. 'Excavations at Bramdean, Hampshire, 1973-77', *Proc Hampshire Field Club*, 38, pp. 57-74.

Perry, B., 1986. 'Excavations at Bramdean, Hampshire, 1983 and 1984, with some further thoughts of the 'Banjo' syndrome', *Proc Hampshire Field Club*, 42, pp. 35-42.

Phillips, C. W. (ed.), 1970. *The Fenland in Roman Times* (London).

Philpott, R., 1991. *Burial Practices in Roman Britain, an archaeological survey of grave treatment and furnishing AD 43-410*, Br Archaeol Rep, Br ser 219 (Oxford).

Pitt-Rivers, A. H. L. F., 1887. *Excavations in Cranborne Chase, Volume I* (London).

Pitt-Rivers, A. H. L. F., 1888. *Excavations in Cranborne Chase, Volume II* (London).

Quinnell, H., 1986. 'Cornwall during the Iron Age and Roman period', *Cornish Archaeol*, 25, pp. 111-34.

RCHME 1976. *Ancient and Historical Monuments in the County of Gloucester, Vol. 1: Iron Age and Romano-British Monuments in the Gloucestershire Cotswolds* (London).

RCHME 1980. *An Archaeological Atlas of Northamptonshire* (London).

Rippon, S., 1996. *The Gwent Levels: the evolution of a wetland landscape*, Counc Br Archaeol Res Rep 105 (York).

Sellwood, B., 1984. 'The rock types represented by the Town Walls of Silchester, in *Silchester Defences 1974-80*, ed. Fulford, pp. 224-31.

Smith, G. H., 1978. 'Excavations near Hadrian's Wall at Tarraby Lane 1976', *Britannia*, 9, pp. 19-57.

Smith, I., & Simpson, D. D. A., 1960. 'Excavation of three Roman tombs and a prehistoric pit on Overton Down', *Wiltshire Archaeol Mag*, 59, pp. 68-85.

Smith, A. H. V., 1997. 'Provenance of coals from Roman sites in England and Wales', *Britannia*, 28, pp. 297-324.

Speake, G., 1989. *A Saxon Bed Burial on Swallowcliffe Down: excavations by F de M Vatcher* (London).

Stoertz, C., 1997. *Ancient Landscapes of the Yorkshire Wolds* (London).

Swan, V., 1975. 'Oare reconsidered and the origins of Savernake Ware in Wiltshire', *Britannia* 6, pp. 37-61

Todd, M. (ed.), 1989. *Research on Roman Britain* (London).

Tomlin, R. S. O., 1996. 'A five-acre wood in Roman Kent, in *Interpreting Roman London: papers in memory of Hugh Chapman*, ed. J. Bird, M. Hassall & H. Sheldon (Oxford), pp. 209-15.

Toynbee, J., 1971. *Death and Burial in the Roman World* (London).

Trow, S., 1978. 'Excavations at Ditches Hillfort, North Cerney, Gloucestershire, 1982-3', *Trans Bristol & Gloucestershire Archaeol Soc*, 106, pp. 19-85.

Trow, S., & James, S., 1989. 'Ditches Villa, North Cerney: an example of locational conservatism in the early Roman Cotswolds', in *The Economies of Romano-British Villas*, ed. K. Branigan & D. Miles (Sheffield), pp. 83-7.

Tyers, P., 1996. *Roman Pottery in Britain* (London).

Wainwright, G. J., 1969. 'The excavation of a Durotrigian farmstead near Tollard Royal in Cranborne Chase, southern England', *Proc Prehist Soc*, 34, pp. 102-47.

Wainwright, G. J., 1979. *Gussage All Saints: an Iron Age settlement in Dorset* (London).

Webster, G. (ed.), 1988. *Fortress into City: the consolidation of Roman Britain, first century AD* (London).

Wheeler, R. E. M., & Wheeler, T. V., 1932. *Report on the Excavations at Lydney Park, Gloucestershire* (London).

Wheeler, R. E. M., 1943. *Maiden Castle, Dorset* (London).

Williams, J. H., 1971. 'Roman building-materials in south-east England, *Britannia*, 2, pp. 166-95.

Williams, H., 1996. 'Placing the dead in ancient landscapes: the Anglo-Saxon period funerary re-use of earlier monuments and structures', Unpubl Univ Reading MA thesis.

Williams, H., 1998. 'The ancient monument in Romano-British ritual practices', in *TRAC 97*, ed. Forcey, Hawthorne & Witcher, pp. 71-86.

Williamson, T., 1987. 'Early co-axial field systems on the East Anglian boulder clays', *Proc Prehist Soc*, 53, pp. 419-31.

Wilson, D. R., 1993. 'Some thoughts on field archaeology', *AARG News*, no. 6, pp. 7-9.

Woodward, A., & Leach, P., 1993. *The Uley Shrines. Excavation of a ritual complex on West Hill, Uley, Gloucestershire: 1977-9* (London).

Young, C. J., 1977. *The Roman Pottery Industry of the Oxford Region*, Br Archaeol Rep, Br ser 43 (Oxford).

Landscapes in transition: the later Roman and early medieval periods

Stephen Rippon

ABSTRACT

In recent decades new light has been cast upon the impact of the Anglo-Saxons in England. This chapter examines the concept of continuity and discontinuity through the use of documentary, place-name, archaeological and palaeoenvironmental data integrated with evidence from the landscape itself.

KEYWORDS

Continuity, early medieval, land use, late Roman, settlement patterns, settlement types

INTRODUCTION

It has long been argued that the ending of Roman authority over Britain was associated with profound changes in the landscape, with a complex urban hierarchy and civilised countryside of villa-estates being replaced by derelict towns and regenerated woodland. The native population – Gildas' 'wretched survivors' (Winterbottom 1978, XXV.1) – were forced westwards by the Anglo-Saxon newcomers, who then cleared that woodland and created open fields and nucleated villages (*e.g.* Hoskins 1955). However, this traditional view was based upon three very weak strands of evidence: an exceedingly sketchy documentary record, the interpretation of place-name and linguistic evidence, and a very restricted range of archaeological material, notably grave goods from cemetery excavations. The scholarly philosophy was also highly unsatisfactory as the archaeological evidence was used simply to support a documentary-based history of the period dominated by invasion, conquest, kingdom formation and certain legendary (or mythical?) heroic figures (*e.g.* Myres 1986; and see Garwood 1989).

One of the major achievements of landscape archaeology since the 1970s has been to first challenge, and then reject this traditional model. The result was that a paradigm of discontinuity came to be replaced by one of overriding continuity, leading to a certain division in outlook between scholars whose main focus was Anglo-Saxon cemeteries, settlements and material culture, who still viewed the post-Roman period as one of mass folk migration, and those revisionists who argued simply for a political take-over of the native population and their landscape by a new warrior élite. What this paper hopes to show is that through the careful integration of a wide range of evidence, it appears that the transition from Roman Britain to Saxon England was in practice a complex combination of these two processes.

Interdisciplinary study is the key to understanding this difficult period, and this paper will focus on the contribution that landscape studies have made. Firstly, it will be shown how large-scale fieldwork forced traditional views of the late Roman period to be reviewed, and how various strands of evidence were used to postulate that many aspects of the Romano-British landscape survived into the medieval period. Attention will then turn to a critical assessment of what 'continuity' actually means in the context of rural landscapes, which leads to a consideration of two critical issues: what happened to the native Romano-British communities, and, in southern and eastern England, what were the relationships between native and immigrant populations at a site, local and regional level? Attention will then focus on the wider landscape, with particular emphasis on palaeoenvironmental evidence for any changing patterns of land use.

CHANGING VIEWS OF THE LATE- AND POST-ROMAN LANDSCAPE

The 1960s and 1970s saw a profound change in our understanding of the late Roman period, as new techniques that were to become the foundations of landscape archaeology – aerial photography, fieldwalking, open area excavations, and palaeoenvironmental analysis – started to occur on a large scale. The results have transformed our understanding of the late Romano-British landscape. It was realised that the landscape of Roman Britain was more densely populated than previously thought, expanding from Collingwood and Myres' (1937, p. 180) *c.* 1 million, to Salway's (1981, p. 544) 4-6 million (and see Millett 1990, pp. 181-6). Although some scholars see a relatively simple, two-fold division in the Romano-British landscape (along similar lines to traditional upland/lowland or military/civilian divide: *e.g.* Dark & Dark 1997), it is

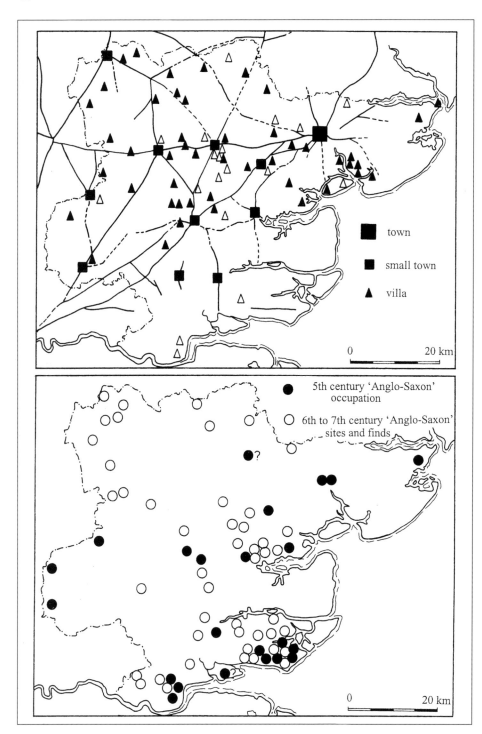

Fig. 4.1a. The distribution of high status Romano-British settlement in Essex, showing its marked bias towards the north and west (after Going 1996). Such local variations in landscape structure can be seen throughout the countryside of Roman Britain.

Fig. 4.1b: The distribution of 'Early Saxon' material in Essex (after Tyler 1996). There is a marked concentration in the south and east, which is particularly clear when only fifth-century sites are considered (cf. the distribution of Romano-British villas and towns in Fig 1a).

increasingly possible to recognise that regional variation in economic systems and social structures occurred at a much more local scale. The countryside of Roman Britain was a complex mosaic with, for example, certain areas of even the south-east lacking a strongly villa-based landscape (e.g. Fig. 4.1; and see Hingley 1989; Jones & Mattingly 1990; Millett 1990, pp. 197-201). This regional variation in settlement structure was particularly pronounced by the fourth century when, for example, the Cotswold landscape around Cirencester, with its high density of palatial villas, socially and economically articulating with

a flourishing urban centre, was very different to the Essex and Suffolk claylands where a few mainly humble villas could be found in a landscape in which both urban and rural settlements were in decline, and fields were going out of use (see below; and see Rippon in press, chs 5-6).

The traditional model, that nucleated medieval villages had their origins in the early Anglo-Saxon colonisation, was similarly not supported by the growing evidence from large-scale survey and excavation. Work on deserted medieval villages was failing to recover evidence for pre-ninth/tenth century occupation of a village character (*e.g.* Wharram Percey, Yorkshire: Beresford & Hurst 1990; Milne & Richards 1992), and where earlier settlements were excavated elsewhere they lacked the size and regularity of medieval villages (*e.g.* Mucking, Essex: Hamerow 1993; West Stow, Suffolk: West 1985). Fieldwalking supported the evidence from excavation in suggesting that settlements associated with fifth- to seventh-century pottery formed a highly dispersed pattern which showed a relatively high degree of mobility (Arnold & Wardle 1981; Hodges 1989; *cf.* Hamerow 1991). In the Midlands and North-east, this came to be replaced by nucleated villages around the end of the millennium (*e.g.* Buckinghamshire: Croft & Mynard 1993, pp. 15-18; Northamptonshire: Foard 1978; Brown & Foard 1998; Hall & Martin 1979; Hall 1988; Lewis *et al.* 1997; Somerset: Aston & Gerrard 1999; Rippon 1997, pp. 159-65), while documentary evidence in the form of charters also suggested a late first millennium A.D. date for village creation in areas such as the West Midlands (*e.g.* Hooke 1985).

As the origin of medieval villages shifted to the end of the millennium, archaeologists increasingly argued for landscape continuity at the end of the Roman period. The idea that the native population was wiped out by plague was dismissed (Todd 1977). A number of important studies suggested that estates continued to function. Finberg's (1955) seminal history of Withington in Gloucestershire led to a number of other studies which postulated continuity in estate structure based on the relationship between Roman villas, medieval churches and estate boundaries described in early medieval charters (*e.g.* Fowler 1975). Bonney (1979) used the relationship between pagan burials and parish boundaries in Wessex to postulate that the latter were based upon earlier estates (but see Goodier 1984), while Leech (1982) observed that the early Roman 'Fosse Way' road in Somerset appeared to cut across a number of parish boundaries, once again suggesting they were of considerable antiquity. On a larger scale, some have even suggested that the *territoria* associated with Romano-British towns survived into the medieval period as administrative units (*e.g.* Great Chesterford in Essex: Bassett 1989b, p. 25; *Verlucio* in Wiltshire: Haslam 1984, p. 103). With Jones' (1979) identification of multiple estates (but see Gregson 1985; Jones 1985), and Davies' (1979) work on the Llandaff charters in south-east Wales, continuity in estate boundaries appears to have occurred across much of Britain (and see Bassett 1997, p. 36; Bassett 1989b, pp. 18-19).

For the boundaries of an estate to have survived implies that it continued to function as an agricultural unit, and if this was the case then field systems should similarly have remained in use. Though Taylor and Fowler (1978) noted a number of instances where Romano-British ditches appear

to have been succeeded by the headlands of open fields, the large-scale replanning of these Midland landscapes from around the ninth/tenth centuries means that evidence for any continuity at the end of the Roman period will have been largely swept away (*e.g.* Brown & Ford 1998, fig. 14). However, extensive areas outside the Midlands never saw this later landscape transformation, and as such have greater potential for landscape continuity.

In areas such as Essex, large-scale excavations in advance of gravel extraction are revealing later prehistoric and Romano-British field systems which, although partly abandoned (and now showing up as crop-marks), appear to follow the general orientation of the medieval and later landscape (*e.g.* Slough House Farm and Chigborough near Heybridge: Wallis & Waughman 1998). Indeed, areas of East Anglia (Bassett 1982; Rippon 1991; Rodwell 1978; Rodwell & Rodwell 1985; Williamson 1987; *cf.* Hinton 1997; and Williamson 1998) (Fig 4.2) and the Midlands (Bassett 1985, 1990) have extensive co-axial field-boundary patterns preserved within the historic landscape which in a number of places appear to pre-date Roman roads, or be Roman in date. Great care must be taken in the interpretation of such evidence as abandoned field boundaries can be re-used in later periods, as appears to have been the case around the fringes of Dartmoor, where parts of a reave system were incorporated into the medieval field pattern (*e.g.* Fleming 1988, pp. 28-9, fig. 30). However, it is unlikely that extensive areas of landscape such as the Scole-Dickleburgh system in Norfolk, which extends for some 14 km, would have been restored had it gone totally out of use and been enveloped by woodland. Rather, for these landscapes to have survived (albeit in a much altered form) implies that the area remained in some sort of agricultural use throughout their existence.

Whilst many archaeologists have increasingly been seeing continuity in the post-Roman landscape, linguists and place-name scholars have retained a more traditional view in arguing that a mass folk migration is the only way of explaining why English came to dominate both spoken language and how features in the landscape are named. In asking 'why aren't we speaking Welsh', Gelling asserts that 'a new language might conceivably be adopted in deference to a new ruling class, but the renaming of the vast majority of settlements is inconceivable without the influx of a mass of peasant settlers' (Gelling 1993, p. 51). However, she later observes that there is no evidence for the wholesale replacement of the native population in western counties such as Devon and Shropshire yet 90 *per cent* of their place-names are English by the tenth century (and see Hooke 1997). That the replacement of British names with English occurred without population replacement in the west suggests that the same could have been true elsewhere as social

Fig 4.2. Landscapes of continuity and discontinuity in south-east Essex. Following a retrogressive analysis (see Williamson 1987) of the field-boundary pattern, three broad landscape zones can be identified (Rippon 1991). In the central area, an irregular landscape results from the post-Roman clearance of woodland (the area has a fairly high density of Roman sites, and at least some of the woodland is itself post-Roman and even post-Conquest in date; Rippon 1999). To the west lies an area of highly rectilinear landscape, at least one element of which has been dated to the Roman period (Rodwell 1966). The survival of elements of the Romano-British road and field system suggest the landscape has remained in some form of agricultural use ever since. In contrast, the more radially arranged landscape around Shoebury has a *terminus post quem* of the fifth century (as the late Romano-British field system at North Shoebury, which had 'Early Saxon' pottery from its upper contexts, was on a different orientation). There is a *terminus ante quem* of the eleventh century when an enclosure, that conforms to the radial landscape, was constructed to the east of St Mary's church. Clearly, these three adjacent landscapes had very different histories in the post-Roman period.

mechanisms – notably the political supremacy and literacy of the new ruling class – led to the gradual re-naming of the landscape (Härke 1997, p. 149; Hines 1990; Powlesland 1997, p. 90). These various processes of migration and assimilation will have occurred in different ways in different places, resulting in marked regional variation in how the landscape was affected, and there is a need to include topics such as rural dialects in the debate (*e.g.* Gay 1999). Ultimately, however, the answer may lie with scientific advances. Härke (1990) has already used skeletal evidence to show that both native and immigrant populations are evident in 'Anglo-Saxon' cemeteries, while the study of genetics, for example, is showing that distinctive traits found in Frisia and Schleswig are rare in Britain and does not support the idea that all English speaking areas were *largely* populated by those who sailed across the English Channel in the fifth and sixth centuries (Evison 1997; Mckie 1993).

This growing emphasis upon continuity came as those scholars who still saw a substantial Germanic (*e.g.* Welch 1985; 1992; Scull 1992, 1993) or Scandinavian (Hines 1984) folk migration in the fifth and sixth centuries, were seeing an increasingly different post-Roman landscape to those who argued that the new burial rites, styles of dress, and other material culture, may not represent the movement of people, but simply the exchange of objects and transmission of ideas (*e.g.* Arnold 1984; Higham 1992; Hodges 1989; and see Crawford 1997; Hamerow 1997; and Hines 1997 for general overviews). However, the problem with this often lively debate is that the various strands of evidence – settlements, estates, field systems, burials, linguistics, etc – are all too often discussed in isolation. The contribution of landscape archaeology is to provide a conceptual, temporal and spatial framework into which the wide range of data relating to this period can be woven together and placed in context.

'CONTINUITY' AND THE ARTICULATION OF POST-ROMAN LANDSCAPES

Settlements and cemeteries, which have produced so much of the data for this period, did not exist in a vacuum but were simply domestic and ritual elements of the broader landscape. One key theme is the nature of that much-used phrase 'continuity'. Any landscape consists of a wide variety of articulated components:

– the natural environment (landform, drainage systems etc)
– settlements (where people lived and worked)
– agriculture, including fields (in which agriculture was practised) and other areas of landed resource (such as meadow and woodland)
– non-agricultural resources (raw material procurement and manufacturing)
– roads and other communication routes (which linked communities living in settlements with each other and their resources)
– ritual foci (where religion and burial was practised)
– social structures (including kinship groups)
– territorial structures (economic and tenurial units within which all the above were articulated)
– demography (including the racial origins of the people who lived in this landscape)

It does not appear that the fifth century was one of great environmental upheaval. Many coastal wetlands were inundated at this time, and while this may in part have been due to a failure to maintain flood defences (a cultural phenomena), there does appear to have been a rise in relative sea-level at this time (Rippon 2000; in press, ch. 7). However, a number of coastal marshes appear to have been largely deserted long before the end of the fourth century (*e.g.* around the Thames Estuary and on Romney Marsh), and while valuable farmland was lost in Fenland and around the Severn Estuary, this formed a small percentage of Britain as a whole. There is also little evidence that lowland Britain suffered a significant climatic deterioration at the end of the Roman period, and if anything the sixth century appears to have been less favourable to agriculture than the fifth (Lamb 1995, p. 165). Overall, any changes seen in most landscapes during the fifth century were, therefore, due to changing socio-economic circumstances.

In a period of cultural upheaval different components of the landscape can experience very different levels of change. Take, for example, a farmstead established by Anglo-Saxon immigrants next to a Romano-British villa which had been abandoned for three months. This would entail demographic discontinuity, but functional continuity of the farmstead, as the three-month gap would have been of little practical significance in landscape exploitation; field boundaries would have survived, crops may still have been in a condition to harvest (and so produce seed for the next year), and livestock may not have wandered too far (and so could have been rounded up). However, if neighbouring villas had also been deserted by their owners shortly before the arrival of the Germanic newcomers, then knowledge of the Romano-British pattern of landownership would probably have been lost, leading to the imposition of a new estate structure on an existing pattern of fields and roads. Thus, agrarian continuity occurred in the context of tenurial discontinuity as the landscape lost only part of its articulation. Indeed, despite all the earlier work on reconstructing continuity in estate structure (see above), the survival of tenurial systems is perhaps one of the landscape features least likely to survive a period of socio-economic disruption as seen at the end of the Roman period.

THE FATE OF ROMANO-BRITISH COMMUNITIES

In viewing the late Roman landscape as a series of articulated components, we must consider two related issues that affected it during the post-Roman period: in all areas of Britain there is the issue of what happened to the native population, and in the south and east of England there is the interaction between any surviving native population and the immigrants (however many there were).

The late fourth/early fifth century is characterised by the collapse of urban culture, manufacturing industry, the market economy, and the need to produce an agricultural surplus to support Roman rule and the non-food producing sectors of society (Esmonde Cleary 1995, p. 20). There is, however, increasing evidence that the landscape of late Roman Britain was changing well before the end of Roman rule. In certain areas there appears to have been a decline in rural prosperity and the intensity of landscape exploitation during the fourth century, as seen, for example, in parts of Hertfordshire (Neal *et al.* 1990, p. 96), northern Kent (Bennett & Williams 1997), Essex (Going 1996; Hodder 1982; Lavender 1993; Wallace 1995; Wallis & Waughman 1998, p. 53), south-east Suffolk (Newman 1992, p. 31), and Yorkshire (Loveluck 1996, p. 28). Of Mucking, in Essex, Going says 'It is ... hard to resist the conclusion that the landscape was effectively *agri deserti* by the later fourth century' (Going 1993a, pp. 20-1).

In such areas, the abandonment of settlements and field systems began well before the 'end of Roman Britain', though in other areas large numbers of Romano-British sites have datable material from the very end of the fourth century. Even if these settlements were suffering some decline during the late fourth century (relative to their wealth in earlier decades), the absence of recognisable material culture after that date does not preclude them from having been occupied well into the fifth century or later (*cf.* Burrow 1981, p. 14). The problem is that with the collapse of pottery production, cessation of coin use (the recently recovered hoard from Patching in Sussex, deposited after A.D. 461, is the latest from 'Roman' Britain: White 1998), and shift from stone to timber methods of construction (see below), it is difficult to determine what happened to these sites after the late Roman period.

The scarcity of distinctive and datable material culture on the few native post-Roman sites that have been excavated (*e.g.* Rahtz *et al.* 1992; Sparey Green 1987; Woodward & Leach 1993, p. 334), suggests that organic materials must have partly replaced the industrial manufacture of metallic and, particularly, ceramic artefacts. What Romano-British material culture survived may also have remained in use far longer than is often thought. On some sites, the worn condition of late fourth-century coins indicates that money-based exchange may have continued for several decades into the fifth century, albeit potentially on a very local scale (*e.g.* Miles 1984, p. 14). The continued use of fourth-century pottery and metal artefacts into the fifth century is more difficult to recognise, but why should people stop using existing artefacts simply because manufacturing had ceased (*e.g.* see Farley 1984, p. 229)? All that we can confidently say is that many Romano-British settlements were abandoned some time between the late fourth century and whenever durable and datable material culture was once again in use on rural sites (which in areas such as Somerset is as late as the tenth century).

It is, therefore, essential that we secure more radiocarbon dates from the latest stratigraphic horizons of sites that were occupied into the fifth century. A good example has recently come from Somerset. At Cheddar Showground, an otherwise undated ditch has yielded a radiocarbon date of 1600+/-45 BP (cal A.D. 346-557) from animal bone recovered from the upper fill; a later recut only contained abraded Romano-British pottery and might otherwise have been regarded as dating to the Roman period (Chris Webster, Somerset County Council, pers. comm., October 1999). An iron-smelting site on Exmoor, which based upon the technology of production appeared to be Romano-British, has recently produced a date of 1520+/-60 BP (cal A.D. 415-650) (Gill Juleff, Univ Exeter, pers. comm., October 1999). Similar surprising results can be obtained through dendrochronology. For example, at Slough House Farm, near Heybridge in Essex, two timber wells, which on typological grounds could have been Romano-British, were constructed from timbers felled in the early sixth and early seventh centuries (Wallis & Waughman 1998, p. 57).

The extent of post-Roman occupation on Roman-period settlements may also have been more widespread than previously assumed. In the south-west of Britain, studies of settlement patterns, and the excavation of individual sites, suggest that while there are signs of settlement retraction in some areas there was no widespread desertion during the early fifth century (*e.g.* Leech 1982; Quinnell 1986; Rose & Preston Jones 1995; Simpson *et al.* 1989). In the east of England, the continued occupation of Romano-British settlements may also have been more common than has often been assumed. For example, a trawl through the recent literature shows that there are numerous sites in one sample county, Essex, where small amounts of fifth- to seventh-century handmade pottery has been recovered from the latest contexts of Romano-British sites (*e.g.* Asheldham: Bedwin 1991; Castle Hedingham: Lavendar 1996; Chignall: Clarke 1998; Coggeshall: Isserlin 1995; Great Dunmow: Lavender 1997; Wickenden 1988; Great Sampford: Garwood 1998; Great Waltham: Tyler & Wickenden 1996; Kelvedon: Eddy 1982; Rodwell 1988; North Shoebury: Wymer & Brown 1995).

Such pottery is poorly dated, and its fabric and style bears little resemblance to late Romano-British manufactured wares, and shares some characteristics with material from mainland Europe. However, this does not mean that it was only used by immigrant populations, as it may have been obtained through exchange and used by the native community (particularly if it was the only pottery being produced at that time). The very small amounts of material involved might suggest that it was simply dropped by casual visitors or users of the site, though bearing in mind the scarcity of material culture on well-excavated post-Roman settlements, a few sherds might be all that survives from continuous occupation. It may be that more careful observation in the field, particularly of the latest areas of stratigraphy (and the ploughsoil!) will reveal that post-Roman use of Romano-British sites is more common that has been previously thought.

NATIVES AND NEWCOMERS

A number of Romano-British settlements have produced more substantial evidence for later occupation in the form of what traditionally have been called 'early Anglo-Saxon' buildings. Although post-built structures of this period may contain a substantial native element to their design (Dixon 1982; James *et al.* 1984; Marshall & Marshall 1993; Powlesland 1997), 'sunken-featured buildings' are generally regarded as being distinctively Germanic. A number of Romano-British structures have been recorded with sunken floors (*e.g.* Dorchester in Dorset: Smith *et al.* 1997; Monkton in Kent: Bennett & Williams 1997), and these are also found on what otherwise appears to be a native post-Roman settlement at Poundbury outside Dorchester (Sparey Green 1987). However, the 'Anglo-Saxon' examples are morphologically so different that where they occur during the fifth century associated with distinctive material culture they are best interpreted as having been constructed by communities of direct Germanic decent, with a memory of their homeland (Hamerow 1997, p. 39).

If fifth-century sunken-featured buildings are regarded as indicative of an immigrant population, and they are found on Romano-British settlements, the key question is the relationship between the two communities. At Heybridge in Essex, for example, the earliest Anglo-Saxon occupation appears to have been contemporary with the final stages of native occupation on this substantial rural settlement (Drury & Wickenden 1982; Langton & Holbrook 1997; Wallis & Waughman 1998, p. 229). At Barton Court Farm, Oxfordshire, Miles (1984, p. 52) argued for a 'butt-jointed' sequence with Saxon colonists settling a recently deserted Romano-British farmstead, though the dating evidence we have cannot rule out the possibility that the two populations lived side by side.

Worn late fourth-century coins from the Romano-British farmstead suggests activity there continued into the fifth century (Fig. 4.3). That the stone buildings were then demolished, presumably because the materials were re-used elsewhere (why else bother demolishing a stone building?), implies occupation continued near by even later. The earliest pottery of a distinctive 'early Saxon' style dates to the mid fifth century and is associated with seven sunken-featured buildings suggesting the presence of Germanic settlers. The dating evidence we have cannot show whether they were contemporary with the final phases of native occupation of the farm (wherever its focus now was). Palaeoenvoronmental evidence from Saxon contexts points to a landscape that remained open (seeing very little woodland/scrub regeneration), with both arable and pastoral farming, but which was used less intensively than in the Roman period, reflecting the need to produce less food (for the market, taxation etc).

Up to eight typologically undiagnostic post-built structures were also recorded at Barton Court Farm. One (Structure C) was stratigraphically and artefactually dated to the early Saxon period, but postholes of another (Structure A) only yielded worn fourth-century material, while the remaining structures yielded no dating evidence: could at least some of these represent the native successors to the stone farmhouse? Ephemeral traces of stratigraphically late timber structures have been noted at other Romano-British villas (*e.g.* Brixworth in Northants: Brown & Foard 1998, p. 73; Gadebridge Park in Hertfordshire: Neal 1974; Latimer in Buckinghamshire: Branigan 1971; Rivenhall in Essex: Rodwell & Rodwell 1985; but see Millett 1987; Shakenoak in Oxfordshire: Brodribb *et al.* 1978), along with a number of urban (*e.g.* Wroxeter in Shropshire: Barker *et al.* 1997) and military sites (*e.g.* Birdoswold on Hadrians Wall: Wilmott 1997, pp. 209-31; York: Phillips & Heywood 1995). On how many early or small-scale excavations were such ephemeral traces of timber buildings overlooked because the focus was on the sequence of stone buildings?

Great care, however, is required in examining the chronology of sites with both Romano-British and 'early Anglo-Saxon' occupation. At the Orsett Cock, Essex, for example, a total of eight excavated sunken-featured buildings occur within and just outside a substantial Romano-British farmstead enclosure. However, the site was largely abandoned by the late fourth century, and the subsequent occupation may date to as late as the sixth century (Carter 1998; Milton 1985; and see Tyers 1996, fig. 2, for the possible extent of the site). Users of the sunken-featured buildings may have been attracted to the site as there were earthworks against which they could tuck their buildings, but there cannot have been functional continuity of this location as a farmstead: the site, and presumably its associated landscape, had lost its articulation as a functioning agricultural system.

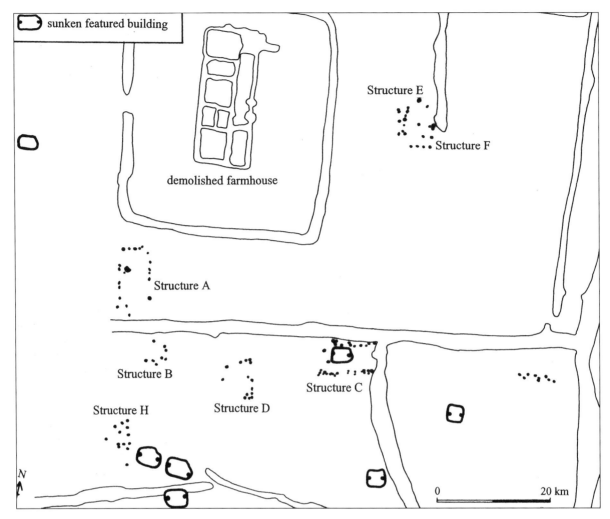

Fig 4.3. Barton Court Farm, Oxfordshire. The Romano-British farmhouse had been demolished before the construction of the 'Anglo-Saxon' sunken featured buildings, though the date of most of typologically undiagnostic posthole structure is unknown. The environmental evidence suggests there cannot have been a long break in the exploitation of the local landscape, though we otherwise know relatively little about other elements to this landscape (such as the fields, roads and territorial structures).

The same appears to have been true with medieval churches that are located on Romano-British sites: in most cases the latter appear to have been in ruins when the former were constructed (Bell 1998; and see Morris 1989; Rodwell & Rodwell 1977), suggesting that these sites were chosen simply for the symbolism that these remains of *Romanitas* possessed (*e.g.* Fulford & Rippon 1994).

On sites such as Barton Court Farm (and Orton Hall Farm near Peterborough: Mackreth 1996), the key question is how any surviving native populations interacted with what do appear to have been the Germanic newcomers (assuming the builders of the fifth-century sunken-featured buildings were immigrants). Our traditional story is of the native and Germanic populations being constantly at war, with the latter soon gaining supremacy. Scull (1992, p. 15), for example, paints a picture of the native population in East Anglia being forced into a handful of unwanted corners and defended sites such as Burgh Castle and the Wighton enclosure. However, in other cases, it is the early Anglo-

Saxon settlements (or at least many of those that have seen large-scale excavation) that were located around the periphery of areas occupied in the Roman period (and which may still have been occupied in the fifth and sixth centuries). At West Stow, Suffolk, for example, the Anglo-Saxon settlement occurs on a gravel terrace with poor soils, in contrast to the Romano-British settlements around the Lark Valley that concentrate along the fertile fen-edge. West (1985, pp. 159-63) has argued that this represents a *shift* in location, due to climatic or sea-level change, though it could have been that the newcomers were simply forced to occupy an area of poor heathland, beyond the core land of a still-functioning native estate (Bell 1989, p. 278; Murphy 1985; Taylor 1983, p. 119). Due to the agencies of discovery (notably large-scale rescue excavations in advance of mineral extraction), there is certainly a marked bias in the distribution of known early Anglo-Saxon settlements towards 'marginal' areas though until other geologies are as thoroughly investigated, it is impossible to say whether the colonists were generally forced to settle poorer land.

Evidence from southern Essex, for example, suggests a more varied picture, as while Mucking appears to lie on an area of poor soil at the fringes of the area settled and farmed during the late Roman period (Hamerow 1992, p. 41; and see Gelling 1976; 1988, pp. 121-3; Going 1996, p. 21), further along the Thames Estuary near Southend-on-Sea the highly fertile brickearths have produced the greatest density of early Anglo-Saxon material from the whole county (Wymer & Brown 1995). Overall, the evidence for fifth-century Saxon occupation in Essex tends to focus in the south and east, notably in coastal areas, away from the villa-dominated boulder clay landscape of northern and western Essex (Fig. 4.1). Is this another example of controlled Anglo-Saxon settlement, as has been argued for in Sussex (Welch 1983)?

Our understanding of this marked spatial variation in the apparent character of the post-Roman landscape in Essex could be pursued by the careful integration of a wide range of evidence. Most large-scale excavations have been carried out in the south and east of the county (the coastal/estuary areas: *e.g.* Hamerow 1993; Wallis & Waughman 1998; Wilkinson 1988; Wymer & Brown 1995), and it is unfortunate that there has been no large-scale fieldwalking in these areas since where this has been carried out the results have been encouraging. Williamson (1986) has studied an area around Saffron Walden in the north-west of the county, where he found that 35 *per cent* of pottery scatters suggestive of settlements occupied at the end of the Roman period were within 200 metres of settlements known to have been occupied in the eleventh century (this figure is actually too low as it excludes a number of locations where chance finds and the pattern of manuring suggest that medieval/modern settlements lie directly over Romano-British sites). Clearly there has been considerable settlement mobility over the intervening 500 years, but there does appear to be a broad continuity in prefered settlement location (most notably in the river valleys rather than on the heavier soils of the interfluvial areas). Earlier work has also suggested that elements of the medieval/modern field and road pattern in this area may date back to at least the Roman period. The north-west of Essex also lacks evidence for fifth-century Anglo-Saxon colonisation (Fig. 4.1a), while the place-name 'Waldon' is derived from 'valley of the Britons' (Bassett 1982, p. 10). There appears to be a strong case for the continuous occupation and exploitation of this landscape by the Romano-British/sub-Roman population, in contrast to the strongly coastal/estuarine distribution of Anglo-Saxon settlement (Drury & Rodwell 1980; Tyler 1996).

Overall, the picture that is emerging is of marked regional variation in the relationships between natives and newcomers. In places, the latter may have forcibly replaced the former, or occupied areas that the natives had abandoned due to political insecurity or the cessation of pressure to farm physically less productive areas. However, during the fifth century, and perhaps much of the sixth, the two communities may have lived side by side, either at a very local (*e.g.* West Stow?), or more regional scale (*e.g.* Essex, Wessex and Yorkshire?: Eagles 1994; Loveluck 1996): such arrangement may even have been agreed by treaty (*e.g.* Sussex?: Welch 1983). The impact that this social geography had on the fifth/sixth-century and later landscape is yet to be fully explored (but see Williamson 1988).

THE BIGGER PICTURE: PATTERNS OF LAND USE

Whatever was occurring at the local level, we must not lose sight of the bigger picture: what was going on in the landscape as a whole (irrespective of the origin of the population)? The occurrence of Romano-British settlements in areas that are now wooded illustrates a degree of post-Roman woodland regeneration (*e.g.* Bellamy 1994), though this need not have occurred during the earlier fifth century (Rippon 1999). Dark (1996) has recently summarised the pollen evidence for this period (and see Bell 1989, pp. 269-70; Bell & Dark 1998). Just thirty-eight sequences were identified with sufficient resolution and dating, most of which were in the north and west: just one (Hockham Mere in Suffolk) lay to the east of a line between Scarborough and Brighton. Despite considerable local variation, some broad regional trends do emerge. In Wales and Scotland most sequences show continuity in landscape exploitation either side of A.D. 400, though around Hadrian's Wall, for example, a recent reassessment of the pollen evidence suggests that there was a phase of abandonment during the earlier fifth century with a reduction of agricultural land use and widespread reversion to woodland (Dark & Dark 1996). However, in an area with a large military garrison this is to be expected, and fits well with the picture that appears to be emerging in lowland Britain in that the more Romanised aspects of the landscape, reliant on social, economic and political links with the Roman empire, were abandoned, whereas the wider rural landscape remained in use. In this respect it is worth stressing that highly Romanised settlements such as towns and villas represented a very small percentage of fourth-century settlements (see Mark Corney, this volume). For example, around *Verulamium* in Hertfordshire, Neal *et al.* argue that 'The general picture which emerges is that of once-rich country houses falling into disrepair or being abandoned, but with associated farms continuing in use, albeit on a run down scale' (Neal *et al.* 1990, p. 96). The whole rationale for the villa-estate system of

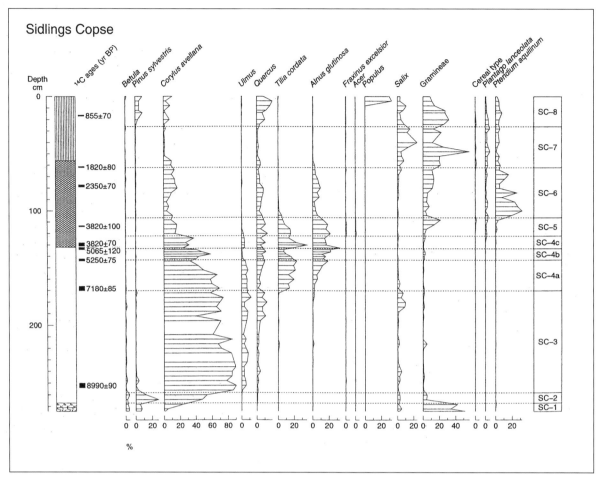

Fig. 4.4: Petra Dark's pollen sequence from Sidlings Copse, Oxfordshire (Bell & Dark 1998, fig. 19.3). There was no post-Roman woodland regeneration though there appears to have been an increase in pastoral activity; the origins of the present, botanically 'ancient', woodland lie after the tenth century.

landscape exploitation had disappeared, resulting in greater dislocation in how the landscape was utilised.

In southern and eastern England there is considerable variation in the pollen evidence, including notable changes in the agricultural emphasis of certain areas (Dark 1996). At Aller Farm, near Stockland in Devon, there was little change. At Hockham Mere in Suffolk there was a minor shift from arable to pasture though the landscape remained open; elsewhere in East Anglia, slight increases in tree/scrub pollen are both brief in duration and poorly dated (*e.g.* Diss Mere in Norfolk and the Mar Dyke in Essex: Peglar *et al.* 1989, p. 218; Wilkinson 1988, pp. 109-14). At Snelsmore, in Berkshire, there is firmer evidence for a limited woodland regeneration, whereas at Sidlings Copse just to the north in Oxfordshire there was an increase in pastoral activity (Fig. 4.4). At Banwell, in Somerset, there appears to have been a slight expansion of woodland just as the adjacent reclaimed wetlands were being flooded (Rippon 2000), though the presence near by of Cadbury Congresbury suggests a wealthy élite that must have been supported by continued agricultural production (Rahtz *et al.* 1992; Rippon 1997, pp. 133-8).

Overall, it appears that the landscape of post-Roman Britain remained *largely* open in the post-Roman period, but with localised regeneration in certain areas.

Most of these pollen sequence have come from peat, but in a number of cases (usually colluvial/alluvial sequences in lakes and river valleys) a more detailed picture emerges from the combination of palaeoenvironmental and lithostratigraphic analysis. In the Chelmer Valley, Essex, the sequence of alluvium and plant macrofossils within a silted-up river channel suggests a continuously-open and cultivated landscape in the surrounding areas, without any woodland regeneration (Murphy 1994, pp. 25-6). At Mickelmere (near Pakenham in Suffolk), the sediments from an infilled lake basin indicate a landscape that also remained largely open during the post-Roman period, and though there was a decrease in cultivation this appears to have been replaced by pasture not woodland (*ibid.,* pp. 29-31). What cultivation there was within the lake's catchment may have shifted from the light Breckland soils to heavier boulder clay, which can be contrasted with fieldwalking evidence in south-east Suffolk (Newman 1992, p. 32), Essex (Williamson 1986), and Northamptonshire which suggests a shift in settlement from the boulder clays towards lighter soils (*e.g.* Bellamy 1994; Brown & Foard 1998; Foard 1978).

A range of palaeo-economic evidence lends further support to this emerging picture of a broad continuity in agricultural practice. On a number of early medieval settlements there are similarities between the range of crops being grown compared to the Roman period. Spelt wheat was still cultivated at the early Anglo-Saxon settlements of Chadwell St Mary, Essex; Gatehampton Farm, Oxfordshire; Mucking, Essex; Springfield Lyons, Essex; Stonea, Cambridgeshire; West Stow, Suffolk; and probably Holloway Lane and Holloway Close in West London, suggesting that there was not a significant break in the cultivation of arable fields (Allen 1995; Lavender 1998; Murphy 1994, p. 27, and see Tyler 1996; Rackham 1994b, p. 126; van der Veen 1993; West 1985).

Animal bone assemblages similarly suggest local changes in the way that what remained a basically open and agriculturally still functioning landscape was exploited. Crabtree (1994) has compared the faunal assemblages from the substantial Romano-British settlement at Icklingham in Suffolk, and nearby Iron Age, Romano-British and early Anglo-Saxon rural settlements at West Stow. At the latter there is a gradual, long term, trend towards sheep and pig: there is no sudden discontinuity, and the kill-pattern is indicative of a self-sufficient or 'producer' site. A greater contrast can be drawn between West Stow and late Roman Icklingham, where cattle were of far greater importance and sheep and pig were poorly represented. However, Icklingham was a 'consumer' settlement, and the meat 'appears to have been obtained through the large-scale late Roman market system in meat products' (*ibid.*, p. 43). These contrasting sites once again show the different post-Roman experiences of mainly high-status sites, dependent on the money-based market economy which collapsed, and rural settlements where 'a case can be made for local continuity in animal husbandry practices' (*ibid.*).

At *Hamwic* (near Southampton), the condition of livestock in the eighth century was good, and the size of both cattle and sheep showed no decrease compared to the Roman period (Bourdillon 1994, pp. 122-3). The size of cattle had increased during the Roman period, as was the case throughout Roman Europe (though not beyond the Empire). If there had been a collapse of livestock husbandry in post-Roman Britain leading to a decrease in animal size, stock could not have been introduced from the Germanic homelands since these areas only ever had smaller stock. It could be argued that if there had been a collapse of livestock husbandry in post-Roman Britain, the Germanic colonists could have then worked to improve the quality of stock, although this argument would beg the question of why this was not done in their homeland. Instead, the good

quality of livestock in eighth-century *Hamwic* suggests that there had not been a significant break in the quality of animal husbandry in Britain.

At first sight, the evidence from pollen, which generally suggests a lack of post-Roman woodland regeneration, is at odds with the results of recent tree ring studies (though most of this data comes from east of a line between York and Southampton, being the area without good pollen evidence: Tyers *et al.* 1996). The value in tree ring studies here is not the date of felling (*i.e.* when the timbers were used), but when the trees started to grow. In mainland Britain there is a notably high number of trees felled and used as late as the ninth century, that started to grow during the first half of the fifth century (though the same is not true of Ireland). However, this need not indicate that formerly agricultural land was being invaded by woodland during the fifth century; these trees that were being felled in the later first millennium A.D. may have been derived from formerly coppiced woodland that was no longer being managed (*ibid.*, p. 20). The management of woodland is something about which we actually know very little, though it may well have continued in certain areas to sustain the demands for contruction and fuel for both domestic and industrial consumption, including iron production which is now attested on a large scale at a number of sites including Exmoor (G. Julleff, pers. comm.) and the northern banks of the Blackwater Estuary in Essex (Wallis & Waughman 1998, pp. 125-6, 227, 233).

Two key conclusions can be drawn from this seemingly disparate set of environmental data. Firstly, there was no widespread woodland regeneration in the immediate post-Roman period, and secondly, there was considerable local variation in how agriculture developed over this period. In places this did include a decrease in the intensity of landscape exploitation, though in many cases this probably reflects localised changes in specific environments, or the fate of individual estates. Overall, the landscapes of post-Roman Britain remain in use.

REGIONAL VARIATION AND THE POST-ROMAN LANDSCAPE

The fourth to sixth centuries undoubtedly saw a major discontinuity in the cultural history of Britain, with many aspects of the Roman socio-economic system disappearing and the eventual emergence of early medieval society. The extent to which this was due to mass folk migration or indigenous development under the influence of a small immigrant élite has been much debated, and will probably only be resolved through more advanced scientific methods such as genetics. That is for the future: there undoubtedly was some immigration, and a key theme of this paper is that we need to understand the marked local and regional variation in how natives and newcomers interacted. This is the key to understanding the post-Roman landscape, and can be achieved through an integrated programme of large-scale fieldwalking, excavation, on- and off-site palaeoenvironmental analysis, and a detailed correlation of crop-mark evidence for deserted landscapes with what survives in the present pattern of roads and field boundaries.

A key issue is the extent to which most of the population would have been embedded in a Romano-British system, and how quickly it declined. Esmonde Cleary sees a sudden, 'catastrophic', change: 'The evidence from the landscape of late Roman Britain is that it was under considerable pressure to produce surpluses to support the army, the bureaucracy, the aristocracy, the townsfolk and others. Quite suddenly, in the early fifth century it stopped' (Esmonde Cleary 1995, p. 22). However, this decline will have impacted most on the more Romanised aspects of the landscape, and there is no reason why the large native population as a whole should have suddenly deserted their landscape during the early fifth century. It is entirely logical that, particularly in more favourable environments, much of the landscape remained in agricultural production for subsistence purposes. Post-Roman native settlement is notoriously difficult to identify, but it is argued here that it may have been far more common for Romano-British settlements to have still been occupied in the fifth or even sixth century than has previously been thought. There was no catastrophe here, just a slight increase in the rate of change in constantly evolving landscapes.

By the mid-fifth century, some Anglo-Saxon colonisation had begun in parts of southern and eastern Britain, though this was far from a simple process of invasion and colonisation (*e.g.* Hamerow 1993, pp. 93-4). The relationships between native and newcomer were varied: as Scull has suggested 'It may not be too fanciful to argue that every region or locality would have seen its own *adventus Saxonum*' (Scull 1992, p. 8). In places, the fifth-century migrants appear to have settled in a landscape either deserted by, or seized from, its native occupants while, elsewhere, the colonists were forced to occupy less favoured parts of the landscape. In a number of regions in southern and eastern England such as central and north-west Essex (see above; Fig. 4.1b), the Chilterns (Bailey 1989; Davis 1982; Hunn 1994), and parts of Sussex (Welch 1971, 1983, 1989) and Wessex (Eagles 1994) substantial areas appear to have been free from fifth-century migration, in contrast to, for example, East Anglia which saw a greater Anglo-Saxon presence from as early as the first half of the fifth century (Carver 1989; Newman 1992). In terms of the debate between those scholars who still see a mass folk migration into Britain during the fifth and sixth centuries (with a residual native population possibly dispossessed and enslaved), and those minimalists who argue simply for an élite take-over, both would appear to be right depending upon which part of the country one is considering.

The immigrant population eventually achieved political supremacy over a landscape which over most of England had remained in agricultural production, though with some changes of emphasis: in places there was a shift from arable to pasture, a trend away from cattle and towards sheep, and perhaps a decline in woodland management. The racial, social and tenurial aspects of landscape may have suffered considerable dislocation, particularly those areas which had been most firmly locked into the earlier political, social and economic system. However, in many cases agricultural production must have been maintained as the landscape continued to evolve until the decision by landowners and communities in the central zone of England to reorganise their landscape through the creation of nucleated villages and open fields. In these areas, it is to this period of transformation that we must look for the origins of the medieval landscape, while elsewhere, the post-Roman period was simply a particularly fluid period in the constantly evolving history of the British landscape.

BIBLIOGRAPHY

Allen, T., 1995. *Lithics and Landscape: archaeological discoveries on the Thames Water Pipeline at Gatehampton Farm, Goring, Oxfordshire 1985-92* (Oxford).

Arnold, C., 1984. *Roman Britain to Anglo-Saxon England* (London).

Arnold, C., & Wardle, P., 1981. 'Early medieval settlement patterns in England', *Medieval Archaeol*, 25, pp. 145-9.

Aston, M., & Gerrard, C., 1999. ' "Unique, traditional and charming": The Shapwick Project, Somerset', *Antiq J*, 79, pp. 1-58.

Bailey, K., 1989. 'The Middle Saxons', in *The Origins of Anglo-Saxon Kindoms*, ed. Bassett, pp. 108-22.

Barker, P., White, R., Pretty, K., Bird, H., & Corbishley, M., 1997. *The Baths Basilica Wroxeter, Excavations 1966-90* (London).

Bassett, S., 1982. *Saffron Walden: excavations and research 1972-80*, Counc Br Archaeol Res Rep 45 (London).

Bassett, S., 1985. 'Beyond the edge of excavation: the topographical context of Goltho', in *Studies in Medieval History Presented to R.H.C. Davis*, ed. H. Mayr-Harting, & R. I. Moore (London), pp. 21-39.

Bassett, S. (ed.), 1989a. *The Origins of Anglo-Saxon Kingdoms* (London & New York).

Bassett, S., 1989b. 'In search of the origins of Anglo-Saxon kingdoms', in *The Origins of Anglo-Saxon Kingdoms*, ed. Bassett, pp. 3-27.

Bassett, S., 1990. 'The Roman and medieval landscape of Wroxeter', in *From Roman Viroconium to Medieval Wroxeter*, ed. P. A. Barker (Worcester), pp. 10-12.

Bassett, S., 1997. 'Continuity and fission in the Anglo-Saxon Landscape: the origins of the Rodings (Essex)', *Landscape History*, 19, pp. 25-42.

Bedwin, O., 1991. 'Asheldham Camp – an early Iron Age hillfort: the 1985 excavation', *Essex Archaeol & Hist*, 22, pp. 13-27.

Bell, M., 1989. 'Environmental archaeology as an index of continuity and change in the medieval landscape', in *The Rural Settlements of Medieval England*, ed. M. Aston, D. Austin, & C. Dyer (Oxford), pp. 269-86.

Bell, M., & Dark, P., 1998. 'Continuity and change: environmental archaeology in historic periods', in *Science in Archaeology: an agenda for the future*, ed. J. Bayley (London), pp. 179-94.

Bell, T., 1998. 'Churches on Roman buildings: Christian associations and Roman masonry in Anglo-Saxon England', *Medieval Archaeol*, 42, pp. 1-18.

Bellamy, B., 1994. 'Anglo-Saxon dispersed sites and woodland in Geddington in the Rockingham Forest, Northamptonshire', *Landscape History*, 16, pp. 31-7.

Bennett, P., & Williams, J., 1997. 'Monkton', *Current Archaeol*, 151, pp. 258-64.

Beresford, M., & Hurst, J., 1990. *Wharram Percy Deserted Medieval Village* (London).

Branigan, K., 1971. *Latimer: Belgic, Roman, Dark Age and Early Modern Farm* (Bristol).

Brodribb, A. C. C., Hands, A. R., & Walker, D. R., 1978. *Excavations at Shakenoak Farm, near Wilcote, Oxfordshire. Part V: Sites K and E* (Oxford).

Bonney, D., 1979. 'Early boundaries and estates in southern England', in *English Medieval Settlement*, ed. P. H. Sawyer (London), pp. 41-51.

Bourdillon, J., 1994. 'The animal provisioning of Saxon Southampton', in *Environment and Economy*, ed. Rackham, pp. 120-5.

Brown, T., & Foard, G., 1998. 'The Saxon landscape: a regional perspective', in *The Archaeology of Landscape*, ed. P. Everson, & T. Williamson (Manchester), pp. 67-94.

Burrow, I. 1981. *Hillforts and Hilltop Settlement in the First to Eighth Centuries AD*, Br Archaeol Rep, Br ser 91 (Oxford).

Carter, G. A., 1998. *Excavations at the Orsett 'Cock' Enclosure, Essex, 1976*, East Anglian Archaeol 86.

Carver, M., 1989. 'Kingship and material culture in early Anglo-Saxon East Anglia', in *The Origins of Anglo-Saxon Kingdoms*, ed. Bassett, pp. 141-58.

Clarke, C. P., 1998. *Excavations to the South of the Chignall Roman Villa, Essex, 1977-81*, East Anglian Archaeol, 83.

Collingwood, R. G., & Myres, J. N. L., 1937. *Roman Britain and the English Settlements* (Oxford).

Crabtree , P. J., 1994. 'Animal exploitation in East Anglian villages', in *Environment and Economy*, ed. Rackham, pp. 40-54.

Crawford, S., 1997. 'Britons, Anglo-Saxons and the Germanic burial ritual', in *Migration and Invasions in Archaeological Explanation*, ed. J. Chapman, & H. Hamerow (Oxford), pp. 45-72.

Croft, R. A., & Mynard, D. C., 1993. *The Changing Landscape of Milton Keynes* (Aylesbury).

Dark, K. R., & Dark, S. P., 1996. 'New archaeological and palynological evidence for a sub-Roman reoccupation of Hadrian's Wall', *Archaeol Aeliana*, 5th ser, 24, pp. 57-72.

Dark, S. P., 1996. 'Palaeoecological evidence for landscape continuity and change in Britain ca A.D. 400-800', in *External Contacts and the Economy of Late Roman and Post-Roman Britain*, ed. K. R. Dark (Woodbridge), pp. 23-51.

Dark, K., & Dark, P., 1997. *The Landscape of Roman Britain* (Stroud).

Davies, W., 1979. *The Llandaff Charters* (Aberystwyth).

Davis, K. R., 1982. *Britons and Saxons: the Chiltern Region 400-700* (Chichester).

Dixon, P. H., 1982. 'How Saxon is the Saxon house?' in *Structural Reconstruction: approaches to the interpretation of the excavated remains of buildings*, ed. P. J. Drury (Oxford), pp. 275-88.

Drury, P., & Rodwell, W., 1980. 'Settlement in the later Iron Age and Roman periods', in *Archaeology in Essex to AD 1500*, ed. D. G. Buckley, Counc Br Archaeol Res Rep 34 (London), pp. 59-75.

Drury, P., & Wickenden, N. P., 1982. 'An early Saxon settlement within the Romano-British small town at Heybridge, Essex', *Medieval Archaeol*, 26, pp. 1-40.

Eagles, B., 1994. 'The archaeological evidence for settlement in the fifth and seventh centuries AD', in *The Medieval Landscape of Wessex*, ed. M. Aston & C. Lewis (Oxford), pp. 13-32.

Eddy, M. R., 1982. *Kelvedon: the origins and development of a Roman small town* (Chelmsford).

Esmonde Cleary, S., 1995. 'Changing constraints on the landscape AD 400-600', in *Landscape and Settlement in Britain AD 400-1066*, ed. D. Hooke & S. Burnell (Exeter), pp. 11-26.

Evison, M., 1997. 'Lo, the conquering hero comes (or not)', *Br Archaeol*, 23, pp. 8-10.

Farley, M., 1984. 'A six hundred metre long section through Caerwent', *Bull Board Celtic Stud*, 31, pp. 209-50.

Finberg, H. P. R., 1955. *Roman and Saxon Withington: a study of continuity* (Leicester).

Fleming, A., 1988. *The Dartmoor Reaves* (London).

Foard, G., 1978. 'Systematic fieldwalking and the investigation of Saxon settlement in Northamptonshire', *World Archaeol*, 9, pp. 357-74.

Fowler, P. J., 1975. 'Continuity in the landscape: some local archaeology in Wiltshire, Somerset and Gloucestershire', in *Recent Work in Rural Archaeology*, ed. P. J. Fowler (Bradford-on-Avon), pp. 121-33.

Fulford, M. G., 1992. 'Iron Age to Roman: a period of radical change on the gravels', in *Developing Landscapes of Lowland Britain*, ed. Fulford & Nichols, pp. 23-38.

Fulford, M. G., & Rippon, S. J., 1994. 'Lowbury Hill, Oxon: a reassessment of the probable Romano-Celtic temple and the Anglo-Saxon barrow', *Archaeol J*, 151, pp. 158-211.

Fulford, M. G., & Nichols, E. (eds), *Developing Landscapes of Lowland Britain*, Soc Antiq Occas Pap 14 (London).

Garwood, A., 1998. 'A late Iron Age and Roman site at Shillingford Field, Great Sampford', *Essex Archaeol & Hist*, 29, pp. 33-47.

Garwood, P., 1989. 'Social transformation and the relations of power in Britain in the late fourth to the sixth centuries', *Scott Archaeol Rev*, 6, pp. 90-106.

Gay, T., 1999. 'Rural dialects and surviving Britons', *Br Archaeol*, 46, p. 18.

Gelling, M., 1976. 'The place-names of the Mucking area', *Panorama* (J Thurrock Local Hist Soc) 19, pp. 7-20.

Gelling, M., 1988. *Signposts to the Past* (2nd edn, Chichester).

Gelling, M., 1993. 'Why aren't we speaking Welsh?', in *Anglo-Saxon Stud in Archaeol & Hist*, 6, pp. 51-6.

Goodier, A., 1984. 'The formation of boundaries in Anglo-Saxon England: a statistical study', *Medieval Archaeol*, 28, pp. 1-21.

Going, C., 1993a. 'The Roman period', in *Excavations at Mucking Volume 1: the site atlas*, ed. A. Clark (London).

Going, C., 1993b. 'The Roman pottery', in *Rivenhall, Vol. 2*, ed. Rodwell & Rodwell, pp. 64-7.

Going, C. J., 1996. 'The Roman countryside', in *The Archaeology of Essex: proceedings of the Writtle conference*, ed. O. Bedwin (Chelmsford), pp. 95-107.

Gregson, N., 1985. 'The multiple estate model: some critical questions', *J Hist Geogr*, 11.iv, pp. 339-51.

Hall, D., 1988. 'The late Saxon countryside: villages and their fields', *Anglo-Saxon Settlements*, ed. D. Hooke (Oxford), pp. 99-122.

Hall, D., & Martin, P., 1979. 'Brixworth, Northamptonshire: an intensive field survey', *J Br Archaeol Assoc*, 132, pp. 1-6.

Hamerow, H., 1991. 'Settlement mobility and the "Middle Saxon Shift": rural settlements and settlement patterns in Anglo-Saxon England', *Anglo-Saxon England*, 20, pp. 1-17.

Hamerow, H., 1992. 'Settlement on the gravels in the Anglo-Saxon period', in *Developing Landscapes of Lowland Britain*, ed. Fulford & Nichols, pp. 39-46.

Hamerow, H., 1993. *Excavations at Mucking Volume 2: the Anglo-Saxon settlement* (London).

Hamerow, H., 1997. 'Migration theory and the Anglo-Saxon "identity crisis" ', in *Migration and Invasions in Archaeological Explanation*, ed. Chapman & Hamerow, pp. 33-44.

Härke, H., 1990. ' "Warrior graves"? The background of the Anglo-Saxon weapon burial rite', *Past Present*, 126, pp. 22-43.

Härke, H., 1997. 'Early Anglo-Saxon social structure', in *The Anglo-Saxons from the Migration Period to the Eighth Century*, ed. Hines, pp. 125-70.

Haslam, J., 1984. 'The towns of Wiltshire', in *Anglo-Saxon Towns in Southern England*, ed. J. Haslam (Chichester), pp. 87-148.

Higham, N., 1992. *Rome, Britain and the Anglo-Saxons* (London).

Hines, J., 1984. *The Scandinavian Character of Anglian England in the pre-Viking Period*, Br Archaeol Rep, Br ser 124 (Oxford).

Hines, J., 1990. 'Philology, archaeology and the *adventus Saxonum vel Anglorum*', in *Britain 400-600: Language and History*, ed. A. Bammesberger & A. Wollmann, A. (Heidelberg), pp. 17-36.

Hines, J. (ed.), 1997. *The Anglo-Saxons from the Migration Period to the Eighth Century: an ethnographic perspective* (Woodbridge).

Hingley, R., 1989. *Rural Settlement in Roman Britain* (London).

Hinton, D. A., 1990. *Archaeology, Economy and Society: England from the fifth to the fifteenth century* (London).

Hinton, D., 1997. 'The "Scole-Dickleburgh field system" examined', *Landscape History*, 19, pp. 5-13.

Hodder, I., 1982. *The Archaeology of the M11: Volume 2. Wendens Ambo: excavation of an Iron Age and Romano-British Settlement* (London).

Hodges, R., 1989. *The Anglo-Saxon Achievement* (London).

Hooke, D., 1985. 'Village development in the West Midlands', in *Medieval Villages, a review of current work*, ed. D. Hooke, Oxford Univ Comm Archaeol Monogr No. 5 (Oxford), pp. 125-54.

Hooke, D., 1997. 'The Anglo-Saxons in England in the seventh and eighth centuries: aspects of location in space', in *The Anglo-Saxons from the Migration Period to the Eighth Century*, ed. Hines, pp 65-99.

Hoskins, W. G. 1955. *The Making of the English Landscape* (London).

Hunn, J. R., 1994. *Reconstruction and Measurement of Landscape Change: a study of six parishes in the St Albans area* (Oxford).

Isserlin, R. M .J., 1995. 'Roman Coggeshall II: excavations at "The Lawns", 1989-93', *Essex Archaeol & Hist*, 26, pp. 82-104.

James, S., Marshall, A., & Millett, M., 1984. 'An early medieval building tradition', *Archaeol J*, 141, pp. 182-215.

Jones, B., & Mattingly, D., 1990. *An Atlas of Roman Britain* (Oxford).

Jones, G. R. J., 1979. 'Multiple estates and early settlement', in *English Medieval Settlement*, ed. Sawyer, pp. 9-34.

Jones, G. R. J., 1985. 'Multiple estates perceived', *J Hist Geog*, 11.iv, pp. 352-63.

Lamb, H. H., 1995. *Climate, History and the Modern World* (2nd edn, London).

Lambrick, G., 1992. 'The development of late prehistoric and Roman farming on the Thames gravels', *Developing Landscapes of Lowland Britain*, ed. Fulford & Nichols, pp. 78-105.

Langton, B., & Holbrook, N., 1997. 'A prehistoric and Roman occupation and burial site at Heybridge: excavations at Langford Road, 1994', *Essex Archaeol & Hist*, 28, pp. 12-46.

Lavender, N. J., 1993. 'A *principia* at Boreham, near Chelmsford, Essex: excavation 1990', *Essex Archaeol & Hist*, 24, pp. 1-21.

Lavendar, N .J., 1996. 'A Roman site at the New Source Works, Castle Hedingham: excavations 1992', *Essex Archaeol & Hist*, 27, pp. 23-34.

Lavender, N., 1997. 'Middle Iron Age and Romano-British settlement at Great Dunmow: excavations at Buildings Farm 1993', *Essex Archaeol & Hist*, 28, pp. 47-92.

Lavender, N., 1998. 'A Saxon building at Chadwell St Mary: excavations at Chadwell St Mary County Primary School 1996', *Essex Archaeol & Hist*, 29, pp. 45-58.

Leech, R., 1982. 'The Roman interlude in the south-west. The dynamics of economics and social change in Romano-British southern Somerset and northern Dorset', in *The Romano-British Countryside: studies in rural settlement and economy*, ed. D. Miles, Br Archaeol Rep, Br ser 103 (i) (Oxford), pp. 209-67.

Lewis, C., Mitchel-Fox, P., & Dyer, C., 1997. *Village, Hamlet and Field* (Manchester).

Loveluck, C., 1996. 'The development of the Anglo-Saxon landscape, economy and society "On Driffield", East Yorkshire, 400-750 AD', *Anglo-Saxon Stud in Archaeol & Hist*, 9, pp. 25-48.

Mackreth, D. F., 1996. *Orton Hall Farm: a Roman and Early Anglo-Saxon Farmstead*, East Anglian Archaeol, 76.

Marshall, A., & Marshall, G., 1993. 'Differentiation, change and continuity in Anglo-Saxon buildings', *Archaeol J*, 150, pp. 366-402.

Mckie, R., 1993. 'Genetic patchwork of an island nation', *Geogr Mag*, 65(vi), pp. 35-8.

Miles, D., 1984. *Archaeology at Barton Court Farm, Abingdon, Oxon*, Counc Br Archaeol Res Rep 50 (London).

Millett, M., 1987. 'The question of continuity: Rivenhall Reviewed', *Archaeol J*, 144, pp. 434-8.

Millett, M., 1990. *The Romanization of Britain* (Cambridge).

Millett, M., & James, S., 1983. 'Excavations at Cowdery's Down, Basingstoke, Hampshire, 1978-81', *Archaeol J*, 140, pp. 151-279.

Milne, G., & Richards, J. D., 1992. *Two Anglo-Saxon Buildings and Associated Finds* (York).

Milton, B., 1985. 'Excavations at Barrington's Farm, Orsett Cock, Thurrock, Essex', *Essex Archaeol & Hist*, 18, pp. 16-33.

Morris, R., 1989. *Churches in the Landscape* (London).

Murphy, P., 1985. 'The cereals and crop weeds', in West, *West Stow*, pp. 100-9.

Murphy, P., 1994. 'The Anglo-Saxon landscape and rural economy: some results from sites in East Anglia and Essex', in *Environment and Economy*, ed. Rackham, pp. 23-39.

Myres, J. N. L., 1986. *The English Settlements* (Oxford).

Neal, D. S., 1974. *The Excavation of the Roman Villa in Gadebridge Park, Hemel Hempstead 1963-8* (London).

Neal, D. S., Wardle, A., & Hunn, J., 1990. *Excavations of the Iron Age, Roman and Medieval Settlement at Gorhambury, St Albans* (London).

Newman, J., 1992. 'The late Roman and Anglo-Saxon settlement pattern in the Sandlings of Suffolk', in *The Age of Sutton Hoo*, ed. M. Carver (Woodbridge), pp. 25-38.

Peglar, S. M., Fritz, S. C., & Birks, H. J. B., 1989. 'Vegetation and landuse history at Diss, Norfolk', *J Ecol*, 77, pp. 203-22.

Phillips, D., & Heywood, B., 1995. *Excavations at York Minster Volume 1: From Roman Fortress to Norman Cathedral. Part 1: the Site* (London).

Powlesland, D., 1997. 'Early Anglo-Saxon settlements, structures, form and layout', in *The Anglo-Saxons from the Migration Period to the Eighth* Century, ed. Hines, pp. 101-24.

Quinnell, H., 1986. 'Cornwall during the Iron Age and the Roman period', *Cornish Archaeol*, 25, pp. 111-34.

Rackham, J. (ed.), 1994a. *Environment and Economy in Anglo-Saxon England*, Counc Br Archaeol Res Rep 89 (York).

Rackham, J., 1994b. 'Economy and environment in Saxon London', in *Environment and Economy*, ed. Rackham, pp. 126-35.

Rahtz, P., Woodward, A., Burrow, I., Everton, A., Watts, L., Hirst, S., Fowler, P., & Gardner, K., 1992. *Cadbury Congresbury 1968-73*, Br Archaeol Rep, Br ser 223 (Oxford).

Rippon, S., 1991. 'Early planned landscapes in south east Essex', *Essex Archaeol & Hist*, 27, pp. 46-60.

Rippon, S., 1997. *The Severn Estuary: landscape evolution and wetland reclamation* (London).

Rippon, S., 1999. 'The Rayleigh Hills in south-east Essex: patterns in the exploitation of a woodland landscape', in *The Essex Landscape: in search of its history*, ed. S. Green (Chelmsford), pp. 20-8.

Rippon, S., 2000. 'The Romano-British exploitation of coastal wetlands: survey and excavation on the North Somerset Levels, 1993-7', *Britannia*, 31, pp. 69-200.

Rippon, S., in press. *The Transformation of Coastal Wetlands: the exploitation and management of marshland landscapes in north west Europe during the Roman and medieval periods* (London).

Rodwell, K., 1988. *The Prehistoric and Roman Settlement at Kelvedon, Essex*, Counc Br Archaeol Res Rep 63 (London).

Rodwell, W., 1966. 'Wickford: interim report', *Trans Essex Archaeol Soc*, 3rd ser, 2.ii, pp. 96-7.

Rodwell, W., 1978. 'Relict landscapes in Essex', in *Early Land Allotment*, ed. H. C. Bowen & P. J. Fowler (Oxford), pp. 89-98.

Rodwell, W., 1993. 'The early Anglo-Saxon pottery', in *Rivenhall, Vol. 2*, ed. Rodwell & Rodwell, pp. 73-8.

Rodwell, W. J., & Rodwell, K. A., 1977. *Historic Churches: A Wasting Asset*, Counc Br Archaeol Res Rep 19 (London).

Rodwell, W. J., & Rodwell, K. A., 1985. *Rivenhall: investigations of a villa, church and village, 1950-1977*, Counc Br Archaeol Res Rep 55 (London).

Rodwell, W. J., & Rodwell, K. A. (eds), 1985. *Rivenhall: investigations of a villa, church and village, 1950-1977, Vol. 2*, Counc Br Archaeol Res Rep 80 (York).

Rose, P., & Preston Jones, A., 1995. 'Changes in the Cornish countryside AD 400-1100', in *Landscape and Settlement*, ed. Hooke & Burnell, pp. 51-68.

Salway, P., 1981. *Roman Britain* (Oxford).

Scull, C., 1992. 'Before Sutton Hoo: structures of power and society in early East Anglia', in *The Age of Sutton Hoo*, ed. Carver, pp. 3-23.

Scull, C., 1993. 'Archaeology, early Anglo-Saxon society and the origins of Anglo-Saxon kingdoms', *Anglo-Saxon Stud in Archaeol & Hist*, 6, pp. 65-82.

Simpson, S. J., Griffith, F. M., & Holbrook, N., 1989. 'The prehistoric, Roman and early post-Roman site at Hayes Farm, Clyst Honiton, *Proc Devon Archaeol Soc*, 47, pp. 1-28.

Smith, R. J. C., Healy, F., Allen, M. J., Morris, E. L., Barnes, I., & Woodward, P. J., 1997. *Excavations Along the Route of the Dorchester By-Pass, Dorset, 1986-8* (Salisbury).

Sparey Green, C., 1987. *Excavations at Poundbury, Vol. 1: the Settlements* (Dorchester).

Taylor, C., 1983. *Village and Farmstead* (London).

Taylor, C., & Fowler, P., 1978. 'Roman fields into medieval furlongs', in *Early Land Allotment in the British Isles*, ed. Bowen & Fowler, pp. 159-62.

Todd, M., 1977. '*Famosa Pestis* and fifth-century Britain', *Britannia*, 8, pp. 319-25.

Turner, J., 1979. 'The environment of north-east England during Roman times as shown by pollen analysis', *J Archaeol Sci*, 6, pp. 285-90.

Tyler, S., 1996. 'Early Saxon Essex AD 400-700', in *The Archaeology of Essex*, ed. Bedwin, pp. 108-16.

Tyler, S., & Wickenden, N.P., 1996. 'A late Roman and Saxon settlement at Great Waltham', *Essex Archaeol & Hist*, 27, pp. 84-91.

Tyers, I., Hillam, J., & Groves, C., 1996. 'Trees and woodland in the Saxon period: the dendrochronological evidence', in *Environment and Economy*, ed. Rackham, pp. 12-22.

van der Veen, M., 1993. 'Grain impressions in early Anglo-Saxon pottery from Mucking', in Hamerow, *Excavations at Mucking Volume 2*, p. 80.

Wallace, C., 1995. 'A Roman rural shrine at Boreham? The Bulls Lodge excavation of 1990 re-interpreted', *Essex Archaeol & Hist*, 26, pp. 264-7.

Wallis, S., & Waughman, M., 1998. *Archaeology and Landscape in the Lower Blackwater Valley*, East Anglian Archaeol, 82.

Welch, M., 1971. 'Late Roman and Saxons in Sussex', *Britannia* 2, pp. 232-7.

Welch, M., 1983. *Early Anglo-Saxon Sussex*, Br Archaeol Rep, Br ser 112 (Oxford).

Welch, M., 1984. 'Rural settlement patterns in the early and Middle Anglo-Saxon periods', *Landscape History*, 7, pp. 13-24.

Welch, M., 1989. 'The kingdom of the South Saxons: the origins', in *The Origins of Anglo-Saxon Kingdoms*, ed. Bassett, pp. 75-83.

Welch, M., 1992. *Anglo-Saxon England* (London).

West, S., 1985. *West Stow: the Anglo-Saxon village*, East Anglian Archaeol, 24.

White, S., 1998. 'The Patching Hoard', *Medieval Archaeol*, 42, pp. 88-93.

Wickenden, N. P., 1988. *Excavations at Great Dunmow, Essex*, East Anglian Archaeol, 41.

Wilkinson, T. J., 1988. *Archaeology and Environment in South Essex*, East Anglian Archaeol, 42.

Williamson, T., 1986. 'The development of settlement in north west Essex: the results of a recent fieldwalking survey', *Essex Archaeol & Hist*, 17, pp. 120-32.

Williamson, T., 1987. 'Early co-axial field systems on the east Anglian Boulder Clays', *Proc Prehis Soc*, 53, pp. 419-31.

Williamson, T., 1988. 'Explaining regional landscapes: woodland and champion in southern and eastern England', *Landscape History*, 10, pp. 5-14.

Williamson, T., 1998. 'The "Scole-Dickleburgh field system" revisited', *Landscape History*, 20, pp. 19-28.

Winterbottom, M. (ed. & trans.), 1978. *Gildas: The Ruin of Britain and other works* (Chichester).

Woodward, A., & Leach, P., 1993. *The Uley Shrines: excavation of a ritual complex on West Hill, Uley, Gloucestershire: 1977-9* (London).

Wymer, J., & Brown, N., 1995: *Excavations at North Shoebury: settlement and economy in south-east Essex 1500 BC - AD 1500*, East Anglian Archaeol, 75.

Landscapes of monasticism

James Bond

ABSTRACT

The nature of the earliest monastic foundations and the expansion and distribution of the monastic orders in Europe are considered as a background to the locations and forms of Celtic, Anglo-Saxon and post-Conquest monastic settlements in Britain. Approaches to the study of the impact of the monasteries upon the wider landscape through the management of estates and granges are summarised.

KEYWORDS

Celtic, Anglo-Saxon, medieval, monasteries, estates, granges.

INTRODUCTION

The impact of medieval monasteries upon the landscape has generally been underestimated. From a twentieth-century and largely post-Christian perspective monastic communities can seem introspective, even eccentric organisations, which have bequeathed to us some magnificent churches and some picturesque ruins, but which seem to have little relevance to the major themes of settlement and land use. Even Hoskins, in his inspirational study which laid the very foundations of landscape history as an academic discipline, dismissed monastic buildings with a seven-line paragraph and a plate of Rievaulx; although the text of his chapter on 'The Colonisation of Medieval England' did contain many passing acknowledgements of the role of the monks, particularly the Cistercians, in marshland drainage, woodland clearance, sheep farming and village depopulation (Hoskins 1955, pp. 80-1, 85).

Yet monasteries were a distinctive form of settlement in their own right. More than any other type of medieval settlement, they were influenced by ideologies as much as by practical needs. Believing that closer communion with God was possible only by rejecting the distractions of the world, many monastic communities shunned already-inhabited places and deliberately settled in locations of extreme difficulty and inaccessibility. This tradition goes back to the very earliest origins of monasticism, to the desert retreats of the hermit fathers in the third century, and the ideal was pursued across Europe from the dizzy rock pinnacles of the Meteora in northern Greece, where the only access for visitors and

supplies was by winch and cable, to the rain-sodden and wind-blasted rocks of Skellig Michael off the westernmost shore of Ireland. Few sites in Britain achieved quite these extremes, but the search for seclusion is still evident, in offshore islands like Iona and Lindisfarne, in the marshes of Glastonbury and Crowland and in the upland valleys of Cwmhir and Strata Florida.

Monasteries were also numerous: by the high-water mark of the mid-fourteenth century there were over a thousand abbeys, priories and friaries in England and Wales alone, leaving aside the preceptories, commanderies and camerae of the military orders, granges, and a wide range of quasi-monastic hospitals and colleges. Their choice of sites and the architecture and plans of their buildings and precincts reflected both the ideology and the practical requirements of communities with particular regulations of life. Their needs placed demands upon the resources of the land, for food, water, fuel and building materials. In consequence, even the most deliberately secluded communities could hardly avoid becoming focal points in the landscape, as landmarks and route centres.

Most importantly of all, monasteries came to have rights of exploitation over perhaps as much as a quarter of the whole country. Many of them were endowed from the time of their first foundation with lands which were intended to provide sustenance and income to support the community. As landholders they enjoyed a security of tenure which few secular lords could hope to emulate. They were able to take the long-term view, and had both opportunity and incentive to invest part of their capital in developing and improving their landed properties. We thus find monastic communities engaged in an enormous range of economic activities: the improvement of agricultural production, the management and clearance of woodland, drainage and reclamation of marshland, enclosure of parks and gardens, creation of rabbit warrens, planting of orchards and vineyards, diversion of watercourses, construction of mills and fisheries, building churches, houses, barns, cattle-sheds, sheepcotes and dovecotes, exploiting mines and quarries, removing and replanning villages, acquiring urban property and founding new towns.

It is impossible within the confines of this brief paper to review the monastic contribution to the landscape in all its aspects, or even to offer more than an incidental acknowledgement of the progress made by scholars in this field during the lifetime of the Society whose twenty-first anniversary this volume commemorates. However, I would like to consider six particular areas where there are still major questions to be asked and where we should be looking to make progress in the future.

(I) THE EXPANSION OF THE MONASTIC ORDERS IN EUROPE

The first point to be emphasised is that we are not dealing with an insular phenomenon. The monastic orders were arguably the first truly multi-national organisations since the disintegration of the Roman empire. Yet for most orders we still lack even the most basic statistics of the numbers of houses, or maps of their distribution on the European scale. We still understand far too little about the chronology of their expansion across the Continent and the social, political and religious factors which influenced it. In 1938 Joan Evans listed and mapped the priories of the Cluniac order as a background to her study of the role of Cluny in the development of Romanesque architecture (Evans 1938). For long this stood alone. Until the late 1970s the only other major order to be subjected to mapping throughout Europe was the Cistercians (Van der Meer 1965; Donkin 1967, 1978). Further surveys have since been carried out, both of orders which spread widely through Europe, such as the Carthusians (Aston 1993) and Premonstratensians (Bond 1993a) and of others which remained more localised, such as the Grandmontines (Hutchison 1989) and Gilbertines (Golding 1995). These surveys have pointed to some interesting variations in distribution, which in turn raise questions about the factors influencing those distributions. It comes as no great surprise to find most orders tending to show relatively heavy concentrations of houses around their points of origin: the Cistercians in Burgundy, the Carthusians around the Alps of Savoy and Piedmont; the Premonstratensians in northern France. Other aspects are more difficult to explain. Why were the Premonstratensians and Carthusians so successful in the Low Countries, where the Cistercians made relatively limited impact? Why were the Cistercians so much more successful in central, western and southern France and in Italy than the Premonstratensians? How did the Cistercians come to spread fairly evenly throughout northern Spain, whereas neither Carthusians nor Premonstratensians managed to penetrate into Galicia, the Carthusian effort being concentrated in Catalonia and the Premonstratensians in Old Castile? Why did the Gilbertines not expand outside England, or the Grandmontines make little impact outside France? To what extent did the earlier settlement of Benedictine monasteries present local barriers to the expansion of the new orders? Conversely, did

the areas shunned by the Benedictines offer vacuums for the new orders to settle? The distribution of all the orders is affected by a wide range of social, political, economic and geographical factors, as well as idiosyncratic personal ones. Any individual operating from the British Isles who contemplates such questions quickly comes to realise that problems of language and access to sources present very considerable difficulties. Despite the enormous Continental literature on monasticism, few countries can offer a published database comparable with the gazetteers of Knowles and Hadcock (1971) for England and Wales, Cowan and Easson (1976) for Scotland or Gwynn and Hadcock (1970) for Ireland, or the two Ordnance Survey maps of Monastic Britain and their Irish counterpart (Ordnance Survey 1954, 1955, 1977). The limitations of my own exploratory work on the Premonstratensians were underlined by Fr Bernard Ardura's survey and gazetteer, published shortly after, which provided a much fuller picture of the order's houses in France (Ardura 1993). Further understanding of the distribution and chronology of the major orders on the European scale is a task which can be achieved only with organised European co-operation.

(II) CHOICES OF SETTLEMENT LOCATION

The expansion of the various strands of monasticism is more than just a matter of dots on maps. The early ideals of isolation which characterised some groups have already been mentioned; but to what extent were those ideals compromised or their characteristics modified as the monastic orders expanded into new areas? The siting of some early Benedictine houses on the Continent reflected the traditional yearning for the desert. St Benedict's own monastery of Monte Cassino stands on top of a mountain rising 500 metres out of the plain. St Guilhem-le-Désert is concealed within a deep gorge in the Hérault Garrigues. It would be difficult to find sites much more evocative of remoteness and isolation than the abbey of St Martin-du-Canigou on its Pyrenean mountain-top (Pl. 5.I), or San Juan de la Peña, perched precariously on a ledge under the shadow of an overhanging rock face, or St Mathieu in Finistère (Pl. 5.II), open to the full fury of the Atlantic on the westernmost promontory of Brittany. Even in the well-settled countryside of eleventh-century Normandy, Benedictine abbeys like Cérisy-la-Forêt, Jumièges and Bec seem isolated by English standards. While some English Benedictine monasteries, including Crowland, Great Malvern, Sandwell, Tewkesbury and Thorney, developed from sites initially chosen by hermits, it is much harder in this country to find isolated sites like Bardney or St Benet of Hulme, still surrounded by fields. English Benedictine monasticism became to a much greater extent an

Plate 5.I. Inaccessible locations: the Benedictine abbey of St Martin-du-Canigou in the Pyrenees, settled by monks from Ripoll (Catalonia) around the beginning of the eleventh century.

urban phenomenon. This may result from the tolerance or active encouragement of trading communities growing up outside the monastic gates, rather than a deliberate intention of locating monasteries in pre-existing towns; but, whatever the reason, the difference is an important one, and deserves further investigation.

Similar changes of style across both geographical and temporal thresholds characterise some of the other orders. The Carthusians established themselves in a site of supreme inaccessibility at La Grande Chartreuse, and many of their early houses in England, like Witham and Hinton, reflect a continuing search for seclusion. Why, then, do their later English houses, London, Coventry and Hull, gravitate towards suburban locations? The Rule of St Augustine had been adopted by communities of regular canons in Italy and France during the later eleventh century, and soon after 1100 new Augustinian houses were being founded in England; but the sheer flexibility of the rule meant that it became a convenient catch-all for labelling a wide miscellany of pre-existing communities, from hermitages and old secular minsters to hospital foundations (Robinson 1980). As a result, Augustinian houses have an almost infinite range of siting characteristics throughout Europe. However, the sites chosen by some of the reformed orders of canons reveal more significant differences. In western Europe, the Premonstratensians, heavily influenced by the Cistercians, tended towards a more isolated contemplative life-style, whereas in central and

eastern Europe they retained more of the evangelical mission of the order's founder, St Norbert, and the proportion of major houses sited in larger centres of population is much greater. Contrasts are also revealed in sites occupied by the mendicant orders. In England the Franciscan and Dominican friars settled deliberately in the larger towns, their mission aimed at the urban masses. Yet in Ireland, while most of the more important urban centres contained friaries, many more seem to be in remote and isolated locations. When the Carmelites first settled in England in the 1240s most of their early houses were isolated, reflecting the hermit origins of the order, but subsequent foundations, influenced by the other orders of friars, were almost exclusively in towns.

(III) THE ORIGINS OF MONASTICISM IN THE BRITISH ISLES: THE CELTIC TRADITION

It is not known for certain when monasteries first appeared in the British Isles. Foundation traditions recorded in later monastic chronicles are notoriously unreliable. The reputation of antiquity, however spurious, lent prestige and attracted benefactions and pilgrims; but few scholars today would accept the claims of Glastonbury Abbey to have been founded by Joseph of Arimathea in A.D. 63 or by King Lucius in the second century. The biographies of the earliest British and Irish holy men emphasised their role as roving missionaries and teachers rather than contemplatives.

Plate 5.II. Exposed locations: the abbey of St Mathieu, Finistère, near the westernmost point of the Breton mainland, a late sixth-century Celtic foundation which subsequently adopted the Benedictine rule.

Nevertheless, it seems likely that some settled communities of hermits, monks or priests were beginning to appear by the later fifth century, and they soon became a feature of the Celtic west.

The strongest evidence comes from Ireland, where monasticism underwent a particularly vigorous expansion between the sixth and eighth centuries and a wide range of monastic settlements developed (Ryan 1972; Hurley 1982; Edwards 1990, pp. 99-131; Ó Cróinín 1995, pp. 147-229). Some communities, following the ascetic ideal, deliberately limited their size and economic potential by clinging precariously to remote and inaccessible offshore islands such as Skellig Michael. Others were better placed to expand, developing round or oval walled enclosures which would ultimately contain a multiplicity of cells, several churches, high crosses and round towers (Norman & St Joseph 1969, pp. 90-129). Following Richard Bradley's paper at the Birmingham conference, some discussion took place on the persistent employment of circular enclosures by early societies. It remains a matter of speculation how far the generally rounded shape of the Irish monastic precincts was an acknowledgement of pre-Christian religious practice, a direct inheritance from secular ring-forts, or was merely a pragmatic response to the need to accommodate the maximum internal space for the minimum length (and therefore effort and expense) of perimeter walling. By the sixth century the influence of the larger monasteries had already spread beyond their enclosure walls: they had become the hub of networks of scattered churches, and had tangible links with other monasteries through traditions of common founders. They were beginning to acquire landed estates. Some monastic communities also attracted large peripheral settlements of farmers, stonecarvers, metalworkers, scribes and students. In Robin Butlin's words, 'there is ... a case to be made for regarding the largest of these monasteries as constituting some form of town' (Butlin 1977, pp. 20-5; see also Swan 1985; Graham 1998 pp. 20-5). By the ninth century, Cogitosus, biographer of St Brigid, was describing the monastic complex of Kildare as 'a great metropolitan city', and other sites such as Armagh, Cashel, Kells and Downpatrick were also developing as proto-urban centres. The influence of Irish missionary monks such as Columbanus and Gallus in spreading monastic colonies across the countryside of France, Switzerland and northern Italy in the late sixth and seventh centuries is well attested.

The situation is more complex in Britain, where 'Celtic' monasteries in the west and north were variously affected by local, Roman, Gaulish, Breton and Irish influences, and often then overlain by Anglo-Saxon settlements. Bede's description of the mission of Ninian (d. c. A.D. 432) to Whithorn, written sixty years after the Synod of Whitby (664), pointedly emphasises his links with the Roman church rather than the insular Celtic church. Welsh traditions from the early seventh century indicate the importance of the great monastic school reputedly founded by Illtyd (c. 425-505) at Llantwit

Plate 5.V. The bounds of a late Saxon monastic property: this green lane along the western margin of Eynsham parish can be identified with the 'way' *(weg)* on the boundary perambulation of lands granted by Æthelmaer for the foundation of Eynsham Abbey, Oxfordshire, recited in a confirmation charter by King Æthelred in 1005.

Plate 5.VI. Benedictine landscapes: the setting of Tewkesbury Abbey Gloucestershire, typifies that of many southern English Benedictine houses, in low-lying, well-watered, anciently-settled countryside surrounded by rich arable land and meadows, but with access to upland pasture and woodland within a day's journey.

Plate 6.II. Halton Gill, Littondale. A hamlet of ten holdings had developed here on Fountains Abbey's property by 1496 (Michelmore 1974, p. 22).

Plate 6.I. Vaccary Country: Mallerstang chase, Westmorland. Looking towards Castlethwaite, described in 1324 as 'a close of meadow *(pratt)'* which was of old a vaccary' (PRO, SC6/1044/6, m.2).

Plate 6.V. Troutbeck Park, Westmorland: a seigneurial deer-park at the head of a Lakeland valley, enclosed before 1272. Income from grazing in the park is recorded from 1283 and it had become a gentry stock farm by the sixteenth century (Farrer 1924, pp. 40-7; Parsons 1993, p. 117).

Plate 12.III. Abraham Darby's iron bridge spanning the Severn Gorge at Ironbridge near Telford.

Plate 12.IV. Limestone walling near Malham in the Yorkshire Dales National Park.

Plate 5.III. The débris of a Celtic monastery: inscribed memorial stones and crosses of the late ninth to early eleventh century in the church of Llantwit Major Glamorgan, site of Illtyd's monastic school.

Major, and the numerous ninth- to eleventh-century crosses in the church there (Pl. 5.III) attest to the continuing ecclesiastical importance of the site. The Irish influence is well documented in Columba's settlement of Iona in 563, Fursey's foundation of a monastery at *Cnobheresburg* in East Anglia (probably Burgh Castle near Yarmouth) soon after 630, and Aidan's mission to Lindisfarne in 634, and it is likely that Irish monks were instrumental in the foundation of other early monasteries in western Britain between the fifth and seventh centuries, such as Glastonbury and Malmesbury. The occupation of offshore islands such as Bardsey, Holyhead, Priestholm and Caldey reflect the continuing ascetic and eremetic tradition.

Hagiologies sometimes provide sketches of early monastic enclosures with their cells, oratories and cemeteries. However, as Susan Pearce has observed,

no agreed set of features, discernible in the archaeological record, has [yet] emerged by which a British monastic settlement may be recognised. The sites involved, in both the South-West and Wales, have virtually no surviving remains earlier than the Norman period ... Consequently the interpretation of excavated structures inevitably tends to rely upon the very much fuller evidence of Irish monasticism, the direct relevance of which is uncertain (Pearce 1978, p. 76).

Even the most famous sites present many difficulties. Ralegh Radford's interpretations of his pioneer excavations at Glastonbury and Tintagel, which he believed had demonstrated fifth-century monastic occupation, have both been called into question in recent years. Certainly Glastonbury's less extravagant traditions suggest a British or Irish foundation around the fifth century, and Radford believed that he had found here evidence for an early *vallum monasterii*, cemetery, mausolea and wattle oratories beneath the buildings of the Benedictine abbey; yet there is no unambigious evidence of occupation here before the seventh century whereas excavations on the summit of Glastonbury Tor have demonstrated late fifth- and sixth-century buildings which may represent an earlier monastic settlement of more eremetic character (Rahtz 1993). By contrast, there is little hagiographical tradition or clear documentation for an early monastery at Tintagel. Although occupation of the Tintagel island in the late fifth and sixth centuries is not in question, this site now seems more likely to represent the summer stronghold of a local ruler, whereas the identification of sixth-century graves within the isolated oval churchyard on the mainland points to an alternative focus of early Christian activity there (Thomas 1993). Undoubtedly many early colonies of monks and clerics once existed which are today wholly undocumented, but their archaeological recognition is often controversial: do the concentrations of early Christian inscribed stones at sites like Kirkmadrine, Margam and Lundy signify monastic sites, or merely lay cemeteries? The status of sites was itself subject to change: many which began as genuine monastic foundations lapsed into loose-knit communities of secular clerics, or passed into secular hands. Evidence for other possible early monastic sites in the north and south-west has been summarised by Thomas (1971, pp. 20-47) and Pearce (1978, pp. 76-85), while the evidence for Cornwall has received critical examination in more detail from Olson (1989).

The most extensive recent archaeological work has been at Whithorn, the supposed site of Ninian's stone church named *Candida Casa* by Bede. Much controversy still surrounds the origins of the Christian community at Whithorn. Excavations undertaken between between the 1970s and 1990s revealed a new settlement established around the late fifth century, which may already have adopted the distinctive double-oval plan reflecting the linkage of ecclesiastical and secular trading settlement by the mid-sixth century. The site was replanned after it became a Northumbrian minster and episcopal see around 730. The buildings were destroyed around 845 and, following the subsequent restoration, Whithorn began its evolution towards a new status as a monastic town. By the eleventh century the settlement was expanding over newly-drained ground to the south, developing more vigorous trades and

industries, and revealing strong Irish and Norse influences (Hill 1997).

The appearance of the first monastic communities had immediate implications for the wider landscape. While a solitary hermit or a small peripatetic group might hope to survive on the offerings of the faithful, larger communities permanently settled in one place needed to be sustained by more reliable means. Monastic discipline ensured resources of co-operative labour, and monastic founders had the wider contacts to facilitate the introduction of new technology. The biographies of many early Irish, Welsh and Breton holy men record the burning of scrub, the felling of trees, the construction of sea-dykes to assist reclamation, the planting of hedges, the building of field walls, experiments with ploughs, the construction of corn driers and watermills, the introduction of new strains of fruit, and the dissemination of crafts such as bee-keeping (Morris 1973, pp. 432-40). Adamnan's seventh-century Life of Columba makes passing allusions to the sowing of barley, harvesting and threshing, a barn with grain sufficient to sustain the community for a year, baking bread, the keeping of sheep and cattle, the monks building a cashel, importing wattles and timber for building and collecting reeds for thatching (Anderson & Anderson 1991). Although such sources are often riddled with anomalies and anachronisms, there is nothing inherently improbable in their message that the early monasteries played a significant role in the revival of dark-age agriculture. The fostering of industrial activity is also apparent from the archaeological evidence of early glass- and bronze-working at Iona and Whithorn.

The practical subsistence needs of the monks must have had a significant impact upon the landscape, but a more distinctive signature came from the concept of sanctity itself. Between the fifth and twelfth centuries the entire promontory of the Machars around Ninian's shrine at Whithorn became, in effect, a sanctified landscape, with hermitages, cemeteries, inscribed memorial stones, a distinctive group of crosses, and pilgrimage chapels at suitable landing-points on the coast such as the Isle of Whithorn and Chapel Finian at Mochrum. A similar concentration of memorial stones, cemeteries, holy wells and chapels distinguishes the territory around St David's in Pembrokeshire. Glastonbury also acquired a halo of peripheral chapels and hermitages extending between the royal centres of Cheddar to the north and Somerton to the south.

(IV) ANGLO-SAXON MONASTERIES

The spread of monasticism through Anglo-Saxon England is rather better documented, from the time of Augustine's mission to Kent in 597. Bede states that religious communities were still rare in England in 640, commenting that those wishing to

Plate 5.IV. Deerhurst Priory church, Gloucestershire, one of the few late seventh-century minsters to remain in use as a regular monastic settlement after the Norman Conquest without comprehensive rebuilding: the later medieval windows are inserted through Anglo-Saxon masonry.

enter conventional life often travelled to France for the purpose. In fact the first major period of Anglo-Saxon monastic foundations seems to have taken place during the seventh century, supported by rulers such as Oswy (641-70) and Ecgfrith (670-85) in Northumbria, Æthelred I (675-704) in Mercia and Ine (688-726) in Wessex. A lull of two and a half centuries ensued, when only a handful of new foundations were made. Following the first Viking raid on Lindisfarne in 793, many of the early monasteries were looted and burned by Norse and Danish plunderers, but those disruptions cannot be held solely responsible for the hiatus. Excavations at both Jarrow and Monkwearmouth have revealed extensive burning, but here the finger of blame could equally be pointed at later Scottish incursions (Cramp 1969, pp. 24-5); whereas Hartlepool has produced no evidence for wanton destruction whatsoever, despite the monastery's vulnerable coastal location (Daniels 1988). Once the first fervour had passed, complacency followed by apathy were probably bigger enemies of monastic life than the Vikings.

The second great period of Anglo-Saxon monasticism began with King Alfred's foundations of Athelney and Shaftesbury soon after his defeat of the Danes in 878; but it did not really pick up momentum until the second half of the tenth century, when King Edgar gave his active support to a reform movement spearheaded by Dunstan at Glastonbury and Canterbury, Æthelwold at Abingdon and Winchester, and Oswald at Worcester. Over thirty monasteries were newly founded or re-established under strict Benedictine rule at this time, along with half a dozen nunneries. However, the impetus was once more on the wane through the early eleventh century. At the time of the Norman Conquest monastic settlements were still almost restricted to three main areas, Wessex, the Severn basin and around the Fens. Monastic life would not be re-established north of the Trent until the mission of Reinfrid, Ælfwig and Ealdwine to Jarrow, Monkwearmouth and Whitby in 1077.

Upstanding buildings from seventh- and eighth-century Anglo-Saxon monasteries are, not surprisingly, scarce. Those few early churches surviving reasonably intact are either in places where monastic life was not resumed (Brixworth, Bradwell-on-Sea), or where it never regained sufficient vigour to attempt comprehensive rebuilding (Deerhurst Pl. 5.IV). Elsewhere the evidence is confined mainly to crypts (Ripon, Hexham, Repton) and to sculptural fragments. Until the late 1970s only ten Anglo-Saxon monastic sites dating from before the tenth-century reform had received any sort of archaeological investigation, and only four late Anglo-Saxon monasteries (the evidence is reviewed by Cramp 1976). Partial plans of early monastic complexes revealed at Hartlepool and Whitby suggested that the first generation of Anglo-Saxon monasteries had more in common with the scattered cells of

Celtic communities than with the organised claustral plans of the later Benedictines. When did the developed claustral plan first appear? The cartographic depiction on the St Gall plan of c. 820 is well known. In England there is, as yet, little clear evidence for its adoption before the tenth-century reform. However, claims have been made for an eighth-century cloister at St Augustine's, Canterbury (Potts 1934), and Richard Gem, acknowledging the special importance of this site, has recently pointed to the possible parallel of Lorsch in Germany, where a monastery founded by the English missionary Boniface in the 760s employed a claustral plan from the outset (Gem 1997, pp. 104).

The identification of the earlier monastic settlements presents many problems. Even the names of some documented sites can no longer be recognised in the present landscape: where were the monasteries of *Icanho* , founded by St Botolph in 654, *Pægnalæch* , where Bishop Tuda of Lindisfarne was buried in 664, *Penitanham* founded by Abbess Cuthswith on land given in 693 by King Oshere of the Hwicce, or *Cornu Vallis*, named in 716?[1] Many monastic settlements of the seventh and early eighth centuries were double communities of monks and nuns, but there was no standard rule at this time, and they varied greatly in size, organisation and plan. There is a considerable grey area between 'proper' monastic communities and the miscellany of minsters and *clasau* occupied by various sorts of secular clerics, as well as a number of dubious foundations which may be no more than fictional devices for avoiding the payment of secular dues. The difficulties of distinguishing the earlier monasteries from contemporary aristocratic settlements have been underlined by the recent debate over Flixborough in Lincolnshire (Whitwell 1991): are the finds of writing implements, an alphabetical ring and the naming of a nun on a lead plaque possibly from a relic chest, sufficient to identify the site as genuinely monastic, and if so, can it be identified with the monastery of West Halton (the neighbouring village) founded by St Etheldreda around 670?

Evidence from archaeological excavation again hints at the exploitation of the surrounding countryside, though at present it is available for only a very small number of the early sites. Animal bones from Hartlepool reveal a preponderance of lambs and calves, which may imply a specialised monastic farm geared to meat production (prior to the enforcement of Benedictine regulations in the tenth century there seems to have been no particular inhibition about meat-eating); pigs, domestic geese and poultry were also kept, and fish were caught from local rivers, estuaries and shallow coastal waters; conditions did not favour the preservation of botanical remains, but plumstones were present and querns indicate the processing of cereals (Daniels 1988). A pollen sample from Monkwearmouth indicated the presence of waste ground with hazel, birch and willow scrub, but was conspicuously devoid of larger woodland trees (Cramp 1969, p. 59). Hartlepool was a centre for silver-, lead- and bronze-working, while evidence of glass-working has come from Jarrow. Few archaeological explorations of abbeys of the later reform period have yet looked beyond the churches to the domestic buildings and the wider environment, apart from Graham Keevil's recent work at Eynsham, as yet unpublished.

Charters record the acquisition of specific properties by monasteries from the early seventh century onwards, and although many of the nominally early charters are highly suspect, the provision of more critical editions by recent historians has helped to separate the wheat from the chaff. Attempts have been made to define the fluctuating landholdings of Abingdon (Stenton 1913), Christ Church, Canterbury (Brooks 1984) and Glastonbury (Costen 1992) before the reform. Reliable documentation for the acquisition and management of estates increases markedly after the tenth century. Monastic chronicles begin to describe woodland clearances and the diversion of watercourses. Boundary perambulations attached to charters give glimpses of the contemporary landscape, documenting the spread of features such as watermills and fisheries (colour Pl. 5.V.).

(V) SANCTITY REVIVED: THE RE-ESTABLISHMENT OF ANCIENT MONASTIC SITES

The resurrection of lapsed monasteries was a feature of the tenth-century reform, but to what extent did traditions of sanctity attached to ancient but abandoned monastic or ecclesiastical sites still attract founders in the post-Conquest period? The nostalgic pilgrimage of the Norman Reinfrid and his two English colleagues to re-establish monastic life in the ruins of Jarrow, Monkwearmouth and Whitby suggests that the impulse was still a strong one. The re-establishment of the see of Whithorn, the building of its Romanesque cathedral in the middle of the twelfth century and the introduction of Premonstratensian canons in 1177 underline the continuing multi-faceted role of an ancient Christian site.

The founders of several Benedictine and Cluniac abbeys after the Norman Conquest seem to have been influenced by such traditions. When Gilbert of Ghent established a Benedictine community at Bardney in Lincolnshire in 1087, he chose the site specifically because of Bede's reference to the place as an important ancient monastery, though it had lain abandoned since 870 (Dugdale, *Mon. Angl.*, I. 628-30). Driven out of Whitby by persecution and piracy, Abbot Stephen persuaded the king in 1078 to grant him and his monks the site of St Cedd's seventh-century monastery at Lastingham, only to find that this place too was infested with brigands, prompting a further move into the relative safety of York. Much Wenlock, Reading and Leominster were also founded on the sites of abandoned Anglo-Saxon monasteries or nunneries. Tantalising glimpses of high-status late Saxon occupation beneath the Cluniac abbey at Lewes have suggested that this too may occupy an undocumented earlier monastic or aristocratic site. The fill of a ditch beneath the infirmary chapel contained rock crystal, cast glass inlay and gold leaf. The ditch was intersected by foundations for a tenth-century building with a deep shaft containing a thick layer of fish bones – perhaps a *sacrarium* for the disposal of remains of ritual meals and spoiled consecrated items. The bones included swan and porpoise (Lyne 1997).

Even the Cistercians, despite their professed preference for sites far from human habitation, were not wholly immune from the pull of ancient sanctity. In Wales and the Marches at least half a dozen Cistercian abbeys have traditions of nearby hermitages or Celtic *clasau* as predecessors, and both Welsh founders and Marcher lords alike seem to have been drawn towards such sites, though perhaps for divergent motives, the former out of respect for ancient traditions, the latter from a wish to extinguish them (Bond forthcoming).

(VI) MONASTIC ESTATES AFTER THE NORMAN CONQUEST

It is in the management of their estates that the monasteries had the most profound effects upon the wider landscape (colour Pl. 5.VI); yet the landed properties of most monastic houses remain largely uninvestigated. There have been some valuable studies of the economy of particular houses undertaken by historians which have relied almost exclusively upon documentary sources (*e.g.* Colvin, 1939; Finberg 1951; Harvey 1977; Hockey 1970; Kershaw 1973; King 1973; Lomas 1978; Miller 1969; Page 1934; Raban 1977; Raftis 1957; Searle 1974; Smith 1943). As a counterbalance, there have been some detailed surveys of individual structures, notably Walter Horn's fine series of studies of monastic barns (Charles & Horn 1973, 1983; Horn 1963; Horn & Born 1965; Horn & Charles 1966). However, there was little concerted attempt to relate the documentation to the physical evidence until Colin Platt's pioneer study of monastic granges (Platt 1969). The framework of traditional academic disciplines continues to be a barrier rather than an aid to progress. No-one can hope to be equally well versed in all the specialisms now required, and we all feel legitimate trepidation about venturing outside our own field; but academic boundaries should never be allowed to become a straightjacket, and it is a matter for particular regret that historians and archaeologists at times no longer seem to speak a mutually comprehensible language. If we are ever to understand the monastic role in the landscape, multi-disciplinary synthesis will be essential.

Some readers may recall that, at the inaugural conference of our Society twenty-one years ago, I attempted to integrate the documentary, architectural and archaeological evidence for the estates of the Benedictine abbey of Abingdon (Bond 1979). This, together with an earlier survey of the Evesham estates (Bond 1973), was largely a byproduct of the professional responsibilities I then had for compiling county sites and monuments records. As a result both studies tended to be 'site'-orientated, being concerned primarily with the identification and basic recording of individual earthworks and buildings, documented and surviving, on the estate farms. In many ways this was a naive and simplistic approach. Little attempt was made to examine the workings of the estate as a whole, the changes which took place through time, the relationships between buildings and land use, or the respective roles of the monasteries and their tenants. Nevertheless, it was an essential first step towards a deeper understanding. Even the most superficial exploration of the physical evidence raises all sorts of questions. Why were there so many dovecotes on the Evesham Abbey properties, compared with other estates? Why is there so little surviving evidence for livestock housing on monastic estates compared with cereal storage buildings? Why are there far more surviving monastic barns than free-standing granaries? Why are English monastic barns normally entered from the long side, with threshing-floors between opposed doors, while French monastic barns are normally entered from the gable end? Why is there such an enormous variation in the size of monastic barns? Speculations have been offered on this last question (Bond & Weller 1991), but there are few solutions.

Steve Moorhouse has emphasised the need to consider the buildings of the granges in relation to the precise extent of land and resources comprising them (Moorhouse 1989), and the potential of this approach has been exploited with particular success by David Williams in his studies of the Welsh Cistercians (Williams 1984, 1990), which stands as a model for future work. There have also been some useful regional studies elsewhere, notably the work of Bryan Waites on the monastic role in the colonisation of the North York Moors (1962, 1967, 1997). Alternative approaches have been to explore the role of the individual orders: the economy of the Cistercians in particular has been fairly extensively explored (Donkin 1978, q.v. for further references) (Pl. 5.VII). More thematic studies have included numerous contributions on monastic agriculture (*e.g.* Brandon 1972; Day 1950; Farmer 1977, 1983; Keil 1965; Mate 1984; Postles 1979; Smith 1947); on sheep and cattle farming (Donkin 1958a, 1962-

Plate 5.VII. Cistercian landscapes: although the role of the Cistercians as pioneer settlers of new land may have been overstated, the setting of Tintern Abbey, Monmouthshire, in a valley bottom site surrounded by steep wooded hills, reflects their search for isolated locations with potential for economic expansion.

3; Postles 1984; Waites 1980; Whitwell 1904); woodland management and assarting (Donkin 1964; Rackham 1998; Tinsley 1976); marshland exploitation and drainage (Donkin 1958b; Smith 1940); water management (Bond 1989, 1993b); fisheries (Bond 1988, though some of the conclusions there need revision in the light of later work); mills (Keil 1961-7; Lindley 1954, 1956; Bond 1994); the impact of monasteries upon rural settlement (Barley 1957; Donkin 1960); and their role in town planning (Slater 1996, 1998). A handful of monastic farms and granges have been excavated to modern standards, notably Tim Allen's recent work at Abingdon's grange at Dean Court (Allen *et al.* 1994).

Many fundamental questions remain. What differences in management practices can be detected in the landscape between lay and monastic owners, between the different monastic orders, and between monasteries and their tenants, and how did this change and evolve through time? To what extent were the monasteries pioneers in agricultural improvement and in the invention and application of new industrial technology? The past twenty years have seen some exciting advances in all these areas, but the potential for continuing enquiry remains vast.

FOOTNOTE

1. Suggested identifications for *Icanho* have included Iken in Suffolk and a location near Boston (Knowles & Hadcock 1971, p. 475). I am grateful to Della Hooke for calling my attention to a suggested identification of *Penitanham* with Inkberrow, made by P. Sims-Williams, 1976. *Cornu Vallis* may have been near the mouth of the Humber (Knowles & Hadcock 1971, p. 471).

BIBLIOGRAPHY

Allen, T., *et al.*, 1994. 'A medieval grange of Abingdon Abbey at Dean Court Farm, Cumnor', *Oxoniensia*, 59, pp. 219-448.

Anderson, A. O. & Anderson, M. O. (eds), 1991. *Adomnan's Life of Columba* (2nd edn, Oxford).

Ardura, B., 1993. *Abbayes, Prieurés et Monastères de l'Ordre de Prémontré en France des Origines à nos jours: dictionnaire historique et bibliographique* (Centre Culturel des Prémontrés (Nancy).

Aston, M., 1993. 'The development of the Carthusian order in Europe and Britain: a preliminary study', in *In Search of Cult: archaeological investigations in honour of Philip Rahtz*, ed. M. Carver (Woodbridge), pp. 139-51.

Barley, M. W., 1957. 'Cistercian land clearances in Nottinghamshire: three deserted villages and their moated successor', *Nottingham Medieval Stud*, 1, pp. 75-89.

Bond, C. J., 1973. 'The estates of Evesham Abbey: a preliminary survey of their medieval topography', *Vale of Evesham Hist Soc Res Pap*, 4, pp. 1-62.

Bond, C. J., 1979. 'The reconstruction of the medieval landscape: the estates of Abingdon Abbey', *Landscape History*, 1, pp. 59-75.

Bond, C. J., 1988. 'Monastic fisheries', in *Medieval Fish, Fisheries and Fishponds in England,* ed. M. Aston, Br Archaeol Rep, Br ser 182.i (Oxford), pp. 69-112.

Bond, C.J., 1989. 'Water management in the rural monastery', in *The Archaeology of the Rural Monastery*, ed. R. Gilchrist & H. Mytum, Br Archaeol Rep, Br ser 203 (Oxford), pp. 83-111.

Bond, C.J., 1993a. 'The Premonstratensian order: a preliminary survey of its growth and distribution in medieval Europe', in *In Search of Cult: archaeological investigations in honour of Philip Rahtz*, ed. M. Carver (Woodbridge), pp. 153-85.

Bond, C. J., 1993b. 'Water management in the urban monastery', in *Advances in Monastic Archaeology,* ed. R. Gilchrist & H. Mytum, Br Archaeol Rep, Br ser 227 (Oxford), pp. 43-78.

Bond, C. J., 1994. 'Cistercian mills in England and Wales: a preliminary survey', in *L'Espace Cistercien,* ed. L. Pressouyre, Comité des Travaux Historiques et Scientifiques, Mémoires de la Section d'Archéologie et d'Histoire de l'Art, 5 (Paris), pp. 364-77.

Bond, C.J., forthcoming. 'The location and siting of Cistercian houses in Wales and the West', in *The Cistercians in Wales and the West,* ed. M. Gray & P. Webster (Cardiff).

Bond, C. J., & Weller, J.B., 1991. 'The Somerset barns of Glastonbury Abbey', in *The Archaeology and History of Glastonbury Abbey,* ed. L. Abrams & J. P. Carley (Woodbridge), pp. 57-87.

Brandon, P. F., 1972. 'Cereal yields on the Sussex estates of Battle Abbey during the later Middle Ages', *Econ Hist Rev*, 2nd ser, 25, pp. 403-20.

Brooks, N., 1984. *The Early History of the Church of Canterbury* (Leicester).

Butlin, R. A., 1977. 'Urban and proto-urban settlements in pre-Norman Ireland', in *The Development of the Irish Town* ed. R. A. Butlin (London), pp. 11-27.

Charles, F. W. B., & Horn, W., 1973. 'The cruck-built barn of Leigh Court, Worcestershire', *J Soc Archit Hist*, 32, pp. 5-29.

Charles, F. W. B., & Horn, W., 1983. 'The cruck-built barn of Frocester Court Farm, Gloucestershire', *Soc. Archit Hist* , 42, pp. 211-37.

Colvin, H. M., 1939. 'Dale Abbey: granges, mills and other buildings', *J Derbyshire Archaeol & Nat Hist Soc.*, 60, pp. 142-55.

Costen, M. D, 1992. 'Dunstan, Glastonbury and the economy of Somerset in the tenth century', in *St Dunstan: his Life, Times and Cult,* ed. N. Ramsay, M. Sparks & T. Tatton-Brown (Woodbridge), pp. 25-44.

Cowan, I. B., & Easson, D. E., 1976. *Medieval Religious Houses: Scotland* (2nd edn, London).

Cramp, R., 1969. 'Excavations at the Saxon monastic sites of Wearmouth and Jarrow, Co. Durham: an interim report', *Medieval Archaeol*, 13, pp. 21-66.

Cramp, R., 1976. 'Monastic sites', in *The Archaeology of Anglo-Saxon England,* ed. D. M. Wilson (Cambridge), pp. 201-52.

Daniels, R., 1988. 'The Anglo-Saxon monastery at Church Close, Hartlepool, Cleveland', *Archaeol J,* 145, pp. 158-210.

Day, L. J. C., 1950. 'The early monastic contribution to medieval farming', *Lincolnshire Hist*, 5, pp. 200-14.

Donkin, R. A., 1958a. 'Cistercian sheep-farming and wool sales in the thirteenth century', *Agric Hist Rev*, 6.i, pp. 2-8.

Donkin, R. A., 1958b. 'The marshland holdings of the English Cistercians before 1350', *Cîteaux in de Nederlanden* , 9, pp. 1-14, 262-75.

Donkin, R. A., 1960. 'Settlement and depopulation on Cistercian estates in the twelfth and thirteenth centuries, especially in Yorkshire', *Bull Inst Hist Res*, 33, pp. 141-65.

Donkin, R. A., 1962-3. 'Cattle on the estates of medieval Cistercian monasteries in England and Wales', *Econ Hist Rev*, 2nd ser, 15, pp. 31-53.

Donkin, R. A., 1964. 'The English Cistercians and assarting, *c*.1128-*c*.1350', *Analecti Sacri Ordinis Cisterciensis* , 20, pp. 49-75.

Donkin, R. A., 1967. 'The growth and distribution of the Cistercian order in medieval Europe', *Studia Monastica,* 9, pp. 275-86.

Donkin, R. A., 1978. *The Cistercians: studies in the geography of medieval England and Wales,* Pontifical Inst Mediaeval Stud, Studies Texts, 38 (Toronto).

Dugdale, Sir W., 1655-73. *Monasticon Anglicanum,* 1846 edn, ed. B. Bandinel, J. Caley & H Ellis (London).

Edwards, N., 1990. *The Archaeology of Early Medieval Ireland* (London).

Evans, J., 1938 *The Romanesque Architecture of the Order of Cluny* (Cambridge).

Farmer, D. L., 1977. 'Grain yields on the Winchester manors in the later Middle Ages', *Econ Hist Rev*, 2nd ser, 30.

Farmer, D. L., 1983. 'Grain yields on Westminster abbey manors, 1271-1410', *Canadian J Hist*, 18, pp. 340-7.

Finberg, H. P. R., 1951. *Tavistock Abbey: a study in the social and economic history of Devon* (Cambridge).

Gem, R., (ed.), 1997. *St Augustine's Abbey, Canterbury* (London).

Golding, B., 1995 *Gilbert of Sempringham and the Gilbertine Order, c.1130-1300* (Oxford).

Graham, B. J., 1998 'The town and the monastery: early medieval urbanisation in Ireland, AD 800-1150', in *The Church in the Medieval Town,* ed. T. R. Slater & G. Rosser (Aldershot), pp. 131-54.

Gwynn, A., & Hadcock, R. N., 1970. *Medieval Religious Houses: Ireland* (London).

Harvey, B., 1977. *Westminster Abbey and its Estates in the Middle Ages* (Oxford).

Hill, P., 1997. *Whithorn and St Ninian: the excavation of a monastic town, 1984-91* (Stroud).

Hockey, S. F., 1970. *Quarr Abbey and its Lands, 1132-1631* (Leicester).

Horn, W., 1963. 'The great tithe barn of Cholsey, Berkshire', *J Soc Archit Hist*, 22, pp. 13-23.

Horn, W., & Born, E., 1965. *The Barns of the Abbey of Beaulieu at its Granges of Great Coxwell and Beaulieu St Leonards* (Berkeley & Los Angeles).

Horn, W., & Charles, F. W. B., 1966. 'The cruck-built barn of Middle Littleton in Worcestershire, England', *J Soc Archit Hist*, 25, pp. 221-39.

Hoskins, W. G., 1955. *The Making of the English Landscape* (1st edn, London).

Hurley, V., 1982. 'The early church in the south-west of Ireland: settlement and organisation', in *The Early Church in Western Britain and Ireland,* ed. S. M. Pearce, Br Archaeol Rep, Br ser 102 (Oxford), pp. 297-332.

Hutchison, C. A., 1989. *The Hermit Monks of Grandmont* (Cistercian Stud ser, 118 (Kalamazoo, Michigan).

Keil, I. J., 1961-7. 'Mills on the estates of Glastonbury Abbey in the later Middle Ages', *Somerset & Dorset Notes & Queries* , 28, pp. 181-4.

Keil, I. J., 1965. 'Farming on the Dorset estates of Glastonbury Abbey in the early fourteenth century', *Proc Dorset Nat Hist & Archaeol Soc*, 87, pp. 234-47.

Kershaw, I., 1973. *Bolton Priory: the economy of a northern monastery, 1286-1325* (Oxford).

King, E., 1973. *Peterborough Abbey, 1086-1310: a study in the land market* (Cambridge).

Knowles, D. & Hadcock, R. N., 1971. *Medieval Religious Houses: England and Wales* (2nd edn, London).

Lindley, E. S., 1954, 1956. 'Kingswood Abbey, its lands and mills', *Trans Bristol & Gloucs Archaeol Soc*, 73, pp. 115-91; 75, pp. 73-104.

Lomas, R. A., 1978. 'The priory of Durham and its demesnes in the fourteenth and fifteenth centuries', *Econ Hist Rev*, 2nd ser, 31, pp. 339-53.

Lyne, M., 1997. *Lewes Priory: Excavations by Richard Lewis, 1969-82* (Lewes).

Mate, M., 1984. 'Agrarian economy after the Black Death: the manors of Canterbury Cathedral Priory, 1348-91', *Econ Hist Rev*, 2nd ser, 37, pp. 341-54.

Miller, E., 1969. *The Abbey and Bishopric of Ely* (Cambridge).

Moorhouse, S., 1989. 'Monastic estates: their composition and development', in *The Archaeology of Rural Monasteries*, ed. R. Gilchrist & H. Mytum, Br Archaeol Rep, Br ser 203 (Oxford), pp. 29-81.

Morris, J., 1973. *The Age of Arthur: a history of the British Isles from 350 to 650* (London).

Norman, E. R., & St Joseph, J. K. S., 1969. *The Early Development of Irish Society: the evidence of aerial photography* (Cambridge).

Ó Cróinín, D., 1995. *Early Medieval Ireland, 400-1200* (London).

Ordnance Survey, 1954. *Map of Monastic Britain, South Sheet* (2nd edn, Chessington).

Ordnance Survey, 1955. *Map of Monastic Britain, North Sheet* (2nd edn, Southampton).

Ordnance Survey, 1977. *Map of Monastic Ireland* (2nd edn, Dublin).

Olson, L., 1989. *Early Monasteries in Cornwall* (Woodbridge).

Page, F. M., 1934. *The Estates of Crowland Abbey* (Cambridge).

Pearce, S. M., 1978. *The Kingdom of Dumnonia: studies in history and tradition in south western Britain, AD 350-1150* (Padstow).

Platt, C., 1969. *The Monastic Grange in Medieval England: a reassessment* (London).

Postles, D., 1979. 'Grain issues from some properties of Oseney Abbey, 1274-1348', *Oxoniensia*, 44, pp. 30-7.

Postles, D., 1984. 'The Oseney Abbey flock', *Oxoniensia*, 49, pp. 141-52.

Potts, R. U., 1934. 'The plan of St Austin's abbey, Canterbury', *Archaeol Cantiana*, 46, pp. 179-94.

Raban, S., 1977. *The Estates of Thorney and Crowland: a study in medieval monastic land tenure*, Dep Land Economy Occas Pap 7, Univ Cambridge.

Rackham, O., 1998. 'The abbey woods', in *Bury St Edmunds: Medieval Art, Architecture, Archaeology and Economy*, ed. A. Gransden, Br Archaeol Assoc Conf Trans, 20, pp. 139-60.

Raftis, J. A., 1957. *The Estates of Ramsey Abbey: a study in economic growth and organisation* (Pontifical Inst Mediaeval Stud, Studies & Texts, 3 (Toronto).

Rahtz, P., 1993. *Glastonbury* (London).

Robinson, D. M., 1980. *The Geography of Augustinian Settlement*, 2 parts, Br Archaeol Rep, Br series 80 (Oxford).

Ryan, J., 1972. *Irish Monasticism: origins and early development* (2nd edn, Dublin).

Searle, E., 1974. *Lordship and Community: Battle Abbey and its Banlieu, 1066-1538*, Pontifical Inst of Mediaeval Stud, Studies & Texts, 26 (Toronto).

Sims-Williams, R., 1976. 'Cuthswith, seventh-century abbess of Inkberrow, near Worcester, and the Wurzburg manuscript & Jerome on Ecclesiastes', *Anglo-Saxon England* 5, ed. P Clemoes (Cambridge), pp. 1-21.

Slater, T. R., 1996. 'Medieval town-founding on the estates of the Benedictine order in England', in *Power, Profit and Urban Land: landownership in medieval and early-modern northern European towns*, ed. F.-E. Eliassen & G. A. Ersland (London), pp. 70-93.

Slater, T. R., 1998. 'Benedictine town planning in medieval England: evidence from St Albans', in *The Church in the Medieval Town*, ed. T. R. Slater & G. Rosser (Aldershot), pp. 155-76.

Smith, R. A. L., 1940. 'Marsh embankment and sea defence in medieval Kent', *Econ Hist Rev*, 10.i, pp. 29-37.

Smith, R. A. L., 1943. *Canterbury Cathedral Priory: a study in monastic administration* (Cambridge).

Smith, R. A. L., 1947. 'The Benedictine contribution to medieval English agriculture', in *Collected Essays of R.A.L. Smith*, ed. M. D. Knowles (London), pp. 103-16.

Stenton, F. M., 1913. *The Early History of the Abbey of Abingdon* (Reading).

Swan, L., 1985. 'Monastic proto-towns in early medieval Ireland: the evidence of aerial photography, plan analysis and survey', in *The Comparative History of Urban Origins in Non-Roman Europe*, ed. H. B. Clarke & A. Simms, Br Archaeol Rep, Int ser S255 (Oxford), pp. 77-102.

Thomas, C., 1971. *The Early Christian Archaeology of North Britain* (Oxford).

Thomas, C., 1993. *Tintagel, Arthur and Archaeology* (London).

Tinsley, H., 1976. ''Monastic woodland clearance on the Dieulacres estate', *North Staffordshire J Field Stud*, 16, pp. 16-22.

Van der Meer, F., 1965. *Atlas de l'Ordre Cistercien* (Amsterdam/Brussells).

Waites, B., 1962. 'The monastic grange as a factor of the settlement of north-east Yorkshire', *Yorkshire Archaeol J*, 40, pp. 627-56.

Waites, B., 1967. *Moorland and Vale-Land Farming in North-East Yorkshire: the monastic contribution in the thirteenth and fourteenth centuries*, Borthwick Pap 32, Borthwick Inst Hist Res, Univ York (York).

Waites, B., 1980. 'The monasteries of north-east Yorkshire and the medieval wool trade', *Yorkshire Archaeol J*, 52, pp. 111-22.

Waites, B., 1997. *Monasteries and Landscape in North-East England* (Oakham).

Whitwell, A., 1904. 'English monasteries and the wool trade in the thirteenth century', *Vierteljahrschrift für Sozial- und Wirtschaftsgeschichte*, 2, pp. 1-33.

Whitwell, B., 1991. 'Flixborough', *Current Archaeol*, 11 (no. 126), pp. 244-7.

Williams, D. H., 1984. *The Welsh Cistercians*, 2 vols (Caldey).

Williams, D. H., 1990. *Atlas of Cistercian Lands in Wales* (Cardiff).

Hill farming landscapes of medieval northern England

A. J. L. Winchester

ABSTRACT

This paper traces the evolution of settlement and landscape change in the valleys of the Pennine and Lake District hills across the medieval period. The status of these upland areas as hunting forest or free chase meant that the strategies pursued by the great feudal landholders determined the direction of change. Two contrasting types of forest are identified, the 'closed' forests dominated by demesne stock farming, and the forests open to peasant colonisation. Much of the central Pennines was dominated by demesne cattle farms ('vaccaries') or monastic stock farms where upland pastures had been granted to monastic houses. Leasing and subdivision of both lay and monastic stock farms in the later middle ages led to the growth of the small hamlet settlements which are typical of the dales. Elsewhere, in 'open' forests, the lords allowed grazing and settlement by peasant communities by the thirteenth century. Seasonal occupation of shieling grounds developed into permanent settlement as peasant communities carved new farms from the valley sides. The paper concludes by exploring the dynamics of landscape change in the medieval uplands, relating the contrasting origins of settlement to the progress of enclosure and the pressures on woodland.

KEYWORDS

Pennines, Lake District, hunting forests, rural settlement, vaccaries, shielings, hill farming

INTRODUCTION

The wide moorlands of the Pennines, the Lake District fells and the Border hills are pastoral landscapes, where the breeding and rearing of livestock has formed the basis of the economy over many centuries. Farming patterns in the uplands have largely been determined by environmental constraint: altitude and exposure reduce the growing season; high rainfall and low temperatures create acidic, waterlogged soils. The scope for arable cultivation becomes progressively more limited as one moves up the major river valleys, though the cultivation of barley and oats at subsistence level is well attested even in the heart of the hills during the medieval and early-modern periods. In such an environment, the management of grassland, both as pasture for grazing beasts and as meadow to provide the vital crop of hay to see livestock across the winter, formed the heart of the agrarian system.

Yet the common aims of a pastoral economy mask a diversity of settlement and landscape history, which forms the central theme of this paper. In exploring the variety of landscapes in the northern English hills during the medieval centuries, it is useful, first, to distinguish between the inner core of the uplands proper, and an outer zone on the margins of the hills. The upland margin, where the river valleys left the confines of the moors and fells, often coincided with a zone of late-surviving woodland. Place-names containing the element *lēah* are frequent where the land rises slowly to the hills, as in County Durham, along the eastern Pennine edge in Yorkshire, and in the Ribble valley in Lancashire, suggesting that this zone probably contained a frontier of settlement in the late Anglo-Saxon and Norman periods (Watts 1976, pp. 219-21; Smith 1962, p. 279 & map; Winchester 1993). Open-field villages bearing arguably early names (such as OE *tūn*, rarely encountered in the uplands proper) are ringed by dispersed settlements with names indicative of woodland. Wolsingham, at the entrance to upper Weardale, is surrounded by *lēah* names (Bradley, Wiserly, Frosterley, for example, the last a post-Conquest name containing the OFr *forestier*); peripheral to Eggleston in lower Teesdale are Stotley, Barnley and Foggerthwaite (ON *thveit*, 'clearing'); Huddlesceugh and Haresceugh (ON *skogr*, 'wood') lie on the edge of Renwick, on the slopes of the north Pennines; Lorton, on the wide floor of the Cocker valley in the Lake District, was ringed by hamlets carved out of surviving woodland, probably in the century before 1250 (Winchester 1987, pp. 147-8).

Beyond this woodland zone, in the uplands proper, lay the landscapes with which this paper is concerned, where the valleys become narrow fingers of farmland hemmed in by the hills. The comparatively few woodland names probably indicate a predominantly open environment; the absence of *-tūn* place-names suggest comparatively late settlement; and the lack of extensive open fields a pastoral economy. By the sixteenth century the upper dales contained clustered stock-rearing hamlets and scattered farmsteads, set in a landscape of extensive common grazings on the fells and moors. It is to the origins of these hills farms that attention is now turned.

MOORLAND FORESTS

By the time the upland heart of northern England enters the written record in the twelfth and thirteenth centuries, much of the Pennine and Lake District hills appears as hunting forest appendant to lowland cores. Their status as hunting forest is central to an understanding of the evolution of settlement in the uplands across the medieval centuries. Forests or free chases were, in theory at least, the hunting grounds of great landowners, over which they generally exercised direct control. In the uplands of northern England few forests were royal, Knaresborough and High Peak being the exceptions, though some private forests (the forests of Lancaster, Bowland, and Richmondshire) came into the hands of the crown in the later middle ages. A few belonged to ecclesiastical liberties: Allendale was the forest of the archiepiscopal estate of Hexhamshire; Weardale belonged to the prince-bishops of Durham; Furness Fells represented the forest of Furness, granted to Furness Abbey in the mid twelfth century (*NCH*, iii. 37, 72-4; Drury 1978; Wilson 1915, p. 533). But most were in lay ownership in the thirteenth century, attached to large baronial estates anchored on the surrounding lowlands. The fells and dales of the Lake District formed private forests belonging to the baronial estates centred on Millom, Egremont, Cockermouth, Greystoke, Appleby and Kendal (Winchester 1987, pp. 17-22). Down the Pennines, Arkengarthdale, New Forest and Wensleydale were forests belonging to the lordship of Richmondshire; Wyresdale and Bleasdale to the earldom of Lancaster; Bowland, Pendle, Trawden, Accrington and Rossendale to the honour of Clitheroe, to name only the most extensive estates (*VCH Yorkshire I*, 1907, pp. 511-2; *VCH Yorkshire North Riding I*, 1914, pp. 37-8, 200-1; Shaw 1956, *passim*; Smith 1961, p. 8).

The extent to which the owners of these private forests actively exercised their hunting rights or attempted to enforce the laws and customs peculiar to forests and chases is not easy to assess, nor is the extent to which the forests were settled before the thirteenth century. Expansion of settlement in the uplands has often been linked to the Scandinavian colonisation of the ninth and tenth centuries, though the absorption of Norse and Danish words into northern English dialects means that many apparently Scandinavian place-names may have been coined several centuries after their arrival. However, the excavation of a handful of deserted settlements from the Viking period (Ribblehead high in the Pennines behind Ingleborough; Bryant's Gill, at the head of

Kentmere, deep in the heart of the Lake District, and Simy Folds in upper Teesdale) hint at a phase of colonisation deep into the hills (King 1978; Dickinson 1985; Coggins *et al.* 1983). It seems likely that the troubled eleventh century caused a major disruption in the uplands. The excavated Viking sites were, after all, deserted and Domesday Book repeatedly records that estates in the Yorkshire Dales lay waste in 1086. While William the Conqueror's 'Harrying of the North' in 1069-70 was probably concentrated on the lowlands, the re-settlement of these more fertile areas in its aftermath may have drawn population away from the Pennine uplands, leaving them largely uninhabited (Bishop 1962, pp. 5-6; Miller 1976, pp. 5-6).

By the century *c.*1250-1350, when the documentary record becomes sufficiently detailed to allow the history of individual settlements to be traced, the salient feature of the upland forests is that, despite being designated hunting reserves, the lords sought actively to generate income from stock farming, and also saw the uplands as reserves of empty land which could be granted out both to monastic houses and to tenants. The settlement history of the uplands therefore reflects the variety of strategies pursued by the owners of the upland forests in the thirteenth and fourteenth centuries. To understand the medieval landscape of the upland core, a distinction should be drawn between those forests in which exploitation by large landowners was paramount, whether through the creation of demesne stock farms or by grants of hill pasture to religious houses, and those which were open to settlement by peasant communities. In the latter, lords generated income by selling summer grazing rights on the fells, enabling systems of transhumance to develop, or by allowing peasant colonisation during the population growth of the thirteenth and early fourteenth centuries. By *c.*1300 a mosaic of demesne, monastic and peasant exploitation had laid the foundations for the hill farming communities which developed in the uplands across the late medieval and early modern centuries. Settled dales communities, tilling the land for subsistence crop production but living off their flocks and herds, were only part of the picture. There were also specialised stock farms, and shieling grounds and other summer pastures, particularly in the 'hopes' or side valleys deep in the hills, where flocks and herds grazed but where there was no permanent settlement.

VACCARIES

Nothing demonstrates more clearly that the owners of the upland forests viewed their estates not only as hunting reserves, but as reserves of upland pasture from which considerable income might be won, than the frequent references to vaccaries (*vaccariae*) in late medieval documents.

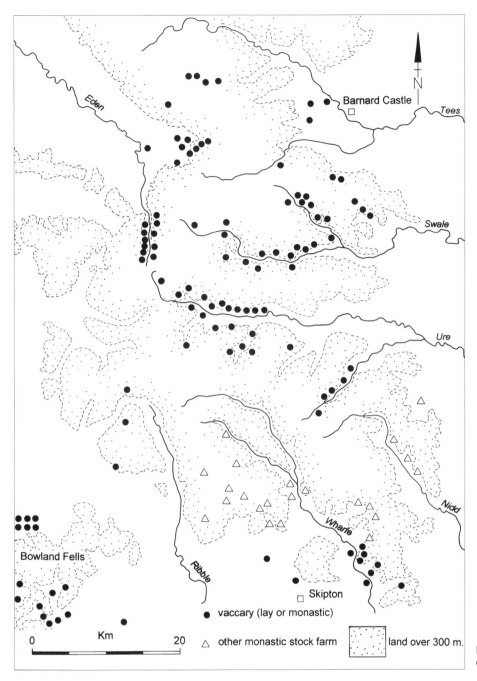

Fig. 6.1. The central Pennines: demesne stock farms

These cattle breeding stations are recorded widely through the uplands of northern England, from the forest of Rothbury in Northumberland, to the forest of Alstonefield in the Staffordshire moorlands (*NCH*, xv. 354; *VCH Staffordshire VII*, 1996, pp. 28, 52). The greatest concentration, however, was in the central Pennines, where whole valleys appear to have been given over to vaccaries (Fig. 6.1). There were twelve vaccaries in the forest of Stainmore at the head of the Eden valley; eleven in the Mallerstang valley (colour Pl. 6.I); nine in Arkengarthdale and a further five in New Forest; thirteen in the forest of Wensleydale; seven in Coverdale; fifteen in the forest of Bowland; eleven in Pendle forest and a further five in Trawden forest; eleven in Rossendale; and twenty in Wyresdale.[1] Over that

wide area, the uplands do, indeed, appear to have been 'cattle country' in the decades before the Black Death (Miller 1976, p. 12).

Although so frequent in records from the Pennines and other upland areas in the fourteenth and fifteenth centuries, the connotations of the term *vaccaria* are far from clear. A handful of thirteenth-century accounts shed direct light on the demesne exploitation of some vaccaries. That at Gatesgarth, at the head of Buttermere in the heart of the Lake District, housed forty milk cows and their followers in the 1280s, generating wealth not only in the form of calves but also from sales of milk (Winchester 1987, pp. 42, 142). The twenty-seven vaccaries in the forests of the Honour of Clitheroe maintained almost 2,500 head of cattle in 1296, most of the individual vaccaries housing around eighty beasts. There the dominant aim was to breed and rear oxen for market (Atkin 1994, pp. 4-5).

Direct demesne exploitation of vaccaries appears to have ceased quite early. Some had already been let in the later thirteenth century, such as those in Arkengarthdale and Wensleydale. There, in 1296, rental income was accounted for against each vaccary, though several in Arkengarthdale were in the lord's hand, unlet (*non dimissa*).[2] By the early fourteenth century most references to vaccaries in estate accounts and extents imply that they had been let to tenants and were generating money income rather than being managed directly for the lords. Gatesgarth had been let to tenants by 1310, as may the vaccaries in the honour of Clitheroe, though their status is not made clear in an extent of 1311 which stated that the 'herbage and agistment' of the vaccaries (*loca vaccarum*) in the forests of Trawden, Pendle, Accrington and Rossendale were worth 10*s.* each (Winchester 1987, p. 142; Farrer 1907, p. 8). Elsewhere, by the 1320s and 1330s, it is clear that vaccaries were in the hands of tenants: named tenants paid money rent for those in Wyresdale and Bleasdale by 1322; the vaccaries in Mallerstang had been put to farm by the following year; and those at Ennerdale and Wasdalehead by 1334 (Farrer 1907, pp. 127-8; Winchester 1987, p. 51).[3] In the quasi-royal forest of Weardale seigneurial control survived until towards the end of the middle ages. Although three of the vaccaries were granted to a lay landowner in 1373, the bishop still had a herd of 936 cattle and 258 horses in Weardale in 1381 (Drury 1978, pp. 95-6).

Whatever the details of the transition from demesne to tenant control, it is clear that many vaccaries developed into small hamlets through a process of subdivision during the fifteenth and sixteenth centuries. The process appears to have been well established by the middle decades of the fifteenth century. In 1436-7 'gressums' (entry fines) were paid by groups of two, three or, in one instance, five tenants for several of the vaccaries in Arkengarthdale, implying that subdivision had occurred by then.[4] Groups of men had taken leases of vaccaries in Coverdale in 1465-6: Henry Lightfoot 'and his associates' farmed Woodale, Thomas Forster and associates Gammersgill, for example.[5] In Wensleydale in the same year several vaccaries had been subdivided into multiple holdings, each paying a standard rent: Marsett vaccary was in the hands of ten tenants, each paying 26*s.* 8*d.*; Burtersett consisted of four holdings at 51*s.* 8*d.* each; Appersett of six at 32*s.* 4*d.*; Gayle of eleven at 26*s.* 8*d.*; Mossdale of four at 25*s.*[6]

The leasing of demesne stock farms in Lancashire, the Yorkshire Dales and the Lake District, their subdivision into smaller holdings (partly as a result of forms of partible inheritance),

and the consequent growth of clustered hamlets, is perhaps the dominant theme in the development of upland communities in the period 1350 to 1550. Sixteenth-century rentals and surveys repeatedly show tenants sharing a common surname holding tenements with regular rents, suggesting deliberate subdivision of a unitary block. The resulting clusters of small farms, often worked by men sharing a common ancestry, stood in marked contrast to the large, unitary farming units of the vaccaries – and they represented the end of direct lordly involvement in farming in many valleys (Shaw 1956, pp. 378-9; Winchester 1987, p. 51; McDonnell 1990; Winchester 2000, pp. 13-16; *cf.* Muir 1998).

MONASTIC STOCK FARMS

The role of monastic houses in the development of the uplands has often been stressed, perhaps to the extent of exaggeration, when the widespread lay exploitation described above is taken into account. However, it is true that extensive blocks of upland pasture had been granted to monasteries by the early thirteenth century, and that these grants yielded considerable income from demesne stock rearing in the hills. The monastic heartland was in the Yorkshire Dales, where the great Cistercian houses of Fountains, Furness and Jervaulx held wide tracts of moorland: Fountains in Nidderdale, Littondale and Malham; Furness around Ribblehead and Ingleborough and in the Winterburn valley; and Jervaulx in upper Wensleydale. The smaller holdings of other houses (Bolton Priory, Byland, Bridlington, Marrick) created a patchwork of monastic property totalling thousands of acres (Winchester 2000, p. 15). Away from the central Pennines, monastic property was more scattered but nevertheless significant. In the Lake District, Furness retained control of much of the Furness Fells around Hawkshead, as well as Brotherilkeld in upper Eskdale and part of Borrowdale. Fountains held the rest of Borrowdale; while the small Cistercian house of Calder was set in its own property on the western edge of the fells (Brownbill 1916, pp. 561-80; Lancaster 1915, pp. 58-64; Dugdale, *Mon. Angl.,* V. 342). In the north Pennines, Hexham held property in Alston Moor, and Durham Priory at Muggleswick; and in the Borders, Newminster had been granted a vast tract of the Cheviots at Kidland in the twelfth century (Hodgson 1840, pp. 43-4; Greenwell 1872, pp. 182-4; Fowler 1878, pp. 73-84)

Most of these upland tracts were retained in hand by the monks to form part of centralised livestock enterprises, rearing not only the sheep for which the monasteries were famous, but also cattle (Donkin 1962). In 1297 Furness Abbey had 5,000 sheep on their granges in Cumberland, Lancashire and Yorkshire, but also 120 oxen and

80 cows on their vaccaries at Newby and Winterburn, and a further 482 oxen and 186 cows in Cumberland and Lancashire.[7] In Wharfedale, Bolton Priory's sheep flock grew from 1,215 in 1296/7 to over 3,000 in the early fourteenth century, and its cattle herd fluctuated between around 370 and 500 in the same period. Its three main landed holdings were integrated into a vigorous pastoral system, the breeding herd of cattle being kept on four vaccaries near the Priory itself; 'geld' cattle and sheep on stock farms and bercaries in Appltreewick (purchased by Bolton in 1300), and sheep on Malham moor (Kershaw 1973, pp. 79-112). Some of this monastic property continued to be exploited directly by the houses through to the sixteenth century. Even St Bees Priory, a small house with few upland possessions, had a flock of over 300 wethers (*multones*) in the Lakeland fells at Loweswater in 1517, the house's fell grazings there complementing lowland sheepwalks where the ewes and hoggs were kept.[8] Wealthier houses continued to run integrated stock farms: three of Bolton Priory's bercaries remained in hand in 1473, while its four vaccaries survived to the Dissolution, and Fountains had sheep flocks on four of its 'lodges' on Malham Moor and in Wharfedale in 1496 (Kershaw 1973, p. 182; Michelmore 1974, pp. 15, 19, 21). On the eastern edge of the North Pennines, Durham Priory's property at Muggleswick and Edmundbyers was similarly integrated with the Priory's lowland estates. Although the number of demesne stocking units at Muggleswick declined, and land was let to tenants in the early fifteenth century, the Prior's stockmen and shepherds still kept two sheep flocks (of over 400 sheep each) and a herd of over 350 oxen and bullocks at Muggleswick in 1452.[9]

Not all the monastic granges and vaccaries in the uplands continued to be managed directly by the monks across the later medieval centuries, however, and many appear to have followed a history of leasing and subdivision comparable to that of the lay vaccaries (colour Pl. 6.II). A phased transition from demesne exploitation to tenant farming occurred on some monastic stock farms. From the mid-fifteenth century Fountains Abbey succeeded in combining income from leasing its upland granges with continuing to make use of its upland properties for its demesne stock. Tenants had to keep a specified number of the abbey's cattle and sheep as part of the terms of their tenancy, the distinction between abbey stockman and tenant thus becoming blurred (Michelmore 1981, p. 196 and *passim*). On Rievaulx Abbey's vaccaries in upper Swaledale, paid stock keepers (akin to the 'feamen' managing Fountains' granges in Craven in the fifteenth century) eventually took over individual vaccaries as tenants. Once leased, the Rievaulx vaccaries rapidly developed into hamlets, each containing between six and fourteen holdings by 1540 (McDonnell 1990, pp. 28, 30).

SHIELING GROUNDS AND PEASANT COLONISATION

Perhaps the salient theme in the landscape history of the medieval uplands lies in the distinction between the 'closed' nature of the forests and chases discussed above, and the 'open' nature of other forests, where lords allowed, and perhaps encouraged, settlement by peasant communities. The contrast is particularly vivid between the vaccary dales of the central Pennines and the colonised valleys of the Lake District and north Pennines.

The chronology and mechanisms of peasant settlement in the uplands are only partially understood. From the Lake District comes clear evidence of the carving out of new farms in remote side valleys in the later thirteenth century, perhaps suggesting that the lower reaches of many dales were already occupied. By *c*.1300, most Lakeland valleys contained populous communities of tenants at will. Where a lordly presence remained, it was usually restricted to the heads of the valleys: an almost identical pattern was to be found, for example, in Buttermere, Ennerdale and Wasdale, where a landscape of peasant farms at the foot of the lake contrasted with demesne vaccaries at the dale head. When population pressure rose again in the century after *c*.1450, the resulting phase of enclosure consisted largely of 'intakes' along the margins of the fells, rather than new farms, again suggesting that most cultivable land had already been taken in from the waste (Winchester 1987, pp. 39-55).

The progress of settlement in the north Pennines was more attenuated. Although there were vaccaries in Weardale and in Lune Forest (Teesdale),[10] peasant colonisation and the leasing of land to tenants appear to have been of greater significance in the evolution of the settlement pattern. In Alston Moor there were communities of thirty-three tenants in Garrigill, thirteen in Ameshaugh, sixteen in Alston, and twenty-two in the Nent valley in 1315, suggesting that most of the settlements recorded in the early seventeenth century had been established by then (Pl. 6.III).[11] By the early fifteenth century substantial acreages were in the hands of tenants in both Allendales and in Weardale. In the Allendales in 1422 a continuing process of colonisation appears to be recorded, with income from assart land (*terra occatio*) (146 acres in East Allendale; 375 acres in West Allendale) being distinguished from 'forest land' (over 250 acres in East Allendale; 86 acres in West Allendale) and land 'newly assarted' or 'of new farm', let according to the custom of the manor.[12] In Weardale twenty-eight named holdings in the upper reaches of the valley west of Westgate and in Rookhope, had been let out to tenants, apparently on a yearly basis, in 1438.[13] A distinctive feature of the north Pennines was the early evidence of lead-mining, with the

Plate 6.III. Foreshield in the Nent valley, Alston Moor. Its name suggests permanent occupation of a former shieling ground. In 1315 twenty-two tenants in 'Nent and Corbygates' were said to hold twenty-two shielings (*scalingae*), but it is not clear whether these were permanent or temporary settlements at that time (PRO, C134/35 (16).

consequent growth of settlements of miners. The lead miners on Alston Moor, who 'dwelt together in their own huts (*shelis*)' in 1356, formed a community separate from the farming folk and enjoyed a considerable measure of self-government.[14]

One process which may have lain behind much peasant colonisation in both Cumbria and the north Pennines is the conversion of summer pastures, at first occupied seasonally, into permanent farms. The final years of seasonal settlement on shieling grounds, to which cattle and their herdsmen removed during the summer 'closed' season, when corn and hay were growing, are recorded in the Border hills and upper Teesdale in the decades either side of 1600 (Ramm *et al.* 1970; McDonnell 1988; Winchester 2000, pp. 85-90). It is generally assumed that these were the last vestiges of a system of upland land use which was formerly more extensive across the northern hills, the frequency of settlement names incorporating terms used of shieling huts ('shiel(d)' or 'scale(s)') suggesting that such farms were former shielings which had come into permanent occupation. Clear hints of such a process are visible in thirteenth-century Cumbria and fifteenth-century Allendale. Wythop, a hidden valley on the northern edge of the Lake District, was settled permanently in the later thirteenth century. Both surviving place-names (Old Scales, 'the old shielings', and Lord's Seat, 'the lord's *sætr* or summer pasture') and the fact that the lord of

Wythop had to buy out the pasture rights of neighbouring land-holders when enclosing his demesne park suggest a transition from shieling ground to settled community. A similar story is found over the fells in the Newlands valley. The name 'Newlands', first recorded in 1318, confirms that this was an area of recent colonisation, and estate accounts from the later thirteenth century record assarting as new land was enclosed. The valley's older name, Rogersett ('Roger's *sætr*'), the farms which bear names incorporating the element 'scale' (Skellgill, Gutherscale, for example), and documentary reference to a shieling at the head of the valley *c*.1270 all point towards the conversion from summer grazing ground to year-round settlement in the later thirteenth century (Winchester 1987, pp. 39-40) (Pl. 6.IV).

A similar story is found in the North Pennines. In Allendale, estate accounts for 1421-2 record income from herbage from six meadows called 'lez Shelez', which are probably to be identified with farms at the head of the valley bearing '-shield' names, which were permanently occupied by 1547 (Winchester 2000, p. 93). The process was even more attenuated in the Border hills, where the lawless reiving society of the sixteenth century delayed settlement until after the union of the Crowns. In north Tynedale, permanent settlement had crept up the main valley and that of the Tarset Burn by 1541 but many of the shieling grounds in the side 'hopes', recorded in the thirteenth century, remained (Harbottle &

Plate 6.IV. A landscape of peasant colonisation: the Newlands valley in the forest of Derwentfells, near Keswick.

Newman 1973, pp. 138-45). In Redesdale several places described as 'pastures' in 1495 had become permanent settlements ('wintersteeds') by 1604. (Winchester 2000, pp. 86-7, 93; *cf.* Charlton & Day 1979, pp. 107-15).

Seasonal settlement in the northern uplands thus appears to have retreated northwards across the middle ages. Vaccaries and monastic stock farms tamed the hunting forests of the central Pennines from the twelfth and thirteenth centuries; a tide of peasant colonisation swept the Cumbrian fells during the later thirteenth century; while the frontier of settlement continued to move up-valley in parts of the north Pennines and Border hills in the fifteenth and sixteenth centuries. By *c.*1550 the northern uplands were a populous landscape, clustered hamlets growing as former vaccaries and monastic stock farms were subdivided, and with industrial by-employment (whether lead-mining in the north Pennines, woodland crafts in the southern Lake District, or textiles in the south Pennines) encouraging cottage settlement.

THE CHANGING FACE OF THE UPLANDS: THE DYNAMICS OF MEDIEVAL LANDSCAPE CHANGE

If these were the broad directions in which settlement patterns evolved, we now turn to explore how the face of the uplands changed in response to the growth of population, settlement and livestock farming across the medieval

centuries. Two facets of landscape change deserve consideration: first, the process of enclosure, by which hill pastures were surrounded by physical boundaries; and, second, the impact on woodland in the uplands.

For much of the medieval period the uplands probably contained comparatively few permanent physical enclosures. In areas of peasant settlement, arable fields and hay meadows had to be protected against grazing stock by a 'head-dyke' or 'ring garth', a substantial and permanent physical enclosure, which encircled the cropland and meadow in the valley bottom. However, the extent of enclosed pasture is more difficult to assess. The more intensive herding of livestock, which was almost certainly a feature of the century before the Black Death (made possible by the abundance of labour, and made necessary by the survival of the wolf in parts of the uplands), may have enabled flocks and herds to be managed in a landscape with few enclosures. By the fifteenth and sixteenth centuries, however, a proliferation of pastoral enclosures seems to have occurred (Winchester 2000, pp. 68-72).

In tracing the evolution of patterns of enclosure, the contrast between demesne or monastic stock farms and areas of peasant settlement again comes to the fore. Contrasting settlement origins were reflected in contrasting landscapes of enclosure, the sites of vaccaries and monastic stock farms of the thirteenth and fourteenth centuries being associated with large enclosures of hill pastures; areas of peasant colonisation with small, valley-bottom enclosures and unenclosed fellsides. In the Lake District, for example, the sites of vaccaries are often associated with the remains of huge fellside enclosures, such as those which survive at Gatesgarthside at the head of Buttermere and around the Coves below the mountains of Haycock and Steeple at the head of Ennerdale Water. In contrast, areas of peasant colonisation, such as the Newlands valley (Pl. 6.IV) were often characterised by small, irregular fields in the valley bottom. The century after 1450 witnessed the 'intaking' of the lower fellsides in many Lake District valleys, as tenants enclosed sections of the wastes close to their farmsteads as pastures, particularly for milk cows in summer and young sheep in winter. Most of the fells remained as unenclosed common, central to the local economy, not only as summer grazing but also as the source of peat for fuel and bracken, heather and rushes for thatch.

In the heartland of vaccary country in the central Pennines large-scale enclosure of valley-side pastures is again found. Perhaps the most distinctive features were the stinted cow pastures belonging to the hamlets into which the vaccaries had evolved by the fifteenth century. Some of these cow pastures, banks of fellside covering several hundred acres in which stock numbers were governed by a numerical limit or 'stint', were separated from the open commons during the sixteenth and early seventeenth centuries. Others, however, appear to be medieval and may be descended from the separate pastures which, presumably, belonged to each vaccary. Similar enclosed pastures surrounded many monastic stock farms: on Fountains Abbey's huge estates in Craven stone walls appear to have divided the limestone pastures before the Dissolution, for example.

The hill country of northern England was overwhelmingly an open environment of grassland, heath or peat moss in the medieval period, as today. Woodland clearance and pastoral farming in the prehistoric period had led to removal of most of the primary woodland cover, soil leaching and waterlogging creating a largely treeless landscape on the mountains and moors. On the valley sides, however, it is likely that significantly more woodland survived in the twelfth century than in the sixteenth. In drawing this discussion to a close, attention is turned to the impact on woodland, as hunting forest was tamed and a hill farming landscape created across the middle ages.

Growth of settlement was accompanied by swelling livestock numbers, increasing pressure on grazing and resulting in the failure of woodland regeneration and, over the long term, in a slow but inexorable reduction in woodland. Evidence of wood-pasture is widespread. Records of income from pannage shed some light both on the extent of woodland before the expansion in cattle and sheep numbers and on the decline of woodland.

Place-names such as Swindale, Gris(e)dale and Swinhope ('pig valley') imply the existence of woodland used for pannage. It is striking that they often refer to small side valleys, perhaps suggesting that little woodland survived elsewhere. Grants of pannage in the uplands are a feature of the twelfth rather than later centuries, and receipts from pannage decline after the thirteenth.[15] With the establishment of vaccaries, monastic sheep ranches and peasant hill farms, cattle and sheep replaced pigs, and their browsing and trampling put further pressure on surviving woodland. We read of woods used as pastures: in 1430 one hundred acres of wood at Wythop was said to be worth nothing 'because it is common pasture for all the tenants of the vill'.[16]

Woodland was a valuable resource to tenant communities, not only for the traditional customary uses around the farm, formalised in rights such as 'haybote' and 'housebote' (the rights to take wood for repairing hedges and houses respectively) but also as winter fodder for livestock. The importance of woodland for 'browse' for cattle is now appreciated: the pollarded ash trees around farms in the Lake District, the holly bushes and 'hollins' names of both that area and the Pennines, and the vestiges of alder pollards and other wood-pasture species in Swaledale are all reminders of the selective and active management of trees as a source of fodder for the cold upland winters (Spray 1981; Winchester 1987, pp. 100-7; Fleming 1997).

Pressure on woodland as a result of grazing highlighted a tension. Lords and tenants alike saw the hill pastures as a valuable resource to be converted into cash through the sale of the animals, their fleeces and hides which had been grown there. Yet woodland remained a vital resource to both lords and tenants which must be protected against the grazing flocks and herds. Forest privileges gave the owners of the private forests control over woodland, in theory to ensure that it survived to provide cover and 'browse' for the deer. In practice, however, the temptations of generating income from commercial use of woodland, notably for charcoal production, proved too strong to resist and lords were increasingly enclosing woods to preserve them from grazing livestock by the later middle ages (McDonnell 1992). Lordly parks were widespread in the uplands by the fourteenth century, some, like the bishop of Durham's great park in Weardale forest and his parks at Wolsingham and Stanhope, covering large areas of valley sides; others, like the parks at Troutbeck and Rydal, whole Lakeland dale-heads (colour Pl. 6.V). Initially game reserves, they rapidly developed into mixed woodland pastures, generating income both from grazing and from sales of wood and timber. For example, both Stanhope and Troutbeck parks had been let for grazing by the early fifteenth century (Drury 1978, pp. 98-101; Farrer 1924, pp. 44-5), and Durham Priory used

Muggleswick park on the margins of the north Pennines as pasture for their own stock, as well as selling substantial numbers of birch and ash trees in the 1420s.[17]

The transition from wood-pasture to a landscape of open hill grazings with enclosed woods brings us back to what was, in theory at least, the primary purposes of the upland forests: the preservation of game for hunting. In most areas forest status was merely a memory, preserved in the name and the institutional structures of forest administration. Foresters continued to be appointed, even if the numbers of deer dwindled and the office therefore became either a sinecure or a synonym for bailiff or reeve. Heavily-settled areas, like Wensleydale and Derwentfells, can have been forests in little more than name by the fifteenth century. By contrast, hunting rights continued to be taken seriously well into the sixteenth century in the royal forest of Bowland and the prince-bishop of Durham's forest of Weardale.[18] Attempts were made to enforce the rules aimed at preserving the game, notably those placing restrictions on dogs and requiring that enclosures were to be low enough to allow deer to pass freely through farmland as well as waste, but reiterations of such regulations came to have an increasingly hollow ring to them as stock rearing replaced the chase as the principal activity in the dales.[19] In the royal forest of Bowland the tension between game preservation and farming was well understood in the sixteenth century. The clearance of woodland, the building of fences which prevented the movement of the deer, and the leasing (and in places, cultivation) of parcels of land which had previously been reserved as herbage for the deer were seen by the manorial jury to pose a serious threat to the survival of the game. 'And yf one evill wynter or grett snawe cum the fallow dere is lyke all to dye for want of meate', they predicted in 1570, and the following winter they duly noted that 273 deer had died through lack of sustenance.[20] The moorland forests of the earlier middle ages had been transformed into hill farming landscapes by the sixteenth century.

The central themes which have run through this survey have been the significance of the legal status of most of the uplands as forest or free chase and, resulting from this status, the contrast between 'closed' and 'open' forests. We now have a reasonably clear picture of the processes by which the hill farming landscapes recorded in surveys and maps from the sixteenth and seventeenth centuries had evolved since the thirteenth century. Implicit in the portrait painted above is the idea that much of the fell country had been 'empty' hunting forest in the twelfth century and that the settlement patterns and landscapes which developed across the medieval centuries were written afresh. The 'prehistory' of the upland forests remains poorly understood. Was forest status a product of the Norman Conquest? Was there a complete break in settlement evolution in the eleventh century, or is it possible to trace elements of continuity from the post-Conquest landscape back to earlier centuries? Were the vaccaries and monastic stock farms new features of the twelfth and thirteenth centuries? If not, what was the nature of the occupation they succeeded? Such questions await the attention of future generations of landscape historians.

FOOTNOTES

1. Stainmore: *Calendar of Inquisitions Post Mortem*, xviii, no. 779; Mallerstang: PRO, SC6/1044/6; Arkengarthdale and New Forest: Brown 1898, p. 38; PRO, SC6/1116/9; PRO, SC6/1085/18; Wensleydale: Brown 1892, pp. 225-6; 1898, pp. 40-1; PRO, SC6/1116/9; Coverdale: PRO, SC6/1085/20; Bowland: Shaw 1956, p. 375; Pendle and Trawden: Farrer 1907, pp. 8, 200-1; Rossendale: Tupling 1927, p. 21; Wyresdale: Farrer 1907, p. 127.
2. PRO, SC6/1116/9.
3. Mallerstang: PRO, SC6/1044/6, m. 2.
4. PRO, SC6/1085/18, m. 2v.
5. PRO, SC6/1085/20, m. 3.
6. *Ibid.*, m. 5.
7. PRO, E143/4/4. I am grateful to Paul Booth for drawing my attention to this document.
8. Cumbria RO, D/Lons/W/St Bees/1.1.
9. DUL, DCD, Enr. Lstk. Acct. 1383-4, Muggleswick Accts 1421-2, 1429-30, 1441-2, 1452-3.
10. Drury 1978, p. 95; Essex RO, D/DL/M.108, m. 3.
11. PRO, C134/35 (16). Comparable numbers of tenants owed suit of court in 1634: PRO, ADM74/1/5, fo. 11.
12. PRO, SC6/1123/12.
13. DUL, CC 190030. For identifications of holdings, see Drury 1978, p. 101.
14. *Calendar of Miscellaneous Inquisitions*, iii, no, 222; vii, no. 159.
15. Winchester 1987, pp. 101-2; *cf.* accounts for Skipton forest, which show substantial sums from pannage in 1267-71 but nothing in 1436-7: PRO, SC6/1087/6; Br Libr, Egerton MS 3144.
16. *Inquisition post mortem*, Robert Louther (copy, Cumbria RO, D/Lec/302).
17. DUL, DCD, Misc. Ch. 6312; Muggleswick Accs.
18. Lancs RO, DDHCl, box 86, Whitewell court rolls; Drury 1978.
19. Restrictions on the height of fences are recorded in the forests of Barden, *temp.* Hen. VIII, Yorkshire Archaeol Soc (Leeds), DD 121/3/1, fo. 60, and Weardale in 1607, PRO, SC2/171/12.
20. Lancs RO, DDHCl, box 86, Whitewell court rolls, nos 4, 11, 12.

ABBREVIATIONS

Cumbria RO Cumbria Record Office
DUL Durham University Library Archives & Special Collections
Essex RO Essex Record Office

Lancs RO Lancashire Record Office
PRO Public Record Office

BIBLIOGRAPHY

Atkin, M. A., 1994. 'Land use and management in the upland demesne of the De Lacy estate of Blackburnshire *c.*1300', *Agric Hist Rev*, 42, pp. 1-19.

Bishop, T. A. M., 1962. 'Norman settlement of Yorkshire', in *Essays in Economic History Vol. II*, ed. E. Carus-Wilson (London), pp. 1-11.

Brown, W. ed., 1892, 1898. *Yorkshire Inquisitions*, vols I and II, Yorkshire Archaeol Soc Rec Ser, 12, 23.

Brownbill, J. ed., 1916, 1919. *Coucher Book of Furness Abbey Volume II (parts ii and iii)*, Chetham Soc, new ser, 76, 78.

Charlton, D. B. & Day, J. C., 1979. 'Excavation and field survey in upper Redesdale, Part II', *Archaeol Aeliana*, 5th ser, 7, pp. 207-33.

Coggins, D., Fairless, K. J., & Batey, C. E., 1983. 'Simy Folds: an early medieval settlement site in upper Teesdale, Co. Durham', *Medieval Archaeol*, 27, pp. 1-26.

Dickinson, S., 1985. 'Bryants Gill, Kentmere: another "Viking period" Ribblehead?', in *The Scandinavians in Cumbria*, ed. J. R. Baldwin & I. D. Whyte, Scott Soc for Northern Stud (Edinburgh), pp. 83-8.

Donkin, R. A., 1962. 'Cattle on the estates of medieval Cistercian monasteries in England and Wales', *Econ Hist Rev*, 2nd ser, 15, pp. 31-53.

Drury, J. L., 1978. 'Durham palatinate forest law and administration, specially in Weardale up to 1440', *Archaeol Aeliana*, 5th ser, 6, pp. 87-105.

Dugdale, Sir W., 1655-73. *Monasticon Anglicanum*, 1846 edn, ed. B. Bandinel, J. Caley & H. Ellis (London).

Farrer, W., 1907. *Lancashire Inquests, Extents and Feudal Aids, II*, Rec Soc Lancashire & Cheshire, 54.

Farrer, W., 1924. *Records Relating to the Barony of Kendale, [II]*, Cumberland & Westmorland Antiq & Archaeol Soc Rec Ser, 5.

Fleming, A., 1997. 'Towards a history of wood pasture in Swaledale (North Yorkshire)', *Landscape History*, 19, pp. 57-73.

Fleming, A., 1998. *Swaledale: valley of the wild river* (Edinburgh).

Fowler, J. T., 1878. *Chartularium abbathiae de novo monasterio, ordinis Cisterciensis, fundatae anno MCXXXVII*, Surtees Soc, 66.

Greenwell, W., 1872. *Feodarium Prioratus Dunelmensis*, Surtees Soc, 58.

Harbottle, B., & Newman, T. G., 1973. 'Excavation and survey on the Starsley Burn, North Tynedale, 1972', *Archaeol Aeliana*, 5th ser, 1, pp. 137-75.

Hodgson, J., 1840. *History of Northumberland Part II, Vol. iii* (Newcastle).

Kershaw, I., 1973. *Bolton Priory: the economy of a northern monastery 1286-1325* (Oxford).

King, A., 1978. 'Gauber High Pasture, Ribblehead: an interim report', in *Viking Age York and the North*, ed. R. A. Hall, Council Br Archaeol (London), pp. 21-5.

Lancaster, W. T., 1915. *Abstracts of the Charters and other Documents contained in the Chartulary of the Cistercian Abbey of Fountains* (Leeds).

McDonnell, J. 1988. 'The role of transhumance in northern England', *Northern Hist*, 24, pp. 1-17.

McDonnell, J., 1990. 'Upland Pennine hamlets', *Northern Hist*, 26, pp. 20-39.

McDonnell, J., 1992. 'Pressures on Yorkshire woodland in the later middle ages', *Northern Hist*, 28, pp. 110-25.

Michelmore, D. J. H. (ed.), 1974. *The Fountains Abbey Rental 1495-6*, priv print.

Michelmore, D. (ed.), 1981. *Fountains Abbey Lease Book*, Yorkshire Archaeol Soc Rec Ser 140.

Miller, E., 1976. 'Farming in northern England during the twelfth and thirteenth centuries', *Northern Hist*, 11, pp. 1-16.

Muir, R., 1998. 'Village evolution in the Yorkshire Dales', *Northern Hist*, 34, pp. 1-16.

NCH A History of Northumberland, 15 vols. 1893-1940. Northumberland Cty Hist Comm (Newcastle upon Tyne).

Parsons, M. A., 1993. 'Pasture farming in Troutbeck, Westmorland, 1550-1750', *Trans Cumberland & Westmorland Antiq & Archaeol Soc*, new ser 93, pp. 115-30.

Ramm, H. G., McDowall, R. W., & Mercer, E., 1970. *Shielings and Bastles* (London).

Shaw, R. C., 1956. *The Royal Forest of Lancaster* (Preston).

Smith, A. H., 1962. *Place-Names of the West Riding of Yorkshire, Part VII*, Engl Place-Name Soc, Vol. 36 (Cambridge).

Smith, R. B., 1961. *Blackburnshire: a study in early Lancashire history* (Leicester).

Spray, M., 1981. 'Holly as fodder in England', *Agric Hist Rev*, 29, pp. 97-110.

Todd, J. M. (ed.), 1997. *The Lanercost Cartulary*, Surtees Soc 203.

Tupling, G. H., 1927. *Economic History of Rossendale*, Chetham Soc, new ser, 86.

VCH Staffordshire VII 1996. *The Victoria County History of the Counties of England: Staffordshire, Vol VII (Leek & the Moorlands)*, ed. M. W. Greenslade (Oxford).

VCH Yorkshire I 1907. *The Victoria County History of the Counties of England: Yorkshire, Vol I*, ed. W. Page (London).

VCH Yorkshire North Riding I 1914. *The Victoria County History of the Counties of England: Yorkshire North Riding, Vol I*, ed. W. Page (London).

Watts, V., 1976. 'Comment on "The evidence of place-names" by Margaret Gelling', in *Medieval Settlement: continuity and change*, ed. P. H. Sawyer (London), pp. 212-22

Wilson, J. (ed.), 1915. *The Register of the Priory of St. Bees*, Surtees Soc 126.

Winchester, A. J. L., 1987. *Landscape and Society in Medieval Cumbria* (Edinburgh).

Winchester, A. J. L., 1993. 'Field, wood and forest: landscapes of medieval Lancashire', in *Lancashire Local Studies in honour of Diana Winterbotham*, ed. A. G. Crosby (Preston), pp. 7-27.

Winchester, A. J. L., 2000. *The Harvest of the Hills: rural life in northern England and the Scottish Borders, 1400-1700* (Edinburgh).

Peoples of wood and plain:
an exploration of national and local regional contrasts

Brian K. Roberts and Stuart Wrathmell

ABSTRACT

This paper reiterates the importance of observing traces of historic and prehistoric human activity – expressed in the distribution of material cultural remains – within the contexts of woodland and open land, and shows the analytical power achieved by placing a regional study within a national perspective. Data from Domesday Book and place-names allow a national reconstruction of woodland and cleared land in the Anglo-Saxon period, and comparison with the distribution of rural settlement in the mid-nineteenth century points towards powerful causal linkages. A short study of the West Midlands argues that the boundaries between woodland and the open land were already well-marked at the time of the Roman conquest – originating earlier – and that the patterns then present were part of landscape developments persisting for over two millennia.

KEYWORDS

Anglo-Saxon cemeteries, clearance, continuity, myth and ritual, Roman forts and roads, rural landscapes and settlement, woodland

INTRODUCTION

In midwinter 1065-6, King Edward the Confessor issued a number of writs by which he declared that the monks of Westminster Abbey were to have the midland estates of Pershore and Deerhurst, royal confirmation that they possessed extensive lands together with associated rights in justice and taxation (Harmer 1952, pp. 363-8). While the formulaic character of these documents cannot be ignored, one clause catches the eye

> mid wuda. 7 mid feldan. mid læse. 7 mid
> hæþe. mid mæden. 7 mid e'i'tu*m*. mid wateru*m*.
> 7 mid weru*m*. (Harmer 1952, No. 102, pp. 366-7).

Over a thousand years later it is still, with a few qualifications, largely intelligible to speakers of English – 'with woodland and with open country, with pasture and with heath, with meadows and with aits (eyots), with waters and with weirs', terms redolent of the landscapes of

Anglo-Saxon England. Over the past five years the present writers, with the support of English Heritage, have been mapping these landscapes, in an exploration of the diversity of rural settlement and agrarian regimes in medieval and later times. A key element to emerge from this work has been the mapping of woodland and open land, *wudu* and *feld,* in later Anglo-Saxon England. This has drawn upon the evidence of place-names as well as the record of Domesday Book, the latter, of course, resulting from decisions made by King William exactly twenty years after the events described above.

The aim of this contribution is primarily to demonstrate the importance of observing traces of human activity – expressed in the distribution of material cultural remains – within the contexts of woodland and open land, insofar as these contexts can be modelled for the last millennium and a half. More generally, we hope that it will demonstrate the analytical power that can be generated by placing a regional study within a national perspective (Thirsk 1987). The area chosen for this demonstration is the West Midlands and Welsh borderlands, a part of the country for which a number of excellent regional studies – archaeological, historical and onamastic – have been published (*inter alia* Gover *et al.* 1936; Darby *et al.* 1954; Hilton 1966; Sylvester 1969; Roberts 1976, pp. 188-231; Ford 1976; Slater & Jarvis 1982; Hooke 1985a; Gelling 1992). It is also a part of the country where the contrast between woodland and open land, in Warwickshire between the wooded Arden and the cleared Feldon regions, has attracted scholarly analysis for many years. Further, the boundary between the two is both sharply defined and yet not the result of any conspicuous physical divide. It seems appropriate, therefore, at the turn of the millennium, to review some of these analyses in the light of our recent national mapping, in order to see how broader horizons can inform the course of regional debate.

WOODLAND IN LATER ANGLO-SAXON ENGLAND

Figure 7.1 is an attempt to map woodland across later Anglo-Saxon England. The primary layer of

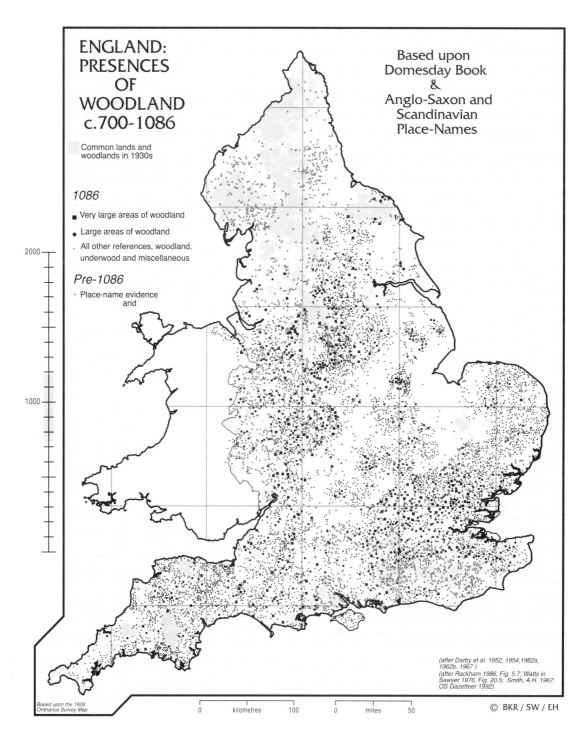

Fig. 7.1. The presences of woodland A.D. 700 – 1086.

information draws into one map the individual county maps of Domesday woodland created by H. C. Darby and his co-workers. Its key follows his own simple but effective solution to the question of the equivalence of the different formulae: leagues, acres, swine totals and swine renders (Darby 1977, pp. 171-207, fig. 64), by reducing the complexity to three symbols. Of course, the symbols are only crudely scaled, so that the map records the presence of woodland and is not a measure of the real quantity. The difference between this and Darby's own summary map is that Fig. 7.1 records *all* the entries, even

the smallest amounts of woodland and underwood: thus, the aggregated image is 'complete'. There must be slight errors in scaling and conceivably a few of omission, while other errors, those inevitably made by each and every scholar who assembled the original county maps, together with the errors present within Domesday Book itself, must be silently present. Furthermore, the record for Lancashire and parts of Yorkshire is imperfect and indeed is completely absent for the four northern counties. Nevertheless, this synoptic image is stimulating because, however imperfect, it provides a readable and challenging picture of the distribution of woodland and open land at a national scale. When evaluating this distribution it is important to appreciate that the jurors who responded to the harsh questions of the king's officers in 1085-6 possessed no notion of the form in which their responses now appear. The computer-generated image lies far beyond their own perception of Domesday; the fact that it generates a 'meaningful' pattern gives support to our acceptance of the general reliability of their responses.

The interpretation of this map undoubtedly presents difficulties, which can be simply demonstrated by the presence of a single, isolated, large block of woodland that sits in otherwise open countryside in the south-central Midlands. Whilst this woodland is recorded at the great royal manor of Brailes, and has therefore been mapped at that locus, there is evidence that its actual location was some twenty miles to the north-west, at Tanworth in the Forest of Arden. This location was suggested by Dugdale (1656, pp. 426, 556) as early as the seventeenth century. There are undoubtedly similar cases throughout the West Midlands, though the problem is far less acute than in the Weald, where woodland of 1086 has the appearance of being wholly peripheral because it was systematically recorded at estate centres rather than at geographically correct locations. Furthermore, the version of the distribution presented here, including post-1086 and pre-1086 place-name data, obfuscates the fact that the 1086 distribution tends to be dominated by the smaller symbols, and that only in limited areas are there significant concentrations of the larger symbols. This aspect, only latent within Fig. 7.1, has been greatly enhanced in a colour version by an appropriate use of different shades of green (Roberts & Wrathmell 2000). In the woodland of the eastern Midlands this manipulation even suggests the existence of core areas, centring on tracts with extensive woodlands, which grade away in all directions into countrysides dominated by small woods and underwoods, eventually to merge with wholly cleared tracts.

Such skewed information can, however, be detected by comparing the Domesday records with a second layer of information initially derived from Rackham's map of Anglo-Saxon place-names indicative of woodland (Rackham 1986, fig. 5.7). Of course, the precise meanings of place-names are as fraught with questions as are the entries of 1086. Nevertheless, the work of such scholars as Mawer and Stenton (1929), Smith (1956), Eckwall (1960), Hilton (1966), Gelling (1978, 1984 and 1992) and Cameron (1996) has established a sound basis for interpretation. In particular Gelling's careful 1978 assembly and analysis of the accumulating evidence creates a foundation for use of the results of this difficult field by non-specialists. For the Midlands she has suggested that there are even subtle variations in the meaning of the element -lēah (-ley) depending on whether it is located amid cleared land or woodland,

although establishing the temporal range of word use and name formation is, as Cox showed, singularly difficult (Gelling 1978, pp. 106-29; Cox 1973). As Rackham's original map did not wholly include the evidence from the most northerly counties the distribution of the four names has been extended to the Scottish border using additional data (Watts 1976, figs 20.4 and 20.4; Armstrong *et al.* 1950, map; Smith 1967, map; Fraser 1968). What emerges is a pastiche, but a challenge to place-name scholars to undertake the worthwhile task of assembling reliable national maps. Finally, a further layer of Fig. 7.1 draws together the evidence for both woodland and open rough grazing land, normally common grazings, from the series of county maps created by L. D. Stamp and his colleagues in the Land Utilisation Survey undertaken during the 1930s (Stamp 1937-44). The combination of woodland and rough pasture may be questioned, but given the problems of a scale range extending from blocks which are near county size to items which appear on the map as no more than a single pixel, differentiation between the two usages was impractical. The result, which draws together evidence from three time periods, is a bold synoptic picture.

The place-names used to compile Fig. 7.1 are thought to have been formed mainly between the mid-eighth and the mid-tenth centuries (Gelling 1992, p. 6). Therefore, as a time-bar shows, the data on early woodland cover three hundred years or more. Such chronological imprecision may be for some readers a matter of concern: it is not one shared by the writers, since our purpose is to explore long-term patterning in the landscape at this national scale. Nor, in such a diachronic analysis, are we reluctant to compare late Anglo-Saxon woodland with mid-nineteenth-century rural settlement, as shown in Fig. 7.2. The methodology used in the construction of this map has been described elsewhere (Roberts & Wrathmell 2000): in summary, in a map based upon the Ordnance Survey Old Series one-inch to one-mile maps, the shading and dots show variation in the intensity of dispersed and nucleated settlement in the middle decades of the nineteenth century (Margary 1975-81). Each dot represents a nucleation, subjectively size-graded, extending from large towns such as Birmingham to the small village/large hamlet threshold. The absence of shading marks the regions where nucleation rather than dispersion was the dominant settlement form; the deepest shading marks those regions which had dispersed settlement of the highest intensity. What appears here is a simplification of a full colour version. It will be immediately apparent that there was a central tract of English countryside – which we have termed the Central Province – where nucleation was preponderant, and two outer bands – the North and West and the South-eastern Provinces – which were characterised by varying intensities of dispersed settlement. These

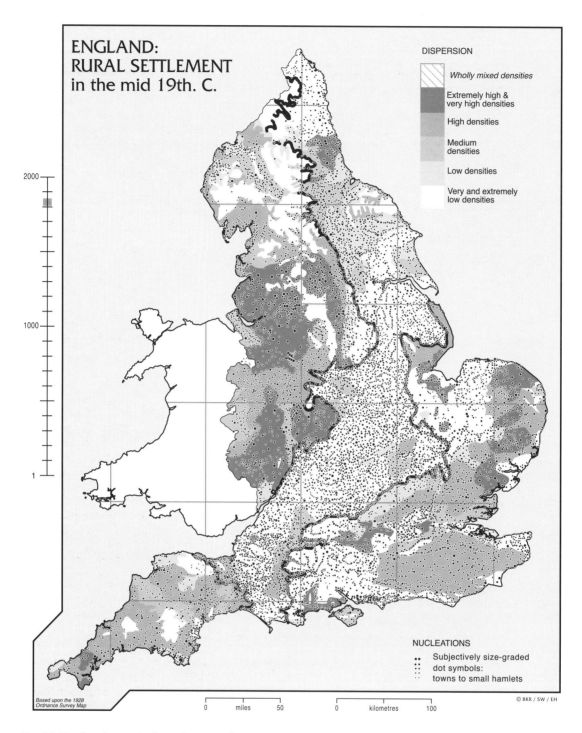

Fig. 7.2. Rural settlement in the mid-nineteenth century

correspond to Rackham's 'planned landscapes' and 'ancient landscapes' (Rackham 1986, fig. 1.3). Further, a comparison of Figs 7.1 and 7.2 shows a marked correlation between regions of late surviving Anglo-Saxon woodland and nineteenth-century dispersed settlement on the one hand and, on the other, regions of open land and nucleated settlement.

WOODLAND, OPEN LAND AND MEDIEVAL SETTLEMENT IN THE WEST MIDLANDS

These correlations are nowhere better defined than in the West Midlands, seen in Fig. 7.3, extracted from the national maps excluding only the commons and woodlands of the 1930s. It has been suggested that the differences between

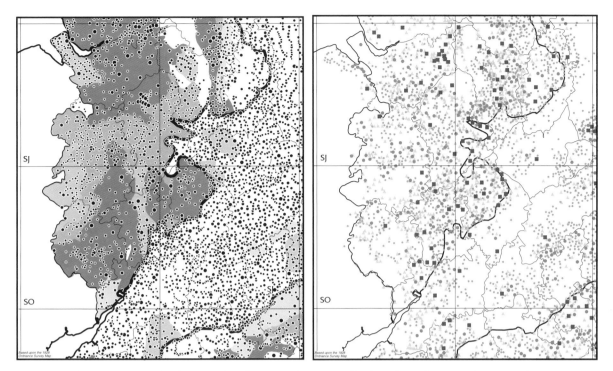

Fig. 7.3. Rural settlement in England. 3a: Rural settlement in the West Midlands in the mid-nineteenth century. 3b: Pre-Conquest woodlands in the West Midlands. Shading and symbols as in Fig. 7.2.

woodland and open land, settlement forms and agrarian systems became more marked during later Anglo-Saxon times (Dyer 1996, p. 121), as the trend in the open land, towards fewer and larger settlement nucleations gathered pace, to facilitate the operation of large townfield cultivation. The contrasts are certainly evident in Hooke's analyses of the boundary descriptions attached to pre-Conquest charters, which record subdivided and common arable from the tenth century (Hooke 1981, pp. 58-9; 1996, p. 106). The descriptions of boundaries in the Feldon show that cultivation had frequently reached the edges of estates; in woodland it had not (Hooke 1981, p. 59; 1985a, p. 126). In some Feldon communities arable land came to represent 80 *per cent* or even 90 *per cent* of the township area (Dyer 1996, p. 122). Farmsteads and houses on the boundaries of Feldon estates were still being recorded in later Anglo-Saxon charters, indicating that the process of nucleation had not yet been fully achieved (Hooke 1985a, pp. 135-8; 1985b, pp. 141-5); but far fewer were recorded than in the woodland areas (*ibid.*). It is generally agreed that the trend towards settlement nucleation and large open townfields was linked to high population densities in the open land (Hooke 1981, p. 62; 1985a, p. 134; Dyer 1996, 119), a matter to which we will return.

In Fig. 7.4 we have selected for more detailed analysis a small portion of the West Midlands stretch of the boundary between the Central Province and the Northern and Western Province. In the map of woodland in 1086 (Fig. 7.4b), the symbols differentiate between those manors with recorded woodland and those without, and in the former case provide a crude subjective differentiation of the quantity. A dashed line sketches the break between the two categories, giving local substance to a boundary between open and wooded countrysides that can be seen regionally in Fig. 7.3. However, a parish by parish study allowed a reassessment of the likely location of this woodland within each territory, using local place-names as indicators. Arrows suggest where adjustments are needed: namely, where the woodland of 1086 was located at some distance from the locus of the estate given by the place-name recorded in 1086, a problem noted nationally in connection with Fig. 7.1. The shaded area of the map suggests in broad terms where the woods were. Finally, the identification of a break between Anglo-Saxon place-names in -*tūn* and in -*lēah* (following Gelling 1978, pp. 126-8) provides another indicator of this important boundary between land largely free of woodland and land within which cultivation represented cleared land set amid wooded countrysides. The three differing measures of this boundary converge in a subtle way that can be assessed only through studies at the level of the individual parish and township.

Two other maps in Fig. 7.4 again represent convergent evidence because they are drawn from wholly distinct and chronologically separated sources. At bottom right (Fig. 7.4d) is a map using the complex coding system for rural settlement devised by one of the authors: opaque to the uninitiated it represents a record of the settlement characteristics found within the area in the second

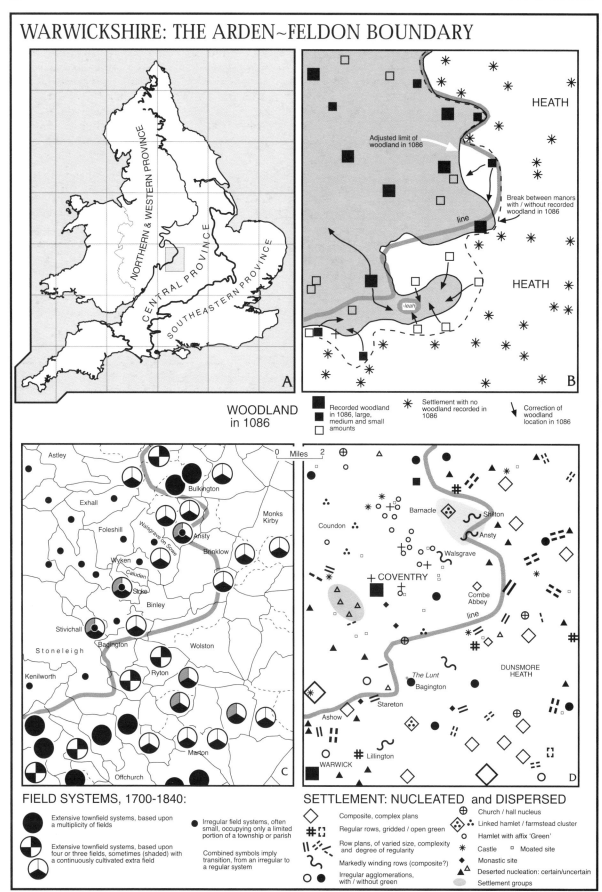

Fig. 7.4. The Arden-Feldon boundary.

half of the nineteenth century, part of the county picture at that time (Roberts 1982, p. 127). In essence, the larger and more compact the symbol, the more nucleated is the settlement represented, and vice versa. In detail the varied symbols reflect the diverse and deep-seated social and economic factors at work during the settlements' development. To analyse and explain them, each must be securely located within the appropriate feudal and tenurial frameworks as well as in time and space. It is worth emphasising again the manner in which this nineteenth-century distribution, for this is what has been mapped, is essentially congruent with data mapped for the pre-Norman period, eight hundred, perhaps even a thousand and more years earlier. The power of these antecedent patterns to act as formative controls on all subsequent developments should not be underestimated. The Ansty-Shilton-Barnacle group were described in 1316 as *una villa*, 'one vill' (*VCH Warwickshire VIII* 1969, p. 4) but by the nineteenth century comprised two villages based upon winding rows and a linked hamlet cluster. There is more here than mere confusion over administrative arrangements: between the early fourteenth and the nineteenth centuries significant and important changes have occurred in this settlement complex straddling the ancient border between woodland and champion.

The map of field systems (Fig. 7.4c), drawing upon a meticulous analysis by David Pannett, also incorporates important changes suggested by the *Victoria County History*, so that the three-field system at Ansty can be seen to have developed from an earlier irregular system (Roberts 1973, p. 202, fig. 5.4; *VCH Warwickshire VIII* 1969, pp. 46-7). An irregular system, possibly based upon subdivided furlongs cropped individually and perhaps mixed with closes, appears to have evolved into a system of three fields created by grouping the furlongs for the purposes of cropping. As late as 1649 the strips of Ansty fields were so intermixed with those of Shilton that the magistrates were still trying to sort them out (*ibid.*, p. 46). Similar changes in the field arrangements are documented at Stoke (*ibid.*, pp. 99-100) and Stivichall (*ibid.*, p. 94) further south, while the group of small depopulated settlements spanning the Coventry-Stoneleigh boundary, which appear as no more than farmstead names on the six-inch maps, hint at similar underlying complexities (*ibid.*, pp. 48-50). In both of these hamlet groupings there is evidence for territorial ambiguity, revealed by the existence of disputes about the settlements' affiliations to adjacent administrative units and, while one developed successfully, the other has been subjected to depopulation. These observations of changes in a complex frontier zone have wider implications. If, as has been postulated, small-scale Anglo-Saxon hamlets, with simple communal field systems subjected to a form of communal cultivation, preceded the rise of large nucleated villages with field systems organised on a township or parish

basis, then the winding rows, the linked hamlet and linked farmstead clusters and church hamlets of this frontier, together with the changes in these which can be documented, give us one measure of what had been happening silently elsewhere in the Midlands during the centuries before 1086. This frontier zone between Feldon and the Arden woodlands is a reminder of the sheer complexity required of any model to 'explain' the growth of nucleated villages and their field systems. In this small area settlements were responding to the presence of a growing and successful great town at Coventry, the organisational impact of Cistercian houses at Stoneleigh and Combe, the presence of ancient royal estates, the presence of forest industries and grazing reserves, as well as accretive intaking by freehold tenants (Hilton 1966, pp. 7-23)

WOODLAND AND OPEN LAND IN THE WEST MIDLANDS DURING ANGLO-SAXON TIMES

The evidence summarised above suggests that the impact of the late Anglo-Saxon woodland/open land boundary in the West Midlands persisted for eight hundred years. An even greater longevity was proposed by W. J. Ford, in his analysis of Warwickshire Avon settlement almost a quarter of a century ago:

> The division of this region into two essentially contrasting parts, the Feldon, or open country of the south, and the forest lands of the Arden to the north, has been a pattern discernible since Roman times (Ford 1976, p. 274).

His conclusions have been endorsed by other scholars working on the region. Della Hooke, for example, has noted the spatial relationship between land extensively cultivated in Anglo-Saxon times, and settlement sites associated with Romano-British farms. The territory around the Fosse Way was 'a region in which clearance and development was already well established by the early Anglo-Saxon period' (Hooke 1981, pp. 50, 52, 59-62 and fig. 14). Similarly, Christopher Dyer (1996, p. 121) has suggested that the characteristics of the Feldon communities represent an inheritance from Roman times. Such broad conclusions imply continuity in land use from Roman to medieval times, both in the cultivated lands of the Feldon and in the woodlands to the north and west, and their implications deserve more detailed consideration. We can begin with W. J. Ford's comparative analysis of the distribution of pagan Anglo-Saxon burials in the West Midlands and the woodland/open land contrasts provided by place-name evidence. He found that 'the relationship of pagan Anglo-Saxon cemeteries to known areas of woodland is virtually one of complete contrast' (Ford 1976, pp. 275-6). The same is largely true for the relevant distributions plotted on our

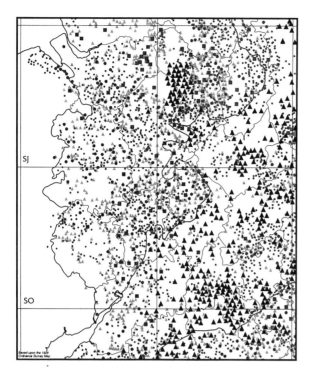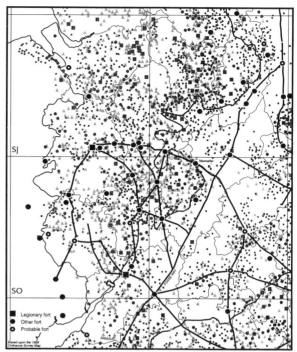

Fig. 7.5. Anglo-Saxon cemeteries. 5a: Pre-Conquest woodland and early Anglo-Saxon burials in the West Midlands. The Anglo-Saxon material is from Jones 1990, fig. 3.1, after Campbell, Ekwall, Jackson & Smith. 5b: Pre-Conquest woodland and Julio-Claudian military sites, Roman sites after Frere 1991, fig. 2. The woodland symbols and sources are the same as in Fig. 7.1.

national woodland map, an extract of which is shown here in Fig. 7.5a. Early Anglo-Saxon burials are confined to areas that appear to have contained relatively little woodland in the mid-eighth to mid-eleventh centuries.

It is necessary, therefore, to consider the patterns of human activity that may lie behind these mapped distributions. A simplistic view might be that 'Anglo-Saxon' peoples occupied the open lands whilst the contemporary 'British' population was confined to the woodlands. It is one which cannot be sustained. Both Ford and Gelling have emphasised how small the 'Anglo-Saxon' population must have been even in the open land, given the small numbers of early Anglo-Saxon burials which have been recovered; they have argued that the post-Roman British population must have constituted the bulk of the Feldon dwellers, despite their archaeological invisibility (Gelling 1992, pp. 31, 40-41, 48, 53). Continuity of land use is further implied in Ford's observation that the earliest Anglo-Saxon settlements were in the vicinity of Roman settlements (Ford 1976, p. 274). The open land, visible both in the densities of Romano-British occupation (Hooke 1981, fig.14) and as gaps in the Anglo-Saxon woodland record, would not have remained open for long without the continued activities of sizeable communities to undertake the farming practices which would repress woodland regeneration.

Equally, there is no reason to suppose a wholly British rather than an Anglo-Saxon presence in the woodlands. Margaret Gelling (1992, p. 29) has implied that an absence of early Anglo-Saxon burials in some West Midland counties means that the pre-Christian Anglo-Saxons did not penetrate those areas. This does not, however, accord with the cluster of pagan Anglo-Saxon place-names around Wednesbury, south of Lichfield (*ibid.,* p. 92; Ford 1976, p. 276). Gelling (1992, p. 94) speculated that the clustering of these names might indicate an area of late surviving paganism on the assumption that the full Anglo-Saxon 'occupation' of the Wednesbury area was late in coming. It may well be the case that pagan belief and ritual survived longer in the woodlands than in the open land, since religious and social controls would have been more difficult to enforce there. Even so, it is entirely possible that Anglo-Saxon control of this area came as early as in the Feldon. In this reading, the presence or absence of early Anglo-Saxon burials would not be an indication of territory occupied and controlled by discrete ethnic groups. Rather, it would indicate different kinds of activities in the different environmental contexts of woodland and Feldon. The linkage between estate centres in the Feldon and outlying associated territories in the woodland has already been noted in the case of Brailes. There are many others. For example, Hooke cites an eighth-century charter which records an estate with open land near Old Stratford, in the Avon valley, and with areas of wooded countryside (*ruris siluatici*) at Nuthurst, deep within Arden (Hooke 1996, p. 106). Ford (1976, pp. 280-82 and fig. 26.4) has plotted lines of settlement linkages in the West Midlands extending from the Feldon to the woodlands. These would have provided Anglo-Saxon folk groupings with seasonal grazing.

Hooke (1985a, pp. 138-41 and fig. 10.10; 1998, p. 161, fig. 55) has recorded the trackways that mark the lines of transhumance. Thus the people represented by the early Anglo-Saxon burials are likely to have been controlling the use of the woodlands, even if the people who herded the stock back and forth were drawn largely from the native post-Roman population.

Besides the grazing, various other woodland resources were no doubt exploited in Anglo-Saxon times. Hunting grounds are documented (Hooke 1996, p. 106); timber would have been acquired for buildings and fuel, and a wide range of crafts and industries would have been supported there, again perhaps on a seasonal basis. That the permanent population of the woodlands would have been much smaller and more scattered than that of the Feldon is a matter of significance for those who attempt population estimates for Roman Britain and Anglo-Saxon England. Pre-Conquest charter boundary descriptions record more scattered farmsteads in Arden than in the Feldon, frequently with *-worth* names suggesting enclosures in the woodland (Hooke 1985, pp. 138, 141). Furthermore, in the light of the Wednesbury group of pagan names, parts of the woodland may have been cult centres, with particular deities associated with specific stretches of woodland and groves. In earlier centuries, according to Tacitus, there were numerous examples of woodland and groves used as cult centres by the German peoples: 'they make sacred woods and groves, and call by the names of gods that hidden presence which they see only in awe' (Tacitus, *Germany*, 9). Attempts have been made to link the Godiva legend, located at Coventry in the Arden woodland, with pagan ritual (*VCH Warwickshire VIII* 1969, pp. 242-7). Particularly appealing in this context is the cult of Nerthus or Mother Earth, common to various peoples of northern Germany (including the *Anglii*): it was centred on an island off the coast, in a sacred grove with a hidden lake (Tacitus, *Germany*, 40). While the idea of such links has been repudiated by Davidson (1960, p. 87), and Hutton (1997, pp. 408-27) has warned of the dangers of assuming an unwarranted antiquity for most such survivals, the Wednesbury cluster of names may well indicate such a woodland cult centre, and may account for the establishment of the Mercian see at Lichfield, just north of the cluster, as a response by Christian missionaries (Gelling 1992, p. 96).

Despite the emphasis we have placed on the woodland/open land contrast in the West Midlands, it would be wrong to regard each of these regions as a uniform entity, or indeed as possessing impermeable boundaries. The open land of the Central Province can be seen in Fig. 7.1 to have been a predominant but not universal characteristic of that territory: in the eleventh century there were still significant patches of woodland, though many of these were later incorporated into the pattern of extensive townfields. Harold Fox's study of the Midland

'wold' regions, which extend marginally into Warwickshire, has indicated that they possessed distinctive wood-pasture resources until the eleventh and twelfth centuries, when they were being assimilated into the surrounding, predominantly arable systems (Fox 1989, pp. 81, 85, 89, 101). Similarly, there were many variations in the Anglo-Saxon woodland region. Hooke (1981, p. 53, figs 11-13), for example, has plotted hedges and enclosure features mentioned in charter boundary descriptions, and has noted marked concentrations in central Worcestershire, as against the north-west of the county where there were extensive woodlands but far fewer indications of enclosure, and where there may have been far less assarting activity. In some parts of the woodland there were small areas of open field, associated with hamlets; elsewhere, as at Oldberrow, there had been far less development by the time of Domesday Book (Hooke 1985a, pp. 143-5).

WOODLAND AND OPEN LAND IN THE ROMAN PERIOD

Returning to Ford's general conclusion about the patterning of woodland and open land in Warwickshire, there is also evidence for the stability of the main boundary from Roman to early Anglo-Saxon times. The contrast is clear between those parts of his study area which have produced concentrations of Romano-British settlement traces, and those parts where such traces are sparse, where the only significant Romano-British activity in the archaeological record is in the form of industries which would have relied upon managed, coppiced woodland for fuel. The contrast is also evident in place-names. To the west of the Fosse Way – and west of the woodland/open land boundary – the Romano-British names of a line of stations along Watling Street survived to be adopted into the English language: from *Manduessedum* (Mancetter), meaning 'horse chariot', to Wroxeter (Rivet 1979, pp. 411-12; Gelling 1992, pp. 55-6). They include *Letocetum*, meaning 'grey wood', attached to the Roman station at Wall, recorded in post-Roman times as *Caer Luitcoed* and surviving in the name Lichfield (Rivet 1979, pp. 387-8; Gelling 1992, pp. 59-61, 72-3). East of the Fosse Way, in the open land, however, there were no such name survivals, a contrast which again could be argued to derive from different experiences of woodland and open land dwellers.

More fundamentally, the patterning of woodland and open land may have been a major consideration in the Roman conquest of Britain and the structures which that conquest produced (Fig. 7.5b). At least in the minds of Roman historians, the legions had usually no difficulty in gaining rapid and effective control of open land, but found enemies who used woodland as a basis for resistance far harder to overcome. When, for example, Germanicus crossed the River Weser in A.D. 16, he found that some of his enemies had occupied woodland which was sacred to the god Hercules. Tacitus records his exhortation to his troops, to the effect that, if they used the correct tactics, they could fight just as well in woodland as in open land: *Non campos modo militi Romano ad proelium bonos, sed si ratio adsit, silvas et saltus* (Tacitus, *Annals* II. 14). The implication is, of course, that his troops were unsure of their chances of success in woodland, understandably in view of the earlier destruction of Varus' legions in the Teutoburgian Forest, where the tribunes and chief centurions had been slaughtered at altars in the groves (*ibid.*, I. 61). And, in Britain, Caesar had met considerable resistance from Cassivellaunus in the tracts of forest to the north of London (Caesar, *Gallic War* V, 19), where extensive woodland survived throughout the first millennium A.D. (Fig. 7.1).

Sheppard Frere (1991, pp. 56-7) mapped the principal structural elements which he attributed to the Julio-Claudian province of Britain, and identified the Fosse Way as the base line for its frontier. Figure 7.5b indicates that, in the West Midlands, the Fosse Way skirts the areas which we have postulated as woodland, and would have formed the arterial route through the principal tract of open, cultivated land. West of the Fosse Way, there appears to have been an intricate network of roads and forts, including Watling Street, which could be seen as the means of controlling the well-wooded areas, of dividing them into manageable blocks. The disposition of the early province was determined not by some vague concept of 'lowland' Britain, but by the actual patterns of woodland and open land that had direct strategic implications for the army commanders.

We have already discussed the religious significance of woodland to the peoples of Germany who opposed Rome. In Britain, it led Suetonius Paulinus to take his legions to Anglesey, to demolish the sacred groves there (Tacitus, *Annals* XIV, 30). As has been argued for the early Anglo-Saxon period, the woodlands of the West Midlands might similarly have contained cult centres in the first century A.D. The curious name of Mancetter, 'horse-chariot', has been suggested by Gelling (1992, pp. 55-6) as having sporting connections; it might alternatively have a religious significance: as Rivet noted cryptically 'some local legend may be involved' (1969, p. 412). Mancetter lies on the well-defined edge of the Warwickshire woodland, and is also one of the locations postulated for the battle between Suetonius Paulinus and Boudicca: 'The description suggests a sudden change from open plain to thick woodland' (Webster 1978, p. 97 and fig. 5). Further south, on the woodland edge near Baginton (Fig. 7.4d), is *The Lunt*, the location of another Roman station. It seems to have been occupied for less than twenty years, beginning with the Boudiccan revolt (Hobley 1975, p. 3). The famous

and unique circular structure within the fort, which caused the eastern defences to take a sinuous course around it, was identified by the excavator as a possible gyrus for cavalry training, or a *vivarium* for empounding wild animals (Hobley 1973, pp. 32-4). Neither of these suggestions explains the apparent need for it to be within the fort's defences. Webster (1978, pp. 109-11) has suggested it was used for sorting and grading horses captured after the Boudiccan revolt, and for training the better sort for military use. But why was the training/sorting ring built *within* the defences, and why was the entrance placed towards the interior of the fort, behind the *principia*, rather than facing a gateway? Returning to the religious theme, Tacitus records that the peoples of Germany were particularly attracted to divination, and placed greatest reliance on white horses which were kept in the sacred woods and groves, and which had never been used for mundane purposes. The horses were yoked to a sacred chariot, and their neighing or snorting was observed and interpreted by accompanying elders or priests (Tacitus, *Germany*, X). Might the 'horse-chariot' of Mancetter be a reference to similar rituals? Would it be too fanciful to suggest that the woodlands of the West Midlands contained sacred groves with horses that were used for divination, and that these animals were taken under control by the Romans at *The Lunt* in the aftermath of the Boudiccan revolt? The entrance to the gyrus seems to be carefully aligned to the southern end of a long building initially called 'Barrack Block 3', but which, as the excavator concluded, showed none of the hallmarks of a barrack block. It could have been stabling for 'special' horses. Immediately to the north was a granary (Hobley 1973, pp. 27-8; 1975, fig.1).

C. E. Stevens (1976, pp. 240-2) identified a possible area of sacred woodland in central Devon on the basis of the distribution of place-names incorporating the word *nemeton*, although his comment that this topic might be more use to the novelist rather than the prehistorian highlights the problems of dealing with such issues. They are, nevertheless, worth some consideration. A further case in question would be that of *Vernemetum*, Willoughby on the Wolds, Nottinghamshire, the 'very sacred grove' or 'the great sacred grove' (Rivet 1969, p. 495), perhaps already set amid tracts of largely cleared land (Wager 1998).

CONCLUSION

'Woodland', comprising of course timbered tracts, degraded areas and heathlands – something we have not discussed here – was not simply and only under-developed open land; it was used for specific purposes by the its occupants, purposes which could not be fulfilled by the resources of the open land. Similarly 'open land' must have contained many local woodland survivals (Wager

1998). It is hardly new to argue that in Roman and Anglo-Saxon times the woodlands were extensive, but it is new to suggest there is evidence that the boundaries between them and the open land were already well marked by the time of the Roman conquest, and that the patterns then present were part of landscape developments persisting for two or more millennia. Furthermore, we would argue that the varying rhythms of human activity to which these patterns gave rise are in some ways more fundamental than the chronological distinctions – Roman, Anglo-Saxon, medieval – which archaeologists perceive in surviving material culture. The implications of this argument for the reading of prehistoric cultural remains are considerable.

BIBLIOGRAPHY

Armstrong, A. M., Mawer, A., Stenton, F. M., & Dickens, B., 1950. *The Place-Names of Cumberland*, Engl Place-Name Soc, 20, 21 and 22 (Cambridge).

Caesar, *Gallic War*, trans. H. J. Edwards (Cambridge, Mass.).

Cameron, K., 1996. *English Place-Names* (London).

Cox, B., 1973. 'The place-names of the earliest English records', *Engl Place-Name Soc J*, 8, pp. 12-66.

Darby, H. C., *et al.* (ed.), 1952-77. *The Domesday Geography of England*, 7 vols, (Cambridge): *The Domesday Geography of Eastern England*, 1952; *The Domesday Geography of Midland England*, 1954; *The Domesday Geography of South-East England*, 1962a; *The Domesday Geography of Northern England*, 1962b; *The Domesday Geography of South-West England*, 1967; *Domesday Gazetteer*, 1975; *Domsday England*, 1977 (Cambridge).

Davidson, H. E., 1960. *Patterns of Folklore* (repr 1978; Ipswich & Totowa, N.J., U.S.A.).

Dugdale, W. Sir, 1656. *The Antiquities of Warwickshire* (London).

Dyer, C., 1996. 'Rural settlements in medieval Warwickshire', *Trans Birmingham & Warwickshire Archaeol Soc*, 100, pp. 117-32.

Eckwall, E., 1960. *The Concise Oxford Dictionary of English Place-Names* (4th edn, Oxford).

Ford, W. J., 1976. 'Some settlement patterns in the central region of the Warwickshire Avon', in *Medieval Settlement*, ed. Sawyer, pp. 274-94.

Fox, H. S. A., 1989. 'The people of the wolds in English settlement history', in *The Rural Settlements of Medieval England*, ed. M. Aston, D. Austin & C. Dyer (Oxford), pp. 77-101.

Fraser, C. M., 1968. *The Northumberland Lay Subsidy Roll of 1296* (Newcastle upon Tyne).

Frere, S., 1987, 1991. *Britannia* (3rd edn 1987, repr 1991, London).

Gelling, M., 1978. *Signposts to the Past* (London).

Gelling, M., 1984. *Place-Names in the Landscape* (London).

Gelling, M., 1992. *The West Midlands in the Early Middle Ages* (Leicester).

Gover, J. E. B., Mawer, A., & Stenton, F. M., 1936. *The Place-Names of Warwickshire*, Engl Place-Name Soc, 13 (Cambridge).

Harmer, F. M., 1952. *Anglo-Saxon Writs* (Manchester).

Hilton, R. H., 1966. *A Medieval Society: the West Midlands at the end of the thirteenth century* (London).

Hobley, B., 1973. 'Excavations at "The Lunt" Roman military site, second interim report', *Trans Birmingham & Warwickshire Archaeol Soc*, 85, for 1971-3, pp. 7-92.

Hobley, B., 1975. "The Lunt" Roman fort and training school for Roman cavalry, Baginton, Warwickshire', *Trans Birmingham & Warwickshire Archaeol Soc*, 87, pp. 1-56.

Hooke, D., 1981. 'Open-field agriculture – the evidence from the pre-Conquest charters of the West Midlands', in *The Origins of Open Field Agriculture*, ed. T. Rowley (London), pp. 39-63.

Hooke, D., 1985a. 'Village development in the West Midlands', in *Medieval Villages*, ed. D. Hooke, Oxford Univ Comm Archaeol Monogr no. 5 (Oxford), pp. 125-54.

Hooke, D., 1985b. *The Anglo-Saxon Landscape: the Kingdom of the Hwicce* (Manchester).

Hooke, D., 1996. 'Reconstructing Anglo-Saxon landscapes in Warwickshire', *Trans Birmingham & Warwickshire Archaeol Soc*, 100, pp. 99-116.

Hooke, D., 1998. *The Landscape of Anglo-Saxon England* (London & Washington).

Hutton, R., 1997. *The Stations of the Sun* (Oxford).

Jones, G. R. J., 1990. 'Celts, Saxons and Scandinavians', in *An Historical Geography of England and Wales*, 2nd edn, ed. R. A. Dodgshon & R. A. Butlin (London), pp. 45-68.

Margary, H. (publ), 1975-1981. *The Old Series Ordnance Survey Maps of England and Wales*, 8 vols (Lympne Castle, Kent).

Mawer, A., & Stenton, F. M., 1929. *Introduction to the Survey of English Place-Names*, Part 1, Engl Place-Name Soc, 1 (Cambridge).

Rackham, O., 1986. *The History of the British Countryside* (London).

Rivet, A. L. F., 1979. *The Place-Names of Roman Britain* (London).

Roberts, B. K., 1973. 'Field systems of the West Midlands', in *Studies of Field Systems in the British Isles*, ed. A. R. H. Baker & R. A. Butlin (Cambridge), pp. 188-231.

Roberts, 1982. 'Village forms in Warwickshire: a preliminary discussion', in *Field and Forest: an historical geography of Warwickshire and Worcestershire*, ed. T. R. Slater & P. J. Jarvis (Norwich), pp. 125-46.

Roberts. B. K., & Wrathmell, S., 2000. *An Atlas of Rural Settlement in England*, Engl Heritage (London).

Sawyer, P. H. (ed.), 1976. *Medieval Settlement: Continuity and Change* (London).

Smith, A. H., 1956. *English Place-Name Elements*, 2 vols, Engl Place-Name Soc, 25 and 26 (Cambridge).

Smith, A. H., 1967. *The Place-Names of Westmorland*, Engl Place-Name Soc, 42 and 43 (Cambridge).

Stamp, L. D. (ed.), 1937-44. *The Land of Britain*, County Fascicles, R Geogr Soc (London).

Stamp, L. D. (ed.), 1962. *The Land of Britain: its Use and Misuse* (3rd edn, enlarged, London).

Strevens, C. E., 1976. 'The sacred wood', in *To Illustrate the Monuments*, ed. J. V. S. Megaw (London).

Sylvester, D., 1969. *The Rural Landscape of the Welsh Borderland* (London).

Tacitus, *Annals, Books I-III*, trans. J. Jackson. (Cambridge, Mass.).

Tacitus, *Gemany*, trans. M. Hutton (Cambridge, Mass.).

Thirsk, J., 1987. *England's Agricultural Regions and Agrarian History, 1500-1750* (London).

Wager, S. J., 1998. *Woods, Wolds and Groves: the woodland of medieval Warwickshire*, Br Archaeol Rep, Br ser 269 (Oxford).

Watts, V. E., 1976. 'Comment on "The evidence of place-names" by Margaret Gelling', in *Medieval Settlement*, ed. Sawyer, pp. 212-22.

Webster, G., 1978. *Boudicca* (London).

Wilcox. H. A., 1933. *The Woodlands and Marshlands of England* (London).

VCH Warwickshire VIII, 1969. *The Victoria History of the County of Warwick*, 8, ed. W. B. Stephens, Inst Hist Research (Oxford).

Understanding the landscape of towns

T. R. Slater

ABSTRACT

This paper examines developments in understanding the landscape of towns since the 1970s, the role of rescue archaeology resulting from urban growth in the 1960s-1980s, and the effect of urban conservation planning. The introduction of town-plan analysis in a British and European context is also discussed.

KEYWORDS

Atlases, rescue archaeology, town-plan analysis, urban growth

INTRODUCTION

Analysis of the landscape of towns has been conspicuous by its absence in the pages of *Landscape History*. In twenty-one years there have been only five papers dealing with urban topics; three on Anglo-Saxon towns in England, one on nineteenth-century Welsh towns, and one, incongruously, on a nineteenth-century Himalayan hill-town (Atkin 1985; Carter 1982; Haslam 1987; 1988; Rawat 1994). This absence of the urban in landscape studies must be seen as one of the consequences of the intellectual origins of English landscape history. The cult of the picturesque from the eighteenth century; the equating of the cultivated, enclosed countryside of lowland England with notions of Englishness (Matless 1998), together with a longing for the rural past consequent on the development of capitalistic industry, has meant that 'landscape' as a term tends to be equated with notions of rurality and the countryside, rather than with the urban and towns. The two are perceived oppositionally, rather than as two parts of the same landscape. One influential example is the polemical writing of the concluding chapter of Hoskins's *The Making of the English Landscape* (1955) which makes clear that, in the author's eyes, the urban and the industrial have little place in landscape studies except as a lament for better times past. It is no surprise to find that, in the series of county volumes that were being published through the 1970s under Hoskins's editorship, urban landscapes were confined to a single chapter in each volume (an 'othering' of the urban from the otherwise temporal structure of these books) where writers could do little more than sample the rich diversity of medieval, early modern and industrial townscapes in their county. Otherwise excellent county historical atlases have similar structures (Wade-Martins 1993; Leslie & Short 1999). Consequently, in reviewing the progress made in understanding the physical landscape of pre-industrial towns and cities in the past two decades, it is necessary to look elsewhere for analyses and descriptions that have enhanced our understanding.

SYNTHESIS

Beginning with the general, the mid-1970s was a period in which a number of popular books were published, from a variety of academic perspectives, which attempted to summarise the advances made in urban studies over the previous two decades. Historian Susan Reynolds relegated the topographical aspect of English medieval towns to nine pages at the end of her textbook (Reynolds 1977, pp.188-96). However, the previous year, historical geographers Michael Aston and James Bond had provided a popular account of the full chronological history of English urban landscapes from the prehistoric period to the present, richly illustrated with maps and plans (Aston & Bond 1976). In the same year, Colin Platt's equally well-illustrated book provided a judicious blend of building history, social history and archaeology for a general audience (Platt 1976). The topography of the English medieval town has continued to be well served by such summarising volumes in the two decades since, though almost all have been concerned to provide an overview of the rich evidence provided by urban archaeological excavations (Carver 1987; Ottaway 1992; Schofield & Vince 1994).

It is, of course, the archaeological evidence that has continued to dominate most discussion of urban landscape change though, since the slowdown in large-scale rescue excavations from the late 1980s, more attention has subsequently been paid to interdisciplinary studies which set that archaeological evidence in historical, social, architectural and geographical contexts. The sheer quantity of new archaeological evidence through the 1970s and 1980s led to the publication of other synthesising books which concentrated on particular temporal periods. Thus a new revised edition of Wacher's volume on the larger Roman towns appeared in 1995 (Wacher 1995), joining his book on the small towns published with Barry Burnham five years previously (Burnham & Wacher 1990). Together, they form a comprehensive survey of the evidence for the landscape of Roman towns in Britain.

Clarke and Ambrosiani's (1991) survey of towns in the Viking age is unusual in taking a wider north-European perspective of the whole Baltic, North, and Irish Sea coastlands, whilst Haslam's (1984) collection of essays on the Anglo-Saxon towns of southern England are stimulating, controversial and annoying in equal measure.

Soulsby (1983) provided a survey of the historical and archaeological evidence for medieval Welsh towns, largely in the form of a comprehensive gazetteer, but the book is marred by poor cartography. The landscape of medieval Scottish towns is even less well served, despite a considerable increase in the number of archaeological excavations taking place there. The collection of essays edited by Lynch et al. (1988), has some topographical material, as does Ewan's (1990) survey of the fourteenth century. The Scottish burgh survey is bringing together historical and archaeological material for selected towns (Torrie & Coleman 1996), but a review of the archaeology and landscape of Scottish medieval towns as a whole is badly needed. By contrast, revisionist studies of Irish urban landscapes, stimulated by the excavation of the spectacular archaeological deposits of Norse Dublin, are legion. Graham (1993) has provided a national summary from an historical geographical viewpoint and Barry (1987) does the same from an archaeological perspective. Clarke (1990) usefully edited a collection of journal articles on Dublin, many of them with a topographical or buildings focus, into a single book. The most comprehensive medieval urban landscape research, blending historical and archaeological evidence, and informed by plan analysis, is probably that published by Bradley (1985, 1990) deriving from his work with the Urban Archaeology Survey of Ireland. The new *Cambridge Urban History of Britain* (Palliser 2000; Clark 2000) provides a new benchmark of synthesis and contains much topographical material in wider social and economic contexts, though the series excludes Ireland. Clearly, the study of the pre-modern urban landscape has been well served by synthesising texts over the past two decades and we can move on to ask what are the debates and themes that have exercised researchers over this period?

TEMPORAL THEMES AND DEBATES

For the Roman urban landscape, three debates predominate. First, interesting and still controversial statistical work by Faulkner (2000) on the building fabric has attempted to both chart the long-term decline of Roman towns in Britain from the early third century, to differentiate between the fortunes of particular towns, and to describe the very different landscape to be found in the military-bureaucratic towns of the fourth century. Secondly, there is discussion on the consequences for towns of the conversion to Christianity. Here Charles Thomas's book (1981) has been the stimulus for new research and findings on burial grounds (where the excavations at Poundbury, outside Dorchester, have brought new insights), church buildings (Morris 1989, pp. 6-45), the administrative landscape (Bassett 1992a; 1992b), and the preservation of *romanitas* through the migration period (Brooks 2000). Thirdly, there has been continuing debate and controversy about the end of Roman Britain and whether there was a consequent decay of towns or continuity in many aspects of life and landscape. Esmonde Cleary (1989) usefully brings much of the evidence together. Twenty years ago many researchers were suggesting that there were numerous elements of continuity in the life and landscape of towns between the Roman and Anglo-Saxon periods. As more urban excavations were evaluated and published the pendulum gradually swung and a new consensus had emerged that, in Britain, almost all Roman towns lost their urban functions and were re-established in the seventh or eighth centuries. The recent publication of the final reports on the excavations at Wroxeter by Barker et al. (1997) and Webster (1999), though already well known from interim reports, has re-ignited the debate by stating that the evidence suggests that Wroxeter continued as a functioning town into the seventh century (White 2000) and that there is similar evidence elsewhere.

For the early medieval period, a time of consolidating new archaeological knowledge about international trading emporia of the eighth and ninth centuries (the *wics*), and about the *burh* settlements of the late ninth and tenth centuries, has been followed by the posing of new questions as to the economic, social and political significance of these towns in the consolidation of the English kingdom. Undoubtedly, the five key places in providing the data for these new interpretations and debates have been London, Southampton, Winchester, York and Dublin, and most of the data have been archaeological. The numerous and extensive excavations in the City of London, Southwark and Westminster have seen at least four major advances in our understanding of the early medieval urban landscape. First, the changing character of the Thames waterfront has been revealed, with its increasingly sophisticated carpentry and massive increase in scale. This knowledge has been integrated into a wider understanding of waterfront developments in north and west European cities in this period (Milne & Hobley 1981; Milne 1992; Good et al. 1991). Secondly, has been the discovery of middle

Saxon *Londonwic*, to the west of the city, centred on Aldwych (Vince 1990, pp. 13-25). Thirdly has been the consequent re-evaluation of Alfredian London and the move back into the city walls; and fourth has been the detailed investigation of the site of London Bridge and the trans-pontine suburb at Southwark (Dyson & Schofield 1984; Vince 1990).

The excavations at Winchester in the 1970s were among the first to suggest the necessity for a re-evaluation of the urban landscapes of the early medieval period. They were especially significant in transforming our understanding of the nature of the *burhs* founded by Alfred. Winchester showed for the first time that many of these places were carefully planned towns, laid out without reference to earlier Roman streets and buildings, and with a distinctive topography of their own (Biddle & Hill 1971). Other excavations revealed the long building history of the cathedral church and its preceding 'old minster' in this same period (Biddle 1970). Full publication of the excavations is still awaited, but the framework is now well known from summary articles.

The excavations at *Hamwic* (middle Saxon Southampton) were already well known in the late 1970s and have continued to provide the yardstick for such international trading emporia in Britain. The town is now known to have been at least 50 *per cent* bigger than thought in 1969 and, like the other *wics*, it was a densely-occupied settlement of at least 45 ha with timber houses/workshops built around a grid of gravel streets (Brisbane 1988; Ottaway 1992, pp. 122-7). Ipswich was of similar significance, but few of the results from the excavations there have reached publication.

At York it was the excavations at Coppergate of part of the Viking age settlement of *Jorvik*, subsequently enshrined in the Jorvik Centre museum, which have dominated both academic and popular perception of the early medieval city (Hall 1984). The waterlogged deposits provided enormous quantities of environmental data as well as stunning evidence for the built structures of houses and craft workshops (Hall 1988). More recently, Anglian York (*Eoferwic*) has been located further to the south of the city centre.

The excavations in Dublin were on-going at much the same time as those in York and revealed a similar Viking age town from the waterlogged deposits. There, however, the discoveries were attended by political controversy and for some time there was the likelihood that nothing would be properly excavated and analysed (Heffernen 1988). The publication of the excavations demonstrated the very short life of buildings in the tenth and eleventh centuries, requiring rebuilding every twenty or thirty years (Wallace 1992). Excavations in Waterford, another of the Viking *wics* on the Irish Sea coast, have shown a similar pattern of development. A parallel debate in Irish urban historiography has been over the

role played by monasteries in the emergence of towns in the eleventh century and their uniquely 'Irish' characteristics. Most commentators have suggested that in both their plans and in their socio-ecomomic and political status, Irish monastic towns are peculiarly Irish (Doherty 1985). Brian Graham has recently tried to reattach these places to a broader European context by suggesting that they are simply a variant of a wider urban type (Graham 1998).

There have, of course, been many other important early medieval urban excavations. The changing topography of late Saxon Norwich is now much better appreciated thanks to a long series of excavations in the city (Ottaway 1992, pp. 155-61), and similarly with Lincoln (Steane & Vince 1993). Both these cities are important for our understanding of the topographical consequences of the Norman Conquest. Thus far, the landscape evidence for urban change in the eleventh century has not been consolidated. Rowley's volumes on the Normans (1983, 1999), with their single chapters on towns, is perhaps the nearest we get. The impact and disruption of the Norman rebuilding of cathedrals and monasteries in towns are well illustrated by the Winchester excavations on the Cathedral Green. At York, and at Norwich, the new cathedrals were on new alignments and, with enlarged precincts eventually becoming bounded by walls and separate jurisdictions, the thrust of urban expansion was redirected.

The urban castles were even more disruptive, of course, as the evidence of demolished houses recorded in Domesday Book demonstrates. Again, the excavations in Norwich (Brisbane 1988; Ottaway 1992) have done much to show the scale of earth-moving and ditch-digging in the centre of a very prosperous and populous town. At Worcester, the new castle took up a large part of the cathedral priory's precinct, while in Hereford, and at Warwick, churches were in the way and were consequently demolished. The successive enlargement of these urban castles taking in even more urban land is well shown by the case of Gloucester (Hurst 1984) (Fig. 8.1). Earth-moving was nothing new, of course, as recent work on Worcester has shown. There the bishop had organised the townspeople to infill the substantial Roman ditch to allow the town to be expanded in the tenth or eleventh century (Baker *et al.* 1992) (Fig. 8.2). More research on what we might term 'the ground-works' of urban development processes is badly needed.

The Normans were not content simply to build, or rebuild, these townscape-dominant buildings, they also expanded many towns with new market places, streets and plots, notably at Hereford, Northampton, Nottingham and Warwick, as well as the huge quasi-rectangular grid-planned extension to Bury St Edmunds. Planning new towns from scratch was therefore a very small step further. Recent research by Lilley (1995, 1999)

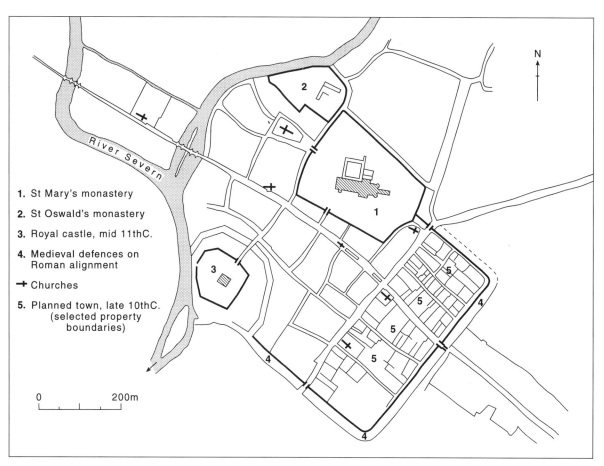

1. St Mary's monastery

2. St Oswald's monastery

3. Royal castle, mid 11thC.

4. Medieval defences on Roman alignment

✚ Churches

5. Planned town, late 10thC. (selected property boundaries)

0   200m

Fig. 8.1. Early medieval Gloucester: institutions and town planning (based on Baker & Holt 2001).

in Hampshire and south Wales has begun to reveal the enormous variety of plan forms laid out by Norman landholders in these areas and to show that the towns were carefully devised for their location and expectations. A single landholder often laid out very different town plans in different places: the de Redvers family, Earls of Devon, for example, had both an impressive quasi-rectangular grid-plan town at Newport, Isle of Wight, founded in 1189-91, where commerce was the predominant motive for foundation, and a classic 'castle town' at Plympton, Devon, founded in the 1140s, and dominated by a huge motte and bailey which was the administrative centre of the honour (Bearman 1994). The latter was especially characteristic of the Norman conquest of south Wales and the Marches, and the grander plans of towns such as Carmarthen, Haverfordwest and Monmouth were preceded by much smaller castle towns, often established within the outer bailey of the castle (Soulsby 1983; Lilley 1995).

For the period of rapid urban development from the eleventh to the thirteenth century, topographical research in the past two decades has sought to flesh out the framework provided by Maurice Beresford's still-admired volume on medieval new towns (Beresford 1967). There has also been much work on the social and economic development of towns in this period so that different sources of evidence can now be combined to provide a rich texture of urban life

and landscape. In terms of topography, one body of work comes from historical geographers and will be considered separately below, but archaeologists have also been exploring the landscape of the high medieval town.

To begin with, the large number of county-based 'implications of development' reports published in the 1970s and 1980s (*e.g.* Rodwell 1974; Leech 1981) provided useful reviews of the topographic development of smaller market towns, though most were not aware of the evidence of plan analysis. More recently, the much more detailed surveys commissioned by English Heritage of particular cities have begun to be published, but they concentrate exclusively on the archaeological evidence (see Lowther *et al.* 1993 for example) with the specific aim of providing guidance to planning authorities. By contrast, the Urban Archaeological Survey of Ireland is much more encompassing in its written and cartographic evidence, but is unpublished.

URBAN BUILDINGS

There has been an increasing interest in researching the third dimension of the urban landscape over the past twenty years, but our understanding of rural buildings, and European research on urban buildings, is still well in advance of our knowledge of British townscapes. Perhaps

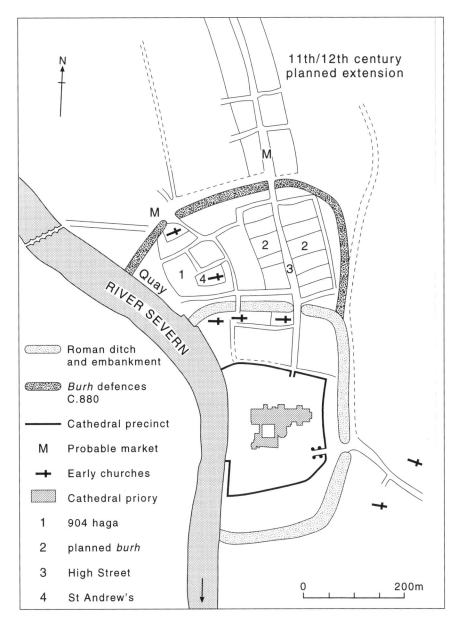

11th/12th century
planned extension

N

M

M

Quay

2

2

1 4 3

RIVER SEVERN

Roman ditch
and embankment

Burh defences
C.880

Cathedral precinct

M   Probable market

+   Early churches

Cathedral priory

1   904 haga

2   planned *burh*

3   High Street

4   St Andrew's

0   200m

Fig. 8.2. Early medieval
Worcester: cathedral precinct
and town planning (based on
Baker & Holt 2001).

the best-known medieval urban buildings are
churches, but it is only in the last quarter-century
that churches have begun to be put into their
social, economic, and landscape settings. Richard
Morris's volume (1989, pp. 168-226) was
something of a landmark in synthesising what had
been learnt up to then. Important themes have
included the multiplicity of lay-founded churches
in Anglo-Saxon towns, which contrast with single-
parish later-established towns; the possible
significance of distinctive church dedications; the
formation of parish boundaries in the later Anglo-
Saxon period; and the relationship between
church and market place. More recently, there
has been a considerable debate about the role of
minster churches in the development of market
towns in the later Anglo-Saxon period. Blair's early
work on the little Oxfordshire town of Bampton
(Blair 1998) has been developed and refined in
many papers and book chapters to the extent that
it is becoming the new orthodoxy (Blair 1988,
1992, 1996), but some authors still say that the

royal *villa regalis* was of equal or superior
significance in the development of an urban
economy.

Archaeologists have excavated and analysed
extensive sections of urban defences dating from
the Anglo-Saxon to the later medieval but there
has been no synthesising account to supersede
Turner's (1971) early account for England and
Wales. It may be that the sheer volume of material
now available has deterred such a summary,
though Jones and Bond (1987) go some way to
making good the deficiency. Amongst the single
city excavations, pride of place should properly
go to those uncovering the Anglo-Saxon defences
of Hereford (Shoesmith 1982) and to the
excavation and survey of the upstanding walls
and gates of York (RCHME 1972). Ireland has been
better served in that, though there have been far
fewer excavations, the landscape, historical and
cartographic evidence has been thoroughly
surveyed by A. Thomas (1992).

Research on medieval urban housing is still notable for its general absence, though there have been some important advances in recent years. Schofield's fine study of London houses (1994) concentrates on the grander houses of the later medieval capital for the most part, whereas Goodburn's work (Milne 1992) on the earlier archaeological evidence for London, amassed from many excavations, shows that the development of timber-framed construction for housing in the later twelfth century must have transformed the urban landscape in two ways. First, buildings became as valuable as land in towns because they now lasted for more than twenty or twenty-five years; and secondly, multi-storey living became possible since two- or three-storey buildings could be constructed. A consequence of this development was that urban populations were able to increase substantially without recourse to extending urban built-up areas. Elsewhere, a major research project has been conducted on The Rows of Chester to try to ascertain their origin (Brown 1999), whilst other extensive urban excavation programmes in cities such as Exeter, Norwich, Winchester and York have provided material for synthesis. Pearson is now beginning to expand her important work on Kentish medieval houses (1994) into towns such as Faversham and Sandwich and the Vernacular Architecture Group has undertaken surveys of late medieval urban buildings in towns such as Bury St Edmunds, Lavenham and Lincoln in the tradition pioneered by Pantin (1947) many decades ago. Urban inns are a specialised category of building in which interest has revived recently: for example a multi-disciplinary study of a fourteenth-century Oxford inn looks to wider connotations (Munby 1992) whilst Smith's (1992, pp. 135-54) study of Hertfordshire towns has sections on urban inns, and on the specialised warehouse and shop buildings found in the middle of market places.

TOWN PLANS

The distinctive contribution of historical geography to studies of the urban landscape comes from town-plan analysis. The early work of M. R .G. Conzen (1960, 1962, 1968) provided a firm foundation upon which others have continued to build. Slater's work (1980) on the metrological analysis of plot series has provided new insights into the planning of medieval new towns in the twelfth and thirteenth centuries, developing many of the themes propounded by Beresford (1967). The rich documentation and well-preserved townscape of Stratford-upon-Avon was especially important in establishing the practicalities of these techniques of analysis (Slater 1987, 1998a). Some of his detailed case studies of smaller towns in the West Midlands have shown the remarkable inventiveness of those responsible for laying out and developing the towns. They

have also demonstrated the truth of Conzen's ideas on the composite nature of the plan of even quite small towns. Places such as Bridgnorth (Slater 1990), Ludlow (Slater 1987, 1988) or Burton-upon-Trent (Slater 1996a) were developed in as many as seven or eight different phases, most of which are clearly inscribed in the town plan (Fig. 8.3). Burton is especially instructive in this respect since the documentation of the town's abbey cartulary shows that the semi-rectangular street plan with associated plot series was developed in six separate phases over a period of just over a century, each consisting of a single street (Slater 1996a). Burton and Stratford also demonstrate the way in which earlier elements of the countryside were incorporated into town plans rather than go to the expense of removing them. In Burton the principal example is a droveway down to the Trent meadows (Fig. 8.3), and in Stratford the ridge and furrow of open-field furlongs are inscribed in the plan. The underlying gravel terraces also provided constraints for the planners who, sensibly, did not develop land on the flood plain.

These, and other studies (Slater 1985, 1988, 1998b) use Conzen's concept of the 'plan-unit' – an area of morphological homogeneity – to suggest chronologies of plan development. They can do no more unless the techniques of plan analysis are combined with historical and archaeological material in multi-disciplinary studies to provide firmer chronological foundations. In the 1990s a number of such studies on much larger English shire towns have been undertaken at the University of Birmingham. Some of the results of a major study of Gloucester and Worcester have been published (Baker *et al.* 1992; Baker & Slater 1992) and the full analysis should be in print soon (Baker & Holt 2001) (Fig. 8.1). The Worcester study was especially notable for firmly locating the famous 899 lease (Whitelock 1979) (Fig. 8.2). It also suggests that the topographical and archaeological evidence confirms the historical evidence of the charters that *hagas* in the *burh* were quite large areas of land (Hooke 1980) and that the typical long narrow burgages of the high medieval period are subdivisions of these properties. Gloucester provides important evidence on the build-up of properties on the market streets of the later medieval city and both cities have added material evidence on the debate about the origins of urban parish boundaries (Baker & Holt 1998).

Baker has also undertaken detailed multi-disciplinary research on Shrewsbury. Here, the evolution of a series of large plots sloping down from Pride Hill to the Severn on the north side of the meander core proved especially interesting and many of the stone-built cellars and foundations of medieval halls were found embedded in later rebuildings which had subsequently been much subdivided (Baker *et al.* 1993). Meanwhile, Lilley was tackling the largest medieval midland metropolis of Coventry in a

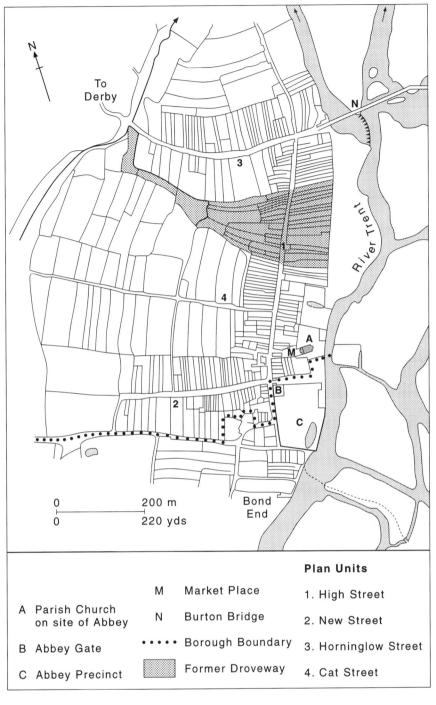

Plan Units

A Parish Church on site of Abbey

B Abbey Gate

C Abbey Precinct

M Market Place

N Burton Bridge

••••• Borough Boundary

▨ Former Droveway

1. High Street

2. New Street

3. Horninglow Street

4. Cat Street

Fig. 8.3. Burton-on-Trent: plan units and relict droveway (based on Slater 1996a).

doctoral study which again used multi-disciplinary sources (Lilley 1994a). This work provided the best evidence yet for the location of the enigmatic, but important, ring-work castle of the Earls of Chester at the heart of the city. It provided more detailed evidence for the character and chronology of the planned extension of the town over part of the earl's park in Much and Little Park Streets (Lilley 1998a), and it demonstrated that it was almost certainly the Benedictine abbey, founded by Leofric and Godiva in 1043 (Demidowicz 1994), that was responsible for the earliest development of the town about a large triangular market place at the west gate of the abbey precinct (Lilley 1994b, 1998b).

GEOMETRICAL KNOWLEDGE AND ORTHOGONAL PLANNING

The most significant symbol of urban planning to the eyes of those looking back from the twentieth century was the rectangular, geometrically precise grid plan. Thanks to the writing of planning historians in just about every European language realm, the grid of streets at right angles to one another is the recognised link in the continuity of the 'civilising' idea of planning between Roman times and the Renaissance. In the British Isles, however, the grid plan was exceptional, even amongst the numerous planned new towns of the twelfth and thirteenth centuries. Most towns continued to be laid out with a single 'High Street'

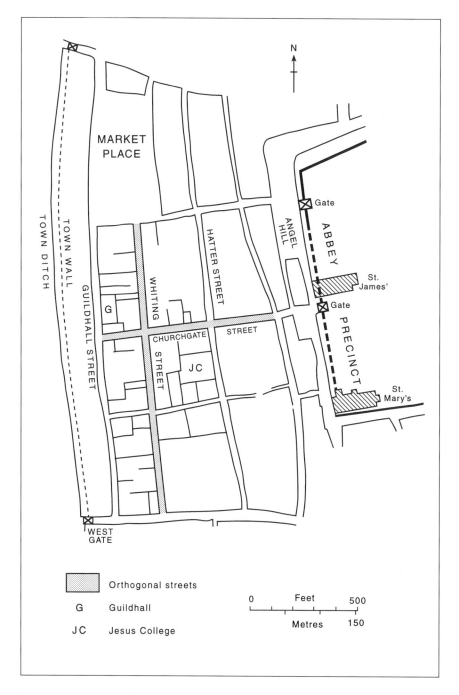

Fig. 8.4. The orthogonal cross of streets in Bury St Edmunds (based on Slater 1999).

layout, with a broadened street market place and rectangular plots on each side of the street.

True grid plans required geometrical knowledge on the part of those charged with laying out the town and, thanks to recent research by Burnett (1987, 1997) we have begun to understand the way in which this knowledge was transferred from the Islamic world, through the monasteries of the Mediterranean, to northern Europe. Here the key centre was the cathedral *scolasticus* at Liège. In the eleventh century a number of clerics trained at Liège were appointed to bishoprics and abbacies in England where they encouraged the diffusion of this new knowledge of geometry, as well as of astronomy, astrology and medicine. One of these Lotharinginian clerics was Giso, Bishop of Bath and Wells, and one of

his wealthy tenants, Fastrad, perhaps himself a Lotharingian, was the father of Adelard of Bath. Adelard was to become one of the greatest scholars of the twelfth century, responsible for the rediscovery of the principles of Euclidian geometry (Burnett 1987).

This specialised knowledge was used first in places with high-status lords, especially ecclesiastical lords. Bury St Edmunds, for example, was a monastic town which had an extensive library of mathematical manuscripts, including copies of Adelard's principal works (Burnett 1997). It is probably no accident, therefore, that its mid-eleventh-century town plan was an extensive grid which, whilst not generally orthogonal, had at its core two streets, which linked abbey gateway to market place, and which had been laid out at

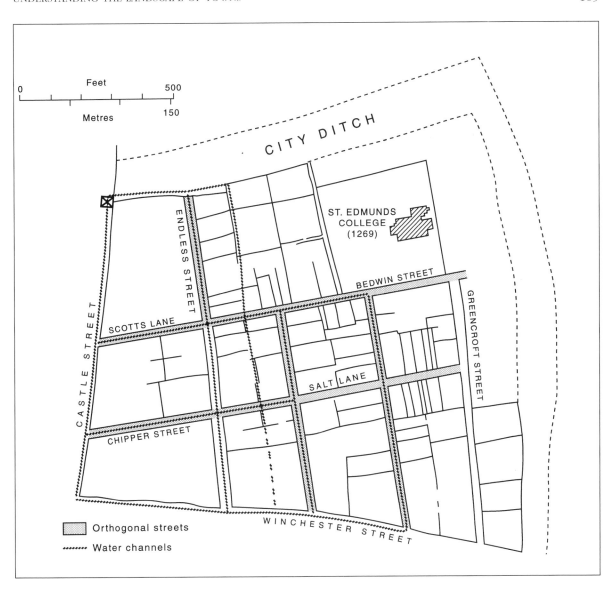

Fig. 8.5. The St Edmund's district of Salisbury showing water channels and orthogonal streets laid out in the 1260s; the ditch is a later addition authorised in 1367 (based on Slater 1999).

right angles to one another (Slater 1999) (Fig. 8.4). Orthogonal grid layouts are not found until the development of New Salisbury. Even here, the earliest phases of the town, dating from the 1220s, do not use orthogonal geometry. It is only with the development of the northern part of the city, adjacent to the collegiate church of St Edmund, in the 1260s, that the streets were laid out at right angles to one another (Fig. 8.5). King Edward I's Welsh bastide at Flint, and the newly sited port at New Winchelsea are late thirteenth-century examples of orthogonal planning (Beresford 1967).

In Gascony, and in the eastern European towns laid out under German law codes, in contrast with Britain, the orthogonal grid plan is almost ubiquitous from the later thirteenth century onwards. Towns in these regions were not developed by ecclesiastical lords. However, in both regions royal authority was critical and, in the same way that Adelard of Bath became the teacher of Henry II in England (Burnett 1997), other European royal houses, in their reliance on

monks and clergy for literary services to the state, were another channel for the diffusion of geometrical knowledge into practical planning.

Gascony was still, in part, within the purview of the English crown in the thirteenth century, hence its inclusion in Beresford's (1967) survey of new town founding. His work has now been supplemented by Lauret et al.'s (1988) analysis of the buildings and plans of this group of planned towns. Their distinguishing of two major, and two minor, sub-regional plan types is an important advance in our understanding of medieval town planning in this region. Bucher's (1979) careful analysis of Grenade-sur-Garrone, showing that its design was reliant on Euclidian geometry, added a further dimension to the story. The chronology and complexity of medieval planning is completed with Friedman's (1988) brilliant exposition of the planning of the Florentine new towns of San Giovanni Valdarno and Terranuova Bracciolini, in Tuscany, where, uniquely, sine geometry was used to determine the layout of street blocks in 1299 and 1337 respectively.

HISTORIC TOWNS ATLASES

This review of research on urban landscapes cannot conclude without some mention of the European Historic Towns Atlases. The British Historic Towns Atlas (Lobel 1969, 1975, 1989) was the first to begin publication. The long-term research and publication programme was devised under the aegis of the International Historical Congress. Of the British Atlas volumes, only the third, on medieval London, falls within the review period of this chapter but it epitomises the problems of the British Atlas as a whole. The aims of the atlas programme are deceptively simple; namely, to publish three plans of each selected city. First, an accurate cadastral plan in four colours at a scale of 1:2 500 based on the first accurately surveyed plan of the period immediately before industrial development (nominally c. 1830); secondly a regional map of the town at a scale of 1:2 5000; and thirdly a modern town plan at a scale of 1:5 000. The British Atlas volumes provide neither of the latter resources but do give additional maps of street names, parish and secular administrative boundaries and contours. They also provide substantial historical essays on the towns concerned. However, very few of these essays have a specific topographical focus and they relate to the maps only marginally. The London volume is especially at fault here since the text makes reference to the rapidly growing knowledge about the topography of Westminster, The Strand and Southwark, whilst the maps are confined to the City of London within the walls.

The atlas, despite its superficial beauty, resulting in generally eulogistic reviews, is a deeply flawed work (Slater 1996b). This is mainly because of the failure to assess critically the maps on which the enterprise was based. The atlas maps are based on different source maps of different dates which are not distinguished one from another. They also map with spurious accuracy an urban landscape that was poorly represented on the original source maps. These, for good reason, were often privately-surveyed plans of the late eighteenth century which did not have the accuracy of later Ordnance Survey plans, especially behind the street-frontage properties. By the time the latter were published in the second half of the nineteenth century many, if not most, British towns had already been transformed by a century or more of industrial growth. Any use of the British Atlas needs considerable care therefore. Other European countries have learnt from the mistakes of the British Atlas, and the similar mistakes made by the German atlas (Stoob 1973-93). In particular, the Irish Historic Towns Atlas, which began regular publication in 1986, is a model of accuracy and good editorial practice. It covers the whole of the island of Ireland and the first eight fascicles (Andrews *et al.* 1986-1999) have been carefully selected to represent the diversity of Irish town types. Paradoxically it was the British Ordnance Survey which provided for Ireland what it did not for Britain, namely accurate large-scale plans of Irish towns for the period 1832-42, before industrialisation had gathered pace.

CONCLUSIONS

Despite the comparative lack of academic interest in urban landscapes on the part of contributors to *Landscape History*, the past quarter century has been a period in which our knowledge of the pre-modern, or pre-industrial town in the British Isles has grown substantially. In terms of empirical information, archaeology has clearly been the driving force in expanding knowledge. Excavations in many historic towns and cities have revolutionised our understanding of the landscape of early medieval towns, as well as refining, or redefining, chronologies and providing information on living standards, commerce, trade and industry. Social and economic historians have often proved more adept at using these new empirical data to draw wider conclusions and redefine frameworks of knowledge about towns. Until quite recently, historical geographers have tended to use their techniques of analysis in isolation. The past fifteen years have seen a welcome growth of interdisciplinary studies and a growing propensity to use this variety of modes of analysis, and of data, on larger and more significant towns in the urban hierarchy. As a result of this work we now have a better understanding of medieval urban layouts, and of the way in which medieval towns were planned and developed in specific phases with distinct layouts and chronologies. We might hope that the spurious categorisation of complex town plans as 'organic' might soon be consigned to the dustbin of superseded ideas.

Knowledge of most categories of medieval urban buildings has also improved substantially. There are new ways of seeing even that much studied building type, the English parish church. Other ecclesiastical buildings are now better understood, again thanks to interdisciplinary studies, and many individual domestic, commercial and industrial building types have been studied in depth. The major revolution in our knowledge of buildings has been the recognition of the late twelfth century as a period in which urban building techniques were transformed. What is missing here is the synthesising of these case studies of different types on a regional or national basis so that we have a better understanding of their evolution through time and space. The other priority must be to integrate studies of the landscapes of medieval towns of England and Wales, first into studies of the British Isles (and it is Scotland, not Ireland, which is the poor relation here) and then into Europe-wide surveys. Towns, much more so than the countryside, are part of social, cultural and economic systems which are international in their scope and influences. Our knowledge systems should similarly be international and interdisciplinary wherever they can.

BIBLIOGRAPHY

Andrews, J. H., Clarke, H. B., & Simms, A. (eds), 1986-99. *Irish Historic Towns Atlas 1-9* (Dublin).

Aston, M., & Bond, J., 1976. *The Landscape of Towns* (London).

Atkin, M., 1985. 'The Anglo-Saxon urban landscape in East Anglia', *Landscape History*, 7, pp. 27-40.

Baker, N. J., Dalwood, H., Holt, R., Mundy, C., & Taylor, G., 1992. 'From Roman to medieval Worcester: development and planning in the Anglo-Saxon city', *Antiquity*, 66, pp. 65-74.

Baker, N. J., Lawson, J. B., Maxwell, R., and Smith, J. T., 1993. 'Further work on Pride Hill, Shrewsbury', *Trans Shropshire Archaeol & Hist Soc*, 68, pp. 3-64.

Baker, N. J., & Slater T. R., 1992. 'Morphological regions in English medieval towns', in *Urban Landscapes. International Perspectives*, ed. J. W. R. Whitehand & P. J. Larkham (London & New York), pp. 43-68.

Baker, N. J., & Holt, R., 1998. 'The origins of urban parish boundaries', in *The Church in the Medieval Town*, ed. T. R. Slater & G. Rosser (Aldershot), pp. 209-35.

Baker, N. J., & Holt, R., 2001. *Urban Growth and the Medieval Church: Gloucester and Worcester* (Aldershot).

Barker, P. A., White, R. H., Pretty, K. B., Bird, H., & Corbishley, M. J., 1997. *Wroxeter, Shropshire: the Baths Basilica, Excavations 1966-90*, Engl Heritage Archaeol Rep, new ser 8 (London).

Barry, T. B., 1987. *The Archaeology of Medieval Ireland* (London & New York).

Bassett, S., 1992a. 'Medieval ecclesiastical organisation in the vicinity of Wroxeter and its British antecedents', *J Br Archaeol Assoc*, 145, pp. 1-28.

Bassett, S., 1992b. 'Church and diocese in the West Midlands: the transition from British to Anglo-Saxon control', in *Pastoral Care before the Parish*, ed. J. Blair & R. Sharpe (Leicester & London), pp. 13-40.

Bearman, R., 1994. *Charters of the Redvers Family and the Earldom of Devon, 1090-1217*, Devon & Cornwall Rec Soc, new ser 37 (Exeter).

Beresford, M. W., 1967. *New Towns of the Middle Ages. Town Plantation in England, Wales and Gascony* (London).

Biddle, M., 1970. 'Excavations at Winchester 1969. Eighth interim report', *Antiq J*, 50, pp. 277-326.

Biddle, M. (ed.), 1976. *Winchester in the Early Middle Ages* (Oxford).

Biddle, M., & Hill, D., 1971. 'Late-Saxon planned towns', *Antiq J*, 51, pp. 70-85.

Blair, J., 1988. 'Minster churches in the landscape', in *Anglo-Saxon Settlements*, ed D. Hooke (Oxford), pp. 35-58.

Blair, J., 1992. 'Anglo-Saxon minsters: a topographical review', in *Pastoral Care before the Parish*, ed. Blair & Sharpe, pp. 267-84.

Blair, J., 1996. 'Palaces or minsters? Northampton and Cheddar reconsidered', *Anglo-Saxon England*, 25, pp. 97-121.

Blair, J., 1998. 'Bampton: an Anglo-Saxon minster', *Current Archaeol*, 160, pp. 124-30.

Bradley, J., 1985. 'Planned Anglo-Norman towns in Ireland', in *The Comparative History of Urban Origins in Non-Roman Europe*, ed. H. B. Clarke & A. Simms (Oxford), pp. 411-67.

Bradley, J., 1990. 'The role of town-plan analysis in the study of the Irish town', in *The Built Form of Western Cities*, ed. T. R. Slater (Leicester & London), pp. 39-59.

Brisbane, M., 1988. 'Hamwic (Saxon Southampton): an eighth-century port and production centre', in *The Rebirth of Towns in The West*, ed. R. Hodges & B. Hobley Counc Br Archaeol Res Rep 68 (London).

Brooks, N. P., 2000. 'Rome, Canterbury and the construction of English identity', in *Rome and the Early Christian West. Essays in honour of D.A. Bullough*, ed. J. Smith (Leiden).

Brown, A. (ed.), 1999. *The Rows of Chester. The Chester Rows Research Project*, Engl Heritage Archaeol Rep 16 (London).

Bucher, F., 1979. 'Medieval architectural design methods, 800-1560', *Gesta*, 11, pp. 37-51.

Burnett, C. (ed.), 1987. *Adelard of Bath. An English scientist and Arabist of the early twelfth century*, Surveys and Texts 14 (London).

Burnett, C., 1997. *The Introduction of Arabic Learning into England* (London).

Burnham, B. C., & Wacher, J., 1990. *The 'Small Towns' of Roman Britain* (London).

Carter, H., 1982. 'The internal structure of Welsh towns in the nineteenth century: changing townscapes', *Landscape History*, 4, pp. 47-60.

Carver, M., 1987. *Underneath English Towns. Interpreting Urban Archaeology* (London).

Clark, P. (ed.), 2000. *The Cambridge Urban History of Britain. Volume 2: 1540-1840* (Cambridge).

Clarke, H., & Ambrosiani, B., 1991. *Towns in the Viking Age* (Leicester & London).

Clarke, H. (ed.), 1990. *Medieval Dublin. The Making of a Metropolis* (Dublin).

Conzen, M. R. G., 1960. *Alnwick, Northumberland. A Study in Town-Plan Analysis*, Publ Inst Br Geogr, 27 (London).

Conzen, M. R. G., 1962. 'The plan analysis of an English city centre', in *Proceedings of the IGU Symposium in Urban Geography Lund 1960*, ed. K. Norborg (Lund), pp. 383-414.

Conzen, M. R. G., 1968. 'The use of town plans in the study of urban history', in *The Study of Urban History*, ed. H. J. Dyos (London), pp. 113-30.

Demidowicz, G. (ed.), 1994. *Coventry's First Cathedral* (Stamford).

Deveson, A., 1998. 'Medieval Whitchurch: the origins of a new town', *Proc Hampshire Field Club & Archaeol Soc*, 53, pp. 121-36.

Doherty, C., 1985. 'Monastic towns in Ireland', in *The Comparative History of Urban Origins in Non-Roman Europe*, ed. H. B. Clarke & A. Simms, Br Archaeol Rep, Int ser 255 (Oxford), pp. 45-76.

Dyson, T., & Schofield, J., 1984. 'Saxon London', in *Anglo-Saxon Towns of Southern England*, ed. J. Haslam (Chichester).

Esmonde Cleary, A. S., 1989. *The Ending of Roman Britain* (London).

Ewan, E., 1990. *Townlife in Fourteenth-century Scotland* (Edinburgh).

Faulkner, N., 2000. 'Change and decline in late Romano-British towns', in *Urban Decline 100-1600*, ed. T. R. Slater (Aldershot), pp. 25-50.

Friedman, D., 1988. *Florentine New Towns: Urban Design in the Late Middle Ages* (Cambridge, Mass.).

Good, G. L., Jones, R. H., & Ponsford, M. W. (eds), 1991. *Waterfront Archaeology*, Counc Br Archaeol Res Rep 74 (London).

Graham, B. J., 1993. 'The high Middle Ages: *c.* 1100 to *c.* 1350', in *An Historical Geography of Ireland*, ed. B. J. Graham & L. J. Proudfoot (London), pp. 58-98.

Graham, B. J., 1998. 'The town and the monastery: early medieval urbanisation in Ireland, AD 800-1150', in *The Church in the Medieval Town*, ed. Slater & Rosser, pp. 131-55.

Hall, R. A., 1984. *The Viking Dig* (London).

Hall, R. A., 1988. 'York 700-1050', in *The Re-birth of Towns in the West*, ed. R. Hodges & B. Hobley, Counc Br Archaeol Res Rep 68 (London), pp. 125-32.

Haslam, J. (ed.), 1984. *Anglo-Saxon Towns in Southern England* (Chichester).

Haslam, J., 1987. 'The second *burh* of Nottingham', *Landscape History*, 9, pp. 45-52.

Haslam, J., 1988. 'The Anglo-Saxon *burh* at *Wigingamere*', *Landscape History*, 10, pp. 25-36.

Heffernen, T. F., 1988. *Wood Quay. The Clash Over Dublin's Viking Past* (Austin, Texas).

Hooke, D., 1980. 'The hinterland and routeways of Anglo-Saxon Worcester: the charter evidence', in *Medieval Worcester. An Archaeological Framework*, ed. M. O. H. Carver, Trans Worcester Archaeol Soc, 3rd ser, 7, pp. 38-49.

Hoskins, W. G., 1955. *The Making of the English Landscape* (London).

Hurst, H., 1984. 'The archaeology of Gloucester Castle: an introduction', *Trans Bristol & Gloucestershire Archaeol Soc*, 102, pp. 73-108.

Jones, M. J., & Bond, C. J., 1987. 'Urban defences', in *Urban Archaeology in Britain*, ed. J. Schofield & R. Leech, Counc Br Archaeol Res Rep 61 (London), pp. 95-8.

Lauret, A., Malebranche, R., & Seraphin, G., 1988. *Bastides: Villes Nouvelles du Moyen Age* (Toulouse).

Leech, R., 1981. *Historic Towns in Gloucestershire* (Bristol).

Leslie, K. & Short, B. (eds), 1999. *An Historical Atlas of Sussex* (Chichester).

Lilley, K. D., 1994a. 'Medieval Coventry: a study in town-plan analysis', Unpubl Univ of Birmingham PhD thesis.

Lilley, K. D., 1994b. 'Coventry's topographical development; the impact of the priory', in *Coventry's First Cathedral*, ed. Demidowicz, pp. 72-96.

Lilley, K. D., 1995. *The Norman Town in Dyfed, a Preliminary Study of Urban Form*, Urban Morphology Res Monogr ser 1 (Birmingham).

Lilley, K. D., 1998a. 'Urban design in medieval Coventry: the planning of Much and Little Park street within the Earl of Chester's fee', *Midland History*, 23, pp. 1-20.

Lilley, K. D., 1998b. ' Trading places: monastic initiative and the development of high-medieval Coventry', in *The Church in the Medieval Town*, ed. Slater & Rosser, pp. 177-208.

Lilley, K. D., 1999. *Norman Towns in Southern England. Urban morphogenesis in Hampshire and the Isle of Wight 1066-1215*, Urban Morphol Res Monogr ser 5 (Birmingham).

Lobel, M. D. (ed.), 1969. *Historic Towns I* (London & Oxford).

Lobel, M. D. (ed.), 1975. *Historic Towns II* (London).

Lobel, M. D. (ed.), 1989. *Historic Towns III. The City of London from Prehistoric Times to c. 1520* (London).

Lowther, P., Ebbatson, L., Ellison, M., & Millett, M. (1993) 'The city of Durham: an archaeological survey', *Durham Archaeol J*, 9, pp. 27-119.

Lynch, M., Spearman, M., & Stell, G. (eds), 1988. *The Scottish Medieval Town* (Edinburgh).

Mc Neill, P. G. & MacQueen, H. L., 1996. *Atlas of Scottish History to 1707* (Edinburgh).

Matless, D., 1998. *Landscape and Englishness* (London).

Milne, G., 1987. 'Waterfront archaeology in British towns', in *Urban Archaeology in Britain*, ed. Schofield & Leech, Counc Br Archaeol Res Rep 61.

Milne, G., 1992. *Timber Building Techniques in London c. 900 – c. 1400: an archaeological study of waterfront installations and related material*, London & Middlesex Archaeol Soc Sp Pap, 15 (London).

Milne, G., & Hobley, B. (eds), 1981. *Waterfront Archaeology in Britain and Northern Europe*, Counc Br Archaeol Res Rep 41 (London).

Morris, R., 1989. *Churches in the Landscape* (London).

Munby, J., 1992. 'Zacharias's: a fourteenth-century Oxford New Inn and the origins of the urban inn', *Oxoniensia*, 57, pp. 245-310.

Ottaway, P., 1992. *Archaeology in British Towns from the Emperor Claudius to the Black Death* (London & New York).

Palliser, D. M. (ed.), 2000. *The Cambridge Urban History of Britain. Volume 1: c. 600-c. 1540* (Cambridge).

Pantin, W. A., 1947. 'The development of domestic architecture in Oxford', *Antiq J*, 27, pp. 120-50.

Pearson, S., 1994. *The Medieval Houses of Kent. An Historical Analysis* (London).

Platt, C., 1976. *The English Medieval Town* (London).

Rawat, A. S., 1994. 'The history, growth and decay of Naini Tal – a tourist township in the central Himalaya', *Landscape History*, 16, pp. 67-76.

RCHME 1972. Royal Commission on Historical Monuments England. *The City of York II. The Defences* (London).

Reynolds, S., 1977. *An Introduction to the History of Medieval Towns* (Oxford).

Rodwell, K., 1974. *Historic Towns in Oxfordshire* (Oxford).

Rowley, T., 1983. *The Norman Heritage* (London).

Rowley, T., 1999. *The Normans* (London).

Schofield, J., 1994. *Medieval London Houses* (New Haven, CT).

Schofield, J., & Vince, A., 1994. *Medieval Towns* (Leicester).

Shoesmith, R., 1982. *Hereford City Excavations, I. Excavations on and close to the Defences*, Counc Br Archaeol Res Rep 46 (London).

Slater, T. R., 1980. 'The analysis of burgage patterns in medieval towns', *Area*, 13, pp. 211-16.

Slater, T. R., 1985. 'Medieval new town and port: a plan analysis of Hedon, East Yorkshire', *Yorkshire Archaeol J*, 57, pp. 23-41.

Slater, T. R., 1987. 'Ideal and reality in English episcopal medieval town planning', *Trans Inst Br Geogr*, new ser, 12, pp. 191-203.

Slater, T. R., 1988. 'English medieval town planning', in *Urban Historical Geography: Recent Progress in Britain and Germany*, ed. D. Denecke & G. Shaw (Cambridge), pp. 93-108.

Slater, T. R., 1990. 'English medieval town plans with composite plans: evidence from the Midlands', in *The Built Form of Western Cities*, ed. Slater, pp. 60-82.

Slater, T. R., 1996a. 'Medieval town-founding on the estates of the Benedictine Order in England', in *Power, Profit and Urban Land, Landownership in Medieval and Early-Modern European Towns*, ed. F-E. Eliassen & G.A. Ersland (London), pp. 70-92.

Slater, T. R., 1996b. 'The European Historic Towns Atlas', *J Urban Hist*, 22, pp. 739-49.

Slater, T. R., 1998a. Domesday village to medieval town: the topography of medieval Stratford-upon-Avon', in *The History of an English Borough. Stratford-upon-Avon 1196-1996*, ed. R. Bearman (Stroud), pp. 30-42.

Slater, T. R., 1998b. 'The Benedictine Order and medieval town planning: the case of St Albans', in *The Church in the Medieval Town*, ed. Slater & Rosser, pp. 155-76.

Slater, T. R., 1999. 'Geometry and medieval town planning', *Urban Morphol*, 3, pp. 107-11.

Smith, J. T., 1992. *English Houses 1200-1800. The Hertfordshire Evidence* (London).

Soulsby, I., 1983. *The Towns of Medieval Wales* (Chichester).

Steane, K., & Vince, A., 1993. 'Post-Roman Lincoln: archaeological evidence for activity in Lincoln in the 5th-9th centuries', in *Pre-Viking Lindsey*, ed. A. Vince (Lincoln).

Stoob, H. (ed.), 1973-93. *Deutscher Städteatlas I-V* (Dortmund).

Thomas, A., 1992. *The Walled Towns of Ireland* (2 vols) (Dublin).

Thomas, C., 1981. *Christianity in Roman Britain to AD 500* (London).

Torrie, E. P. & Coleman, R., 1996. *Historic Hamilton* (Edinburgh).

Turner, H. L., 1971. *Town Defences in England and Wales* (Newton Abbot).

Vince, A., 1990. *Saxon London. An Archaeological Investigation* (London).

Wacher, J., 1995. *The Towns of Roman Britain* (London, 2nd revised edn).

Wade-Martins, P., 1993. *An Historical Atlas of Norfolk* (Norwich).

Wallace, P. F., 1992. *The Viking Age Buildings of Dublin* (2 vols) (Dublin).

Webster, G., 2000. *Wroxeter: Excavation of the Roman Baths and Macellum, 1955-85*, Engl Heritage Archaeol Rep 19.1 (London).

White, R., 2000. 'Wroxeter and the transformation of late-Roman urbanism', in *Towns in Decline, 100-1600*, ed. Slater, pp. 96-119.

Whitelock, D. (ed.), 1979. *English Historical Documents* (London, 2nd edn).

The rural landscape: 1500 – 1900, the neglected centuries.

Tom Williamson

ABSTRACT

The eighteenth and nineteenth centuries saw the real 'making of the English landscape' with the demise of traditional farming pays and the emergence of a simpler pattern in which the largely arable south and east is contrasted with the largely pastoral north, west and midlands. The impact of agricultural change on the rural landscape is explored, together with the way that such change influenced our understanding of the medieval and post-medieval periods.

KEYWORDS:

Enclosure, landownership, estates, farming patterns

INTRODUCTION

Most of the papers presented in this volume are concerned with the landscape history of relatively remote periods of time: with prehistory, the Roman period, or the middle ages. Landscape historians have certainly not ignored the post-medieval centuries but this selection is by no means unrepresentative: the majority of articles and books published on the English landscape deal primarily with the period before the fifteenth century. Yet the rural landscape – the pattern of fields and roads, vernacular buildings, many upstanding earthworks – was in fact largely created in the period after 1450. In particular, while historians might argue about the precise figures, at a reasonable estimate around 60 *per cent* of the walled and hedged landscape of England post-dates 1450, and around 30 *per cent* post-dates 1750. Moreover, the various 'traditional' landscapes whose destruction was so lamented by Hoskins in the 1950s, and which have recently been categorised and mapped by the Countryside Commission, were very substantially the product of the post-medieval centuries. Many achieved their particular character as late as the eighteenth or nineteenth century. The grass 'shires' of the Midlands for example, the great fox-hunting countries of Leicestershire, Rutland or Northamptonshire, described eloquently by the writer Surtees as consisting of 'grass, grass, grass, nothing but grass for miles and miles' (Carr 1976,

p. 27); the landscape of flimsy hawthorn hedges and wide arable fields of the chalklands of southern and eastern England; or more local and idiosyncratic landscapes like that of the East Anglian Breckland, with its lines of twisted Scots pines, originally the hedges – 'deal rows' – planted at enclosure in the early nineteenth century. Even the early-enclosed landscapes of the south-east and west of England – Rackham's 'ancient countryside' (Rackham 1976, pp. 15-17) – did not simply stop developing at the end of the middle ages. Ancient they certainly are, but these landscapes contain abundant traces of a much more recent history. Many such districts once had open fields, which were for the most part removed piecemeal, in the period between *c.* 1450 and 1750: while the later eighteenth and early nineteenth centuries saw field rationalisation and hedge removal and realignment on some scale, the wholesale removal of pollards, and the enclosure of innumerable greens and commons.

There are many stories that can be read in the post-medieval landscape but in this short paper I shall merely highlight two: the steady growth of large landed estates, owned by wealthy individuals as absolute private property; and the replacement of small-scale peasant cultivators by larger capitalist farms, specialised producers for the market. The two were distinct processes but so intimately connected that they are hard to disentangle. Their joint impact on the English landscape was immense.

THE PATTERN OF FARMING

Let me begin with the second of these two processes. The English countryside in the period up to the early or mid-fourteenth century had two main characteristics. It was chronically over-populated, with farmers in some districts subsisting on less than ten acres; and it was poorly specialised, in that most cultivators practised mixed farming, producing a relatively small surplus for sale. True, some recent research has tended to emphasise the opposite view, seeing a high degree of local variation in farming. But the evidence for market specialisation comes principally from large manorial demesnes, and is unlikely to be representative of the economies of the broad mass of farmers who cultivated the

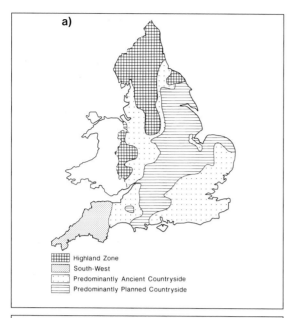

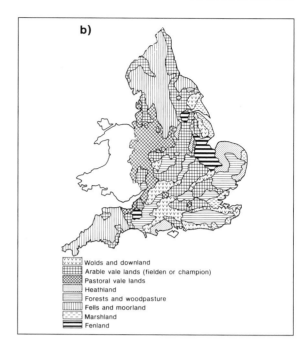

Fig. 9.1. Regions in England
a. Rackham's simplified landscape regions.
b. Early modern farming regions, as defined by Thirsk (1987).
c. Farming regions in 1851, according to James Caird (1852).
    To the east of the dark line were the 'chief corn districts of
    England'; to the west, areas dominated by grazing and
    dairying.

majority of the land area of England. Certainly, ploughland was extensive in all areas which in later years were to be devoted to grass.

The centuries after *c.* 1400, however, saw a steady growth both in farm size, and in the degree of regional specialisation – topics which have received considerable attention from scholars such as Joan Thirsk and Eric Kerridge (Kerridge 1967; Thirsk 1987). Although most farmers continued, to some extent, to be mixed farmers, regions increasingly specialised in the production of certain commodities, and a complex mosaic of farming 'countries' emerged which was maintained, with relatively little alteration, into the eighteenth century. Most landscape historians carry around in their heads an image of Rackham's familiar map of England, showing the distribution

of 'planned' and 'ancient' countryside (Rackham 1976, p. 16) (Fig. 9.1a). Fewer, perhaps, have internalised the equally important map of early-modern farming regions, a map more familiar to students of agricultural history (Fig. 9.1b).

Fewer still, I suspect, carry within them a map showing the next key transformation in England's agricultural geography, most clearly (if oversimply) expressed by James Caird in his *English Agriculture* of 1852 (Caird 1852, p. i) (Fig. 9.1c). In the period of the 'agricultural revolution' – roughly, in the century after 1750 – the complex mosaic of early-modern farming regions disintegrated, to be replaced by a rather simpler pattern, a version of which persists to this day. By the mid-nineteenth century arable farming was largely concentrated in the east of England, with pasture farming dominating in the west. Areas of eastern England which had, in the early modern period, been devoted to livestock farming now became arable; much of Midlands, in contrast, moved from being a primarily arable to a primarily pastoral countryside.

The economic explanations for these successive transformations in agrarian geography are extremely complex and cannot be discussed here; the maps presented here represent very broad generalisations with, in particular, Caird rather overemphasising the extent of arable in many areas of the South-east. But both contain at least a grain of truth, and help explain several important aspects of English landscape history. To begin with, we should note that the predominantly arable areas of England in the period before the eighteenth century were those which were, by and large, enclosed latest: that is, they approximate more or less to Rackham's area of 'predominantly planned countryside'. Early-enclosed regions in general correspond with pasture-farming districts. We should also note, however, that many of these districts had not *always* been characterised by landscapes of enclosed fields (Roden 1973, pp. 325-38; Skipper 1989). In many, open fields of a kind had been widespread in the middle ages, but had disappeared steadily in the course of the fifteenth, sixteenth and seventeenth centuries, through gradual piecemeal enclosure. The field systems of these areas were generally of 'irregular' form and were often only poorly regulated. The intermixture of holdings was less extreme than in the Midlands: lands could be consolidated and enclosed with relative ease (Yelling 1977, pp. 88-93).

We should also note that while to some extent the pattern of early-modern farming regions corresponds to the distribution of different soil types, this is only true up to a point. The 'wold and downland' and 'heathland' farming systems were largely found on light soils – chalk and sands – where open fields co-existed with extensive areas of sheepwalk, on which large flocks were grazed by day (Allison 1957). Folded by night on the arable, they provided the steady flow of nutrients necessary to keep these light soils in heart. The bulk of England's arable land in the sixteenth century, however, lay in the Midlands, on heavy clay soils poorly suited to cereal cultivation. Evidently, clayland farmers in areas of anciently-enclosed fields, or in areas where open fields were of irregular form and particularly susceptible to piecemeal enclosure, came to specialise at an early date in livestock production. On the clays of the Midlands, in contrast, they did not. Presumably enclosure was much more difficult here, given the complex intermixture of rights and properties which characterised 'regular' open field systems. Enclosure for pasture did take place here in the fifteenth and sixteenth centuries but it was often a traumatic process, associated with the depopulation of settlements. The rate of enclosure increased markedly in the second half of the seventeenth century but even in 1700 the Midlands remained a predominantly open, arable region.

The next 'transformation' of agricultural geography changed all this, however. In the period of low population growth, and poor agricultural prices, in the first half of the eighteenth century, enclosure and conversion to grass continued apace in the Midlands (Broad 1980). What is curious – and deserving of more attention from economic historians – is that even as population and prices recovered in the late eighteenth century enclosure and conversion continued here – indeed, accelerated. The middle decades of the eighteenth century saw the elaboration of, and growing familiarity with, new legal forms which could remove even the most complex of common field systems, parliamentary enclosure, and in the 1760s, 1770s and '80s vast areas of the Midlands were divided by hawthorn hedges and laid to grass (Turner 1980; Mingay 1997, pp. 20-31). The incumbents who supplied the 1801 Crop Returns often remarked on the change: the vicar of Breedon on the Hill in Leicestershire typically remarked how

> Within the last 30 years almost all the country north-west of Leicester to the extremity of the county has been enclosed: by which means the land is become in a higher state of cultivation than formerly; but on account of a great proportion of it being converted into pasturage much less food is produced than when it was more generally in tillage (List & Index Soc 1982, p. 53).

It will be apparent from the above account that up until the start of the eighteenth century most enclosure in England was concerned with conversion of open fields on heavy soils to pasture. Indeed, it is probable that this was true even up until the 1780s or 90s. Enclosure was essential if open field farmers were to shift to primarily pastoral pursuits. In arable areas, in contrast, there was much less to be gained from enclosure before the introduction of the new cropping patterns of the 'agricultural revolution': the elimination of fallows and the institution of rotations combining grain crops with clover and roots. Enclosure was not *essential* for the adoption of the new rotations; that is a myth propagated by eighteenth-century improvers, and open field farmers could, and frequently did, adopt the new crops, in some cases recasting their field systems accordingly (Havinden 1961). But innovators nevertheless faced problems. The 1839 tithe file for Great Milton, south-east of Oxford, typically commented how the

> Arbitrary and antiquated customs of open field husbandry present here as they do universally a bar to improved cultivation and check the enterprise of the farmer. The routine of two crops and a fallow is adhered to on the strong open lands but the occupiers on the lighter soils venture upon the innovations of turnips and artificial grasses. They do so however on sufferance as the nonconformity of any one of the open field farmers would place them in peril of a return to the old course of crops (Kain 1986, p. 398).

Enclosure thus became increasingly desirable in arable districts in the course of the eighteenth century. But there was another factor here. The new crops reduced the need for the great areas of heath and sheepwalk which had formed such an important element in 'sheep-corn' systems: much of this was common land, and could only be reclaimed and put to arable use after enclosure. Thus it was that the great upland wolds of Yorkshire and Lincolnshire, and the heaths of north-west Norfolk, fell to the plough: gradually at first, and then in a frenzy of enclosure activity which peaked during the Napoleonic Wars (Turner 1980). By this time, however, the Midland open fields had already been largely enclosed and laid to grass: much of the Midland plain comprises soils 'too strong and too harsh' for turnip to be grown successfully (Pitt 1813, p. 97).

The simple maps presented in Fig. 9.1 thus help explain, in broad regional terms, the history of enclosure in England. Readers might like to think about them when examining other features of the countryside, such as patterns of settlement. But of equal importance in the development of the post-medieval landscape, and intimately connected to the progress of enclosure, was the increasing dominance of England by large landed estates, and the concomitant decline of the small owner-occupier, in the period after c.1450.

THE DISTRIBUTION OF LARGE ESTATES

It is a commonplace that we can only really speculate about the distribution of landed wealth in England in the period between 1086, when Domesday Book was compiled, and 1873, when the 'New Domesday' was produced (Clemenson 1982; Thompson 1966; Becket 1986, pp. 43-90; Clay 1985, pp. 119-98). Attempts to estimate changing patterns of possession in the intervening period are, moreover, rendered problematic by the fact that between these two dates the whole idea of 'ownership' changed fundamentally. In the early middle ages absolute ownership of landed property, in the modern sense, did not really exist. A manor might be said to be the property of its lord but even customary tenants had a presumptive right to pass their farms by inheritance, according to the custom of the manor; while by the twelfth century an active land market in customary land had developed. Feudal superiors, and even the monarch, could also in some senses be considered to have property rights in the land. The key developments of the late fourteenth and fifteenth centuries – again too complex to be discussed here – were the emergence of modern concepts of property and ownership, and of a complex geography of landownership.

In some places, and in some districts, numerous small freeholders could be found. In others, copyholders held on terms of such security that they might almost have been freeholders. But in others places many farmers held by copyholds (or other forms of tenure) which were much less secure, and here the proprietary rights of a manorial lord were correspondingly stronger, so that he became the effective owner of the land in question, in the modern sense, and the farmers his tenants (Kerridge 1967). The origins of such local, and regional, variations would repay further research. They were evidently determined in part by antecedent structures – by the various forms of customary tenure which had developed in the early middle ages. In part they were structured by the varied ways in which the balance of power between the feudal class and the peasant cultivators had been negotiated during the crisis of the late middle ages. But whatever their particular origins, patterns of ownership did not

remain stable and unchanging thereafter and there was, by common consent, a steady drift of land from small owners to large (Clemenson 1982; Thompson 1966; Becket 1986, pp. 43-90; Clay 1985, pp. 119-98).

The beneficiaries of this process changed over time. So far as the evidence goes, in the sixteenth and early seventeenth centuries both local gentry and great landowners seem to have been the main gainers. In the period after the Restoration of 1660, however, the very largest estates seem to have benefited. From the late eighteenth century, the local gentry once again may have been in the ascendancy. Either way, the attrition of small landowners seems to have been greatest in periods of agricultural recession, especially in the late seventeenth and early eighteenth century, a period of low population growth.

What was particularly important in the development of England's diverse landscapes was that large estates were not evenly distributed. In part this was because of the varied distribution of the antecedent tenurial forms already discussed. But it was also because, as Joan Thirsk (1970) has argued, the different forms of agrarian economy which developed from late medieval times tended to foster particular kinds of land owning structure. In general, arable farming tended, over time, to encourage the emergence of large farms and large landed estates. Pasture farming districts, in contrast, especially those involved in dairying and rearing, rather than fattening and grazing, were associated with small family farms and a more diverse property structure, featuring greater numbers of minor gentry and small owner-occupiers. Thirsk's suggestions have recently been criticised and it is arguable that the distinction between arable and pasture districts was too crudely drawn (Overton 1996, pp. 50-62). Other factors certainly operated. In particular, large estates came to characterise areas of comparatively poor land – that is, areas in which, given the character of sixteenth- and seventeenth-century agricultural technology, yields were low and land values likewise. It was easier to accumulate a large estate where land was cheap than where it was expensive. Whatever the precise balance of factors involved, large estates tended to be a particular feature of sheep-corn regions such as the Wolds of Lincolnshire and Yorkshire, the 'Good Sands' of north-west Norfolk, the East Anglian Breckland, the Cotswolds and most of the Downland areas of England. The 'wood-pasture' countrysides of the south and east and of the west, in contrast, were not for the most part characterised by great estates; nor were those arable districts located in areas of particularly fertile and therefore expensive land, such as Flegg in north-east Norfolk. By the eighteenth century, however, it was not only soil fertility and agricultural rents which determined land prices: and thus there were few really large estates in the vicinity of London, although innumerable small gentry properties, and 'villa' residences, existed in this area of favoured residence.

To add further to this complex picture, *within* many regions there was a distinction between the principal river valleys, where good soil and abundant water supplies had encouraged early settlement, in which communities were large and landownership divided, and drift-covered uplands, in which large estates often acquired a monopoly share of the land at an early date. This distinction was often a major factor in deciding the chronology of enclosure (Fox 1993; Wade Martins & Williamson 1999b, pp. 34-55). Indeed, although in broad, regional terms the chronology of enclosure was primarily linked to the patterns of agrarian change already described, at a *local* level it was closely connected with patterns of ownership. Enclosure was always easiest to achieve where fewer proprietors were involved, and easiest of all where a township was owned in its entirety by a single individual. Indeed, enclosure was often achieved by systematic engrossment – by the simple expedient of buying out all the other proprietors in a village. In the eighteenth century, in particular, engrossment was often carried out with a single-minded aggression, and not just for economic reasons. Landowners aspired not simply to a large estate, but to a continuous, compact, uninterrupted one, in which the totality of the environment could be controlled: and used to express the fact of the undivided ownership to which all aspired. Land close to the mansion might thus be bought at any price. As one land agent commented, concerning the proposed purchase of a neighbouring farm:

> If we cannot purchase on terms we would, we must purchase on the terms we can, as from its contiguity [the farm in question] is extremely desirable, and to have a disagreeable neighbour, so near, would be superlatively vexatious (Clay 1985, p. 79).

LANDSCAPES OF IMPROVEMENT

The combined effects of enclosure, and the growth of large landed estates, were many. The erection of great mansions, and the laying out of elaborate parks, have attracted particular attention, and have been discussed at length elsewhere. Others have perhaps received less attention from landscape historians. Variations in ownership had, for example, major effects upon the development of settlement, and nineteenth-century commentators made much of the distinction between 'closed' and 'open' parishes (Holderness 1972; Mills 1980; Neave 1993). The former, owned by one or a small number of owners, tended to exhibit slow or negative demographic growth in the seventeenth, eighteenth and nineteenth centuries; 'open' parishes in multiple ownership, in contrast, tended to grow more rapidly, and, in addition, generally supported a more diverse economy, with a larger number of public houses, chapels, and shops. There were a number of reasons for these differences. Landowners and their agents preferred to deal with a small number of large tenants, able to weather the storms of periodic recession and to invest in stocking and equipping farms adequately, rather than with a plethora of small holders. An estate with fewer tenants, moreover, required less management and demanded lower repair and maintenance costs than one with innumerable small farms. In addition, large numbers of cottages meant large numbers of labourers and their families, all potential claimants for Poor Relief through sickness, old age or illegitimate pregnancy. As the poor rates were paid by the proprietors and principal tenants in a parish, monopoly landowners had an understandable interest in limiting or even reducing the size of villages, while large numbers of cottages, once again, meant high repair costs. A shortage of accommodation caused few problems for the landowner: labour was simply imported from neighbouring 'open' communities. Landowners' control of settlements was not, however, simply an economic matter. Sprawling villages full of alehouses and dissenters offended the aesthetic sensibilities of the rich: estate villages were, to varying degrees, often landscaped in suitably aesthetic manner, especially from the late eighteenth century.

The effects of monopoly ownership could be dramatic. In 1730 Sir Marmaduke Constable of Everingham in the East Riding of Yorkshire typically described to his steward how he 'would rather have my cottages diminished, than increased, though I am now in Everingham at or about the number I would be at'. Ten years later he noted that 'Few houses and good is what I propose at Everingham' (Neave 1993, p. 134). Like that of many neighbouring Wold villages, the population of Everingham fell fast in the late seventeenth and early eighteenth centuries. There were fifty-seven households here in 1672, but only twenty-seven in 1743 (Neave 1993, p. 135). The association between monopoly landownership and settlement contraction is one reason why villages cleared for emparking in the eighteenth century had usually already experienced a degree of earlier contraction. It is also a good reason why we should not always assume that areas of desertion within parks date from the time of emparking: some represent the sites of farms and cottages which had disappeared long before the park was laid out (Williamson 1998, pp. 132-3).

The planting of trees and woods was another major consequence of enclosure and the rise of great estates. The area under trees in England had unquestionably declined steadily in the early middle ages, and probably continued to decline into the seventeenth century. Large areas of midland England, and of the 'sheep-corn' areas of heath and wold and down, had by this time been devoid of woodland for centuries. But in the period after 1660, in particular, the rate of planting increased. Landowners' motives were complex. Forestry was a good way of using marginal land which had, before enclosure, been used by commoners as rough grazing. But tree-planting had important symbolic functions. Plantations symbolised the ownership of land by large landowners, and also confidence in the continuity of that ownership. As Worlidge explained in 1669:

> What can be more pleasant than to have the bounds and limits of your property preserved and continued from age to age by the testimony of such living and growing witnesses? (Worlidge 1669, p. 72).

A small freeholder might plant a few trees in his hedgerows, but on a farm of 100 acres it was impossible to put aside ten acres or more for forestry. Only those with broad acres could tie up land in this way for perhaps two generations. Contemporaries read the landscape in this light and assumed that abundant plantations signalled the presence of a gentleman's estate. Moreover, trees could only be established on enclosed ground. Planting on commons, or within unenclosed open fields, was impossible, because of the rights enjoyed by the local community to forage over them. Commoners would simply uproot the young trees, or their livestock destroy them through grazing. Hence the second essential rule of the eighteenth-century landscape: that plantations indicated land held in severalty.

Plantations and other forms of tree-planting were vested with further meanings by contemporaries (Daniels 1988; Williamson 1995, pp. 124-40). Royalist propaganda after the Restoration had exaggerated the extent of felling in royal parks and on royalist estates, and this had fostered an association between felling and republicanism and, conversely, between planting and loyalty to the restored monarchy. In a more general sense planting showed confidence in the new political dispensation – long-term investments were safer now that the right to private property was guaranteed by a parliament of the propertied. Planting was also a patriotic duty, providing timber for the navy which would protect Protestant Britain and its trading interests from enemies and rivals, at a time when England was frequently at war. Changing attitudes to nature and, more mundanely, changing fashions in shooting (the growing enthusiasm for hunting pheasants) also played a part in the growth in tree-planting in the post-Restoration period. As with the impact of landownership on rural settlement, economic motivations were thus only part of the story: planting was a complex business.

Indeed, in general terms it is arguable that one of the real contributions that landscape history can make to wider academic debates is to demonstrate the mixed and varied motives underlying estate management. Economic

historians generally interpret the activities of great estates primarily in economic terms. They also tend to disaggregate the motivation behind various forms of landscape change, categorising some as 'rational' and economic, others as aesthetic and recreational. Examination of the landscape, in contrast, encourages us to see park-making, control of settlement, enclosure, tree-planting and reclamation as interconnected phenomenon, and all informed by a wide range of motives. Contemporary language is one immediate clue to this: the word 'improvement' was used indiscriminately for enclosure, reclamation, tree-planting, or the laying out of a landscape park.

One aspect of all this is worthy of particular attention. I have noted above that the classic 'agricultural revolution' of the textbooks – turnips, marling, four-course rotations and the rest – was essentially a phenomenon of the light soil, 'sheep-corn' areas of England. I have also noted that these were districts in which, by the seventeenth century, large landed estates were particularly prominent. In traditional historiography the story of the agricultural revolution is told in terms of great aristocratic improvers – 'Turnip' Townshend, Coke of Holkham, Sir Christopher Sykes – and their tenants, 'gentlemen farmers' with extensive enclosed farms of 400 acres or more. Needless to say, the estates of the individuals in question were all on the light soils of eastern England where, in many places, the landscape was indeed being transformed. Arthur Young, typically, described the changes which they had brought about in north-west Norfolk:

> All the country from Holkham to Houghton was a wild sheep walk before the spirit of improvement seized the inhabitants ... Instead of boundless wilds and uncultivated wastes inhabited by scare anything but sheep, the country is all cut up into enclosures, cultivated in a most husbandlike manner, well peopled, and yielding an hundred times the produce that it did in its former state (Young 1771, p. 1).

These changes, however, were only one aspect of a much wider process of agrarian change in the period after 1750, at the heart of which lay that fundamental transformation of England's agrarian geography already described. The changes on the light soils certainly increased grain production, but even after 'improvement' yields from these areas often remained unimpressive and, more importantly, were only maintained by considerable inputs of labour and capital. The population of England's growing urban and industrial areas was really fed by bringing into cultivation areas of eastern England particularly suited by climate for arable cultivation, but which, for reasons, above all, of poor drainage, had previously engaged mainly in pasture farming: the Fens, and the fertile claylands of Essex, Suffolk and Norfolk (compare, again, Figs 9.1b and 9.1c). Improvements in fen drainage in the period after

1790, and the spread of under-drainage on the clays, ensured that by 1850s both were primarily arable regions (Wade Martins & Williamson 1999b, pp. 49-55, 61-7). The claylands of Suffolk, for example, had been largely under grass in the early eighteenth century. By 1849 the Raynbirds could describe them as 'one of the finest corn districts in England' (Raynbird & Raynbird 1849, p. 7). This transformation had itself major effects upon the local landscape, with the widespread rationalisation of field boundaries and the wholesale removal of pollarded trees. Under-drainage and field rationalisation do not, however, figure large in conventional histories of the agricultural revolution: these improvements were a phenomenon of areas not characterised by large landed estates, but by small proprietors and absentee landlords, and the changes in question were the work of small farmers rather than great aristocratic improvers. They were consequently ignored by writers like Young and have thus generally been neglected by modern historians, although not all élite commentators were blind to the changes taking place here. One, writing in the 1840s, remarked of the Suffolk claylands:

> I cannot but look with surprise at the altered appearance of the country when I pass through and consider the enormous cost of the labour which has been expended by the tenantry in clearing, draining, and breaking up pastures &c. (Raynbird & Raynbird 1849, p. 127).

Conversely, many of the principal 'improvements' effected by the great aristocratic landowners and their tenants on the light lands of southern and eastern England achieved relatively little in the medium or long term. Some techniques were introduced by fashionable improvers into areas to which they were unsuited and, after much expense, were quietly abandoned – the late and unsuccessful spread of water-meadow irrigation into the eastern counties being one striking example (Wade Martins & Williamson 1999a). More importantly, much of the reclamation of heaths and sheep walks carried out in the late eighteenth and early nineteenth centuries, which so mesmerised contemporaries, was of little real benefit: much of this activity was, indeed, motivated less by rational economic considerations than by a fashionable desire to improve, to demonstrate paternal concern and social responsibility. When in 1774 Thomas de Grey bemoaned the costs of enclosing the heaths at Tottington in Breckland, he observed candidly that the 'great expense ... would but ill answer, unless there was a real satisfaction in employing the labourers and bringing forth a ragged dirty parish to a neatness of cultivation' (NRO Walsingham WLS XXLVII/19, 415X5). Here, typically, enclosure and reclamation were part and parcel of a wider scheme of landscape improvement, featuring tree-planting and emparking.

In some districts, such as the East Anglian Breckland, large areas of reclaimed land were abandoned to rough pasture again in the aftermath of the Napoleonic War; and with the onset of agricultural recession in the 1880s and '90s retrenchment began in earnest. As one commentator observed of this region in 1885, 'On the light soils, fields which once grew good crops of wheat and barley were put down to rye-grass worth 1s to 2s an acre and devoted to the rearing of game'. This was because 'when prices of corn were high and labour cheap it paid to fertilise these lands with clay ... spreading a hundred loads to the acre. At present, this is out of the question' (BPP 1895, XIV. 310).

CONCLUSION

The perspectives of landscape history can thus throw light on a number of issues of importance to those working in more 'mainstream' disciplines, especially economic history. It is arguable, for example, that the chronology and distribution of enclosure in the post-medieval period is hard to understand without some knowledge of the antecedent structures – of field systems and landholding patterns – in different regions; or as a phenomenon distinct from the wider patterns of landscape and land use change described above. Similarly, the classic 'agricultural revolution' of the text books is best understood as only one, regionally limited, aspect of agrarian change in the eighteenth and nineteenth centuries. And it was part of a wider package of improvements effected by large landowners on the light lands of eastern England, which included emparking, large-scale tree-planting, and changes to the pattern of settlement. Young and other fashionable writers were mesmerised by the scale of these changes; meanwhile, arguably, the real 'revolution' in arable production was taking place elsewhere.

Landscape historians and archaeologists studying much earlier periods might also benefit from maintaining at least a passing interest in the post-medieval centuries, for at least two reasons. Firstly, an examination of the principal changes affecting the different regions of England during these comparatively recent periods can throw much light upon – or at least, raise interesting questions about – some of those earlier transformations of the landscape which have long fascinated archaeologists. To take but one example: if the landscape of the 'champion' Midlands, nucleated villages and extensive, 'regular' open fields, really came into existence because this was the prime area of arable production in Romano-British and early Anglo-Saxon times, then it is interesting that in the post-medieval centuries this region's history was dominated by one theme – a steady shift out of arable and into grass, a use to which all contemporary commentators seem to have agreed its soils were best suited.

Secondly, an awareness of post-medieval developments is important because the changes effected by enclosure, successive transformations in agricultural geography, and the growth of large estates have had a very material impact not only on the patterning and distribution of data from earlier periods, but also on our whole perception of what characterises the landscapes of the more remote past. The discipline's long obsession with the Midland landscape – deserted medieval villages, ridge and furrow, etc – is partly at least a consequence of the fact that post-medieval changes saw much of this region put down to grass, thus preserving, in obviously 'archaeological' form, earthwork traces of the former landscape (Harrison *et al.* 1965) (although how far a *medieval* landscape is perhaps open to question: most of this archaeology post-dates 1450, much post-dates 1600). Other post-medieval changes served to obliterate, wholesale, earthwork traces of medieval and earlier landscapes, most notably the expansion of arable farming across large areas of eastern England in the period after 1750. We should never underestimate the height of the tide of reclamation and improvement which, directed by fashionable aristocratic enthusiasm, swept across some of the most unpropitious terrain in England during the late eighteenth and early nineteenth centuries, flattening in its path prehistoric earthworks formerly preserved under the turf and heather of the sheepwalks.

Many other aspects of the rural landscape underwent radical change in the post-medieval centuries, and it is perhaps worth emphasising this at a time when so much expensive research into the landscape, funded in particular by English Heritage, is based on nineteenth-century maps. In particular, the widespread assumption that settlement forms and patterns existing in the nineteenth century can in any simple or direct way inform us about the early medieval landscape is at least questionable. Broad regional distinctions in settlement – between the Midlands and the South-east, for example – were clearly unaffected by later developments but more detailed variations could be, and often were. The drastic demographic changes of the fifteenth century certainly worked to alter regional settlement character, converting hamlet-based patterns to widely dispersed farms in parts of Devon, for example (Fox 1983). But settlement did not stop changing in the period after 1550, and it is a moot point, for example, how many areas of 'medieval' desertion are of much more recent date, the consequence of landowner's policies to limit or reduce settlement size, or the result of a local or regional shift into pasture farming. Susan Neave's important work in the East Riding of Yorkshire, for example, demonstrated that

> Many settlements decreased in size between the mid-seventeenth and mid-eighteenth centuries, and a large number of 'shrunken village' earthworks date from this period of contraction. Although the population of many townships increased again in the late eighteenth and early nineteenth centuries, this was largely due to the establishment of post-enclosure farmsteads away from village centres (Neave 1993, p. 135).

Documentary research in other areas, including Bedfordshire (Tranter 1966) and Gloucestershire (Percival 1972) suggests that the East Riding experience was by no means unique. In terms of settlement morphology and settlement patterns, as with much else, the complex changes occurring in the period after *c*.1450 may have contributed more to the forms recorded on mid-nineteenth-century maps than many landscape historians currently recognise.

ABBREVIATIONS

NRO = Norfolk Record Office
BPP = British Parliamentary Papers.

BIBLIOGRAPHY

Allison, K. J., 1957. 'The sheep-corn husbandry of Norfolk in the sixteenth and seventeenth Centuries', *Agric Hist Rev*, 5, pp. 12-30.

Beckett, J. V., 1986. *The Aristocracy in England 1660-1914* (Oxford).

Broad, J., 1980. 'Alternate husbandry and permanent pasture in the midlands, 1650-1800', *Agric Hist Rev*, 28, pp. 77-89.

Caird, J., 1852. *English Agriculture in 1851* (London).

Carr, R., 1976. *English Fox Hunting: a history* (London).

Clay, C., 1985. 'Landlords and estate management in England', in *The Agrarian History of England and Wales Vol V.II, 1640-1750*, ed. J. Thirsk (Cambridge), pp. 119-250.

Clemenson, H., 1982. *English Country Houses and Landed Estates* (London).

Daniels, S., 1988. 'The political iconography of woodland in later eighteenth-century England', in *The Iconography of Landscape*, ed D. Cosgrove & S. Daniels (Cambridge), pp. 51-72.

Fox, H., 1983. 'Contraction: desertion and dwindling of dispersed settlement in a Devon parish', *Medieval Village Res Group Ann Rep*, 31, pp. 40-2.

Fox, H., 1993. 'The people of the Wolds in English settlement history', in *The Rural Settlements of Medieval England: studies dedicated to Maurice Beresford and John Hurst*, ed M. Aston, D. Austin & C. Dyer (Oxford), pp. 77-104.

Harrison, M. J., Meade, W. R., & Pannett, D. J., 1965. 'A midland ridge and furrow map', *Geog J*, 131, pp. 366-9.

Havinden, M., 1961. 'Agricultural progress in open-field Oxfordshire', *Agric Hist Rev*, 9, pp. 73-83.

Holderness, B. A., 1972. '"Open" and "closed" parishes in the eighteenth and nineteenth centuries', *Agric Hist Rev*, 20, pp. 126-39.

Kain, R. J. P., 1986. *An Atlas and Index of the Tithe Files of Mid Nineteenth-Century England and Wales* (Cambridge).

Kerridge, E., 1967. *The Agricultural Revolution* (London).

List & Index Society, 1982. *Volume 190: Home Office Acreage Returns (HO67). List and Analysis Part II: Jersey-Somerset, 1801.*

Mills, D. R., 1980. *Lord and Peasant in Nineteenth-Century Britain* (London).

Mingay, E., 1997. *Parliamentary Enclosure in England: an introduction to its causes, incidence and impact* (London).

Neave, S., 1993. 'Rural settlement contraction in the East Riding of Yorkshire between the mid seventeenth and mid eighteenth centuries', *Agric Hist Rev*, 41, pp.124-36.

Overton, M., 1996. *Agricultural Revolution in England* (Cambridge).

Percival, A., 1972 'Gloucestershire village populations', *Local Population Stud*, 8, Appendix.

Pitt, W., 1813. *General View of the Agriculture of the County of Northampton* (London).

Rackham, O., 1976. Trees and Woodlands in the English Landscape (London)

Raynbird, W., & Raynbird, H., 1849. *The Agriculture of Suffolk* (London).

Roden, D., 1973. 'Field systems of the Chiltern Hills and their environs', in *Studies of Field Systems in the British Isles*, ed A. H. R. Baker & R. A. Butlin (Cambridge), pp. 325-74.

Skipper, K., 1989. 'Wood-pasture: the landscape of the Norfolk claylands in the early modern period', Centre East Anglian Stud, unpubl Univ East Anglia MA thesis.

Thirsk, J., 1970. 'Seventeenth-century agriculture and social change', in *Land, Church and People, essays presented to Professor H. P. R. Finberg*, ed. J. Thirsk, *Agric Hist Rev*, 18 supp (Reading), pp. 148-77.

Thirsk, J., 1987. *England's Agricultural Regions and Agrarian History 1500-1750* (London).

Thompson, F. M. L., 1966. 'The social distribution of landed property in England since the sixteenth century', *Econ Hist Rev*, 19, pp. 505-17.

Tranter, N. L., 1966. 'Demographic change in Bedfordshire from 1670 to 1800', unpubl Univ Nottingham PhD thesis.

Turner, M., 1980. *English Parliamentary Enclosure: its historical geography and economic history* (Folkstone).

Wade Martins, S., & Williamson, T., 1999a. 'Inappropriate technology? The history of "floating" in the north and east of England', in *Water Management in the English Landscape: field, marsh and meadow*, ed. H. Cook & T. Williamson (Edinburgh), pp. 196-209.

Wade Martins, & Williamson, T., 1999b. *Roots of Change: Farming and the Landscape in East Anglia 1700-1870*, Br Agric Hist Soc Monogr (Exeter).

Williamson, T., 1995. *Polite Landscapes: gardens and society in eighteenth-century England* (Stroud).

Williamson, T., 1998. *The Archaeology of the Landscape Park*, Br Archaeol Rep, Br ser 238 (Oxford).

Wordie, J. R., 1983. 'The chronology of English enclosure, 1500-1914', *Econ Hist Rev*, 36, pp. 483-505.

Worlidge, J., 1669. *Systema Agriculturae* (London).

Yelling, J. A., 1977. *Common Field and Enclosure in England 1450-1850* (London).

Young, A., 1771. *The Farmer's Tour through the East of England* (London).

Post-medieval industrial landscapes: their interpretation and management

Marilyn Palmer

ABSTRACT

This paper discusses the attitude of landscape historians and archaeologists towards industry in the landscape. It emphasises that industrial activity was a feature of many landscapes, urban and rural, and looks at the importance of continuity as well as change in industrial development, taking examples from the textile and mining industries. It considers the problems of recording and conserving industrial landscapes in the face of environmental pressures to reuse derelict and contaminated land.

KEYWORDS

Industrial landscapes, industrial archaeology, cultural resource management

INTRODUCTION

The practice of industry is almost as old as humanity itself: archaeological evidence of attempts to turn natural resources into useful items occur in all periods. Yet, whilst we can observe and admire the manipulation of both organic and mineral resources on a substantial scale from classical times onwards, this scale nowhere matches the momentous changes in economic activity which took place in the eighteenth and nineteenth centuries, with which this paper is concerned. The so-called 'industrial revolution' was first experienced in Britain but then very rapidly elsewhere in the world. The effect on the landscape was profound, as raw materials were exploited at a rate never previously dreamed of: canals and railways were driven through town and countryside alike, and the settlement pattern was transformed as new communities arose wherever a workforce was needed and towns expanded faster than ever before. It cannot be denied that in many areas of the country the landscape underwent an unprecedented, and rarely welcome, transformation. Nonetheless, the depth of change has, in many cases, been overstated, as argued, for example, for the textile industries (Palmer 1994a) and a new generation of social and economic historians has re-visited the work of their predecessors (*e.g.* Berg 1994; Timmins 1993).

Whereas nearly every landscape had always contained some industrial element, in these two centuries it becomes possible to talk about 'industrial landscapes', *i.e.* those in which the practice of industry appears to be the dominant factor in their creation and in their 'human' role. One can thus talk about the mining landscapes of south-west England, the Black Country or south Wales, the textile landscapes of the Pennine districts of Lancashire and Yorkshire, and the colliery landscapes of north-east England. But has the term 'landscape' correct meaning in this context? Or are we really talking about individual sites in a particular geographical region? The individual sites do, however, become industrial landscapes when we move beyond them to consider the human manipulation of space for economic ends. Indeed, the harnessing of power sources, particularly water power, has a regional impact which goes beyond an individual site: transport networks link individual centres of production to national or international markets; industrial settlements often exhibit evidence of the means of control and surveillance practised by employers to exploit their workforce. In effect, industrial landscapes are a complex amalgam: they must be studied not just for their economic or technological significance, but for what they reveal about the cultural environment of our working forebears.

LANDSCAPE HISTORIANS AND THE IMPACT OF INDUSTRIAL DEVELOPMENT

Industrialisation and landscape: to many early practitioners of landscape history, the two terms were irreconcilable. Industrialisation destroyed the traditional landscape and traditional communities – W. G. Hoskins used the term 'tormented landscape' to describe the area around St Helens in Lancashire in his seminal *The Making of the English Landscape* (Hoskins 1955, p. 223). Between the new industrial towns, he says,

> stretched miles of torn and poisoned countryside – the mountains of waste from mining and other industries; the sheets of sullen water, known as 'flashes', which had their origins in subsidence of the surface as the result of mining below; the disused pitshafts; the derelict and stagnant canals (*ibid.*, p. 229).

Yet, once living in Devon, he was clearly attracted by the new subject of industrial archaeology and published various articles on it in *The Western Morning News*, eventually published as an essay on industrial archaeology in *Old Devon* (Hoskins 1966). He saw that the essence of the subject was the same interrelationship between fieldwork and documentary research which he himself had practised for decades. It must be said, however, that the examples of industrial archaeology which he cited in *Old Devon* were in a rural or small-town context and he was not faced with industrialisation on a large scale as he would have been in Lancashire or the Black Country. Nevertheless, he did appreciate the grandeur of some industrial scenes in the same way that contemporaries had: there is a similarity in Webb's description of his tour of Ferreday's ironworks in Bilston in 1810-11:

> Plain narrative is inadequate to compare what I felt at this wonderful combination of the ingenious productions of man! I was not only astonished by the works of art, but Nature had also contributed to add terror to the scene, by the earth smoking at different places in consequence of the burning coalpits, by which these works are surrounded ... The awfulness of the scene reminded me of the description of Cyclops forging thunder for Jupiter (Webb 1812, p. 186)

with Hoskins' own words:

> There is a point when industrial ugliness becomes sublime. And indeed the new landscape produced some fine dramatic compositions, such as the railway viaduct over the smoking town of Stockport; or the sight of Bradford at night from the moorland hills to the north; or the smoky silhouette of Nottingham on a winter evening as seen from the south-bound train on the Eastern Region line; or the city of Sheffield in full blast on a murky morning (Hoskins 1955, p. 232).

What Hoskins disliked was the tedium of many industrial landscapes:

> The Leicestershire industrial landscape nowhere attains the grandeur of the north, or the dramatic and demented ugliness of the Potteries or the Black Country. It is profoundly dull, as one might expect from factories making such prosaic things as vests and pants, boots and shoes, biscuits and bricks (Hoskins 1957, pp. 84-5).

Much of this tedium he attributed to 'a new class of speculator who made conditions even worse than they need have been by extracting high profits out of the unprecedented demand for cheap houses' (Hoskins 1955, p. 226). His dislike of the legacy of 'this particular class of parasite', as he describes the speculator, is perhaps summed up in his view of south Wigston, next door to his Leicestershire home village of Wigston Magna, which was built as a speculative development of factories and over 600 identical brick houses in terraced rows by Orson Wright in the 1880s:

> The sight of south Wigston on a wet and foggy Sunday afternoon in November is an experience one is glad to have had. It reaches the rock-bottom of English provincial life; and there is something profoundly moving about it (Hoskins 1957, p. 84).

Hoskins, then, both resented the intrusion of large-scale industrialisation into the self-sufficient village community and yet saw the potential of industrial archaeology to recreate a particular stage in the development of past society. Interestingly, the year Hoskins initiated *The Making of the English Landscape* series with his own book was the same year that Michael Rix coined the term 'industrial archaeology' in print for the first time in an article in *The Amateur Historian* (Rix 1955). This is the first generally accepted use of the term, despite efforts to claim earlier origins for it. Rix was referring to the physical evidence of the industry of the past two centuries, in his case in the Black Country, not evidence for earlier industry. There has been disagreement over the restricted timespan he and others gave to the term 'industrial archaeology', as will be discussed later, but it is now generally accepted that its practitioners concentrate on the period when the manufacture of goods ceased to be at the level of domestic or craft production and moved into industrial or capitalist production. When this happened varied from industry to industry but the period 1700-1900 is a reasonable compromise.

It is striking how, subsequently, many other landscape historians and archaeologists failed to value the impact of industry on the landscape: in the Dent *Archaeology in the Field* series, we have *Fields in the English Landscape* (Taylor 1975), *Trees and Woodland in the British Landscape* (Rackham 1976), *The Landscape of Towns* (Aston & Bond 1976) and *Villages in the Landscape* (Rowley 1978). Not until 1982 did Dent publish Barrie Trinder's *The Making of the Industrial Landscape* (Trinder 1982) which in fact did not form part of the *Archaeology in the Field* series. By contrast, in the regional studies which followed Hoskins' *The Making of the English Landscape*, industry in the landscape fared a little better. *The Cornish Landscape* (Balchin 1983) considered the impact of the mining of tin and copper and the quarrying of china clay, slate and granite on the landscapes of the extreme south-west, while Arthur Raistrick – a geologist by training and later a pioneer of industrial archaeology – provided two chapters on 'Landscapes of the industrial revolution' in the West Yorkshire volume (Raistrick 1970). D. M. Palliser's *The Staffordshire Landscape* (1976) tackled both the Black Country and the Six Towns, while the jacket of the hardback edition boldly proclaims the industrial nature of much of the region by an illustration of the M6 motorway crossing the Tame Valley Canal near West Bromwich.

Many other landscape historians, though, concentrated on the formation of the landscape in earlier periods and preferred to leave alone the complexities of the effect of industrialisation. Even in 1998, the studies presented to Christopher Taylor as *The Archaeology of Landscape* make no mention of this important facet of Britain's past, having a *terminus post quem* of *c.*1700 (Everson & Williamson 1998) despite the quantity of survey work on industrial landscapes carried out by the RCHME of which Chris Taylor was such a valued member (but also a pupil of W. G. Hoskins who had noted Hoskins 'obvious dislike of industry' in the annotated edition of *The Making of the English Landscape* in 1988). The RCHME's work on industrial landscapes has at least been acknowledged in one of the last publications to emerge from that organisation prior to its amalgamation with English Heritage, *Unravelling the Landscape* (Bowden 1999), perhaps influenced by the amount of time the editor had himself spent surveying and investigating industrial landscapes in Cumbria and Northumberland. Equally, it must be admitted that many industrial archaeologists have ignored the context of the monuments they cherish and have tended to produce site-specific work rather than studies of whole industrial landscapes, but, as in landscape archaeology as a whole, this too has now begun to change.

INDUSTRIAL ARCHAEOLOGISTS AND LANDSCAPE HISTORY

Unlike other branches of archaeology, industrial archaeology came into being with a specific mission – to record and, where possible, to preserve some of the monuments of the British industrial revolution at a time of wholesale redevelopment, particularly in urban areas. The first books written on the subject were concerned to explain the significance of these monuments in relation to past industrial processes rather than their cultural significance as part of a landscape. Angus Buchanan's seminal *Industrial Archaeology in Britain* (Buchanan 1972) treats the subject industry by industry, as did Neil Cossons in *The B.P. Book of Industrial Archaeology* (Cossons 1975). Many of the authors of the David and Charles series of regional studies in industrial archaeology followed suit, while also providing extensive gazetteers of sites – after all, industrial archaeologists were still very much at the stage of discovering what remained from earlier periods of industry.

Arthur Raistrick was perhaps the first industrial archaeologist to break out of this mould and to carry out what would now be recognised as landscape archaeology. He argued that the discipline should cover the study of industry from prehistory to the present, but also recognised the importance of what he described as the integration of man at work and his immediate environment:

by investigation, recording and preservation, we are trying to demonstrate and display the progress

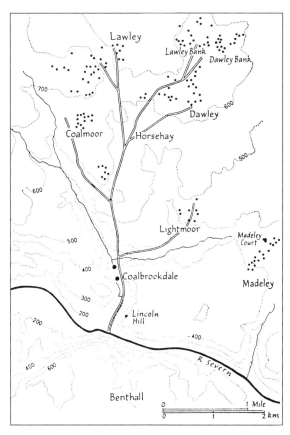

Fig. 10.1. An early example of a map showing linkages between sites: tramways between ironstone and coal pits, and the furnaces at Coalbrookdale, *c.*1750 (from Raistrick 1972, reproduced by permission of Eyre Methuen).

through the centuries of the material environment of man's working life and the increasing skills in manipulating the raw materials of that environment (Raistrick 1972, p. 13).

He abandoned the thematic treatment for a period one, and, with his background, as both geologist and landscape historian of West Yorkshire, paid far more attention to the role of industry in altering the landscape. Furthermore, unlike many of his predecessors in industrial archaeology, he carried out actual survey and recording work as well as documentary research, and the maps in his book demonstrate linkages between individual sites, such as the tramways which carried materials between the ironstone mines, coal pits and the ironworks at both Low Moor in Yorkshire and Coalbrookdale in Shropshire (Fig. 10.1) and artificial watercourses which supplied water to lead mines for both pumping and processing on Grassington Moor (*ibid.* 1972).

Raistrick's attention to fieldwork inspired the next generation of industrial archaeologists, which includes the author. Like him, I worked with small teams of amateur enthusiasts on a wide variety of industrial sites, trying to understand the field remains but also making use of available documentary material to put these in an wider context. I first discussed this approach in an article entitled 'Industrial landscapes of the eighteenth and nineteenth centuries' in Michael Reed's

Discovering Past Landscapes (Palmer 1984), and stressed the value of a variety of different types of documentary sources for understanding industrial sites: to show this, two case studies were offered, the coal and iron community of Moira on the Derbyshire-Leicestershire border and the extensive lead- and copper-mining sett of Esgair Hir in what was then Cardiganshire. With my fellow editor of *Industrial Archaeology Review*, Peter Neaverson, I followed this by a contribution to Michael Reed's *History of the British Landscape* series, *Industry in the Landscape, 1700-1900* (Palmer & Neaverson 1994), in which we sought to describe the various kinds of industrial landscapes which had existed over the past two centuries, identifying the features of those landscapes which still existed in the hope that our readers would learn to recognise these pointers to the past and understand both their function and the contexts with which they should be associated. This approach was essentially archaeological and geographical rather than historical, aiming to complement rather than compete with Barrie Trinder's mainly historical approach to the evolution of the industrial landscape (Trinder 1982). *The Making of the Industrial Landscape* made extensive use of contemporary sources to illuminate the impact of industry on the landscape in the period 1700-1900. Dr Trinder was at pains to point out that industry is only one theme among many in the complex history of the English landscape, and that it needs to be seen in the context of many centuries of man's activities (*ibid.*, p. 5).

A similar plea for setting industrial activity in the wider context has been made by David Crossley of Sheffield University. In his important contribution, 'Early Industrial Landscapes', to the Royal Archaeological Institute's *Building on the Past* (Crossley 1994), he argued that since the archaeological verification of the technology of early industry has been sufficient over the past thirty years for the nature of most of the main developments to have emerged, the emphasis of enquiry should now be extended to establish the place of occupations in the wider landscape. In an archaeological sense, it is only recently that this has become possible.

In its early days, industrial archaeology was largely the province of amateurs – often professionals in their own field, but not archaeologists – who sought to study and protect individual sites and structures in which they were interested. They simply did not have the resources to tackle anything on a larger scale. The growing professionalisation of archaeology in the 1980s and 1990s has affected industrial archaeology no less than other branches of archaeology, and it would be fair to say that less fieldwork than previously is now carried out by the volunteer community, even if this is still a key element in cultural resource management of industrial sites. The growth of contract archaeology as a result of the widespread application of PPG 15 and 16 has

led to much more multi-period work, and often specific work on industrial sites as can be seen from the pages of *Industrial Archaeology Review*. English Heritage, seeking to review the list of scheduled monuments by means of the Monuments Protection Programme (MPP), found it necessary to set up a special programme to deal with industrial sites and the work of their contractors has contributed greatly to our knowledge of industrial sites and landscapes, especially those concerned with mining and the manufacture of raw materials such as lime and glass (Stocker 1995). Finally, the three Royal Commissions on Historical Monuments have undertaken surveys of industrial landscapes on a scale which was just not possible for the pioneers of industrial archaeology. As Paul Everson, Head of Archaeological Projects with the RCHME before its amalgamation with English Heritage, has said:

> For RCHME (and certainly for our colleagues in the Royal Commissions in Scotland and Wales, and for many other public bodies) survey of industrial landscapes has been an increasingly important element in the fieldwork timetable. It has touched many primary industries – coal and charcoal, iron, copper, lead tin, alum – as well as gunpowder and explosives, in all regions of England. And it has appeared to become increasingly complex and ambitious, both as a consequence of a growing awareness by the staff involved of the understanding such landscapes have to offer but more particularly because of the expectations of the public sector customers by whose requests or commissions such surveys have increasingly been prompted (Everson 1995, p. 21).

Such increased professional activity has resulted in a far greater understanding of the nature and scope of industrial landscapes. The remainder of this paper will discuss the key advances which have been made.

ANALYSING INDUSTRIAL LANDSCAPES

Industrial landscapes are a physical record of the way in which people carried out various kinds of industrial activity in the past. They therefore include buildings, not as discrete entities in themselves but in their relationship to one another and to their topographical setting – in other words, their spatial distribution. Different industrial processes are represented by often distinctive buildings which the industrial archaeologist must learn to recognise. These may survive intact or as ruins: the landscapes may also include earthwork remains or buried structures, particularly those associated with extractive industries. One of the major reasons for studying industrial landscapes is to transform such a collection of individual sites and structures into a coherent whole with meaning in both technological and cultural terms. Technologically, the important elements are the linkages between the various field monuments:

these may be physical in the form of watercourses supplying power or transport networks, or functional in the way in which structures were placed to facilitate the processing or manufacturing process (see Malaws 1997). Culturally, these interrelationships can reveal systems of industrial organisation and social relationships, particularly those between the employer and his workforce. These spatial relationships are horizontal ones, manifested on the surface of the land. There are also vertical or sequential relationships which are equally components in the industrial landscape, the results of both technological and cultural change through time. The task of the industrial archaeologist is to analyse the industrial landscape in terms of both the spatial and sequential relationships of structures and features to illuminate the process of industrialisation.

In our recent book *Industrial Archaeology: Principles and Practice* (1998), Peter Neaverson and I have argued that there are three stages in the process of analysing the industrial landscape: (i) determining the reasons for the location of particular industrial enterprises; (ii) interpreting the changes to them through time; and (iii) examining their spatial relationship both with each other and with the development pattern of settlements and transport systems.

Firstly, then, the existence of industrial activity in a particular area is normally governed by the interaction between three groups of factors, namely the presence of natural resources, topographical features and the human agencies which harnessed these for industrial production. As the location of industry has been the subject of considerable research among historical geographers (*e.g.* Smith 1971; Grant 1987), comment here can be brief. Among topographical features, though, the natural gradient of the land is extremely important as it influences the provision of both power and transport. Early industrial development often took a linear form, utilising either water-power sites along streams and rivers or methods of transport which were dependent on gradient. Previous research tended to concentrate either on a single site or the transport element itself, ignoring the totality of the landscape with its interdependent features. New standards were set with the publication of two books from the Royal Commission on Ancient and Historic Monuments in Wales (RCAHMW), one on horse-drawn railways in the Brecon Forest (Fig. 10.2) and the other on the Montgomeryshire Canal (Hughes 1988, 1990). In both cases, the linear feature forms the basis for the study of industrial development and settlement patterns along its

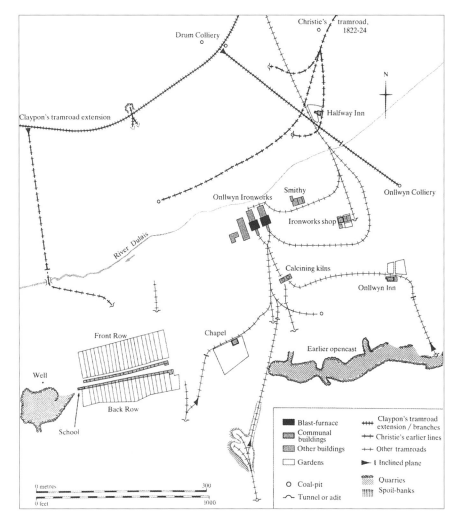

Fig. 10.2. The industrial and social landscape associated with Onllwyn ironworks in the mid-19th century (from Hughes 1990, reproduced by courtesy of RCAHMWales).
© Crown Copyright.

Plate 10.I. The derelict buildings of Old Gang smelt mill in Swaledale, North Yorkshire. Its situation in a valley bottom enabled the use of water power to operate bellows, whilst the valley side provided the route for the condensing flues linking the hearths to the remote chimney.

length. One of David Crossley's research groups carried out a survey in the Sheffield region, demonstrating that on almost 30 miles of five streams and their tributaries, there had been upwards of 115 places where mills once stood, the great majority used by the metal trades, whose water-wheels drove grindstones, forge hammers, rolling mills and wire mills (Crossley 1989, p. v). The importance of conserving water has also been demonstrated in the Coalbrookdale valley in Shropshire, where water-wheels powered blowing engines, forge hammers and grinding mills over a distance of half a mile or so. Here, a tunnel was driven back upstream and water returned to the Upper Furnace Pool by means of a steam-powered pumping engine (Alfrey & Clark 1993). These examples indicate how the intensive study of a river as a power source can put individual sites into a meaningful landscape context. This is equally true of canals and railways, which all too often have been studied as historical entities in themselves (*e.g.* the works of Charles Hadfield) rather than as linear industrial landscapes.

Natural slopes were also important in the siting of a variety of industrial structures. Prevailing wind currents up a suitable slope were used to provide the draught for primitive boles or smelting hearths (Willies & Cranstone 1992). Chimneys were placed on a hillside to provide an artificial draught, with a sloping flue between the furnace and the stack. In some cases, such as lead-smelting, these flues may be very long and also serve a secondary

purpose of allowing vaporised metallic ores to condense on their inner surfaces. These stone-built flues are a striking feature of the landscape of Swaledale, running from smelting mills making use of water power in the valleys to chimneys on the hill-tops (Pl. 10.I). Natural topography was also usefully employed in the location of limekilns and blast furnaces, since both were charged from above and emptied at the base and therefore built against a hillside wherever possible.

Environmental determinism is, however, not solely responsible for the location of industry: human agency has been equally influential. In Britain, the landed élite generally had the power to exploit all the resources of their estates, both above and below ground. This resulted in a pattern of exploitation of mineral resources which reflected seigneurial initiative as much as the existence of raw materials. Landowners might also deter the establishment of manufacturing industry on their estates, preferring to retain the integrity of their closed villages by not encouraging the immigration of industrial workers. The Dukes of Rutland prevented the introduction of the domestic hosiery industry into the Vale of Belvoir in Leicestershire, which therefore presents a totally different landscape from the industrialised villages of the Vale of Trent (Palmer & Neaverson 1992, p. xv). Of course, it has not only been the great landowners who have been responsible for shaping the industrial landscape. The unemployed often squatted on common land and eked out a precarious living by small-scale mining and quarrying. Such settlement was frequent on the fringes of major coalfields, where scattered houses in isolated plots rather than nucleated villages are often still the norm (Trinder 1982, pp. 47-9). The rights of ordinary men to exploit natural resources was both recognised and regulated in certain areas, notably the mining districts of the Forest of Dean, Derbyshire and Cornwall. In the latter, the tinners had the right to divert streams, cut fuel and prospect for tin without hindrance from the landowner. Their disputes were settled by the Stannary Courts and they paid for their privileges by a proportion of their product after smelting. Their stream workings are still an obvious feature in many areas of Devon and Cornwall: those on Caradon Moor have been surveyed by Cornwall Archaeological Unit (Sharpe 1993) and those on Dartmoor by RCHME and the Dartmoor Tinworking Research Group (Austin *et al.* 1989; Gerrard 1994, 1996).

The second stage in analysing an industrial landscape is unravelling the sequential relationships, in other words looking at the processes of change though time. The industrial landscape has to be treated stratigraphically, determining the layers of development and their relationship to each other. This can be tackled strictly archaeologically, as Judith Alfrey and Kate Clark attempted to do with their construction of a Harris matrix to unravel the sequences of development in the limestone industry of Benthall Edge in Shropshire (1993, pp. 5, 38). This is a graphical but highly time-consuming method of analysing change through time and few others have followed their example, but it is essential to recognise that industrial landscapes can change more dramatically in a very short space of time than most other kinds of landscape. For example, archaeological work on the Basset mining sett in Cornwall showed that this tin-mining landscape had been altered radically on three occasions in the twenty-five years between 1875 and 1900 (Palmer & Neaverson 1987).

A highly innovative way of approaching the problem of unravelling sequential relationships in the landscape has recently been explored by two members of The University of Manchester Archaeological Unit, Michael Nevell and John Walker. In *Tameside in Transition* (Nevell & Walker 1999), they have attempted to explain the growth of wealth in the period 1642 to 1870 by relating the physical remains to the particular social groups which can be identified in the two lordships of Ashton and Longdendale. The physical remains were classified according to the English Heritage/RCHME *Thesaurus of Archaeological Monument Types* (RCHME 1996) and over a hundred new site types were identified for the period under discussion, the most common being the farmstead, the textile mill and the terraced house. The three main social groupings of lords, freeholders and tenants had already been identified in the accompanying volume, *Lands and Lordships in Tameside* (Nevell & Walker 1998), and proved equally valid for this period, when the freeholders in particular sought to maximise the potential of their estates and were responsible for the construction of most of the textile sites. Nevell and Walker argue that the products of the three main groups, as identified through the archaeological database, were defined ultimately by landholding rights and that the social structure of this region framed and shaped the nature of the archaeology in the industrial period. It is possible to argue that the methodological framework is too rigid, being constrained partly by the site types defined in the *Thesaurus*, which do not really take into account the adaptation of existing sites for new functions, and partly by a social structure which does not allow for any social fluidity. It is, however, one of the most interesting theoretical perspectives on the archaeology of industrialisation to emerge in recent years and could well be tested in other distinct regions to see if social structure largely accounts for the evolution of a specific industrial landscape.

The third and final stage in analysing the industrial landscape is to consider not just the individual features within it but their relationship with each other. Only by doing this can sequences of production and methods of industrial organisation be established. The nature of early industry, particularly its dependence on both human resources and water power, meant that different stages of production were often widely dispersed in the landscape yet were at the same time inseparably linked. In the lead-mining industry of the Pennines, the actual mining was usually an upland process, as can be seen in the landscape of hushes and bellpits in Arkengarthdale north of Swaledale. Dressing of ore was usually carried out fairly close to the mine to save transporting waste materials, and rough barracks or rows of cottages up by isolated mines suggest that the miners lived on the spot, only returning home for a short time at weekends. Smelting, however, required both water power and fuel, and so was generally a valley-based process, and Arthur Raistrick identified the sites of many smelting mills in the valleys of Swaledale and Wensleydale (Raistrick 1975).

Similar networks also operated in the iron industry, where charcoal from coppiced woodlands and ironstone from mines were taken to water-power sites for smelting into pig iron. Crossley (1994) discussed the historical work which had been carried out on the use of woodland as a resource for fuel in the smelting of iron (*e.g.* Hammersley 1973; Lindsay 1975; and Cleere & Crossley 1985, p. 135) and of non-ferrous metals (Kiernan 1989; Gledhill 1992), but pointed out that insufficient archaeological survey work had been carried out to identify relict coppice in surviving woods. Coincidentally, the RCHME undertook an important survey of the Furness

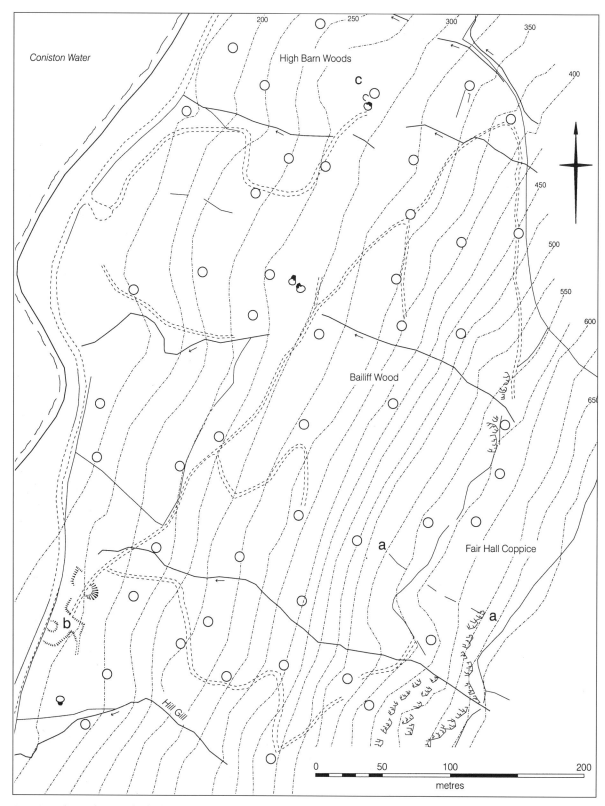

Fig. 10.3. Charcoal pitsteads, bark peelers' huts and trackways in woods to the east of Coniston Water, Cumbria (from Bowden 2000). © Crown Copyright NMR.

district of Cumbria, partly at the request of the Lake District National Park Authority for planning purposes. The aim of the survey was to identify the relationships in the landscape between the surviving iron furnaces, the associated charcoal pitsteads and the sledways and tracks used for transporting the fuel. The charcoal sites were all in the woodland and Fig. 10.3 shows the results of the survey in one area of woodland, consisting of Bailiff Wood, High Barn Woods and Fair Hall Coppice on the eastern side of Coniston Water. This woodland occupied very steep ground and was divided up by dry-stone walls, now in a ruinous condition. The pitsteads were even distributed throughout all three woods and were terraced into the ground to provide a flat platform for charcoal-burning. Most of them were served by tracks which traversed the slopes in a series of zigzags, linking to a main route out of the woods. It is probable that the charcoal was transported by boat across Coniston Water to furnaces such as Duddon on the western shore. These furnaces here remained charcoal-based long after coke had been adopted elsewhere: Duddon furnace worked until 1867, while Backbarrow was only converted to coke in the early twentieth century. For this reason, considerable archaeological evidence remains not just of the furnaces but also of the related woodland industries, including remnants of the

huts occupied by the charcoal-burners and other itinerant woodland workers. The RCHME survey has therefore not only revealed an important cultural landscape but also, much as Crossley advocated, advanced the methodology of the study of industrial landscapes by identifying linkages between fuel supplies and industrial processes (Bowden forthcoming).

An equally innovative and technically demanding survey has been carried out by RCHME on the extensive and complex site of the Royal Gunpowder Factory at Waltham Abbey in Essex. It exemplified the problems of determining both spatial and sequential relationships in the landscape, since it included a multiplicity of different buildings and earthworks and had a chronological depth from the mid-seventeenth to the end of the twentieth century. Whilst the form of gunpowder mills is comparatively well known (Crocker 1986: Buchanan 1996), the earthworks and structures associated with the manufacture of explosives, having always been under government control, were very little understood. To minimise the risk of explosions, many of the buildings were linked by waterways, while others were screened by earthworks or woodland for similar reasons. The RCHME survey included not only field recording but an extensive survey of the considerable quantity of documentary material

Plate 10.II. The textile mill landscape at Milnsbridge in the Colne valley, West Yorkshire. The saw-toothed roofs of the single-storey weaving sheds contrast with the multi-storey spinning mills.

available, necessary for understanding the function of the numerous components within this complex landscape (Everson 1995; Cocroft, *Dangerous Energy*, forthcoming; summary in Bowden 1999, pp. 152-4).

Transport networks of various kinds provided a vital link between different stages of a process, as, for example, David Hey has shown in his invaluable work on packhorse routes (Hey 1980). In Yorkshire, some trains of packhorses carried ore to the smelt mills whist others distributed the raw materials of the textile industry, which was equally dispersed in the Pennine landscape. Most of the weavers' cottages were in hillside locations, often in groups around a farmhouse which were known as 'weaving folds'. Although some of those surviving are of seventeenth-century date, many others were built during the nineteenth century and indicate the continuity of domestic-based handloom weaving alongside powered spinning. Mills down in the valleys had made use of water power, first for fulling cloth as early as the twelfth century and for carding and spinning by the end of the eighteenth, but the adoption of power for weaving was a long drawn-out process. This spatial distinction between the powered and hand processes created paired settlements, with mill communities such as Hebden Bridge and Milnsbridge (Pl. 10.II) in the valleys and weaving villages like Heptonstall on the hill-tops. This kind of pairing was gradually brought to an end in the second half of the nineteenth century by further technological innovation as steam power replaced water power and integrated, valley-bottom mill complexes were built which included all processes from carding to weaving and dyeing under one roof. Contemporary written accounts overemphasise the immediate adoption of a factory system in textile production, whereas the landscape evidence clearly indicates the differences in the pace of technological progress (see Giles & Goodall 1992, pp. 166-99, and Palmer & Neaverson 1994, pp. 94-118).

The methods of the landscape historian or archaeologist have therefore helped to create a more subtle and refined understanding of industrial development than would have been possible from documentary evidence alone.

THE MANAGEMENT OF INDUSTRIAL LANDSCAPES

Most of the landscapes discussed in this paper are extant landscapes, representing in many cases the most recent development of tracts of land. It is therefore relevant to end this brief analysis with some consideration concerning the potential and problems of conserving such landscapes. Some are spectacular in nature, such as the Delabole Quarry in Cornwall or the copper-tainted wasteland of Parys Mountain on Anglesey; others have use as a leisure facility, notably the canal

system and the numerous man-made reservoirs which supplied waterways, mining sites and textile mills.

More have a purely local amenity value, for what is derelict land to some is an adventure playground to others. How many of these landscapes can or should be preserved?

The buzz-phrase in conservation circles is 'sustainable development' (Clark 1994, p. 87). This is defined as development which meets the aspirations of the present generation without compromising the ability of future generations to satisfy their own aspirations – in other words, we need to consider if what we do now compromises the future as well as the past. This concept is particularly applicable to industrial landscapes, where the tendency has been to sweep away what reminded people of exploitation and sweated labour. In addition, relict industrial landscapes have two other problems: dereliction and contamination. Dealing with the latter has resulted in the destruction of many industrial landscapes which may have been contaminated with heavy metals and the debris of other industrial processes; this was one of the many problems with the Waltham Abbey gunpowder works recorded by RCHME. Landscapes of metalliferous mining have been deemed a particular hazard and the removal or burial of waste heaps have been instrumental in the destruction of much archaeological evidence. The lead-mining landscapes around Minera in Clwyd, Van in Dyfed, and Snailbeach in Shropshire have been transformed by land reclamation work, although archaeological evaluations were carried out in advance of the work and some isolated features retained (Palmer 1994b). Cornwall has also been particularly vulnerable to another off-shoot of the Green Movement, the rehabilitation of derelict land, much of it funded from European sources and therefore welcome in an area of high unemployment. Reclamation has involved the capping of shafts for safety reasons, which can involve the destruction of surface archaeology (Sharpe 1995). Both these initiatives have attracted short-term funding for archaeological work and the consolidation of industrial structures but the long-term result has been the sudden transformation of a historic landscape which has evolved over a long period. Nevertheless, the tin-mining area of Camborne-Redruth in Cornwall is on the list of potential World Heritage Sites currently being presented to ICOMOS (DCMS 1999), demonstrating the growing awareness in Britain of the international significance of several of its industrial landscapes, the Derwent Valley of Derbyshire being another (Menuge 1993).

It is perhaps fortunate that many important industrial landscapes lie within National Parks. The Park authorities have demonstrated an enlightened approach towards their management, adopting a policy of 'consolidate as found', preventing further deterioration by the stabilisation of standing

Plate 10.III. Cobbs Engine House, Windmill End. A consolidated beam engine house is a feature of a relict coal-mining landscape, recolonised by nature and providing a leisure resource in the Black Country.

structures but not attempting to re-create their original appearance (White 1991). Land acquisition by the National Trust, particularly coastline as a result of Enterprise Neptune, has brought many industrial landscapes under its protective umbrella. These incorporate monuments ranging from early nineteenth-century engine houses in Cornwall to post-World War Two weapons-testing structures at Orford Ness in Suffolk (Buchanan 1996; Wainwright 1996). The Trust's policy, like that of the National Parks, has been to create an inventory of archaeological structures in its care and, in selected cases, to consolidate rather than rebuild them.

Industrial landscapes outside the protection of National Parks and the National Trust depend for their survival on the attitude of local authorities. Many of these, however, have come to realise the cultural significance of industrial landscapes, especially in areas where industrial activity is now little more than a memory. A classic example is the Ironbridge Gorge in Shropshire, where the creation of a new town to revitalise the economy of the run-down East Shropshire coalfield threatened a landscape often described as 'the cradle of the industrial revolution' and later recognised as a World Heritage Site. The area has now become a series of museums within a landscape, preserving the infrastructure of settlements, water supply systems and transport links which were the context of its iron, coal and clay industries. Other derelict landscapes have been made freely accessible by local authorities as Country Parks, preserving major features of past industry but without elaborate interpretation or curatorial input. A good example is Windmill End in the Black Country, once a coal-producing and iron-working landscape intersected by canals (Pl. 10.III) (Palmer & Neaverson 1994, pp. 188-92). But the utilisation of industrial landscapes as a cultural resource in this way only succeeds if they are within easy reach of large centres of population, thereby investing them with an economic value. The lack of incentive for similar initiatives in remote areas which are not National Parks, such as the lead-mining landscapes of central Wales or the Pennines, places them at risk. A Register of Historic Landscapes can only draw attention to their importance, not provide the resources to manage them, and their long-term survival hangs in the balance.

It is therefore apparent that the management of industrial landscapes is a patchwork of different initiatives, ranging from the very local to the wide expanses in the care of the National Trust and the National Parks. The greatest threat, however, is the current concern not just to treat contaminated land, which is justifiable, but also to use short-term funds to 'prettify' what is classed as derelict land, thereby destroying the historic evolution of the landscape and its value as a cultural resource (Palmer 1994b, p. 50). However, attention is finally being paid to the ecological value of such landscapes, which are often home to a variety of rare plants which colonise disturbed ground (DOE 1994; Box 1999). English Nature may prove more useful in the conservation of relict industrial landscapes than English Heritage!

CONCLUSION

Studies of the evolution of the cultural landscape all too often make only passing mention of industrialisation, regarding it as destructive of an idealised rural environment. But, as Hoskins himself acknowledged in his later work, industry had long been integrated into the countryside. Corn and fulling mills were clustered along rivers, while streams powered blast furnaces and forges, themselves linked by sledways to charcoal-burning sites concealed within the woodlands. Many industrial structures were sited to take advantage of natural features such as gradients or the direction of the prevailing wind, while the dispersed pattern of settlement ensured that most available natural resources like brick clay and limestone were worked locally on a small scale. But from the late seventeenth century onwards,

the pace of change increased and wholly industrial landscapes began to evolve, both rural and urban. Unattractive as these may appear to people who feel that landscape should be an aesthetically pleasing experience, we cannot ignore their existence if we are using the landscape as a means of determining change in the human condition.

This paper has tried to demonstrate that archaeologists with an interest in the industrial period – this is perhaps a more preferable term than 'industrial archaeologists' now that the study of the recent past is both accepted and practised by professional if not by academic archaeologists – have moved away from their previous concentration on isolated monuments. They are seeking to put these features, be they buildings, earthworks or buried remains, in a proper landscape context and to understand their spatial and sequential relationships. As we enter the twenty-first century, we can no longer afford to pass over the impact of industrialisation on the landscape of the last two centuries, and I am grateful to the Society for Landscape Studies that I was asked to produce a paper for this volume on a topic which has been noticeably absent from most previous publications on landscape history and archaeology.

ACKNOWLEDGEMENTS

Some of my early thoughts on the subject of industrial landscapes were rehearsed when I gave the fourth Hoskins lecture at St Anne's College, Oxford, in 1994 and I am grateful to the Principal, Mrs Ruth Deech, for inviting me to participate in that distinguished series. I am also grateful to my friends among the staff both of the former RCHME and RCAHMW for discussing industrial landscapes with me, and also for

supplying two of the illustrations. Finally, I would like to acknowledge the assistance of my fellow Editor of *Industrial Archaeology Review*, Peter Neaverson, in much of the practical work which underlies this paper, and also my colleague at the University of Leicester, Dr Neil Christie, for his perceptive comments on a first draft of this paper.

BIBLIOGRAPHY

Alfrey, J., & Clark, K., 1993. *The Landscape of Industry: patterns of change in the Ironbridge Gorge* (London).
Aston, M., & Bond, J., 1976. *The Landscape of Towns* (London).
Austin, D., Gerrard, G. A. M., & Greeves, T. A. P., 1989. 'Tin and agriculture in the Middle Ages and beyond: landscape archaeology in St. Neot parish, Cornwall', *Cornish Archaeol*, 28, pp. 5-21.
Balchin, W. G. V., 1983. *The Cornish Landscape* (London); revised edition of his *Cornwall: an illustrated essay on the history of the landscape* (1972).
Berg, M., 1994. *The Age of Manufactures 1700-1820* (London).
Bowden, M. (ed.), 1999. *Unravelling the Landscape: an inquisitive approach to archaeology* (Stroud).
Bowden, M. (ed.), 2000. *Furness Iron: the physical remains of the iron industry of Furness and southern Lakeland*, Engl Heritage (London).
Box, J., 1999. 'Nature conservation of post-industrial landscapes', *Ind Archaeol Rev*, 21,2, pp. 137-46.
Buchanan, R. A., 1972. *Industrial Archaeology in Britain* (Harmondsworth).
Buchanan R. A., 1996. 'Landscape with Engines', in *The Remains of Distant Times*, ed. D. Morgan Evans, P. Salway & D. Thackray (London). pp. 84-91.
Buchanan, B. J., (ed.), 1996. *Gunpowder: the history of an international technology* (Bath).

Clark, K., 1994. 'Sustainable Development and the Historic Environment', in *Rescuing the Historic Environment*, ed. H. Swain (Hertford).
Cleere, H., & Crossley, D. W., 1985. *The Iron Industry of the Weald* (Leicester).
Cocroft, W., forthcoming. *Dangerous Energy: the archaeology of gunpowder and military explosives manufacture* (London).
Cossons, N., 1975, 1983, 1993. *The BP Book of Industrial Archaeology* (Newton Abbot).
Crocker, G., 1986. *The Gunpowder Industry* (Princes Risborough).
Crossley, D. (ed.), 1989. *Water Power on Sheffield Rivers* (Sheffield).
Crossley, D., 1994. 'Early industrial landscapes', in *Building on the Past*, ed. D. Vyner (London), pp. 244-63.
DCMS 1999. Department for Culture, Media and Sport. *World Heritage Sites: the tentative list of the United Kingdom of Great Britain and Northern Ireland* (London).
DOE, 1994. *The Reclamation and Management of Metalliferous Mining Sites* (Dep Environ Miner Div) HMSO, London).
Everson, P., 1995. 'The survey of complex industrial landscapes', in *Managing the Industrial Heritage*, ed. M. Palmer & P. A. Neaverson (Leicester), pp. 21-8.

Everson, P., & Williamson, T. (eds.), 1998. *The Archaeology of Landscape* (Manchester).

Gerrard, S., 1994. 'The Dartmoor tin industry: an archaeological perspective', *Proc Devon Archaeol Soc*, 53, pp. 173-98.

Gerrard, S., 1996. 'The early south-western tin industry: an archaeological view', in *Mining and Metallurgy in South-West Britain*, ed. P. Newman (Matlock Bath), pp. 67-83.

Giles, C., 1986. *Rural Houses of West Yorkshire* (London).

Giles, C., & Goodall, I., 1992. *Yorkshire Textile Mills 1770-1930* (London).

Gledhill, T., 1992. 'Smelting and woodland in Swaledale', in *Boles and Smeltmills*, ed. L. M. Willies and D. Cranstone (Matlock Bath), pp. 62-4.

Grant, E. G., 1987. 'Industry: landscape and location', in *Landscape and Culture*, ed. J. M. Wagstaff (Oxford), pp. 96-117.

Hammersley, G., 1973. 'The charcoal iron industry and its fuel', *Econ Hist Rev*, ser 2, 26, pp. 593-613.

Hey, D., 1980. *Packmen, Carriers and Packhorse Roads* (Leicester).

Hoskins, W. G., 1955. *The Making of the English Landscape* (London) (Book Club Associates edn, 1981).

Hoskins, W. G., 1955, 1988 edn. *The Making of the English Landscape with an introduction and commentary by Christopher Taylor* (London).

Hoskins, W. G., 1957. *Leicestershire: an illustrated essay on the history of the landscape*, (London).

Hoskins, W. G., 1966. *Old Devon* (Newton Abbot).

Hughes, S., 1988. *The Archaeology of the Montgomeryshire Canal* (revised edn, Aberystwyth).

Hughes, S., 1990. *The Brecon Forest Tramroads: the archaeology of an early railway system* (Aberystwyth).

Kiernan, D. T., 1989. *The Derbyshire Lead Industry in the 16th Century* (Chesterfield).

Lindsay, J. M., 1975. 'Charcoal iron smelting and its fuel supply: the example of Lorn Furnace, Argyllshire, 1753-1875', *J Hist Geogr*, 1, pp. 283-98.

Malaws, B. A., 1997. 'Process recording at industrial sites', *Ind Archaeol Rev*, 16, pp. 75-98.

Menuge, A., 1993. 'The cotton mills of the Derbyshire Derwent and its tributaries', *Ind Archaeol Rev*, 16, 1, pp. 38-61.

Nevell, M., & Walker, J., 1998. *Lands and Lordships in Tameside: Tameside in transition, 1348-1642* (Tameside).

Nevell, M., & Walker, J., 1999. *Tameside in Transition: the archaeology of the Industrial Revolution in two north west lordships, 1642-1870* (Tameside).

Palliser, D. M., 1976. *The Staffordshire Landscape* (London).

Palmer, M., 1984. 'Industrial landscapes of the eighteenth and nineteenth centuries', in *Discovering Past Landscapes*, ed. M. Reed (London).

Palmer, M., 1994a. 'Industrial archaeology: continuity and change', *Ind Archaeol Rev*, 16,2, pp. 135-56.

Palmer, M., 1994b. 'Mining landscapes and the problems of contaminated land', in *Rescuing the Historic Environment*, ed. Swain, pp. 45-50.

Palmer, M., & Neaverson, P. A., 1987. *The Basset Mines: their history and industrial archaeology* (Sheffield).

Palmer, M., & Neaverson, P. A., 1992. *Industrial Landscapes of the East Midlands* (Chichester).

Palmer, M., & Neaverson P. A., 1994. *Industry in the Landscape, 1700-1900* (London).

Palmer, M., & Neaverson P. A., 1998. *Industrial Archaeology: Principles and Practice* (London).

Rackham, O., 1976. *Trees and Woodland in the British Landscape* (London).

Raistrick, A., 1970. *West Riding of Yorkshire* (London).

Raistrick, A., 1972. *Industrial Archaeology: An Historical Survey* (London).

Raistrick, A., 1975. *The Lead Industry of Wensleydale and Swaledale: Vol. 2: The Smelting Mills* (Ashbourne).

RCHME 1996. Royal Commission on Historical Monuments England. *Thesaurus of Monument Types* (London).

Rix, M., 1955. 'Industrial archaeology', *Amateur Historian*, 2,8, pp. 225-9.

Rowley, T., 1978. *Villages in the Landscape* (London).

Sharpe, A., 1993. *Minions: an Archaeological Survey of the Caradon Mining District* (2nd edn, Truro).

Sharpe, A., 1995. 'Developments under derelict land grants: the potential, the problems', in *Managing the Industrial Heritage*, ed. Palmer & Neaverson, pp. 133-6.

Smith, D., 1971. *Industrial Location: an Economic Geographical Analysis* (2nd edn, New York).

Stocker, D., 1995. 'Industrial archaeology and the Monuments Protection Programme', in *Managing the Industrial Landscape*, ed. Palmer & Neaverson (Leicester), pp. 105-14.

Taylor, C., 1975. *Fields in the English Landscape* (London).

Timmins, J. G., 1977. *Handloom Weavers' Cottages in Central Lancashire* (Lancaster).

Timmins, G., 1993. *The Last Shift: the decline of handloom weaving in nineteenth century Lancashire* (Manchester).

Trinder, B., 1982. *The Making of the Industrial Landscape* (London).

Wainwright, A., 1996. 'Orford Ness', in *The Remains of Distant Times*, ed. D. Morgan Evans, P. Salway & D. Thackray (London), pp. 198-210.

Webb, D. C., 1812. *Observations and Remarks during Four Excursions made to Various Parts of Great Britain in the Years 1810-1811* (London).

White, R. F., 1991. 'Arresting decay: archaeology in the Yorkshire Dales', in *Archaeology in National Parks*, ed. R. F. White & R. Iles (Leyburn), pp. 55-64.

Willies, L. M. & Cranstone, D. (eds), 1992. *Boles and Smeltmills* (Matlock Bath).

The discovery of landscape

John Chandler

ABSTRACT

This paper summarises academic and lay attitudes to landscapes from the medieval period to the twentieth century. It explores the process of discovering the history of landscape, including late medieval and Tudor travellers, the development of cartography, the landscape element in county and regional historiography, the growth of antiquarianism, the Victorian climate of nostalgia for vanishing landscapes through to the work of landscape pioneers and the marriage of disciplines.

KEYWORDS

Landscape, historiography, perception of landscape

'Matford Lane, still so-called,' wrote W. G. Hoskins as he gazed out of his study window, 'has a right-angled bend in it, quite inexplicable as there are no physical obstacles to make it bend like this; so I assume that it was contrived to run around some Saxon estate that already existed' (Hoskins 1977, pp. 15-16). Hoskins (Pl. 11.I) had moved back to Exeter in 1968, and for me, re-reading that passage three decades on after years of puzzling over bends in roads, his words brought a shock of recognition. I realised that Matford Lane in 1968 was part of my experience too. By then, and for several years, I had been walking along it most days on my way home from school in Exeter to the bus stop. My copy of his *Devon* was purchased in 1969, so like many of my contemporaries working in this field I have lived in his shadow all my adult life.

Hoskins famously wrote that, when as a child his curiosity in landscape features was first aroused, he would borrow library books, 'but they never answered my questions or even seemed aware that such questions might be asked' (Hoskins 1967, p. 16). And when in 1955 he published *The Making of the English Landscape* he claimed that, 'there is not one book which deals with the historical evolution of the landscape as we know it' (Hoskins 1955, p. 13). Few landscape historians would dissent from the view that the defining moment for their discipline came at some point during the 1950s, when Hoskins, Beresford and Finberg produced for a popular audience their syntheses of the ideas fomenting in their own minds and in those of their academic colleagues (Finberg 1952; Hoskins 1955; Beresford 1957). But alongside the papers surveying

progress since those pioneering days, room should perhaps be found in this volume for a glance backwards, to the 'prehistory' of landscape history. Was there, in fact, landscape history before Hoskins, and if not, why not?

If for a new discipline to be launched it takes the charisma and enthusiasm of an individual, distilled into a book which captures the popular imagination, then Hoskins should take much of the credit. There would in that case (apart from some maverick exceptions to be considered later) be no landscape historians before Hoskins. Tributes to him penned around the time of his death (*e.g.* Phythian-Adams 1992), and more recent assessments (especially Muir 1999, pp. 27-37) have explored the germination of *The Making of the English Landscape*, and have seen it as in part a response to the destructive enemy raids on Exeter and Plymouth in 1941-2.

Richard Muir (*ibid.*) has suggested that Hoskins underplayed the groundwork achieved before the war by historical geographers such as Clifford Darby. Indeed, after the war, in 1951, Darby had published an important paper on 'The Changing English Landscape', four years before Hoskins's book (cited by Butlin 1993, p. 133). Historical geographers themselves, when considering the origins of landscape studies, point to the work of Carl Sauer in the United States who, under the influence of German concepts of *landschaft*, was writing about cultural and morphological aspects of landscape during the 1920s and 1930s (Cosgrove 1985, pp. 56-7; Butlin 1993, pp.131-2; Atkins *et al.* 1998, pp. 274-6). It is notable, too, that a popular textbook on historical geography, which anticipated *The Making of the English Landscape* by a year, defined its subject's themes as:

> the distribution of peoples, the patterns of settlement, the soil and vegetation zones that develop as fields and pasture replace forest, marsh and moor – the study of these lead back in most areas to much earlier ages than the present. The great themes are also those rapid changes in a region that man's increasing ability to adapt himself to his environment and to modify it bring about: the changing patterns of agriculture, of industry, of communications and trade, of population densities, and the resultant changes in the evaluation of natural resources and of space relations (Mitchell 1954, pp. 14-15).

Hoskins owed a considerable debt also, as Muir (1999) notes, to field archaeologists such as Cyril

Plate 11.1. William Hoskins viewing the landscape

Fox, Jacquetta Hawkes and O. G. S. Crawford, who was in turn influenced by Heywood Sumner. Indeed reading now one of Sumner's essays, 'A Winter Walk in the New Forest', for example, which was first published in 1925 (reprinted in Cunliffe 1985, pp. 61-70) we are immediately transported into the stylistic and intellectual world which Hoskins and Beresford were to make their own a generation later:

> Similar, though lesser, pit diggings may be found on other hilltops near here ..., where we know that these diggings date back, at least, to medieval times by the name given to this place in New Forest Perambulations of Edward I, 'Putts in Merkynggeslade,' and of Charles II, 'The Pits,' and infer that heathstone was the material sought for, by present-day experience that this stone may still be found here. Such sites as these are both intriguing and baffling to one who trusts excavation to provide documents – things that teach ... (*ibid.*, pp. 68-9).

But Sumner never attempted the subject on the scale demanded, for instance, by Harold Fox's excellent definition of landscape history as exploring, 'the pivotal nature of human landscapes both as artefacts made by people and also as influences on behaviour – that is, the study of landscapes *in societies* ... (Fox 1996, p. 273; *cf.*

Muir 1999, p. 299: 'Landscape ... is about the settings of human existence and development'). Against this yardstick even the antecedents whom Hoskins *et al.* acknowledge – the field archaeologist Hadrian Allcroft, or the historian F. W. Maitland – seem to fail the test. They fall short of Fox's criteria because they approach landscape history specifics without placing them in their broader historical context.

Nevertheless, taking our lead from Hoskins and his reviser Christopher Taylor (Hoskins 1967, p. 17; Taylor 1997, p. 9), we do well to regard *Domesday Book and Beyond* by Maitland as in some sense a catalyst. His interest in Domesday studies was stimulated in part by the work of another pioneer, Frederic Seebohm (1833-1912), whose seminal *The English Village Community: an Essay in Economic History* (1883) extrapolated from a map of the open fields of Hitchin (Hertfordshire), where he lived, a theory about the origins of English settlement. Maitland disagreed with the theory, but like Seebohm (and of course like Hoskins later on) was keen on maps. At one point in describing the Domesday survey Maitland commented: 'Two little fragments of "the original one-inch ordnance map" will be more eloquent than would be many paragraphs of written discourse' (Maitland 1897, p. 39). The happy term 'palimpsest' (literally a paper or parchment erased and rewritten) was already in figurative use in other areas of Victorian thought before Maitland applied it to the map, in an essay on place-names published in 1889:

> Now I cannot but think that some evidence about these things might yet be discovered in that most wonderful of all palimpsests, the map of England, could we but decipher it; and though I can do but very little towards the accomplishment of this end, I may be able to throw out a suggestion ... (Maitland 1911, vol. 2, p. 87).

Maitland was also a visionary. At the end of his great work, published in 1897, he wrote:

> A century hence the student's materials will not be in the shape in which he finds them now ... . Instead of a few photographed village maps, there will be many; the history of land-measures and of field-systems will have been elaborated. Above all, by slow degrees the thoughts of our forefathers, their common thoughts about common things, will have become thinkable once more (Maitland 1897, p. 596).

Maitland is regarded by historians still as among the greatest of their number, and his premature death in 1906, when aged 56, was universally lamented (see Elton 1985). His work, so familiar to us, on pre-Conquest England in the light of Domesday Book, was only one of many achievements, in the fields also of medieval and legal history, the Selden Society and the prolific editing of records. But his more personal life is important, too, since it may provide the clue to his nascent interest in landscape and maps as evidence for the history of early societies. The grandson of a churchman and son of a lawyer, he was related by marriage to such diverse talents as Sir Leslie Stephen, Ralph Vaughan Williams and H. A. L. Fisher, as well as the families of Josiah Wedgwood and Charles Darwin. His interests included music, walking and cycling. His widow subsequently married her kinsman, Darwin's son and collaborator, the botanist Sir Francis Darwin (see Freeman 1978; Vaughan Williams 1964, pp. 35-6).

Darwinism, and its perceived threat to religion and authority, was a key intellectual issue during the 1870s and 1880s (see Wilson 1999, ch. 9 for a stimulating recent discussion), and the idea that evolutionary theory could be reconciled to the Christian doctrine of Creation and a Creator was only adopted by many within the Church of England after Frederick Temple, an avowed Darwinian, became archbishop of Canterbury in 1896 (Chadwick 1970, pp. 23-4). Maitland, an establishment figure at Cambridge, but also a controversial agnostic (Elton 1985, pp. 15, 73) moved within a mainly agnostic circle of friends and relations who had been very close to Darwin himself. Leslie Stephen had renounced holy orders in 1875, after more than a decade of

disillusionment and disbelief, calling Thomas Hardy to witness the legal document (Wilson 1999, p. 8). Even those scholars, historians included, who retained their faith, were influenced by the scientific revolution. Seebohm was a staunch Quaker, but in the preface to his book (*ibid.*, p. ix) he couched his quest in terms of the nature of the *economic evolution* [my italics] which had taken place in England since the English conquest. To Maitland, the unbeliever, the contrast between theories of natural selection and evolution on the one hand, and the Biblical account of creation on the other, must have been particularly stimulating.

Lateral thinking, as we might term it, was one characteristic of the Darwin circle which Maitland manifested in his work. An example, one of many which might be quoted, concerns Darwin's son Sir George (to become Maitland's widow's brother-in-law), who was the first to apply statistical techniques to genealogies and surname lists in an attempt to determine the frequency through history of marriages between first cousins, and so to study the effects of human inbreeding (Lasker 1985, p. 6). Since his parents, Mr and Mrs Charles Darwin, were themselves first cousins, this was a matter close to his heart.

But in the context of landscape history a much more important contribution of Darwinian theory than lateral thinking, for many of the natural sciences, especially geology and palaeontology, was that it finally toppled that old shibboleth, Catastrophism. This was the attempt by a French scholar, Georges Cuvier, to reconcile the Biblical account of creation with current thinking on fossils, by asserting that the present state of nature and landscape were the direct consequence of Noah's flood (see Allen 1978, pp. 69-70). As an explanation of landscape irregularities the theory had antecedents as far back as Thomas Burnett in 1684 (Simpson 1986, p. 57).

Perceptions of landscape based on religious dogma undoubtedly offer one, and perhaps the most cogent, reason, for the failure of landscape studies to take their place within the broader spectrum of the Victorians' intellectual exploration of the past. Until late in the century religious orthodoxy was all-pervading among local antiquarians and historians, many of whom were themselves Anglican clergymen. The social composition of the early printing clubs (forerunners of record societies), and the national and local archaeological societies, has been studied by Phillipa Levine, who has shown that in nearly half the Victorian local societies of this type the clergy accounted for 30 *per cent* or more of the membership (Levine 1986, pp. 184-5). Indeed the Tractarian movement and ecclesiologists of the 1830s and 1840s spawned not only the Camden Society, but lay behind many of the early county societies, for whose members the minutiae of church architecture offered an abiding fascination (Clarke 1938, pp. 75-6; Piggott 1976, pp. 174-83).

Even for those society members drawn from the nobility and county gentry who were not of the cloth, a university education (Oxford or Cambridge) was virtually *de rigueur*, for which professed Anglicanism was essential (Levine 1986, pp. 8-10). The snobbery extended not only to academic background, but more particularly to social position. One candidate for the Society of Antiquaries, Charles Roach Smith, an expert on Roman London, was nearly rejected when a letter to the acting secretary pointed out that he was 'in business' (Levine 1986, p. 21).

Social division at all levels within and between the emerging historical disciplines was a barrier to any form of cross-disciplinary research. In two respects, specialism and élitism, this militated against the possibility of landscape history. The central thesis of Levine's study is the gradual divergence through the later nineteenth century of disciplines previously linked by social and even family connections – antiquarianism, archaeology and history. By Maitland's time there was a caucus of professional, academic historians in universities and the national archive collections who took little interest in 'mere antiquarianism' (Levine 1986, pp. 29-30). Archaeologists were in general amateurs, not university men, whose digging concentrated on prehistoric and Roman remains. They had, therefore, little time for historical sources. General Pitt Rivers, the most progressive excavator of his day, went so far as to remark that, 'the evidence that can be derived from them [historical sources] appears to be of the weakest possible description' (quoted by Bowden 1991, p. 160).

Antiquarianism at its worst, as manifested in the county societies, had become the occupation of leisured and moneyed enthusiasts, who enjoyed social occasions centred on the museum, lecture hall, field trip and dinner table, who accumulated artefacts and made lists, and who revelled with chauvinistic pride in their own locality (Levine 1986, pp. 59-61). By their nature and attitude antiquarians at the end of the nineteenth century were for the most part backward-looking and unreceptive to change. In itself, antiquarianism as a pursuit did not *need* to be narrow-minded, as perusal of county journals of the period makes plain. Contributors were tireless collectors of disparate and obscure information about the past, in areas such as folklore, genealogy, architectural details and heraldry. But their mentality was not to bring the various strands together, so as to make more than a sum of the parts. Worse, their élitism might have the effect of deterring those of a different background, with imagination and new ideas.

A case study will illustrate this (see Chandler 1996). The nature writer Richard Jefferies (1848-87) was brought up the son of a small farmer near Swindon, and his early enthusiasm was for local history, which as a cub reporter on small-town weekly newspapers he was able to indulge in various series of articles. Through a kindly but

misplaced attempt at patronage he was invited in 1873 (another speaker having declined) to lecture at short notice on the history of Swindon to the Wiltshire Archaeological and Natural History Society at their annual meeting. At the time approximately 90 *per cent* of the society's members were nobility, gentry or clergy, with most of the remainder drawn from the professions. Jefferies was not a member, and did not therefore have access to the society's library. Intimidated by the occasion, no doubt, he gave a dull, derivative lecture along antiquarian lines, and committed a social gaffe at the end (Jefferies 1874).

Not long after this experience he gave up local history research, and twice described the precise moment when he realised that he was on a hiding to nothing. He had travelled to London in connection with some local topic. He proposed, he told a correspondent, to include in his work, 'all that could be learnt in the British Museum Library'. Soon, gazing at the shelves of folio county histories and aware of thousands of pamphlets, deeds and unindexed documents, he realised his folly. 'At the thought', he wrote, 'the dome overhead seemed to descend upon my head like a vast extinguisher, putting out the vital spark of hope ... The truth forced itself upon me that it was utterly impossible to write the history of little Okebourne Wick. No mortal mind could achieve it ...' That is from one, recently discovered account (Jefferies 1985); the other is more philosophical, and includes the telling remark:

> Nothing will ever be found in it [the library]. Those original grains of true thought were found beside the stream, the sea, in the sunlight, at the shady verge of woods. Let us leave this beating and turning over of empty straw; let us return to the stream and the hills; let us ponder by night in view of the stars (Jefferies 1884).

I have focussed on Jefferies, not because he would necessarily have distinguished himself as a landscape historian, but because his experience is a graphic illustration of the stultifying effect of Victorian antiquarianism. How many others like him, by virtue of class and education, were denied the opportunity to develop their enthusiasm for landscape and the countryside within and beyond the jejune historical disciplines of the day? Jefferies has become one of a number of authors now categorised as part of a 'rural tradition' of writing (see Keith 1974), which can be traced back to Izaak Walton in the seventeenth century. Some were conscious that they were writing within a tradition – Edward Thomas, for instance, wrote the classic biography of Jefferies – while others, including Jefferies himself, or Gilbert White or John Clare, would perhaps have regarded themselves as *sui generis*.

I do not propose to discuss this rural tradition further, but it does signal to us, and to anyone musing on my topic, 'the discovery of landscape', that were we to become deflected from our fairly narrow definitions of landscape studies, and leave the antiquarian/ historical tradition, we should rapidly become overwhelmed. When asked, the University of Bristol computer told me unflinchingly that there were 805 books in the library containing the word 'landscape' in their titles. Leaving aside the many anodyne and fairly meaningless appearances of the word in recent book titles (an alternative, perhaps, to the other vogue word, 'heritage'), a large proportion of 'landscape' books are about planning, painting, poetry, or garden design.

In pursuit of landscape history we may draw a distinction between the aesthetic appreciation and portrayal of real or imaginary landscapes on the one hand, and the explanation of real landscapes in the context of human activity on the other. But although we are concerned with the latter, we need also to have some awareness of landscape in literature and art from the seventeenth to the nineteenth century, if only to understand the cultural mindset within which topographical writers during this period were working. A few generalisations will suffice.

The words 'landscape', 'scenery', and the 'picturesque' all derive from *representations* of (usually) the countryside, not from the actual countryside so depicted. A landscape was originally a work of art, scenery a theatre prop, and the picturesque a view suitable as a subject for a picture. This distinction is plainly seen in topographical writers, such as Celia Fiennes, when she wrote in about 1703: 'The commons all about Epsham [Epsom] is very good aire and shews the country like a landskip, woods, plains, inclosures, and great ponds' (Morris 1947, p. 353). Educated tourists in search of the picturesque, therefore, appreciated a view, when they found it, because it resembled the classical, literary and mythological ideals to be found in a picture or a poem (Andrews 1989, pp. 3-4). Richard Payne Knight in 1805 noted that, 'a person conversant with the writings of Theocritus and Virgil will relish pastoral scenery more than one unacquainted with such poetry'. So viewing landscapes required knowledge and intellectual effort on the part of the viewer, but it was knowledge of the classics, poetry, and paintings. One is reminded of Hoskins 150 years later, writing: 'One needs to be a botanist, a physical geographer, and a naturalist, as well as an historian, to be able to feel certain that one has all the facts right before allowing the imagination to play over the small details of a scene' (Hoskins 1988, p. 18). The principle is the same, but the knowledge required for landscape appreciation is in totally different fields.

The quest for pastoral landscapes, and the popularity of nature poems, such as James Thomson's *The Seasons* (1730), are generally attributed first to the increasingly unpleasant living conditions in large towns, necessitating a country retreat for those who could afford it, and later to the dramatic changes to the countryside resulting from enclosure (Thomas 1984, pp. 243-54; Bermingham 1987, pp. 9-11). Thus a rural arcadia or utopia was conjured up by nostalgic imaginations, derived from Biblical and Classical notions of a Garden of Eden, a golden age; and real landscapes were judged according to how well they could be made to fit the illusion.

Much topographical writing, particularly of the eighteenth century, fits within or sits alongside this literary tradition. The published results of picturesque tours generally have the words 'historical, topographical and descriptive' (or similar) in their titles, and such productions were sometimes by noted topographers, who included William Coxe, Robert Clutterbuck, T. D. Fosbrooke, Francis Grose, Sir Richard Colt Hoare and Stebbing Shaw (see Andrews 1989, bibliography). Edward Brayley and John Britton between 1801 and 1814 produced the multi-volume series, *The Beauties of England and Wales*. But, given what has been said above, an eighteenth-century topographer, asked why he did not explore landscape with the precision that he traced a manorial descent or transcribed an epitaph, would have replied that landscape was a philosophical or aesthetic ideal, and had no bearing on the description of actual places.

Conversely, persons of aesthetic judgement ridiculed and caricatured the narrow-mindedness of topographers. Examples abound in contemporary fiction of the antiquary as a stock figure of derision, beginning with John Earle's *Microcosmography* of 1628 (cited by Levine 1987, p. 100), through Sir Walter Scott's Jonathan Oldbuck, to Bill Stumps in *The Pickwick Papers* and Mr Simpkinson (probably a caricature of John Britton) in Barham's *Ingoldsby Legends* (Piggott 1976, pp. 132-62, 184-7). An extreme form of satire was *a New Description of Merryland, containing a Topographical, Geographical, and Natural History of that Country*, published anonymously in Bath by Thomas Stretzer in 1741. It is a work of topographical pornography, an extended *double entendre* which describes the female anatomy in landscape terms familiar to readers of Stukeley, whose work it parodies.

Local antiquaries and topographers were rampant throughout the English countryside during the eighteenth and nineteenth centuries, and their work has been admirably and thoroughly chronicled in a recent *festschrift* (Currie & Lewis 1994). They were men (and very occasionally women) of a very broad range of intellectual attainment, mostly writing from the standpoint of the class to which they belonged or, as Finberg shrewdly noted (Finberg & Skipp 1967, p. 74), would have liked to belong, but didn't. Had they evolved a discipline of landscape history, it would have been what is now called the landscape of power; since, as Cosgrove argues (1985), the visual power of landscape paralleled the real power of the landowners. But of course, for the most part they did not take this prospect. They were constrained, I suggest, by three widely held assumptions which could not be dislodged until the nineteenth century. The first I have already discussed: the disjunction between landscape as an aesthetic ideal and as a topographical reality.

The second assumption, which was touched on in discussing the Darwinian revolution, has been explored in detail by Sir Keith Thomas (1984). This was the anthropocentric view of the world derived from Biblical theology, which preached that the relationship between man and nature throughout human history since the Fall was God's punishment. Tudor and Stuart churchmen, according to Thomas (1984, p. 18), 'did not hesitate to represent the world's physical attributes as a direct response to Adam's sin. "Cursed is the ground for thy sake" (*Genesis* iii. 17)'. Although this harsh view was softened in the eighteenth century, so that the natural world became more benign, it was still generally regarded that everything, animal, vegetable and mineral, was placed there by the Creator to benefit or torment mankind. This view prevailed, despite occasional awkward observations to the contrary by astronomers, botanists and zoologists (*ibid.*, pp. 168-9). And, by implication, if everything existed for mankind to exploit, farmers and landowners (the agents of landscape modification) were failing in their Christian duty if they did not cultivate their estates to the limits of their potential (*ibid.*, pp. 254-5).

There was not much room in this philosophy for curiosity about landscape history. As the then President of this Society, Paul Harvey, remarked at the tenth anniversary conference of the Society of Landscape Studies:

> The student of landscape history has at least this advantage, that the past ages that produced the written records, at least until the eighteenth century, had not the slightest interest in landscape ... If people in the past were uninterested in landscape they will not have been trying to mislead each other (and thus us) about it in their written documents (Harvey 1991, p. 49).

The third restraint on innovation which topographers of the seventeenth and eighteenth centuries laboured under was that the ground rules for their literary genre had already been laid. The longevity of William Camden's *Britannia* was extraordinary – first published (in Latin) in 1586, it was frequently revised up to the first English translation in 1610. It was thoroughly revised within Camden's original framework by a team of scholars in 1695, and appeared again in revised editions in 1722 and 1789, and reprinted in 1806. How damning a reflection on the lack of innovative thought within a discipline could there be than that the same basic textbook remained in use for 220 years! (see Piggott 1976, pp. 33-53; also Parry 1995, pp. 331-57, who takes a more benign view than mine). The habitual plagiarism

of county mapmakers during the same period tells a similar story.

Camden adhered firmly to the anthropocentric view of nature described above, claiming (here in Edmund Gibson's 1695 version) that: '[Britain] is the master-piece of Nature, perform'd when she was in her best and gayest humour; which she placed as a little world by it self, by the side of the greater, for the diversion of mankind' (quoted in Piggott 1976, p. 48). Camden's first love, and principal theme in compiling *Britannia*, was the evidence for Roman Britain, in order to bring Britain within the orbit of the nations of the classical world. Consequently, he had little interest in the middle ages, 'so overcast with darke clouds or rather thicke foggs of ignorance, that every little sparke of liberall learning seemed wonderful' (*ibid.*, pp. 43, 38).

I have probably gone as far as I need on this wild goose chase, looking for glimmers of landscape history where none, by the definitions given when I set out, appear to exist. It is my contention that until the end of the nineteenth century the intellectual conditions were not really right for our discipline to emerge. That said, it would be strange if there were no iconoclasts who, although their ideas were not followed up in their lifetimes or by their successors, can be seen with hindsight to have foreshadowed the work of Hoskins and his fellows, which was my starting point. I should like to end by very briefly singling out three: John Aubrey, John Leland and Thomas Burton.

The reputation of John Aubrey (1625-97) as a pithy but scatty biographer belies a man of wide attainments, and extraordinary mental dexterity ('ingeniose', to use his term). His experiment to discover the proportion of downs to clayland in Wiltshire is well known. He worked out the respective areas on a copy of Speed's county map, cut the map up with scissors, made two piles of the pieces, and weighed them on a goldsmith's balance – and then (true to character) lost the result. Michael Hunter, in his 1975 study of Aubrey, made an impassioned and convincing plea that the maggotty-headed gossip-monger of the *Brief Lives* should be taken seriously, and examined in detail his antiquarian methods and assumptions.

More recently, the cause has been taken up by Graham Parry (1995, pp. 275-300), who distinguishes Aubrey from contemporary antiquarian thought by his, 'movement away from documentary evidences to an emphasis on fieldwork, the study of sites and monuments *in situ*, and the development of an idea of "comparative antiquity"' (*ibid.*, p. 277). To this attempt to catalogue change, particularly gradual change (evolution, one might almost say), he marshalled folklore, oral tradition, etymology, scientific experiment and a host of other sources of evidence to explain the phenomena which he observed (Hunter 1975, pp. 162-78). Nor was he inhibited by the Biblical teaching on creation.

Against a discussion of earthquakes and their geological consequences he glossed the remark that, 'the world is much older, than is commonly supposed' (cited in Hunter *op. cit.*, p. 59; see also Parry 1995, p. 281).

The preface to Aubrey's manuscript collections on Wiltshire, entitled, 'An Essay towards the Description of the North Division of Wiltshire', illustrates well his attitude to the task, and is something of a literary *tour de force*. This extract imparts the flavour of the essay:

> But as Pythagoras did guesse at the vastnesse of Hercules' stature by the length of his foote, so among the Ruines are Remaynes enough left for a man to give a guesse what noble buildings, etc, were made by the Piety, Charity, and Magnanimity of our Forefathers ... These Remaynes are *tanquam tabulata naufragii* ['like the planks of a wrecked ship'] that after the Revolution of so many yeares and governments have escaped the teeth of Time and (which is more dangerous) the hands of mistaken zeale. So that the retrieving of these forgotten things from oblivion in some sort resembles the Art of a Conjuror who makes those walke and appeare that have layen in their graves many hundreds of yeares: and represents as it were to the eie, the places, customs and Fashions, that were of old Time ... Let us imagine then what kind of countrie this was in the time of the Ancient Britons ... (Aubrey & Jackson 1862, p. 4).

More than a century earlier John Leland (*c.* 1503-52) had travelled England and Wales under Henry VIII collecting notes of remarkable perspicacity for various topographical and historical projects which (like Aubrey) he never brought to fruition. Had insanity not struck in 1547, rendering him incapable of further work, he might indeed have edited away much of what we now find most valuable and revealing in his work. The substance of his notes was widely copied, used and (sometimes) plagiarised by later writers, notably Camden, but his underlying method, and the astuteness of his observations, were seldom matched by those of his successors. He observed earthwork remains of urban decay, crop-marks, rivers impeded by human intervention, and the economic effects of specific land use. He chronicled buildings, old and new, looked for and tried to understand antiquities, even to the extent of probing a hill-fort by excavation (Chandler 1993, pp. xxi-xxiii).

Alongside this, he employed a whole battery of evidence to explain the appearance of a settlement on his route. Here he is at his best (I have modernised the English):

> The town of Winchcombe lies due east of a small valley, and its single main street climbs gently towards the west. There is no doubt that the town was walled; the wall may be seen in several places, especially on the south side towards Sudeley Castle, and it is recorded also in the *Life of St Cenelm*. There was a fortress or castle right next to the south side of St Peter's ... The parish church (according to documents at Winchcombe Abbey), was later known as Ivy-castle, and its site is now occupied by a few poor houses and gardens. I suspect that the reason for the name Ivy-castle is that when the old building fell into ruin, ivy grew up its walls. The last Prior of Winchcombe told me that he had heard of a fort or castle once existing in the east or north-east part of the town (Chandler 1993, pp. 168-9).

A close reading of this description (not untypical of many passages in Leland) reveals the range of sources which make up the synthesis, including a literary work, archives, oral evidence, place-names, fieldwork and personal observation. Here, I suggest, Leland comes close to meeting the criteria we have set for the landscape historian.

My third accolade would go to Thomas Burton (d. 1437), a Cistercian monk and sometime abbot of Meaux Abbey in East Yorkshire, whose work has been described by Antonia Gransden (1980, pp. 81-3; 1982, pp. 355-71). She regards his chronicle of Meaux as, 'the most comprehensive and scholarly of the local histories written in medieval England' (Gransden 1980, p. 81). He too employed a variety of sources – literary works, documents, reliable witnesses and his own observations – and as a former bursar of his house he was well equipped to understand the texts at his disposal. Burton described the effects of erosion and silting on the Holderness levels, and how settlements had been washed away or abandoned, though in some cases the ruins could still easily be seen. He described a road which led from the manor of Old Ravenser towards the ruins of the lost town of Ravenser Odd, submerged in the Humber estuary. He noted changes which had been made to watercourses, including the cutting of new channels, and his evidence of town plantation in the East Riding was used extensively by Beresford (1967, pp. 511-16).

Of all the medieval chroniclers and historians described by Gransden he seems to have been the first to try to explain changing landscapes in terms of human and natural intervention. This interest was in part pragmatic – one strand of his research stemmed from his work as bursar, defending the abbey's property and arguing for tax and tithe exemption on land lost to the sea (Gransden 1982, p. 361). Topographical change, therefore, had to be clearly understood and explained, as in the case of the two courses of the River Hull. The abbey's estate of Wyk lay between them, and:

> because the New Hull, on the eastern side of Wyk, was daily increasing, the Old Hull became blocked in the course of time, so that it could hardly be described even as a drain. And so the New Hull, which had formerly been called *Sayercryk*, became a large river, and now separates the estates [wapentakes] of Holderness and Harthill, which means that Wyk should now be regarded as within

the boundary of Harthill. But now the grange at Wyk lies completely in ruins, and can be seen to the present day lying open in a meadow, which still bears the name *Grangwyk*. And another manor house, called *Tuppcottes*, has taken over its lands, but stands on a different site, within the territory of Myton (Bond 1866, p. 169).

If there is any characteristic – beyond their genius to think outside the bounds imposed by their contemporaries – which links these three landscape historians of the fifteenth, sixteenth and seventeenth centuries to each other, and to Maitland and Hoskins of the nineteenth and twentieth, it is perhaps that for each of them their work was a response to some kind of landscape change, and a consequent recognition of loss. For Burton it was the practical consequence of coastal inundation upon his abbey's revenues; for Leland the loss at the dissolution of an ordered countryside based on the monastic estates; and Aubrey continually harked back to a way of rural life wrecked by the Civil War (Parry 1995, p. 276). Maitland and his contemporaries lost their comfortable theocentric world – a bereavement

which led in some cases to extreme depression, even suicide (Wilson 1999, pp. 10-11). Hoskins, perhaps, compensated for the destruction of his beloved Exeter by the *Luftwaffe*, and of the Devon of his childhood by the motor car, by writing *The Making of the English Landscape*.

At around the time of its publication, in 1955, Hoskins recorded three radio talks for the BBC on the theme of the rediscovery of England (printed in Hoskins 1963, pp. 209-29). He described the allure to Leland and the Elizabethans of this 'country waiting to be explored and described', and bemoaned the failure of their successors until recently to carry through their impulse. He ended the last of his talks with the thought that:

> sitting upon the Saxon hedgebank in the afternoon sun, looking over a view as richly orchestrated as a Brahms symphony, it is sufficient for the time being to feel that, much as we know about the topography of England, there is even more we do not know; and that there are endless possibilities of discovery ahead, enough perhaps for another three hundred years of inquiry and affectionate exploration (*ibid.*, p. 229).

ACKNOWLEDGEMENTS

This is a revised version of a paper given at the Society for Landscape Studies 21st Anniversary Conference, Birmingham, 23rd October 1999. I am grateful to participants at the conference for their constructive comments; also for research facilities during the preparation of this paper to the University of Bristol Library; the National Monuments Record Library, Swindon; the British Library; and Bath and Trowbridge Reference Libraries.

BIBLIOGRAPHY

Allen, D. E., 1978. *The Naturalist in Britain: a social history* (Harmondsworth).

Andrews, M., 1989. *The Search for the Picturesque: landscape, aesthetics and tourism in Britain, 1760-1800* (Stanford, California).

Atkins, P., Simmons, I., & Roberts, B., 1998. *People, Land and Time: an historical introduction to the relations between landscape, culture and environment* (London).

Aubrey, J., corrected and enlarged by Jackson, John E., 1862. *Wiltshire: the topographical collections*, Wiltshire Archaeol & Nat Hist Soc (Devizes).

Beresford, M., 1957. *History on the Ground* (London).

Beresford, M., 1967. *New Towns of the Middle Ages: town plantation in England, Wales and Gascony* (London).

Bermingham, A., 1987. *Landscape and Ideology: the English rustic tradition, 1740-1860* (London).

Bond, E. A. (ed.), 1866. *Chronica Monasterii de Melsa ... auctore Thoma de Burton, Abbate ...* vol. 1, Rolls ser, vol. 43.1 (London).

Bowden, M., 1991. *Pitt Rivers: the life and archaeological work ...* (Cambridge).

Butlin, R. A., 1993. *Historical Geography through the Gates of Space and Time* (London).

Chadwick, O., 1970. *The Victorian Church, Part 2* (London).

Chandler, J. (ed.), 1993. *John Leland's Itinerary: travels in Tudor England* (Stroud).

Chandler, J., 1996. 'An uncomfortable antiquary: Richard Jefferies and Victorian local history', *Richard Jefferies Soc J*, 5, pp. 14-24.

Clarke, B. F. L., 1938. *Church Builders of the Nineteenth Century: a study of the Gothic revival in England* (London).

Cosgrove, D., 1985. 'Prospect, perspective and the evolution of the landscape idea', *Trans Inst Br Geogr*, new ser, 10, pp. 45-62.

Cunliffe, B., 1985. *Heywood Sumner's Wessex* (London).

Currie, C. R. J., & Lewis, C. P. (ed.), 1994. *English County Histories: a guide* (Stroud).

Elton, G. R., 1985. *F.W. Maitland* (London).

Finberg, H. P. R., 1952. *The Local Historian and his Theme* (Leicester).

Finberg, H. P. R., & Skipp, V. H. T., 1967. *Local History: Objective and Pursuit* (Newton Abbot).

Fox, H. S. A., 1996. 'Landscape history: the countryside', in *The Oxford Companion to Local and Family History*, ed. D. Hey (Oxford), pp. 266-73.

Freeman, R. B., 1978. *Charles Darwin: a Companion* (Folkestone).

Gransden, A., 1980. 'Antiquarian studies in fifteenth-century England', *Antiq J*, 60, pp. 75-97.

Gransden, A., 1982. *Historical Writing in England, vol. 2: c. 1307 to the early sixteenth century* (London).

Harvey, P. D. A., 1991. 'The documents of landscape history: snares and delusions', *Landscape History*, 13, pp. 47-52.

Hoskins, W. G., 1955. *The Making of the English Landscape* (London).

Hoskins, W. G., 1963. *Provincial England: essays in social and economic history* (London & Basingstoke).

Hoskins, W. G., 1967. *Fieldwork in Local History* (London).

Hoskins, W. G., 1977. *The Making of the English Landscape*; revised edn (London).

Hoskins, W. G., 1988. *The Making of the English Landscape; with an introduction and commentary by Christopher Taylor* (London).

Hunter, M., 1975. *John Aubrey and the Realm of Learning* (London).

Jefferies, R., 1874. 'Swindon, its history and antiquities', *Wiltshire Archaeol & Nat Hist Mag*, 14, pp. 180-6.

Jefferies, R., 1884. 'Pigeons at the British Museum', in *The Life of the Fields*, pp. 215-19.

Jefferies, R., 1985. *The Birth of a Naturalist* (London).

Keith, W. J., 1974. *The Rural Tradition: a study of the non-fiction prose writers of the English countryside* (Toronto).

Lasker, G. W., 1985. *Surnames and Genetic Structure* (Cambridge).

Levine, J. M., 1987. *Humanism and History: origins of modern English historiography* (Ithaca, New York).

Levine, P., 1986. *The Amateur and the Professional: antiquarian, historians and archaeologists in Victorian England, 1838-1886* (Cambridge).

Maitland, F. W., 1897. *Domesday Book and Beyond: three essays in the early history of England* (Cambridge) [citation from Fontana edn, 1960].

Maitland, F. W., 1911. *The Collected Papers of Frederick William Maitland*, ed. H. A. L. Fisher, 3 vols (Cambridge) [quotation is from 'The surnames of English villages', vol. 2, pp. 84-95, originally published in *Archaeol Rev*, Nov. 1889].

Mitchell, J. B., 1954. *Historical Geography* (Teach Yourself Geography series) (London).

Morris, C. (ed.), 1947. *The Journeys of Celia Fiennes* (London).

Muir, R., 1999. *Approaches to Landscape* (London & Basingstoke).

Parry, G., 1995. *The Trophies of Time: English antiquarians of the seventeenth century* (Oxford & London).

Phythian-Adams, C., 1992. 'Hoskins's England: a local historian of genius and the realisation of his theme', *Local Hist*, 22 (4), pp. 170-83.

Piggott, S., 1976. *Ruins in a Landscape: essays in antiquarianism* (Edinburgh).

Seebohm, F., 1883. *The English Village Community: an essay in economic history* (Cambridge).

Simpson, J., 1986. 'God's visible judgements: the Christian dimension of landscape legends', *Landscape History*, 8, pp. 53-8.

Stretzer, T., 1741. *A New Description of Merryland, containing a Topographical, Geographical, and Natural History of that Country* (Bath).

Taylor, C., 1997. 'Dorset and beyond', in *Making English Landscapes*, ed. K. Barker, & T. Darvill, Oxbow Monogr 93 (Oxford), pp. 9-25.

Thomas, K., 1984. *Man and the Natural World: changing attitudes in England, 1500-1800* (Harmondsworth).

Wilson, A. N., 1999. *God's Funeral* (Edinburgh).

Vaughan Williams, U., 1964. *R.V.W.: a Biography of Ralph Vaughan Williams* (Oxford).

The appreciation of landscape history

Della Hooke

ABSTRACT

Changing trends in landscape history are examined: from an initial concern with the influence of humans as expressed physically and visually in the landscape there has been a growing concern with both human cultural impact and our perception of the environment. There has been an awakening across Europe of an interest in protecting Europe's cultural/historical landscapes, an aspect in which the landscape historian should play a prominent role.

KEYWORDS

Conservation, European cultural landscapes, landscape history, landscape pays, traditional land use, woodland usage

INTRODUCTION

When the first volume of *Landscape History* appeared in 1979 it represented an important milestone in recognising the importance of the interdisciplinary approach in understanding landscape evolution. The work of several prominent scholars in the late 1950s had helped to convey their love of landscape to an ever-widening audience. They had been drawn from several disciplines: the most well known of all, the late Professor W. G. Hoskins, was an economic historian but the history of landscape was also firmly established within many university geography departments in the way that historical geography was then interpreted. Paradoxically, it was largely because landscape history required a multi-disciplinary approach that it tended for years to remain upon the fringe of the old-established academic disciplines. However, such was its inescapable importance that it inevitably found a niche in the widening studies of archaeology, history and geography.

The late Professor H. C. Darby, as a geographer, made important contributions to the recognition of early historical landscape regions, firmly based upon an investigation of the Domesday evidence. His interpretation of landscape evolution may have been somewhat influenced by the ideas of the '50s, when there was a general acceptance of the belief that a relatively undeveloped landscape with much surviving woodland, heathland and waterlogged ground was gradually subjected to reclamation and the expansion of farmland from the early medieval period onwards. This view had to be cast aside as evidence mounted of the extent of earlier prehistoric and Roman activity but the landscape regions outlined by Darby and his colleagues (Darby *et al.* 1952-77), involving meticulous analysis of the statistics found in Domesday Book, remain a valid starting point for understanding subsequent landscape change. Within geography, fashions were to change, with a growing emphasis upon man's perception of the landscape, and it was within archaeological and some historical departments that an understanding of landscape evolution tended to find a more welcoming home. The nature of the discipline also changed: simplistic and often deterministic views had long been rejected and the influence of cultural, social and economic factors was gradually appreciated as the complexities of developing landscapes became clearer.

Works such as Hoskin's *The Making of the English Landscape* (1955) have made an indelible impression upon the subject. Dipping into all periods of history, Hoskins extended an interest and love of landscape which had first been fostered in his native Devon to encompass the whole of England. His book was followed by a county series which was sadly never completed but whose volumes marked a notable improvement upon many earlier county topographies. These were usually more concerned with church architecture than surrounding landscapes – although some notable gems remain rich sources of topographical history today and most counties can boast a pre-twentieth-century scholar who has treated the history and, to some extent, the topography, in considerable academic depth and with sensitivity. Hoskins' contribution was to bring landscape history in a readily understandable form to the general public and among this group he remains better known for this one book than for any of his more in-depth studies. His legacy was that he helped to create a ground swell of interest without which any concern cannot thrive. Hopefully, this journal has continued in this tradition.

In recent years another important development has taken place. Awareness of the role of landscape evolution in the formation of the present landscape has steadily grown and has been incorporated into more applied studies. To a certain extent, in the past the academic world tended to view the *application* of knowledge for specific purposes as somewhat inferior to 'pure' research, an attitude eradicated by the present-day need to raise funds and integrate research with its practical implementation. Nevertheless, practical studies were undertaken. The late Dudley Stamp incorporated historical landscape development into his study of farming regions in the interwar years (1930-47, 1950) and the reports published in *The Land of Britain* series are now valuable historical documents in themselves. Today an increasing number of landscape practitioners across Europe are beginning to consider the historic element in the landscape, although progress has been frustratingly slow, not helped by an inadequate database. Although archaeological sites have been listed for many years it is only more recently that this has been extended to incorporate historical landscapes – many counties have no such data on record (Hooke 1999 and in preparation).

For both statutory bodies and much of the general public, it has often been easier to raise concern for plants and wildlife than the more conceptual historic landscape. The media has not helped: programmes on archaeology are popular but few aspire to look at the wider landscape setting, some have tended to play upon the element of 'treasure seeking' rather than in-depth study. There are hardly any programmes dealing with the historical landscape or regional landscapes.[1] There is further tension in the countryside as the latter is displayed increasingly as a place for urban recreation, a playground for all manner of active pursuits. Never has a greater in-depth understanding of rural culture been more essential – and this must include the historical past or the title of 'culture' is a misnomer. The rich inheritance of the rural countryside is unlikely to be appreciated if one is unaware of it: the popularisation of the study should not be a missed opportunity.

LANDSCAPE HISTORY AND ECOLOGY

Studies of past landscapes have now been made more reliable by a wide diversity of archaeological techniques: palynology, studies of molluscs, of early soil horizons, etc, can show how plants and animals adapted to changing environments and can begin to detect the influence of man (Edwards *et al.*, ch. 2, this volume). Many questions remain unanswered: to what degree did climate change contribute to the development of peat in upland marginal areas just at the time at which man was clearing the land of woodland and preventing regeneration by the increased pasturing of stock?

How 'man-made' are the barren moorlands that fringe many of the hill ranges of North Wales (Walker & Taylor 1976; Hooke 1997)? The vegetation history of much later periods remains the subject of debate: while few would wish today to countenance the myth of a thickly wooded rural countryside at the beginning of the Anglo-Saxon period, waiting for the new migrants to tame its wilderness, the density and nature of the woodland cover on the eve of the Norman Conquest is still open to debate. Pollen studies from a small number of sites in lowland England suggest woodland regeneration, where it occurred, to have been a late Anglo-Saxon, early Norman phenomena (Day 1991)[2] and many, like Oliver Rackham, would now argue for the predominance of an open 'savanna'-like landscape over much of the country with next to no truly ancient woodland surviving. Yet recent archaeological studies have revealed the use of oak timber taken from forest-grown trees in the hinterland of London that grew within 'a form of high, dark wildwood' in the A.D. 890s and up to *c.* 1200 (Goodburn 1999).

The traditional management of woodlands, heaths and pastures obviously helped a native flora and fauna to survive over the centuries, even if these, sometimes, only managed to regenerate themselves in spite of man's activities. Indeed, most historical environments were directly created by man's use of the land. Ecological studies have shown how amazingly complex the life cycle of some creatures can be, depending upon the close juxtaposition of one or two species, and any change in land use can upset the delicate pattern. The chalk pastures of southern England have been decimated by the breaking up of new land for arable and this has been marked by more than the recognised destruction of irreplaceable archaeological monuments and early field systems. It has been shown (Thomas & Elms 1998) how the larvae of the Large Blue butterfly feed for several days on thyme and then wait to be found by foraging *Myrmica* ants, mimicking the smell and behaviour of the ant grub. For this to happen the thyme has to grow within 2-3 metres of the foraging ants or the caterpillar will die; moreover, although up to eight species of ant will carry back the caterpillar it will only survive in the nest of one particular species. The caterpillar then eats the ants' grubs and hibernates for eleven months. As it has destroyed the ant colony the next generation of caterpillars must hatch near a new colony. Only some forty sites in Britain are rich enough in thyme to support 1,000 butterflies but there are insufficient host ants at most of them – for the ants the grass must be less than 3 cm tall. To ensure such conditions, no fertiliser must be added to the land or the delicate meadow plants which sustain the butterfly will be shaded out and currently less than 3 *per cent* of the chalk grassland in Britain is free of fertiliser. Grazing is also essential to keep down the rank grasses, but

Plate 12.I. A *bocage* landscape in the Warwickshire Arden. Ancient hedgerows well set with trees surrounding small irregular fields are characteristic of this region.

farmers have abandoned the steep, unfertilised slopes and rabbits have been killed by myxomatosis, still lethal within the rabbit population. Admittedly, the Large Blue is a relic of a time 10,000 years ago when temperatures in southern Britain were higher; many other diminishing species, such as the nightingale, are near the fringe of their favoured habitat zone but others have simply diminished due to changing land use. Knowing how land was managed in the past and the techniques that were in use can offer invaluable advice and guidance – few would question the importance of maintaining biodiversity for future generations.

It is, perhaps, the extent of change that has taken place in the second half of this century that has alerted both landscape planners and the general public to the need for greater vigilance and more effective protective measures. The effects of unmitigated agro-industry can not only drastically change the landscape for ever but alter its ecological base – including, now, such half-understood and fundamental features as genetic make-up. Progress in itself is not 'bad', and it would not be feasible to turn back the clock to an economy that managed to feed smaller populations with hours of back-breaking toil for the many, but the need for continued research remains paramount, including knowledge of historic landscape management.

LANDSCAPE *PAYS* AND COUNTRYSIDE CHARACTER

Few would dispute that much of the joy of the British countryside derives from the variety of its landscape regions, changing within short distances to give a rich panoply of ever-changing vistas. Admittedly largely influenced by geology, these also reveal how man has adapted the natural environment to influence vegetation cover, fieldscapes and settlement patterns. While the present-day landscape can be evaluated from a morphological aspect, categorising the visible scene, only a knowledge of how this was produced over the centuries explains its present-day characteristics, allowing us to understand the implications of change. What we see today is the product of thousands of years of man's interdependency with his surroundings; it is a rich archive and we should be foolish indeed not to heed the lessons of the past. We are also intellectually much poorer if we fail to comprehend the richness of this living legacy and its cultural complexity.

Une individualité géographique ne résulte pas de simples considérations de géologie et de climat. Ce n'est pas une chose donnée d'avance par la nature. Il faut partir de cette idée qu'une contrée est un réservoir ou dorment des énergies dont la nature a déposé le germe, mais dont l'emploi

Plate 12.II. Open views characterise the south Warwickshire *Feldon*. A former open field area, hedgerows in this region may date from late medieval enclosure for stock but most are the result of parliamentary enclosure in the eighteenth and nineteenth centuries when large geometric fields were laid out. Chesterton Roman camp astride the Fosse Way can be seen in the middle distance.

dépend de l'homme. C'est lui qui, en la pliant a son usage, met en lumière son individualité (de la Blache 1911, p. 3).

Recently the Countryside Commission produced its 'Countryside Character' map (Countryside Commission, English Nature 1996) which attempted to identify landscape regions across England each of which displayed a degree of physical and cultural unity. Now, as the newly formed Countryside Agency, it is attempting to fill out the basic data as a guide to those who manage the land. Additionally, more and more counties are undertaking more detailed surveys, most of which involve a degree of historical landscape reconstruction and analysis. These vary in depth: some rely upon the collection of published work but others collect historical information at either 1:50 000 or even 1:10 000 scales. Essentially, all attempt to identify those characteristic features which make individual landscape regions unique. Considerable progress has been made since Rackham (1986) recalled the long-established division in England between the Highland Zone and the Lowland Zone but suggested a contrast within the latter between 'ancient' and 'planned' landscapes. Basically, 'ancient' countryside was an appellative for areas where open field had been absent or enclosed before *c.* 1700, giving a

landscape of ancient hedgerows, but also with many small woods, heath and non-woodland trees, while a 'planned' countryside was one with a strong tradition of open field farming which lasted into the enclosure movement and beyond; in such areas woods are absent or few and large, heaths rare and thorns and elders, shrubs which are ever ready to re-colonise abandoned arable, abound (*ibid.*, pp. 4-5). This division emphasises the present-day situation but fails to clarify the fact that historically 'ancient' landscapes have undergone as much change as any other, and that the 'planned' landscape has been subject to an element of 'planning' or reorganisation at several different stages of history.

The concept of contrasting landscape regions is, of course, by no means a new one. Contrasts between *bocage* and *champagne* or 'champion' landscapes have interested antiquarian historians, travellers and writers for centuries. In the sixteenth century, both John Leland and William Camden noted the contrast between the once-wooded Arden and the open lands of the Feldon in Warwickshire (Toulmin-Smith 1964, V. 47; Camden 1586, II. 329; Hooke 1988) (Pl. 12.I, Pl. 12.II). *The bocage* landscape of small irregular hedged fields, patches of woodland and scattered settlements was aptly described by Marc Bloch (1931) in the 1930s describing the countryside of western Normandy. The work of Darby and his colleagues (Darby *et al.* 1952-77), discussed above, showed how these regional differences could be identified as early as the time of the Domesday survey and, indeed, pre-Conquest charter evidence confirms that they were recognisable at a date before this (Hooke 1998a) and probably much earlier. In some form they must go back into at least the late Iron Age with the clearest distinction between the more infertile and more favoured regions, but probably even then they were already affected by such 'cultural' factors as tribal frontiers or communication routes. Obviously there has been continuous change and regional differences have been more marked at some stages than at others (Fox 1989). In spite of major progress in understanding landscape evolution, especially of settlement patterns, there are still many unanswered problems – concerning the origin of open fields, for instance, for the location of wide areas of cultivated land, however, organised, has always been a major factor determining landscape pattern.

The historical element seems to be the least addressed even in the new landscape divisions of the Countryside Agency although, to be effective, it was essential that this study should remain a landscape précis. The relevance of past landscape management was brought home to the present writer recently when asked to comment upon the view from the summit of the Clent Hills, an outlier of breccia and pebble beds on the southern outskirts of the Black Country. Almost all of the visible countryside around had lain within royal forest in the twelfth century and, apart from nineteenth-century and modern development, is characterised by a similar pattern of dispersed settlement – small manorial nuclei, outlying farms and hamlets set within a pattern of scattered woodland and small hedged fields – in spite of the fact that it is geologically varied, including the Triassic sandstone plateau of north Worcestershire and south-west Staffordshire, outliers of more ancient rock forming prominent hills in Shropshire and intervening clay valleys. The whole area had been pock-marked with medieval hunting parks (Fig. 12.1). Open field had rarely been a significant component in this region although small scattered patches, many subject to early enclosure, had been a characteristic of many parishes. On the more infertile soils, heathland remained extensive into the nineteenth century and woodland survived on steeper slopes. Even industry had early roots in the woodland environment for charcoal from the surrounding woodlands fed the blast furnaces established at Cradley and Hales in the seventeenth century, the forerunners of the Black Country iron-working and metal industries. The trends of twentieth-century agriculture have led to the loss of the irregular field pattern produced largely by medieval assarting over extensive parts of the region, especially on the lighter soils and along alluvial valleys, but the region remains visibly different to the 'champion' areas visible

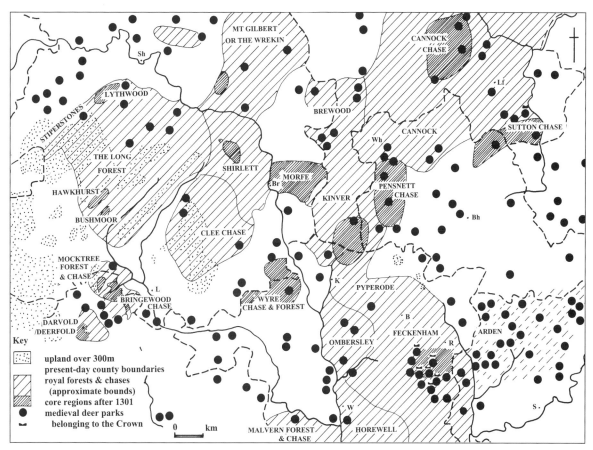

Fig.12.1. Forests, chases and parks in the medieval landscape around the Clent Hills.

beyond – such as the fertile Vale of Evesham where open fields were noted for their high yields of corn throughout medieval times.

The Clent upland was also very much a part of a frontier zone, close to the divide between the Iron Age tribes of the Dobunni and the Cornovii and between the Anglo-Saxon kingdoms of the Magonsæte, the Hwicce and Mercia, but this is a cultural element expressed physically by only a few surviving Iron Age hill-forts. However, the cultural element is one that cannot easily be omitted in our understanding of the landscape. Man is a being of complex intellect. He brings to anything he sees a wide medley of personal emotions, memories and beliefs which affect his interpretation and perception of his surroundings. Neither is the perception of landscape static. In the eighteenth century, if one were rich enough, the choice landscape with which to surround one's home was a quiet pastoral landscape with green meadows and pastures, sinuous lakes and encircling woodland, the latter keeping the rest of the world at bay. A suitable 'ruin' might evoke the perceived qualities and virtues of a bygone classical age. These designed landscapes are still with us today. But by the end of that century many were beginning to find them somewhat boring and they were often replaced by a Victorian exuberance with exotic planting and new glasshouses to house the exhibits being gathered from all around the world by exploratory botanists. Perception of landscape beauty varies with fashion: this century, in the 1950s, a Scotsman, David Linton (Linton 1968), attempted to rank landscapes by a perceived measure of quality and gave his top ranking to landscapes that were most topographically broken – such as the Scottish Highlands.

We are now increasingly concerned with the human 'cultural' aspect in the landscape. One aspect of this is the expression of identity with a specific region, a feeling of 'belonging' influenced by familiarity with and an understanding of an area in which we feel 'at home'. This sense of identity is undoubtedly strengthened by a knowledge of how these regions were shaped in the past – how local industry and farming evolved, how people lived in former times, what people and individuals from that region contributed in the realms of science or the arts.

Looking north-westwards from the Worcestershire Clent Hills, in the far distance the forests and chases of Mount Gilbert, Shirlett and Clee once extended southwards from the Wrekin. Although most of the forests were greatly diminished in extent in the earlier part of the fourteenth century much woodland survived, especially in private woods and chases. Charcoal was used at an early stage in the bloomeries used to produce iron. In this area, the industry had been mainly established on monastic estates: Wenlock (Cluniac) Priory had two iron foundries and ironstone quarries in Shirlett Forest in 1540,

there was a bloomery adjacent to Wombridge Priory and the Cistercian monks of Buildwas had a small iron forge on their demesne in the sixteenth century (Rowley 1972, p. 216; Trinder 1973, p. 15). The availability of charcoal, combined with water power, was a factor in the establishment of charcoal-fired blast furnaces for iron-working in the Border region in the sixteenth and early seventeenth centuries, this method of production almost completely replacing iron-working in bloomeries. The Willey furnace was built soon after 1609 on the margin of Shirlett and a charcoal-fired blast furnace, The Old or Upper Furnace, came into use in Coalbrookdale in 1638 (Riden 1993, pp. 54, 62-3, 59-60) (Fig. 12.2).[3] Woodland was being coppiced within Shirlett by the mid-sixteenth century to provide timber for the expanding iron industry. The industry became firmly established in this area and subsequent technological advances (including the use of coke as fuel), led to the region becoming recognised as the birthplace of the Industrial Revolution.

The effect of the iron industry upon the woodland has been disputed. While Rackham (Rackham 1976, pp. 91-3; 1980, pp. 108-9) argues that careful management was carried out by the ironmasters to ensure fuel supplies (coppicing was being practised in Coalbrookdale by the sixteenth century: Rowley 1972, pp. 217-18), Bayliss (1987, pp. 722-6) argues that the woods of Mocktree and Bringewood were severely depleted by this activity, noting petitions from Ludlow Corporation and the Council of the Marches to the Crown and other landowners in the late sixteenth and seventeenth centuries:[4]

> the iron works in Bringewood and Mocktree have already made so general a west & spoile by all kinds of wood (save a remnant of spring woods as they now dig by the ground and pull out the auld rootes), wch the whole countrey do much grudge at ... (Lord Eure, President of the Council of the Marches, April 1611, cited in Bayliss 1987, p. 723).

However, concentrations of ancient woodland – what little that survives anywhere in the midland region – are still found around Bringewood, Coalbrookdale and Wyre – all areas of charcoal production on a large scale (Fig. 12.2).

While the distinctive landscape characteristics of the Coalbrookdale/Ironbridge area include the presence of both ancient and secondary woodland and a plethora of industrial remains, there is also a strong cultural tradition which demands that it should be firmly placed within an historical context. Without the entrepreneurial skills, investment and enthusiasm of such men as John Wilkinson and Abraham Darby the iron industry of this region would not have reached such an ascendancy. After 1763, Wilkinson pioneered the development of a technique for boring larger iron guns and applied these techniques to steam engine cylinders, applying the Boulton and Watt steam engine to his ironworks at the New Willey Furnace

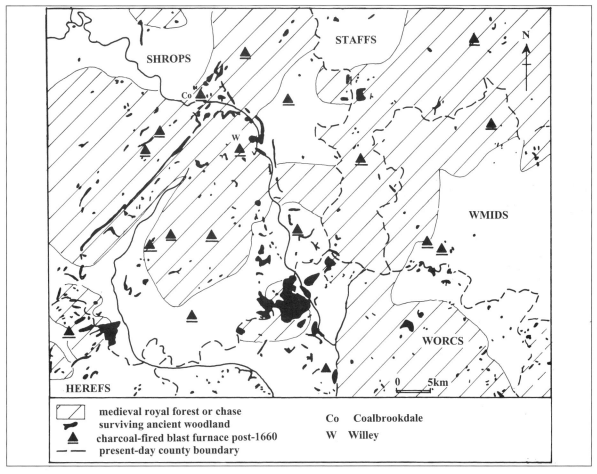

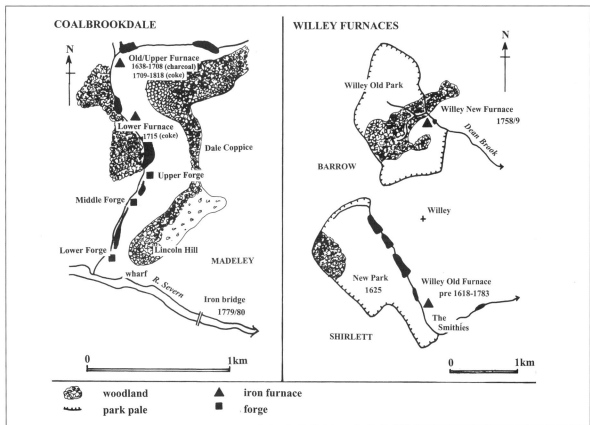

Fig. 12.2. Forest and charcoal-fired blast furnaces in use since 1660 in the Ironbridge region.

in 1776, only the second person to use this for blowing a blast furnace directly; he also developed the world's first coal-cutting machines (Collins & Duckworth 1997). Darby introduced the use of coal instead of charcoal to his ironworks in Coalbrookdale in the early eighteenth century and built the world's first iron bridge to span the gorge in 1779 (colour Pl. 12.III). After his death the Coalbrookdale Company began to expand and to build new works making use of local coal supplies they themselves leased (Alfrey & Clark 1993, pp. 19, 23). The region, too, has a vibrant local culture based on the traditions of the working man and the rise of Methodism. All these factors, together with the rich survival of the physical relics of its industrial past, which include the iron bridge, have promoted it today to the status of a World Heritage site, with both sensitively promoted tourism and associated academic research helping to maintain a strong sense of local identity

An increasing number of studies like that of the Ironbridge area (Hooke 1998b) are being carried out to map and analyse the historical landscape of local regions. These provide the background to present-day landscape assessments and to an understanding of a region's cultural history.

THE PRACTICAL IMPLEMENTATION OF HISTORICAL LANDSCAPE STUDY

Given its position as an advisor to the government and to public bodies the Countryside Agency is in a strong position to further landscape study but other bodies are also implementing practical studies, sometimes with the financial help of English Heritage. In particular, county and district councils are actively offering guidance and preparing management plans which will, hopefully, continue to take the historical landscape evolution into account. Several pioneering surveys which helped to establish the methodologies were those carried out in Oxfordshire for English Heritage (Chadwick, Hooke, & Hitchott 1993; Chadwick 1999), and for Cornwall (Cornwall Co Counc 1996) and Warwickshire (Warwickshire Co Counc n.d. based upon a 1989 survey) for county councils (see, further, Fairclough 1999). Both the Oxfordshire and Warwickshire surveys involved the drawing up of historical land use maps prepared at a scale of 1:50 000 which helped to define the historical landscape regions of the county and to identify those features which still gave such regions a particular character. Briefly, these usually fall into a number of categories (Table 12.1): i) those which are primarily geological or topographic in nature, including soil type; ii) settlement pattern and settlement density, embodying village location, size, form and building material; patterns of routeways; iii) historical land use: farming methods, field size and the nature of field boundaries (Pl. 12.I,

TABLE 12.1. FEATURES CONTRIBUTING TO COUNTRYSIDE CHARACTER

Geological/topographical characteristics
Settlement pattern & density: location, size, form & building material
Communication patterns including roads, railways, canals
Historical land use & present vegetation cover field size & shape; nature of field boundaries; former open field woodland ancient & secondary; common pasture & heath; meadowland
Past & present rural industry including water & windmills: mining etc
Historic Parks & Gardens including medieval deerparks & designed landscapes
Known archaeological features

Pl. 12.IV); the presence of ancient and secondary woodland, heath, meadowland, rural industry; iv) specialised former land use such as former royal forests, chases, historic parks, both medieval hunting parks and later ornamental parks, and gardens (Hooke 1998c). Settlement patterns frequently remain influenced by the changes that occurred in the formative early medieval period when the basic differences between champion and woodland regions started to become more apparent. In the former, increasing nucleation was the dominant pattern throughout the medieval period while, in the latter, continued assarting and squatter settlement merely intensified the dispersed character. Rural industry has been a factor influencing development but in the past tended to fit into the basic pattern of settlement rather than to lead to drastic change. Each period, too, has added its own expressions of social hierarchy, from the modest manor-house to the castle or country house, with the influence of landowners also reflected in the foundation of churches and abbeys. All these elements could be identified through the methods followed in these projects and particularly by the use of historical land use mapping.

Taking such studies into consideration, landscape architects are able to identify detailed character areas which reflect present-day patterns, affected, too, by the more recent elements of change (Worcestershire Co Counc 1999). In the Clent area, for instance, woodland was lost from the more readily cultivable terrains, such as the sandstone plateaus and floodplains, as the forests diminished and ceased to be of value, especially where woods were not protected in chases or parks (most of which were themselves to be enclosed for pasture); modern hedge removal has now produced a pattern of large fields more akin to the landscapes once associated only with early open field agriculture; the settlement pattern,

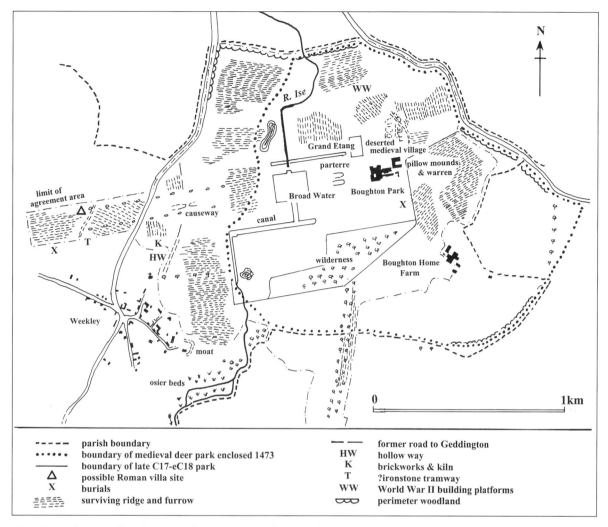

Fig. 12.3. Medieval earthworks at Boughton House, Northamptonshire.

however, often remains dispersed and hints at earlier arrangements. Few would wish to fossilise the landscape 'in aspic' and sensitive guidelines prepared for land managers are able to suggest how regional characteristics may be conserved within modern farming arrangements.

The Countryside Stewardship scheme, initiated by the Countryside Commission and now run by MAFF (Ministry of Agriculture, Fisheries and Food), has been able to target certain threatened landscapes, such as chalk and limestone grassland and lowland heath, for conservation and enhancement by financial aid and some years after its commencement its initial categories were extended to include 'historic landscapes'. In practice, most of these have been historic parklands, although the historical aspect is recognised as an important component of all types of land addressed: waterside meadows, old orchards and ancient grasslands obviously derive their nature from past land management and many are especially rich in historic and archaeological features. The parklands, in particular, often present a multi-layered landscape: medieval field systems are frequently preserved within later parkland, as at Boughton House and Steane Park

in Northamptonshire where the earthworks of ridge and furrow, headlands, deserted medieval village sites and routeways can be recognised (Fig. 12.3) while the features associated with eighteenth-century design, often incorporating elaborate water features and ornate small buildings, add a further overlay. Rich landowners were also able to carry out agricultural improvement and elaborate water irrigation systems have left notable earthwork features in a number of parks, as at Arlington Court in Devon or Clumber Park in Nottinghamshire (a water meadow system is now being partially restored by the National Trust at Sherbourne in Gloucestershire). A number of parks, like Boughton, were used in the Second World War for training purposes and at Basildon Park in Berkshire and Clumber Park there are remains of trial trenches and ammunition stores. Under stewardship, most parks have been subject to detailed archaeological survey and attention is being given to judicious tree-planting, the rebuilding of ha-has, grassland management etc, while increased public access where appropriate is a constant objective.

Similar schemes operate in Wales: here landscape protection under the Tir Cymen scheme concentrated upon grant-aid in certain selected regions but has now been extended under the new Tir Gofal sceme to the whole of Wales. A study of selected historic landscape regions has been carried out on behalf of Cadw and the Countryside Council of Wales to 'demonstrate the nature, level and significance of the historic interest in Welsh landscapes' (CCW n.d; Cadw 1998) and has been directly geared towards GIS recording in its LANDMAP programme, the establishment of a database that combines ecological and cultural information for the purposes of land management. This is designed to be all-embracing and to be evaluative, not just descriptive, putting a value or rating on the landscapes being defined. This approach has been rejected in England by English Heritage but in practise the selection of certain regions as Areas of Outstanding Natural Beauty etc, has already followed this route.

The conservation and maintenance of field boundaries is one objective addressed by Countryside Stewardship for reasons of regional character and wildlife preservation. For the landscape historian, hedges and walls preserve a living record in the present-day landscape of past field systems and land management, making sense of documentary sources and maintaining a strong link with past character. Hedges now also enjoy greater legal protection, resulting from the magnitude of hedgerow loss in recent decades. This is a subject which has been addressed by many private organisations such as Common Ground or the Council for the Protection of Rural England as well as by public bodies, and some local authorities are now recording historic hedgerows on their database (Hooke 1999 and in prep.). Legal protection is now afforded to hedges that mark township boundaries or the bounds of pre-1600 manors, to pre-enclosure hedges (*i.e.* the period before the General Act of 1845), and to recorded hedges in areas where they are a distinctive regional characteristic (if recorded before 1845) (Hedgerow Regulations 1997). Early hedges have a particularly strong ecological value, often containing many different plant species, but even later hedges can act as valuable wildlife corridors in areas which were historically traditionally more open. Obviously conflicting views have occasionally to be considered – in many open field areas hedges were virtually absent in historical times and even the furlongs of individual open fields abutted without lasting physical expression; hedgerow removal in these areas actually *re-instates* an historic landscape but decisions have to be made on the basis of many interests. It is always worth recording in detail the earliest mapped evidence for individual hedges although this does not always go back far enough to capture the origins of hedges resulting from medieval or pre-eighteenth-century enclosure

(Hooke in prep.) (Fig. 12.4).[5]

One project, the replanting of woodland, deliberately changes the present-day landscape and raises questions as to how far one should be allowed to dispense with the past. The Countryside Agency wishes to double England's woodland cover to 15 *per cent* by the year 2050 – a million hectares of new woodland (Countryside Commission 1996). The National Forest has already begun to extend across the East Midlands, linking the former Forest of Needwood in Staffordshire with Charnwood in Leicestershire, but incorporates regions such as the Trent-Meuse lowland which have long been pasture and meadow (Countryside Commission 1994; Hooke 1998d). Elsewhere new community forests organised by statutory authorities are contributing to the programme.

One notable recent step has been an increase in public involvement in the decision-making process, a move fostered by grant-awarding bodies and local councils. An example is the preparation of Parish Appraisals, a move instituted in 1979 (Countryside Agency 1999). Within the area of Stratford-on-Avon District Council in Warwickshire there are, for instance, 113 parishes and almost half of them have signed up to the production of a parish or village appraisal covering all aspects of community life, including housing and transport issues (Stratford Dist Counc n.d.). This involves decisions about what is bad planning and how good points and characteristics can be enhanced by the production of a village design statement. The process is obviously subjective but participants are advised to consider the Council's Local Plan and guidelines; it is here that historical information has been fed in. Obviously, the more informed local people can be about their local landscape the better if rural life is to preserve its quality both visually and socially and if recommendations are to be accepted – and even suggested at grass roots level. Recent results of this process have included some award-winning village plans, including new cottage-style housing in Long Compton which extends along the village street in keeping with the existing historic village plan.

THE EUROPEAN DIMENSION

While England has made major headway in the application of both ecological and cultural information many European countries have made far greater headway in the historical mapping which provides the basic database. In Sweden volumes of the National Atlas have addressed land use and settlement patterns (Helmfrid 1994), Ulf Sporrong (Sporrong *et al.*1995) has described regional landscapes and a detailed study involving historical landscape reconstruction covers much of southern Sweden (Berglund 1991). Similarly, in the Netherlands, detailed historical mapping has been carried out in Zuid-Limburg which identifies

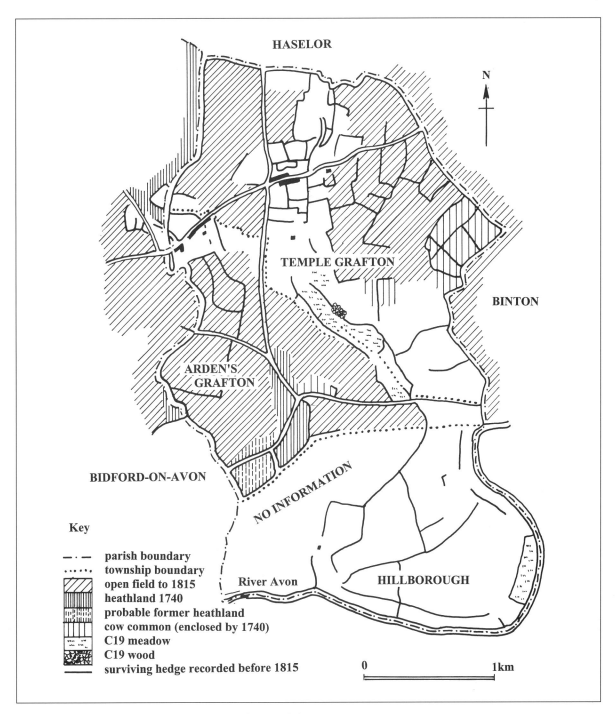

HASELOR

N

TEMPLE GRAFTON

BINTON

ARDEN'S
GRAFTON

BIDFORD-ON-AVON

NO INFORMATION

Key

- . - parish boundary
...... township boundary
open field to 1815
heathland 1740
probable former heathland
cow common (enclosed by 1740)
C19 meadow
C19 wood
surviving hedge recorded before 1815

River Avon

HILLBOROUGH

0   1km

Fig. 12.4. Historical land use in the Avon Valley of Warwickshire.

the historic elements in the landscape of that region (Renes 1988) and, in that country, Jelier Vervloet heads a team in the Agricultural Research Department of Wageningen University that is attempting to map Europe's cultural landscapes on a broad scale. In Denmark a new government financed centre, *Foranderlige Landskaber*, the Centre for Strategic Studies in Cultural Environment, Nature and Landscape History, has been established (for a limited period) to draw together a wide range of interested bodies involved in landscape study. At a more strictly academic level, the *Atles del Comtat de Besalú (785-988)* and the *Atles dels Comtats d'Emúries*

(780-991) are the first of a series of atlases of the Catalan area in Spain mapping early medieval historical features and land use (Bolòs & Hurtado 1998, 1999).

At present a more far-reaching scheme is making its way through the levels of EC administration. Initially two working groups were set up by the Council of Europe, one related to nature conservation in a landscape context, the other to the historic heritage. These have moved from a site-specific attitude to a broader view of landscape. The European Environment Agency for the European Environment Ministers' conference held in Sofia in October 1995 (the Dobris

Assessment) for the first time extended its reference to landscapes and a strategy for Ecological and Landscape Diversity was approved that is being pursued by a forum with representatives from some fifty-five countries. This expressed a hope that the Council of Europe would prepare a European convention on landscape. In 1995 the Congress of Local and Regional Authorities of Europe (CLRAE) set up a Working Group to prepare a European Landscape Convention which has subsequently been put into legal form and was adopted at the fifth plenary session of CLRAE in May 1998 (Council of Europe 1998). This recognises the importance that Europe's citizens attach to their environment and their desire to see the quality of their surroundings safeguarded, especially as this is often already in decline. It is noted that, as an international instrument on landscape, the recommendations of the Convention must be legally binding to have any effect. At the May meeting it was recommended that 'official landscape activities should no longer be merely a field of study or a limited area of action which is the prerogative of certain specialised scientific bodies' but 'the landscape should become a mainstream political subject, since it plays an important role in the well-being of Europe's citizens, for whom it is no longer acceptable that their surroundings are transformed by technical and economic changes on which they have no say'. Should the Convention be approved by the Committee of Ministers it will be put forward for acceptance as an international treaty. In practice, however, there is likely to be at least a three-year delay before sufficient Member States sign up to it.

With this awakening across Europe it is essential that 'cultural' landscapes should embody sufficiently the historical element and that this country should not miss the opportunity to improve the necessary database. Unfortunately, as yet, funding for this is a low priority but liaison between researchers and practitioners must continue and landscape historians should play an active role in formulating future policy decisions.

ACKNOWLEDGEMENTS

I should like to thank Judith Wardlaw at the Institute of Terrestrial Ecology, Furzebrook Research Station, Wareham, for further information on the feeding habits of the *Maculinea* butterfly. I am also grateful to English Heritage, the Countryside Agency, ADAS and Jim Waterson of the Severn Gorge Countryside Trust for involving me in the projects discussed in this paper; and to Cheltenham and Gloucester College of Higher Education for funding a visit to the Council of Europe in Strasbourg.

FOOTNOTES

1. Two recent BBC programmes on early agriculture were a welcome contribution in this field and a another series has recently been filmed but the overall presentation of historical *landscape* material, as opposed to archaeology, remains small and there have been few follow-ups to Hoskins' admirable series.
2. For the implication of hunting reserves upon the protection of woodland in a pre-Norman context see Hooke 1998e. For comments upon the limitations of the evidence see Day 2000.
3. Most of the early charcoal furnaces were in the Weald of Kent but one was built on the edge of the Shropshire coalfield near Shifnal in 1562 and one at Cleobury Mortimer at about the same time; others followed at Lilleshall (1591) and Bringewood (1601) (Rowley 1972, p. 217).

4. This was probably a two-stage process, with coppicing replacing earlier indiscriminate felling – new coppices were being planted in Shropshire in the mid-seventeenth century. Near the Willey furnaces, coppices were planted in Aldenham Park by 1725 (Rowley 1972, pp. 126, 218, fig. 11).
5. There is no documentary or cartographic evidence to prove the date of the hedgerows in the western part of Hillborough township in Temple Grafton before the early Ordnance Survey six-inch map (*c.*1866). This date does not fall into the pre-1845 date required by the regulations although the hedges here are likely to pre-date 1517, the date at which the Inclosure Commission noted enclosure and resultant depopulation in Hillborough (Leadam 1897, II. pp. 405-6).

BIBLIOGRAPHY

Alfrey, J., & Clark, C., 1993. *The Landscape of Industry: patterns of change in the Ironbridge Gorge* (London & New York).

Bayliss, D. G., 1987. 'The effect of Bringewood forge and furnace', *Trans Woolhope Naturalists' Field Club*, 45, pp. 721-9.

Berglund, B. E. (ed.), 1991. *The Cultural Landscape During 6000 Years in Southern Sweden*, Ecol Bull No. 41 (Copenhagen).

de la Blache, V., 1911. *Histoire de France depuis les origines jusque la Révolution, Vol. 1: Tableau de la Géographie de la France* (Paris).

Bloch, M., 1931. *Les Caractères originaux de l'Histoire rurale française* (Oslo).

Bolòs, J., & Hurtado, V., 1998. *Atles del Comtat de Besalú (785-988)* (Barcelona).

Bolòs, J., & Hurtado, V., 1999. *Atles dels Comtats d'Empúries I Peralada (780-991)* (Barcelona).

Cadw: Welsh Historic Monuments 1998. *Register of Landscapes of Outstanding Historic Interest in Wales* (Cardiff).

Camden, W., 1586 (1607). *Britannia*, 1789 edn ed. R. Gough (London).

CCW (Countryside Council for Wales) n.d. *Tirlun Cymru/ The Welsh Landscape: our inheritance and its future protection and enhancement. Consultative document: policy and assessment* (Bangor).

Chadwick, P., 1999. 'Oxfordshire', in *Yesterday's World, Tomorrow's Landscape. The English Heritage Historic Landscape Project 1992-94*, ed. G. Fairclough, G. Lambrick & A. McNab (Engl Heritage, London), pp. 38-42.

Chadwick, P., Hooke, D., & Hitchott, A. (1993). *Historic Landscapes in Oxfordshire, Historic Landscapes Project Draft Report*, unpubl report on behalf of Lawson-Price for English Heritage.

Collins, P., & Duckworth, S., 1997. *An Initial Study of the Case for Including the Broseley area in the Ironbridge Gorge World Heritage Site*, unpubl. rep., Ironbridge Inst.

Cornwall County Council, 1996. *Cornwall Landscape Assessment 1994*.

Council of Europe, Fifth Session, 1998. *The Preliminary Draft European Landscape Convention*, unpubl report (Strasbourg).

Countryside Agency, 1999. *The State of the Countryside*, CA3 (Cheltenham).

Countryside Commission, 1994. *The National Forest – the Strategy*, CCP 468 (Cheltenham).

Countryside Commission, 1996. *Woodland Creation: needs and opportunities in the English countryside* (Cheltenham).

Countryside Commission, English Nature 1996. *The Character of England: landscape, wildlife and natural features* (Cheltenham).

Darby, H. C., *et al*. (ed.), 1952-77. *The Domesday Geography of England*, 7 vols (Cambridge): *The Domesday Geography of Eastern England*, 1952; *The Domesday Geography of Midland England*, 1954; *The Domesday Geography of South-East England*, 1962a; *The Domesday Geography of Northern England*, 1962b; *The Domesday Geography of South-West England*, 1967; *Domesday Gazetteer*, 1975; *Domesday England*, 1977 (Cambridge).

Day, S. P., 1991. 'Post-glacial vegetational history of the Oxford region', *New Phytol*, 119, pp. 445-70.

Day, S. P., 2000. *The Environment of Britain in the First Millennium AD* (London).

Fairclough, G. (ed.), 1999. *Historic Landscape Characterisation, 'The State of the Art'*, ed. G. Fairclough, Engl Heritage (London).

Fox, H. S. A., 1989. 'Peasant farmers, patterns of settlement and pays: transformations in the landscapes of Devon and Cornwall during the later Middle Ages', in Higham, R. (ed.), *Landscape and Townscape in the South West*, pp. 41-73.

Goodburn, D., 1999. 'An image of ancient English woodland', *British Archaeol*, pp. 10-11.

Hedgerow Regulations, the, 1997, Statutory Instrument 1997 No. 1160. London, HMSO; *Guide to the Regulations*, August 1998 reprint, par. 7.22, 7.23.

Helmfrid, S., 1994. *Landscapes and Settlements, National Atlas of Sweden* (Stockholm).

Hooke, D., 1988. 'The Warwickshire Arden: the evolution and future of an historic landscape', *Landscape History*, 10, pp. 51-9.

Hooke, D., 1997. 'Place-names and vegetation history as a key to understanding settlement in the Conwy valley', in *Landscape and Settlement in Medieval Wales*, ed. N. Edwards (Oxford).

Hooke, D., 1998a. *The Landscape of Anglo-Saxon England* (London & Washington).

Hooke, D., 1998b. *The Historic Land Use and Cultural Landscape of the Ironbridge and Coalbrookdale Area*, Unpubl study for The Severn Gorge Countryside Trust.

Hooke, D., 1998c. 'Towards a methodology of reconstructing and assessing historical landscapes', in P. Sereno & M. L. Sturani (eds), *Rural Landscape between State and Local Communities in Europe. Past and Present* (Turin), pp. 283-97.

Hooke, D., 1998d. 'The historical landscape regions of the National Forest', in 'The National Forest: from vision to reality', ed. P. M. Wade, J. Sheail & L. Child, *East Midlands Geogr Spec Issue*, vol, 21, part 1, pp. 23-30.

Hooke, D., 1998e. 'Medieval forests and parks in southern and central England', in *European Woods and Forests, studies in cultural history*, ed. C. Watkins (Wallingford), pp. 19-32.

Hooke, D., 1999. *Historic Landscape Assessment*, unpubl report for Stratford-on-Avon District Council.

Hooke, D., in preparation. 'Hedgerows in the landscape'.

Hoskins, W. G., 1955. *The Making of the English Landscape* (London).

Leadam, I. S., 1897. *The Domesday of Inclosures*, vol. 2, citing the Inclosure Commission Inquiry of 1517, London Hist Soc (London).

Linton, D., 1968. 'The assessment of scenery as a natural resource', *Scott Geogr Mag*, 84, pp. 219-38.

Rackham, O., 1976. *Trees and Woodland in the English Landscape* (London).

Rackham, O., 1980. *Ancient Woodland: its history, vegetation and uses in England* (London).

Rackham, O., 1986. *The History of the Countryside* (London).

Renes, J., 1988. *De Geschiedenis van het Zuidlimburgse Cultuurlandschap* (Assen/Maastricht).

Riden, P., 1993. *A Gazetteer of Charcoal-fired blast Furnaces in Great Britain in use since 1660* (Cardiff).

Rowley, T., 1972. *The Shropshire Landscape* (London).

Sporrong, U., Ekstam, U., & Samuelsson, K., *et al.*, 1995. *Swedish Landscapes* (Stockholm).

Stamp, D. (gen. ed.), 1930-47; 1950. *The Land of Britain, the report of the Land Utilisation Survey of Britain* (multivolume).

Stratford-on-Avon District Counc, n.d. *The Planning Service*.

Thomas, J. A., & Elms G. W.,1998. 'Higher productivity at the cost of increased host-specificity when *Maculinea* butterfly larvae exploit ant colonies through trophallaxis rather than by predation', *Ecol Entomol*, 23, pp. 457-64.

Toulmin-Smith, L. (ed.), 1934. *The Itinerary of John Leland in or about the Years 1535-1543* (London, 1964 edn).

Trinder, B., 1973. *The Industrial Revolution in Shropshire* (Chichester).

Walker, M. F., & Taylor, J. A.,1976. 'Post-Neolithic vegetation changes in the western Rhinogau, Gwynedd, north-west Wales', *Trans Inst Br Geogr*, new ser 1, pp. 323-45.

Warwickshire County Council (n.d.). *Warwickshire Landscape Guidelines*, 3 vols (Warwick). Historical study undertaken 1989.

Worcestershire County Council, May 1999. *Shaping the new Worcestershire*, Supplementary Planning Guidance. Draft Landscape Assessment.

The plus fours in the wardrobe:
a personal view of landscape history

C. C. Taylor

ABSTRACT

The development of landscape history as a proper discipline is traced from its somewhat simple beginnings to the complexities of modern scholarship. Some of the problems of definition and of incorporating material from other forms of study are examined. The paper ends with some personal hopes for the future of the subject.

KEYWORDS

Philosophy, time-scales, education, industrial archaeology, vernacular architecture, military archaeology, gardens, regional studies

When he was a young man, my father had a reputation as a snappy dresser. As this was the 1920s, among his extensive array of clothes were some plus fours which he wore whenever he was in the country. Despite changes in fashion he continued to wear them until the 1950s. Then, regretfully, he packed them away carefully. He always believed that one day plus fours would come back into vogue and he would again lead the world in sartorial elegance. Alas this was not to be and, on his death at over eighty, the plus fours were found still hanging in the wardrobe.

Although not, as is well known, my father's son in matters of dress, this story has some relevance to my time in landscape history. For landscape history represents, in some respects, my metaphorical plus fours. When I was a young man the discipline had only just begun and was then a most fashionable subject with which to be involved. The young enthusiasts of the 1950s and 1960s, all impeccably turned out academically, took up the challenge that had been laid down by the great scholars of a previous generation, among them W. G. Hoskins, H. P. R. Finberg, M. W. Beresford and O. G. S. Crawford. Together, young and old, they developed the new subject, the popularity of which now outstrips that of most other forms of historical research. The attraction of this challenge, and indeed the reason why the new subject became so popular at all levels, was due in large part to the writings of the pioneers, and especially of Hoskins. Their ability to write easily and fluently and in a style that could be understood by almost anybody was as important as the content.

But the other feature which made landscape history attractive to the beginners in the subject in the 1950s was the way in which it was presented. As was the case with the prehistory of V. G. Childe, on which I was brought up (Childe 1940, 1957), and in tune perhaps with post-war euphoria, early landscape history was primarily a relatively simple narrative. So, although we all knew that much remained to be done, we naively assumed that this was really nothing more than tweaking or refining the established outlines. Few workers in the field realised the major changes in fashion, concepts and philosophy that were to occur and that would soon render our simple if elegant intellectual plus fours hopelessly outmoded.

I think that it was this wonderful simplicity that seduced me and many others into landscape history. And nothing assisted that seduction more than Hoskins's *Making of the English Landscape* (1955). Incidentally, I do not think that anyone has ever pointed out that the acronym for *Making of the English Landscape* is MOTEL. The significance of this in my seduction by it remains to be explored. One result of this wonderful simplicity is that some of us who grew up with it and who have seen all of the later changes and advances have harboured a wish that one day it would be possible to rewrite *The Making of the English Landscape* in the original exquisitely simple way, but incorporating all of the new ideas and material. Now we know that this can never be achieved. Landscape history has come of age and has reached the same level of complexity, and perhaps confusion, that characterises other and older forms of historical research (Taylor 1967, 1998). It is thus an appropriate moment twenty-one years after the Society for Landscape History was founded, forty-five years after the publication of *The Making of the English Landscape*, sixty years since I asked my first recorded question on the English landscape and, at the start of a new millennium, to look back briefly and see what has been achieved and forward to what we might do.

Perhaps the most important development in landscape history is that inevitably it has exploded temporally, spatially, thematically and conceptually. In addition it has had an enormous impact on both general education and the continuing debate on the future of the environment. The extension of the time-scale for the history of the man-made landscape has been staggering. Although Crawford was already describing prehistoric landscapes as early as 1924 (Crawford 1924; Crawford & Keiller 1928), his work had little impact, even on the archaeological world. For Hoskins, and the other pioneers of landscape history, the subject really only began with the arrival of the Anglo-Saxons in the early fifth century A.D. Hoskins's *Midland England* (1949), an even more pioneering but less well-known work than *The Making of the English Landscape*, has only two and a quarter pages out of 116 on prehistoric and Roman landscapes. *The Making of the English Landscape* itself has less than 18 out of 235 pages on the same periods. More significantly, Hoskins concluded that 'much ... of the work of ... shaping the landscape by the hungry generations from the Belgae [*sic*] onwards had been lost in weeds, scrub and ruins by the time that the Anglo-Saxon colonists arrived. The work had to begin all over again.' (1955, pp. 36-7). While admitting that a few remains of the prehistoric and Roman past did survive, Hoskins's view of the fifth century was that 'the great majority of the English settlers faced a virgin country' (*ibid.*).

Today landscape history begins with the Mesolithic around 8,000 to 10,000 B.C. It is now known that it was the hunter-gatherer people of that period who began to modify the landscape of Britain (Simmons 1996). And, more significantly, whose work marks the start of a long, almost continuous, process of landscape change, not a short-lived dead-end. Many of us who have observed the development of landscape history have come to regard this extension of its time-scale as the most exciting part of an expanding subject. Even Hoskins, in his later writing, accepted without question the importance of prehistoric landscapes (1977, p. 38). Yet he would have been surprised, and no doubt impressed by his own prophetic wisdom, to see the advances in the studies of prehistoric and Roman landscapes (Fleming 1988; Barrett *et al.* 1991; Bradley *et al.* 1994; Hall & Coles 1994; Barber 1997; RCAHMS 1997; Stoertz 1997). He would surely have been amazed that in a collection of papers on landscape history there could be ones on landscapes of prehistoric memory, and on Roman rural planning (Bradley and Corney, this volume). These papers illustrate well the dynamic nature of our subject over the last half century.

The subject has also expanded temporally towards the present. Partly because of the interests of its pioneers – Hoskins hated anything from the recent past (1949, pp. 103-16; 1955, pp. 231-5; Millward 1992, p. 64) – but more probably because of the way that general history was taught until the 1950s, most early work on landscape history rarely dealt with anything later than the nineteenth century. Now, with the widespread interest in recent times, the subject has begun to concern itself with the understanding of modern landscapes. These include studies of twentieth-century suburbia (Jackson 1991), of modern gardens (Everson 1995), of Forestry Commission landscapes (Skipper & Williamson 1997) and of that most wonderful and beautiful place, Orford Ness, Suffolk, where in the 1950s and 1960s a landscape for testing the route to Armageddon was created (Wainwright 1996).

Landscape history has expanded spatially in at least two very different directions. First, it has reached out far beyond the British Isles into many other countries and continents, changing and evolving as it has been developed by scholars with very different backgrounds and experience (Sporrong *et al.* 1995; Griffiths & Robin 1997; Mills 1997; Rackham & Moody 1997; Seddon 1997). It has also extended into the study of hitherto completely unrecognised landscapes. The most notable of these are buried landscapes which range from tiny fragments, sealed beneath later features, to whole areas covered by deep layers of peat or alluvium, and complete landscapes lying below estuarine deposits (Pryor 1991; Needham & Machlin 1992; Barber 1997; Brown 1997; Rippon 1997).

The content and depth of landscape history have also changed out of all recognition over the last thirty to forty years. In its pioneering stage the subject, especially with its narrative form, was conceived in simple terms as the chronological development of rural or urban landscapes. In this form it brought in apparently relevant information on fields, roads, architecture and so on, as seemed necessary. Now every aspect of the historic landscape, whether it be estates, country houses, forests, farmyards or the landscapes of art has been, is being, or soon will be, subjected to minute examination by scholars who are experts in all of these fields and many others (Rackham 1989; Bettey 1993; Mitchell 1994; Emery 1996; Barnwell & Giles 1997). Such detailed research is vital for the future of landscape history for without it the subject would atrophy and die. But it also has its own dangers. For the landscape historian who is trying to understand the landscape in all its kaleidoscopic fascination is at first overwhelmed and then depressed by the sheer amount of information that is now available and that cannot be assimilated properly. The dates and titles of the publications cited in the Bibliography of this paper give a flavour of the present situation. A much more comprehensive list has been compiled by Richard Muir (1999).

However the greatest changes in landscape history, especially over the last decade or so, have been conceptual. The earlier simple aims and methods have been replaced by new ways of looking at landscapes, by entirely fresh interpretations of them and by the re-examination of past and present attitudes to them (Chandler, this volume). In particular there has been a divergence of approach between those scholars who study the physical evolution of human landscapes and those who study the impact of those landscapes on human thought, perception and political and social organisation. Thus we now have, among others, ritual landscapes, symbolic landscapes, landscapes of the mind and phenomenology (Tuan 1979; Bender 1993; Fumagalli 1994; Tilley 1994). Most, if not all, of these approaches are perfectly valid fields of study for landscape history, although those who have lived through the 'new' geography, the 'new' archaeology and social theory may ask how many of them will last very long. The inevitable drive of each generation to rewrite its history according to the social, political and economic interests of the time, that is according to fashion, casts doubt upon the sustainability of some of the 'new' approaches. Fashion in landscape history is even more ephemeral than in plus fours.

The final change in landscape history is, in many ways, the most important of all. This is its increasing impact in the late twentieth century, and no doubt the early twenty-first century, on the debate on the environment. This has involved general, theoretical, specific and practical advice to local and national government, individuals and institutions, on all aspects of landscape, as well as action through pressure groups of various kinds (Hooke, this volume; Bender 1998). Landscape history has also played a part in education in its widest sense, most of all in that for adults. It is perhaps not without significance that Channel 4's *Time Team*, probably the most popular historical programme on British television since Hoskins's *Landscapes of England* in 1976 and 1978 (Hoskins 1978), is led by someone who would call himself a landscape historian even though paid to be an archaeologist (Taylor 1999).

Yet in spite or perhaps because of the success of landscape history, there are still difficulties both in defining its extent and in incorporating all of its parts. This is particularly so when it embraces the material and results of other disciplines that are also relatively new, some even younger than landscape history itself. The older subjects, which have given so much to landscape history, such as archaeology, geography, place-name studies and architectural history, and even many of the newer applied sciences, such as palaeobotany and the various dating techniques, all seem to have been readily assimilated into landscape history (Dimbleby 1985; Aitken 1990; Needham & Macklin 1992; Pollard 1992; Evans 1999). Some of the newer subjects have not been taken on board so easily, largely, I think, because they, even more than landscape history, have had their own difficulties in progressing beyond what I call their 'nuts and bolts' stage. This was first recognisable in industrial archaeology for although Hoskins, for example, pointed the way towards understanding industrial landscapes (Hoskins 1955, pp. 162-79), many of the first industrial archaeologists, with a few notable exceptions, were so obsessed with finding and describing the 'snuffle-pin gaskets' that their own subject was in

danger of choking to death on its information base. Now industrial archaeology too has come of age and its practitioners and their scholarship play a vital part in landscape history. And nowhere more so than in the work of Marilyn Palmer who, in this volume, has again left us in her debt (Palmer & Neaverson 1994, 1998).

Another subject that has in the past had great difficulty in meeting with landscape history is vernacular architecture, despite, yet again, Hoskins's pioneering work (1955). Regardless of Pantin's advice (1958), much time was spent in the early years of the development of the subject on collecting information. Joints, peg-holes and especially roof types have always figured large in the vernacular architectural literature, even though some of the early students of the subject had already broken free by the 1960s, at least into social history (Smith 1970; Mercer 1975; Machin 1977). In the last decade or so some workers in vernacular architecture have widened the scope of their discipline and have produced results that are directly relevant to landscape history. One thinks here of the specific work of Sarah Pearson on Kent (1998), and the more wide-ranging studies by Matthew Johnson (1993). Yet it is not without significance that there is no paper on vernacular architecture in the present volume.

Another subject with great potential for landscape history, but which has also not developed much beyond the stage of collecting information, is the study of recent military structures. The database is now enormous, but many of its practitioners are still mesmerised by the discovery of yet another Alan Williams Turret or are busy recording the fragments of one more spigot mortar base. Here too, some of its pioneers, among them Henry Wills who mapped the distribution of pillboxes and identified the 1940 Stop Lines, were quick to grasp the wider significance of the details (Wills 1985). Recently Wills's results have been modified and improved to give a much better understanding of the strategies behind the military landscapes of Britain in 1940-42 (Redfern 1999). Although much remains to be done with this subject, and others, both in terms of their own development and of increasing their value to landscape history, there is no doubt that the future is bright.

The very success of landscape history as both a popular subject and an academic discipline means that it is in danger of losing its core values and purpose. Landscape history is now such a broad study that it is difficult to comprehend it all. I feel increasingly in agreement with Groucho Marx who said, in another context, 'I have an explanation for all this but I am not sure that I believe it myself'. No one can be the polymath that we once thought our subject required. This is despite my hopes of twenty-five years ago; another case of taking out the plus fours to give them an airing (Taylor 1974). As a result there is a danger of fragmentation. Landscape historians are increasingly unable to speak to each other about their particular interests. The landscape history of the Norfolk Broads (Williamson 1997) is a long way from that of the Bowmont Valley (Tipping 1998). And the study of the landscapes of art (Rosenthal *et al.* 1997), is far from the analysis of medieval pollen in central Wales (Leighton 1997, p. 99). Yet all these projects, and of course many more, are acceptable aspects of landscape history. Its practitioners therefore need at least to understand their significance and to appreciate their value.

The emergence of what I call 'illustrated history' which purports to be a form of landscape history is also a problem. This often involves the use of pictures or plans of features in the landscape, the better to persuade the reader of the merits of a perfectly valid but non-landscape study. Or, more seriously, to use these illustrations to attract the reader and so provide 'Merely corroborative detail intended to give artistic verisimilitude to an otherwise bald and unconvincing narrative' (Gilbert 1885, Act II). It is not easy to give examples of this without being accused of libel or worse but the use of an aerial photograph of a deserted medieval village to illustrate early fourteenth-century economic decline, while quite acceptable, offends my feeling for the dynamism of landscape history. Such a photograph should be used to tell something of the probable origin, growth and decline of the village, and of others like it, as well as something of the history of the surrounding land before and after the desertion.

More objectionable is the use of the word landscape or landscapes in the titles of books and articles in an attempt to cash in on the success of landscape history. A recent book of essays entitled *Neolithic Landscapes* (Topping 1997), while full of good things on the *archaeology* of the Neolithic period, has almost nothing of significance about its landscape. By devaluing the term landscape in this way I believe that we are in danger of forgetting what Hoskins and the other pioneers of landscape history taught us, that it is landscapes that we are studying and landscapes that we are trying to explain. These landscapes can be actual or perceived, extant or relict, hidden or even destroyed. And to explain them we may, indeed must, use the techniques and methods of geographers, archaeologists, historians, philosophers and many others. But we have to remember that it is the landscape that is our prime concern and, often, that it is that landscape that contains the answers to the questions it poses.

Another aspect of current landscape history that concerns me is the careless use of its vocabulary. A result of this is that some of the fundamental ideas and advances in the subject remain obscure and not properly appreciated. One example must suffice. I sometimes despair of there ever being a proper understanding of what might have been the mechanisms that lay behind the changes to the English landscape in the fifth and sixth centuries A.D. (Rippon, this volume). Despite all of the evidence from archaeology, place-names and documentary sources, the results of some fifty years of careful and detailed research and a wealth of new ideas, eminent and not so eminent scholars of the subject still insist on having Anglo-Saxon 'invaders', 'sweeping in ...', 'advancing across ...' and 'settling down'. The history of early Anglo-Saxon England is still conceived of as a 'Wagon Train' process. The use of these words and others such as 'colonists' and 'penetration' all suggest that Anglo-Saxon people poured into a half-empty countryside, brushing aside all opposition and creating a new landscape. This, as I pointed out earlier, was how Hoskins and his contemporaries saw the fifth century A.D. Now I do not know what happened at this time. There may have been many Anglo-Saxon arrivals or just a few. There may have been millions of Romano-British people or merely two or three hundred thousand. There may have been dire economic circumstances or flourishing markets and trade. The climate may have deteriorated and disease may have been rife. Estates may have survived or have been created anew. Great battles certainly occurred but there may also have been gradual absorption of the existing population. The new language may have been accepted by the majority or imposed by a powerful few. My own view, for what it is worth, is that there was a takeover by a small military and political élite and that the landscape continued to be changed and adapted, as it always had been. What I am sure of is that the continued use of such terms as invaders and settlers conjures up an outdated deterministic view of early Anglo-Saxon England. This view, which some of us have spent a lifetime trying to eliminate, still persists largely because of the vocabulary used by those who should know better. This may appear to be nit-picking and in a way it is. All of us, landscape historians, historical geographers, historians, archaeologists *et al.* are trying to understand the past. So perhaps it does not matter if landscape history is 'misused' in the endeavour to interpret that past. But I am a landscape historian and believe passionately that, as the subject can shed a different light on the past to other forms of historical research, its techniques and philosophies must be rigorously defended and applied.

So much for the past. What of the future of landscape history? I doubt that I shall be here to see much of it; certainly less than I have already seen. And my scholarly plus fours are now so outmoded that it is unlikely that I shall be able to make a significant contribution. Nor is it a good thing to prophesy. In my experience those who do are always wrong. But I do have a few hopes. Some of these are directly related to research in landscape history, others to subjects that have contributed so much to it. Just a handful must suffice here.

The first takes the form of a question to archaeologists. When are they going to discover some of the low-status sites that never seem to appear in the archaeological record, but which must surely greatly outnumber those of high status that they always excavate? In fact, of course, these low-status sites have been found and excavated in increasingly large numbers through the application of PPG 16. But the same system also prevents any proper dissemination of the results, except as brief notes or as abbreviated reports with limited circulation. Certainly there is rarely any overall analysis of the implications for landscape history of such sites. The recent collation and publication of this type of material for parts of Cambridgeshire, although already out of date, is a vivid reminder of the amount of new archaeological evidence for past landscapes now available for landscape historians but difficult of access (Taylor 1997, 1998).

A second future line of enquiry, of interest to me, would be into the landscapes of twentieth-century gardens. Not the great gardens of the famous designers or gardeners for these have already been examined minutely but the multitudes of suburban gardens which collectively occupy so much of our landscape (Taylor 1998, pp. 158-9). A study of their origins and the social, economic, technological and political influences that have formed them would be a splendid project. I have often wished, but have never been allowed, to set the examination question 'Bloom's of Bressingham have had a greater impact on the English landscape than "Capability" Brown. Discuss.'.

My third hope for the future involves a topic that has occupied much of my working life, medieval settlement. This is that the next generation of landscape historians will get nearer to answering the question as to the origins and distribution of dispersed and nucleated rural settlement in England. We have made gigantic strides over the years, as is clear from the work of Chris Dyer and his co-authors (Lewis *et al.* 1997) and of Brian Roberts and Stuart Wrathmell (this volume). But there is still a long way to go, especially in the matter of dispersed settlements. Their beginnings are probably more complicated than those of nucleated settlements.

Another desire is for far more detailed regional studies. Although it has always been axiomatic that landscape history is based on the results of such studies, the inevitable drive for generalisation and synthesis has meant that local and regional differences have often been smoothed over or ignored. Yet no matter how awkward the results of such studies may be to the theories of the generalists, they remain fundamental to landscape history, as Angus Winchester has shown (this volume). Related to this is the requirement for more interdisciplinary work. One of the reasons for the success of landscape history has been its cross-subject approach. However this requires further development as some of the other papers in this volume indicate. I would also like to see more research into the problems of continuity. Many of the papers here, either explicitly or implicitly, have been concerned with continuity. And it is the continuity of the landscape, whether material or mental, actual or imagined, that makes the study of its history so absorbing. Apart from the first Mesolithic peoples, no one has ever lived in a virgin landscape. Fields, tracks, settlements, burials, defence works and so on have all been placed over, around or between something already there or something that was believed or imagined once to have been there.

My final hope is of a different order. It is that our society and journal continue to flourish, as they have over the past twenty-one years. The success of the journal in particular has been due in large measure to its two editors, Margaret Faull and Della Hooke. Margaret took on the mammoth task of getting the new journal off the ground and establishing its credibility. Della built on this and saw that it gained an international reputation. Both must be thanked for what they have done and congratulated on what they have achieved. Our society will be lucky if its future editors can match them.

So landscape history and *Landscape History* enter a new millennium. Both have been with us for a relatively short time yet both have achieved much. Those of us who were present at their inception have now been left behind by their dynamic growth. We shall never be able to rewrite or update that simplistic subject with which we began. Our metaphorical plus fours must remain in the wardrobe, unused and moth-ridden. Our ideas have been superseded, our philosophies changed, our theories overtaken. Yet all this is as it should be. I am always encouraged by a comment by Isaac Azimov (1964): 'Once we learn to expect theories to collapse ... the collapsing theory becomes, not the gray remnant of a broken today, but the herald of a new and brighter tomorrow'.

BIBLIOGRAPHY

Aitken, M. J., 1990. *Science-based Dating Methods in Archaeology* (London).

Azimov, I., 1964. 'Adding a dimension', in *The Nature of Science* (London).

Barber, J. (ed.), 1997. *The Archaeological Excavations of a Prehistoric Landscape: excavations on Arran 1978-81* (Edinburgh).

Barnwell, P. S., & Giles, C., 1997. *English Farmsteads 1750-1914* (Swindon).

Barrett, J., Bradley, R., & Green, M., 1991. *Landscape, Monuments and Society. The Prehistory of Cranborne Chase* (Cambridge).

Bender, B., 1993. *Landscape: Politics and Perspectives* (Oxford).

Bender, B., 1998. *Stonehenge. Naming Space* (Oxford).

Bettey, J. H., 1993. *Estates and the English Countryside* (London).

Bradley, R., Entwhistle, R., & Raymond, F., 1994. *Prehistoric Land Divisions on Salisbury Plain* (London).

Brown, A. G., 1997. *Alluvial Geoarchaeology* (Cambridge).

Childe, V. G., 1940. *Prehistoric Communities of the British Isles* (Edinburgh).

Childe, V. G., 1957. *The Dawn of European Civilization* (6th edn, London).

Crawford, O. G. S., 1924. 'Air survey and archaeology', *Ordnance Survey Prof Pap*, 7.

Crawford, O. G. S., & Keiller, A., 1928. *Wessex from the Air* (Oxford).

Dimbleby, G. W., 1985. *The Palynology of Archaeological Sites* (London).

Emery, A., 1996. *Greater Medieval Houses of England and Wales 1300-1500*, vol. 1 (Cambridge).

Evans, J. G., 1999. *Land and Archaeology* (Stroud).

Everson, P., 1995. 'The Munstead Wood survey', in *Gertude Jekyll: essays on the life of a working amateur*, ed. M. Tooley & P. Arnander (Witton-le-Wear), pp. 71-82.

Fleming, A., 1988. *The Dartmoor Reaves* (London).

Fumagalli, V., 1994. *Landscapes of Fear* (Oxford).

Gilbert, W. G., 1885. *The Mikado* (London).

Griffiths, T., & Robin, L., 1997. *Ecology and Empire* (Edinburgh).

Hall, D., & Coles, J., 1994. *Fenland Survey*, Engl Heritage Archaeol Rep 1 (London).

Hoskins, W. G., 1949. *Midland England* (London).

Hoskins, W. G., 1953. 'The rebuilding of rural England, 1570-1640', *Past and Present*, 4, pp. 44-59.

Hoskins, W. G., 1955. *The Making of the English Landscape* (London).

Hoskins, W. G., 1977. *The Making of the English Landscape* (2nd edn, London).

Hoskins, W. G., 1978. *One Man's England* (London).

Jackson, A. A., 1991. *Semi-Detached London* (Didcot).

Johnson, M., 1993. *Housing Culture* (London).

Leighton, D. K., 1997. *Mynydd Du and Fforest Fawr* (Aberystwyth).

Lewis, C., Mitchell-Fox, P., & Dyer, C., 1997. *Village, Hamlet and Field* (Manchester).

Machin, R., 1977. 'The great rebuilding', *Past and Present*, 77, pp. 33-56.

Mercer, E., 1975. *English Vernacular Houses* (London).

Mills, S. F., 1997. *The American Landscape* (Edinburgh).

Millward, R., 1992. 'William George Hoskins', *Landscape History*, 14, pp. 65-70.

Mitchell, W. J. T. (ed.), 1994. *Landscape and Power* (Chicago).

Muir, R., 1999. *Approaches to Landscape* (London).

Needham, S. P., & Machlin, M., 1992. *Alluvial Archaeology in Britain*, Oxbow Monogr 27 (Oxford).

Palmer, M., & Neaverson, P., 1994. *Industry and the Landscape 1700-1900* (London).

Palmer, M., & Neaverson, P., 1998. *Industrial Archaeology, Principles and Practice* (London).

Pantin, W. A., 1958. 'Monuments or muniments?', *Medieval Archaeol*, 2, pp. 158-68.

Pearson, S., 1998. 'Vernacular buildings in the landscape', in *The Archaeology of Landscape*, ed. P. Everson & T. Williamson (Manchester), pp. 166-82.

Pollard, A. M. (ed.), 1992. *New Developments in Archaeological Science*, Proc Br Academy, 77 (Oxford).

Pryor, F., 1991. *Flag Fen* (London).

Rackham, O., 1989. *The Last Forest* (London).

Rackham, O., & Moody, J., 1997. *The Making of the Cretan Landscape* (Manchester).

RCAHMS 1997. Royal Commission on the Ancient & Historical Monuments of Scotland. *Eastern Dumfriesshire. An Archaeological Landscape* (Edinburgh).

Redfern, N., 1999. 'Anti-invasion defences of Scotland, Wales and Northern Ireland, 1939-45: insights and issues', *Defence Lines*, 12, pp. 6-9.

Rippon, S., 1997. *The Severn Estuary, Landscape Evolution and Wetland Reclamation* (Leicester).

Rosenthal, M., Payne, C., & Wilcox, S. (eds), 1997. *Prospects for the Nation. Recent Essays in British Landscape 1750-1880* (Yale).

Seddon, G., 1997. *Landprints. Reflections on Place Landscape* (Cambridge).

Simmons, I. G., 1996. *The Environmental Impact of Later Mesolithic Cultures* (Edinburgh).

Skipper, K., & Williamson, T., 1997. *Thetford Forest: Making a Landscape, 1922-1997* (Norwich).

Smith, J. T., 1970. 'The evolution of the English peasant house', *J Br Archaeol Soc*, 33, pp. 122-47.

Sporrong, U., Ekstam, U., & Samuelsson, K., 1995. *Swedish Landscapes* (Stockholm).

Stoertz, C., 1997. *Ancient Landscapes of the Yorkshire Wolds* (Swindon).

Taylor, A., 1997. *The Archaeology of Cambridgeshire*, vol. 1 (Cambridge).

Taylor, A., 1998. *The Archaeology of Cambridgeshire*, vol. 2 (Cambridge).

Taylor, C. C., 1967. 'Whiteparish, a study in the development of a forest-edge parish', *Wiltshire Archaeol Mag*, 62, pp. 79-102.

Taylor, C. C., 1974. 'Total archaeology', in *Landscape and Documents*, ed. A. Rogers & T. Rowley (Oxford), pp. 15-26.

Taylor, C. C., 1987. 'Whittlesford, the study of a river-edge village', in *The Rural Settlement of Medieval England*, ed. M. Aston, D. Austin & C. Dyer (Oxford), pp. 202-27.

Taylor, C. C., 1998. *Parks and Gardens of Britain* (Edinburgh).

Taylor, T., 1999. *Behind the Scenes at 'Time Team'* (London).

Tilley, C., 1994. *A Phenomenology of Landscape* (Oxford).

Tipping, R., 1998. 'Towards an environmental history of the Bowmont Valley and the northern Cheviot Hills', *Landscape History*, 20, pp. 41-50.

Topping, P. (ed.), 1997. *Neolithic Landscapes* (Oxford).

Tuan, Y. F., 1979. *Landscapes of Fear* (Oxford).

Wainwright, A., 1996. 'Orford Ness', in *The Remains of Distant Times*, ed. D. Morgan Evans, P. Salway & D. Thackray (London), pp. 198-210.

Williamson, T., 1997. *The Norfolk Broads* (Manchester).

Wills, H., 1985. *Pillboxes* (London).

Notes on contributors

JAMES BOND was trained as an historical geographer at the University of Birmingham. After serving as Archaeological Officer at Worcester County Museum (1964-74) and as Assistant Keeper of the Field Section of Oxfordshire Museum Services (1974-86) he moved to North Somerset, where he now works freelance as a landscape archaeologist. He has been a part-time external tutor for various universities since 1966, and has written and co-authored numerous articles and several books, most recently *Somerset Parks and Gardens: a landscape history* (1998). He is currently working on a book on monastic estates.

RICHARD BRADLEY has been Professor of Archaeology at Reading University since 1987 and has studied prehistoric landscapes in Britain, Spain and Scandinavia. Recent publications include *Altering the Earth* (1993), *Rock Art and the Prehistory of Atlantic Europe* (1997), *The Significance of Monuments* (1998) and *An Archaeology of Natural Places* (2000).

JOHN CHANDLER, BA, PhD, studied classics at Bristol University and trained as a librarian. Freelance since 1988 he combines historical research for archaeological assessments with writing, editing, broadcasting and lecturing. He has written extensively on Wiltshire, has produced editions of John Leland and John Taylor, and is general editor of the Wiltshire Record Society series.

MARK CORNEY is currently Lecturer in Landscape Archaeology at the University of Bristol and a Consultant specialising in earthwork survey and analysis, air photograph interpretation and Iron Age and Roman artefacts. A graduate of the University of Reading he was a Senior Field Investigator for RCHME from 1983-1996. His current interests centre on Romano-British landscapes, the period of c. A.D. 300-600 in north-western Europe and the appliction of earthwork survey and analysis.

KEVIN J. EDWARDS is Professor of Physical Geography in the University of Aberdeen. After graduating from the Universities of St Andrews and Aberdeen, he held posts at The Queen's University of Belfast, at the University of Birmingham and at the University of Sheffield where he was Professor and Head of the Department of Archaeology and Prehistory. His research interests focus on Scotland and the North Atlantic region. His recent publications include *Scotland: Environment and Archaeology, 800 BC-AD 1000* (1977, with Ian Ralston), and *Holocene Environments of Prehistoric Britain* (1999, with Jon Sadler) and he is currently co-editor of *Environmental Archaeology*.

KEN R. HIRONS was a post-doctoral fellow in the School of Geography and Environmental Sciences at the University of Birmingham and is now a consultant in information technology.

DELLA HOOKE read geography at the University of Birmingham and is a Fellow of the Institute for Advanced Research in Arts and Social Science at the University of Birmingham. Her research interests cover many aspects of landscape evolution: studies of pre-Conquest charter evidence include four county volumes on charter boundaries, regional studies which include *The Anglo-Saxon Landscape: the kingdom of the Hwicce* (1985) and, more recently, *The Landscape of Anglo-Saxon England* (1998). She now combines writing with work as a Consultant in Archaeology and Historical Landscapes and is editor of the Society's journal.

TIM LOMAX is a former research student in the School of Geography and Environmental Sciences at the University of Birmingham and is now a school teacher.

YMKE MULDER is a former research student in the Department of Archaeology and Prehistory at the University of Sheffield.

MARILYN PALMER read history at the University of Oxford. She is now Professor of Industrial Archaeology in the School of Archaeological Studies at the University of Leicester. She was a Commissioner with the Royal Commission on the Historical Monuments of England until their amalgamation with English Heritage, for whom she now serves on the Ancient Monuments Advisory Committee. With Peter Neaverson, she has edited *Industrial Archaeology Review* for nearly twenty years, and they have written *Industry in the Landscape, 1700-1900* (1994) and *Industrial Archaeology: Principles and Practice* (1998).

STEPHEN RIPPON is a Lecturer in the Department of Archaeology, School of Geography and Archaeology, at the University of Exeter. Recent publications include *The Gwent Levels: the evolution of a wetland landscape* (1996) and *The Severn Estuary: landscape evolution and wetland reclamation* (1997). His current interests centre upon the landscape archaeology of the Roman and medieval periods.

BRIAN ROBERTS is Professor of Geography at the University of Durham. He has researched extensively upon aspects of settlement in England: his publications include a world review *Landscapes of Settlement* (London, 1996). In collaboration with Stuart Wrathmell and English Heritage he is working upon a national survey of local regional landscapes as a framework for monument protection procedures applied to medieval rural settlements.

TERRY SLATER is a Reader in Historical Geography in the School of Geography and Environmental Sciences at the University of Birmingham. His research interests extend across all aspects of urban landscape studies from medieval town planning to modern suburbia. He has edited, amongst others, The *Making of the Scottish Countryside* (1980); *The Built Form of Western Cities* (1990); *The Church in the Medieval Town* (1998); *Towns in Decline AD 100-1600* (2000) and he is editor of the Urban Morphology Research Group Research Series.

CHRISTOPHER TAYLOR was formerly head of Archaeological Survey for the Royal Commission on the Historical Monuments of England and is a Fellow of the British Academy. He is the author of numerous books on landscape history which include *Village and Farmstead, a history of rural settlement in England* (1983) and a new edition of Hoskins' *The Making of the English Landscape* (1988), bringing the study up to date. His interests cover not just the evolution of settlements and their fields but also garden history, recently publishing *Parks and Gardens of Britain, a landscape history from the air* (1998). He is a former president of the Society for Landscape Studies.

GRAEME WHITTINGTON is Emeritus Professor of Geography in the School of Geography and Geosciences, University of St Andrews. A graduate of Reading University, his research interests lie in Scotland and are concerned with landscape and environmental change. He has published extensively in geographical, archaeological and biological journals.

TOM WILLIAMSON is a Lecturer in Landscape Archaeology at the Centre of East Anglian Studies, University of East Anglia. He has written widely on the history of the English landscape, and on the history of landscape design. His publications include *The Origins of Norfolk* (1993); *Polite Landscapes: Gardens and Society in Eighteenth-Century England* (1995); *The Norfolk Broads: a landscape history* (1997); and *The Archaeology of the Landscape Park* (1998).

ANGUS J. L. WINCHESTER is a geographer turned historian, who teaches in the Department of History at Lancaster University. He has long-standing research interests in landscape history, particularly in Cumbria and other upland areas of Britain. His books include *Landscape and Society in Medieval Cumbria* (1987) and *The Harvest of the Hills: rural life in northern England and the Scottish Borders, 1400-1700* (2000).

STUART WRATHMELL is County Archaeologist for West Yorkshire. He has enjoyed researching the archaeology and history of rural settlement for over thirty years, specialising in the interpretation of excavated buildings and, more recently, in the regional patterning of English rural settlement and agrarian structures. With Brian Roberts, he has recently completed two monographs on rural settlement which are due to be published by English Heritage.

Index

Former counties in brackets where relevant; Unitary Authorities given

Italics indicate illustrations; C = plates in colour section